RECREATING AFRICA

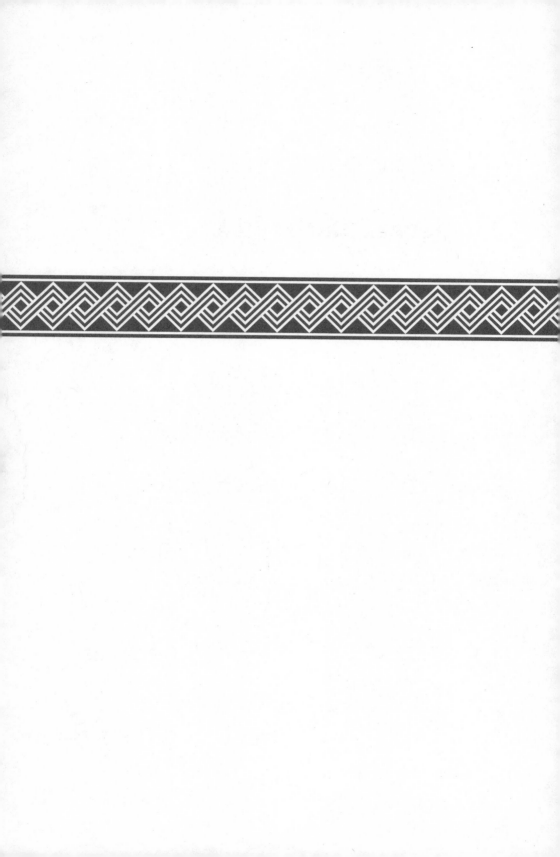

Recreating
AFRICA

Culture, Kinship,
and Religion in the
African-Portuguese
World, 1441–1770

JAMES H. SWEET

THE UNIVERSITY OF NORTH CAROLINA PRESS
Chapel Hill and London

Designed by Jacquline Johnson
Set in Sabon by Tseng Information Systems, Inc.
Manufactured in the United States of America

The paper in this book meets the guidelines for
permanence and durability of the Committee on
Production Guidelines for Book Longevity of the
Council on Library Resources.

The publication of this book was supported in part
by the College of Arts and Sciences of Florida
International University.

Library of Congress Cataloging-in-Publication Data
Sweet, James H. (James Hoke)
Recreating Africa : culture, kinship, and religion
in the African-Portuguese world, 1441–1770 /
by James H. Sweet.
p. cm.
Includes bibliographical references and index.
ISBN 978-0-8078-2808-3 (cloth : alk. paper) —
ISBN 978-0-8078-5482-2 (pbk. : alk. paper)
1. Blacks—Brazil—Religion.   2. Blacks—Brazil—Social
conditions.   3. Slavery and the church—Brazil—
History.   4. Slavery and the church—Catholic
Church—History.   5. Afro-Brazilian cults.   6. Brazil—
Civilization—African influences.   I. Title.
F2659.N4 S94   2003
981'.00496—dc21
2003001194

cloth   07 06 05 04 03   5 4 3 2 1
paper   11 10 09 08 07   7 6 5 4 3

TO LYN, MARGARET, AND ALI

CONTENTS

MAPS, TABLES, & ILLUSTRATIONS

ILLUSTRATIONS

ACKNOWLEDGMENTS

S everal years ago at the American Historical Association meeting in Chicago, I was on my way to dinner with Colin Palmer,
Mary Karasch, and Monica Schuler. As we were leaving the lobby of the hotel,
one of them spotted Philip Curtin across a crowded room. We made our way
to where Curtin was, and Palmer introduced me as one of his students. Curtin's reply, short and pithy, was simply, "Ah, one of my grandchildren!"

As I pondered this some time later, I began to appreciate the deeper meaning of Curtin's comment. I stand on the shoulders of an impressive group of
scholars who fell under the influence of Curtin and Jan Vansina at the University of Wisconsin at Madison in the late 1960s and early 1970s. Some, like
Schuler, Paul Lovejoy, and Joe Miller, were trained as Africanists. Others, like
Palmer, Karasch, and Franklin Knight, were trained primarily as Latin Ameri-
canists. But the common denominator in all of their work is an emphasis on
the breadth and scope of what has come to be called the African diaspora.
Long before there was a discrete field known as "African diaspora" history,
Curtin and Vansina were producing some of the finest diaspora scholars in the
world. More than a few of these scholars have influenced this manuscript. In
recognition of this rich legacy, I begin by thanking two of the "grandfathers"
of African diaspora historical study, Philip Curtin and Jan Vansina.

By far, the most important person in my intellectual development has been
Colin Palmer. Palmer took an interest in me when I was an undergraduate at
the University of North Carolina. Supervising my "duties" as a work-study
student in the department of history, he would often find me dozing with my
head buried in a half-finished crossword puzzle. One day, perhaps curious to
see how shiftless I really was, he asked to read a paper I had written on the
Sandinista revolution in Nicaragua. To his surprise, the paper was engaging

and well written (or so he claims). From that day forward, he has refused to allow me to settle for mediocrity. As an adviser, critic, and friend, he has been unwavering in his support. I can only hope that the publication of this book will in some way justify the energy and time he has invested in me. For everything, I am eternally grateful.

Other mentors and colleagues have been instrumental in helping me along the way. In my first year of graduate school, John Chasteen, beyond being a friendly and insightful critic, emphasized the importance of writing and style to the historian's craft. He improved my writing in ways that I hope will remain our secret. Carter Dougherty and Patrick Rivers were colleagues, critics, and good friends while I was in Chapel Hill. Lydia Lindsey and Carlton Wilson at North Carolina Central University were both immensely helpful in their suggestions when I was writing up the early research that eventually led to this book.

At the City University of New York, I would like to thank David Nasaw for his advice and support when I was a Ph.D. student. Michael Yudell made my move and adjustment to the city far easier. Teofilo Ruiz was an influential teacher, critic, and friend before departing for greener pastures at the University of California–Los Angeles. Ada Ferrer at New York University provided a stimulating seminar on Latin American and Caribbean history and was gracious enough to serve on my oral exam committee. Meg Crahan, Susan Besse, Donald Robotham, and James Oakes served on my dissertation committee, some of them on short notice. Special thanks to Prof. Crahan, who along with Colin Palmer, was one of my primary readers. Her advice and suggestions were invaluable throughout my graduate training.

John Thornton and Linda Heywood read an early draft of the manuscript, providing thorough critiques and suggestions, particularly from the Central African perspective. Thornton read the manuscript a second time for the University of North Carolina Press, again making important suggestions for revision. Thornton also helped with translations of Central African languages and gave me access to several of his forthcoming articles. Although Thornton and I disagree on some of the finer points of Central African religion, he has remained a steadfast supporter of this project, demonstrating a spirit of collegiality and mentorship that will serve as a model as I move forward in my career. His contributions have made this an infinitely better book.

I would also like to thank the Press's second reader, Mary Karasch, whose close and careful reading of the manuscript was instrumental in shaping my revisions. Karasch provided detailed suggestions that have improved the book in countless ways. Others have also commented and made valuable suggestions. Paul Lovejoy and David Richardson provided encouraging comments when they heard me deliver the conference papers that form the cores of Chapters 6 and 7. Joe Miller read portions of the manuscript and provided important feedback. In the book's final stages, Wyatt MacGaffey, Roque Ferreira, and Terry Rey made important contributions. Thanks to them all.

Elaine Maisner, my editor at the University of North Carolina Press, shepherded the manuscript through its various stages, making many useful suggestions along the way. Elaine's patience and enthusiasm made the daunting process of first-time publication a truly enjoyable experience.

As I was conducting the research for the book, I incurred a number of debts. Without the financial support of a Fulbright-Hays Fellowship and a Social Science Research Council International Dissertation Research Fellowship, the research could not have been completed. In Portugal, the staffs of various libraries and archives were consistently helpful. Particular praise is due to the staff of the Arquivo Nacional do Torre de Tombo, whose patience and alacrity were tested daily as I sorted through documents from dozens of Inquisition cases. I also benefited from the goodwill and comraderie of two other Fulbright fellows in Lisbon, Michael Kerlin and Amy Buono. Their companionship and good humor made being away from my family far easier. In Brazil, Aloysio de Oliveira Martins Filho, director of the Arquivo da Curia in Rio, took great interest in my project and made my work there go quickly and smoothly. The staff of the Arquivo Nacional also went above and beyond the call of duty, allowing me access to fragile manumission documents from the eighteenth century, documents that remain badly in need of restoration. Finally, the staff at the Vatican Film Library at Washington University in St. Louis were efficient and courteous.

While professional debts are important to acknowledge, my trajectory as a historian has been influenced primarily by friends and family. Tony Scott and Todd McMasters have been life-long friends and supporters. I could never repay either of them for their decency, loyalty, and good sense. I would be remiss if I did not thank Denny Denison, Clive Harriott, Vinson Jenkins, Dana Lumsden, Susan Morgan, Kiko Nakano, Warren Robinson, James Taylor, Valerie Williams, and Cedric Woods. In ways big and small, you all form the foundation of my historical consciousness. To my family in South Africa, in opening up your hearts and homes to us on a yearly basis, you not only provide respite from the grind of work, but you reaffirm in us the paramount importance of ancestors, family, and kinship. Margaret, Ali, and I are proud to call ourselves Lekoma, Mabale, Motsepe, and Ramaphosa, as well as Sibilsky and Sweet. We are enriched and made larger by you all.

Finally, there are three people whose influence in my life has simply been immeasurable. My mother, Lyn Sweet, dedicated a large portion of her life to raising three irreverent, hell-raising boys. I hope this project will stand as a testimony to her strength and determination in seeing us succeed. My wife, Margaret Mabale, remains the most remarkable person I have ever known. Her personal odyssey is one of utter resilience, itself worthy of a book. The sacrifices she made to ensure that I finished graduate school and completed the research and writing of this book are too numerous to name. Her encouragement and pride in my accomplishments are only one small indication of her amazing selflessness and generosity of spirit. I wish I could somehow repay her for her patience and her love, but I know that I cannot. My nine-year-old daughter, Alexandra, has literally grown up with this project. More than anyone else, she has humanized me and made me appreciate the importance of playing Barbies, riding bikes, and frolicking in the swimming pool—the "real" stuff of human history. For their loyalty and love, I dedicate this book to Lyn, Margaret, and Ali.

RECREATING AFRICA

Introduction

In the past ten years or so, the African diaspora has received a
great deal of attention in scholarly circles. As studies and programs on the so-called "Atlantic World" have come into vogue, the notion
of a single African diaspora has become an attractive way for those studying
peoples of African descent to situate themselves in the broader debate over
the emergence of a "creolized" Atlantic world. Unfortunately, theoretical con-
ceptualizations of the African diaspora have not kept pace with the books,
conferences, scholars, and academic programs that label themselves as such.
The African diaspora often has been uncritically superimposed on the Atlantic World, allowing anyone who studies peoples of African descent to claim
that they are diaspora scholars. Indeed, there seems to be a general consensus
that the so-called "Black Atlantic" is synonymous with the African diaspora.

Recently, several historians have published strong theoretical statements
that depart from this widely held view of the African diaspora.[1] Paul Lovejoy, John Thornton, Colin Palmer, and Michael Gomez are among a new generation of diaspora scholars that Lovejoy calls the "revisionist" school. These
scholars shift the focus of African diaspora studies away from the explicit
study of creolization toward an emphasis on placing Africans and their descendants at the center of their own histories. In theory, this means making
Africa the starting point for any study of Africans in the diaspora, particularly during the era of the slave trade. At the same time, the revisionists argue that students of the diaspora must avoid static, homogenized notions of
an essential "Africa." In tracing the trajectory of slaves from Africa to the
diaspora, scholars should chart the processes of social, cultural, and political
change from specific African ethnic homelands to slave communities in the
colonial Americas. This requires not only a familiarity with the major trends

in African historiography but an acute sensitivity to various African world-views. The goal of the revisionist school is to bring greater specificity to what have previously been termed African "survivals."[2] The African impact in the diaspora went far beyond culturally diluted "survivals"; Africa arrived in the various destinations of the colonial world in all of its social and cultural richness, informing the institutions that Africans created and providing them with a prism through which to interpret and understand their condition as slaves and as freed peoples.

This book contributes to the scholarly revision of the African diaspora, focusing on African peoples and the cultures they created in the Portuguese colonial world between 1441 and 1770. The geographic center of the work unquestionably is Brazil. As the final destination of just over a million Africans, Brazil took in more slaves than any other European colony during the period prior to 1770.[3] As such, the main emphasis of the study is Brazilian slave society. Still, African-Portuguese slavery was not restricted to the sugar plantations and gold mines of Brazil. African workers could be found in all corners of Portugal's far-flung empire—from settlements in North Africa at Ceuta and Mazagão to the colonial possession at Goa on the west coast of present-day India (see Map 1).

While it may appear overly ambitious to study Africans in the entire Portuguese world, or even all of Brazil, this is a study of the beliefs and practices of peoples; not a study of captaincies, colonies, or nation states. By using specific African peoples as the starting point for the study, geographic boundaries have far less meaning. The "flux and reflux" of African slaves, from Lisbon to Madeira to Bahia and back to Lisbon, was not at all unusual.[4] What concerns me are the social and cultural practices that these African slaves carried with them throughout the Portuguese world. Indeed, the tenacity of certain core beliefs actually can be measured more effectively across time and space. The pervasiveness of specific African beliefs and practices across the Portuguese world illustrates the shared cultural backgrounds of peoples, despite the geographic space that separated them.

The chronological watersheds that I use in this study are a reflection of the shifts in the various African regional streams that I see contributing to the African-Portuguese diaspora. John Thornton has argued persuasively that despite the myriad ethnic groups that existed in the primary slaving areas of Africa, the Atlantic coast can be divided into three broad cultural/linguistic regions: Upper Guinea, Lower Guinea, and Central Africa. Within each of these regions peoples shared much in common, resulting in mutual understandings—shared beliefs, values, and customs—both in Africa and in the slave communities of the Americas.[5] For the most part, I adhere to Thornton's regional divisions, but whenever possible, I refer to the more narrowly conceived "ethnic" backgrounds listed in colonial documents. Though problematic, these ethnic signifiers have the potential for illuminating more clearly the historical links between Africa and the various diasporic streams.

The first African regional stream that I discern is the Upper Guinea stream. From 1441, when the first African slaves arrived on Portuguese soil via the Atlantic, until around 1580, slaves from the Upper Guinea coast dominated the slave communities of the Portuguese world. A significant number of these slaves were Muslims, and it is on this facet of their identity that I focus. Around 1580, Upper Guinea was overtaken by Central Africa as the leading producer of Portuguese slaves. As early as the beginning of the sixteenth century, Central Africans were already appearing in significant numbers in Portugal and the Atlantic island of São Tomé, but it is not until the latter part of the century that we can really begin to see a Central African community emerging in the African-Portuguese diaspora. The Central African influence eventually became dominant, particularly in seventeenth-century Brazil. From the arrival of the first large shipments of slaves to Brazil in the middle of the sixteenth century until the end of our study in 1770, better than two out of every three slaves who arrived in Brazil were of Central African origin. During the seventeenth century, the percentage was even higher. For this reason, Central African slaves figure more prominently in this study than any other African peoples.[6]

Despite the overall dominance of Central African slaves, around 1700 a significant number of slaves from Lower Guinea began pouring into Brazil, and their cultural impact was felt across the Portuguese empire. In places like Bahia, Pernambuco, and even Coimbra, these mostly Aja-speaking "Minas" significantly changed the complexion of slave communities. Though the Central Africa stream never ceased to be important, by the middle of the eighteenth century, Lower Guinea slaves were asserting their distinct cultural influences in many regions of the Portuguese world.

The terminal point of this study occurs around 1770, when the Mina slave trade shifted slightly eastward, toward the coast of present-day Nigeria, increasing the numbers of Yoruba and Hausa slaves arriving in Brazil. The year 1770 also marks the end of the period in Brazilian slave history about which we know the least. Though there is an abundance of work on the African presence in Brazil during the nineteenth century, very few scholars have investigated the years when African slaves were being introduced, first to Portugal and later to Brazil. And even fewer scholars have attempted to examine the cultures of those Africans who were dispersed across the Portuguese world. Stuart Schwartz's work on sugar plantations in Bahia is perhaps the most im-

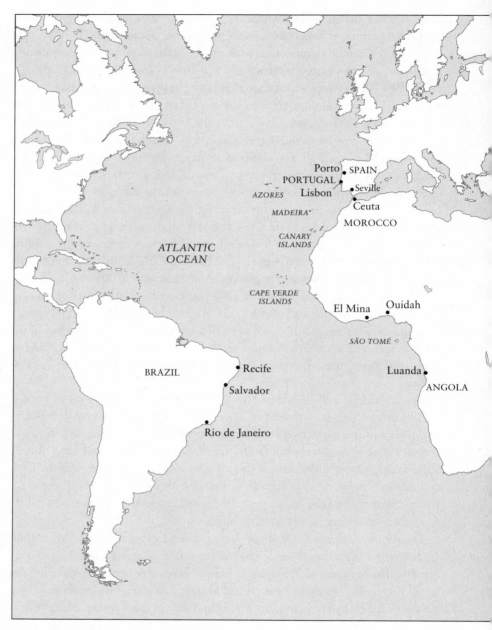

Map 1. The Portuguese Colonial World

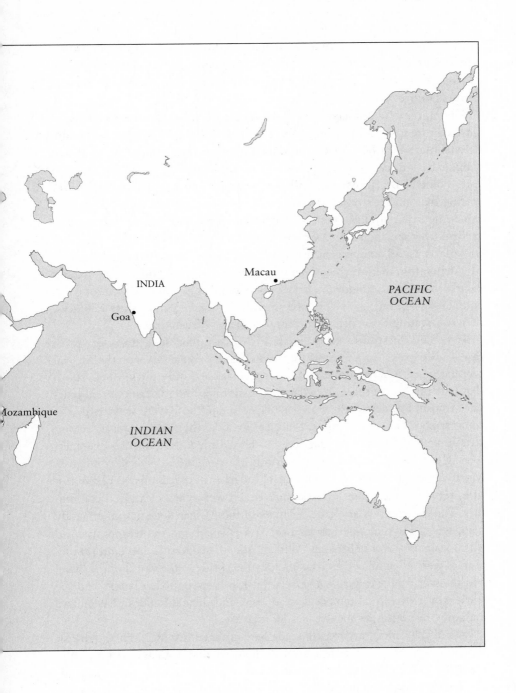

INDIA

Macau

Goa

Mozambique

PACIFIC
OCEAN

INDIAN
OCEAN

portant study of early colonial Brazil and is certainly the most well-known to American readers; but Schwartz's focus is primarily on the economic aspects of sugar production and slavery rather than on the transmission of African cultures to the Americas.[7]

Among the few scholars who have written on the African dimensions of slave culture in Brazil prior to 1770, Luiz Mott, Ronaldo Vainfas, and Laura de Mello e Souza have made the most important contributions.[8] Mott and Vainfas have done pathbreaking works on the sexuality of African slaves in early colonial Brazil. Mott's work, in particular, does an exemplary job of tracing the same-sex practices of slaves from Africa to Brazil. Mott has also done important studies on slave religion, stressing Portuguese-African syncretism over specific African beliefs.[9] Souza's *O diabo e a terra de Santa Cruz* provides a useful comparison of Portuguese, Indian, and African perceptions of witchcraft in the seventeenth and eighteenth centuries. Souza demonstrates clearly that Africans made important contributions to witchcraft discourse in colonial Brazil, but, like Mott, she stresses the syncretism of slave practices, underestimating the continuing centrality of the African past.

By raising questions that originate in Africa rather than in the diaspora, this study departs from most of the works that have been done on the African presence in early slave communities. The central, and most obvious, questions that I am raising are these: To what extent were specific African cultural practices transferred across the broader diaspora, and how were these practices transformed? For our purposes, "culture" includes the customs, ideas, and institutions shared by a particular people—family and kinship formation, child-rearing practices, sexual roles, gender roles, language, and especially religion. Most would agree that religion is one of the most important facets of any culture, revealing the values, mores, and overall worldview of a given community. This was particularly true for most of the African societies under study here, where the dialogue between the spirit world and the temporal world was continuous and unbroken. Political, social, economic, and cultural ideologies were all animated by a cosmology that bridged the world of the living and the world of the spirits. The relationship between living beings and the spirit world explained temporal conditions and dictated codes of behavior, including responses to misfortunes like slavery.

One of the central arguments made here is that resistance among African slaves did not always manifest itself in the ways that scholars have typically understood such challenges. Africans and their descendants frequently addressed the institution of slavery and its attendant uncertainties and pressures with the most potent weapons at their disposal—not muscle and might, but religion and spirituality. I argue that Africans in seventeenth-century Brazil utilized a variety of specific "Angolan," and especially Mbundu, ritual practices and beliefs—divinations, ordeals, ritual burials, dietary restrictions, cures, and so on—as a way of addressing their condition.

These findings challenge widely held notions that African slaves were unable to replicate specific African institutions in the Americas. In seventeenth- and early-eighteenth-century Brazil, African religions were not syncretic or creolized but were independent systems of thought, practiced in parallel to Catholicism. When significant religious mixing did occur, beginning in the eighteenth century, it was most salient among Ganguelas and Minas, or Ndembus and Ardas—not among Africans and Portuguese Catholics. This does not mean that specific African ethnic identities were vanquished after 1700. On the contrary, even as Africans from different ethnic groups found common ground in shared core cultural beliefs, they continued to cling to their specific ethnic pasts. Still, religious and cultural exchanges between Africans of various ethnic backgrounds were part and parcel of a process of Africanization that began in Africa and continued in Brazil, a distinct and intermediate step in the long, slow process of becoming Afro-Brazilian.

Finally, I have found that given the difficulty of everyday life in colonial Brazil, whites were sometimes quick to adopt African religious practices in order to address the secular and temporal needs that Christian prayer and faith could not immediately address. However, most whites were deeply ambivalent in their acceptance of these African religious practices. Although African forms were widely embraced for their effectiveness and power, publicly they were repudiated as the work of the Devil. Ultimately, whites accepted certain African religious practices even as they maintained their essential Catholic cores. Like African slaves, whites engaged in parallel religious practices in accordance with their individual spiritual and secular needs.

The book is divided into three parts. In the first, "The African-Portuguese Diaspora" (Chapters 1–3), I discuss the impacts of slavery on Africans in the Portuguese colonial world, with particular emphasis on Brazil. I argue that despite the re-creation of African kinship structures and some kinlike institutions, the temporal conditions of slavery—breaks in lineage, stolen childhood, death, disease, hunger, low fertility, and physical abuse—were overwhelming and inescapable. Africans re-created communities and kinship structures where they could but, for the most part, were constrained by their masters' hunger for power and wealth.

Part 2, "African Religious Responses," (Chapters 4–8), addresses the ways Africans used religious beliefs and practices to respond to the abuses and uncertainties that they encountered in their everyday lives. Chapter 4 looks at the ways Wolof slaves used their Islamic faith to forge paths of resistance against their masters in sixteenth-century Portugal. The chapter also examines the contradictions in Portuguese policies toward the religious conversion of African slaves, demonstrating how the church uncritically accepted conversion to Catholicism as "normal" while rejecting African desires to convert to other religions (Islam, Anglicanism) as "criminal." Chapter 5 sets a theoretical framework for subsequent chapters, providing an overview of Central African religious beliefs and worldviews. Chapters 6, 7, and 8 demonstrate how Central Africans actually practiced their religions in the Portuguese world, using divination, curing, and rituals assailed as "witchcraft" to address slavery and its attendant misfortunes. These chapters also show how the beliefs of Central Africans continued to flourish, even as new ritual practices of Lower Guinea slaves were introduced into some areas.

Finally, in Part 3, "Africans and the Catholic Church," (Chapters 9 and 10), I attempt to step back and look at the broader impacts of African religious practices in Brazil during the colonial period. Chapters 9 and 10 show that Africans and their descendants were very slow to embrace the Catholic faith, and where they did, they often created a distinct brand of African Catholicism. At the same time, I demonstrate that whites, including some priests, were adopting certain African religious practices, in spite of the church's insistence that African rituals and beliefs were the work of the Devil. This conflict between popular practice and orthodoxy divided the Catholic mission in Brazil. Some priests remained devoutly orthodox, demanding that their adherents obey the laws of the Roman Church. Other priests encouraged their flocks to engage in both African and Catholic religious practices. And still other priests Africanized Catholic rituals in order to withstand the African religious challenge.

Several words of caution are in order here regarding sources and methodology. First, the reader should be aware of the challenges in finding documentation that captures the African cultural past in the early colonial world. Much of the African slave past remains elusive, since the majority of Africans were illiterate, and whites rarely found elements of African culture that they believed were deserving of commentary. This inherent paucity of source material is compounded by the disappearance and deterioration of countless documents over the hundreds of years. The passage of time and nature's elements have not been kind to papers that were written 300 and 400 years ago. The problem of water-damaged, insect-ravaged source materials is particularly acute in Brazil, where the tropical climate has accelerated the process of deterioration. This explains, I believe, the relatively larger number of scholarly studies that concentrate on the slave societies of nineteenth-century Brazil.[10]

The second caveat involves the types of sources used in this project. The backbone of this study are the records of the Portuguese Inquisition. Scholars of European history have noted the inherent problems of working with Inquisition records. The atmosphere of hostility and mistrust that was fostered by the various Inquisitions led to numerous false accusations. As a result of these personal attacks, innocent people were sent before the inquisitors, where they often were tortured and forced to confess to crimes that they did not commit. These forced confessions call into question the extent to which certain practices, like witchcraft, actually occurred. While these concerns are not unimportant to us, we must recognize that many of the specific African practices described in Inquisition cases can be cross-checked and verified through other sources, both in Africa and the broader diaspora. For instance, by comparing missionary reports from Africa with Inquisition cases from Brazil and Portugal, we can show that Portuguese "witchcraft" charges involved activities that were actually very specific African religious practices. In addition, we should also recognize that the Inquisition provided African defendants with a forum to speak for themselves in denunciations, confessions, and interrogations. Often we see Africans making direct references to their African pasts. Finally, we must recognize that African practices were not a particular concern for the Inquisition in Portugal. Indeed, the primary focus of the Inquisition was converted Jews, or "New Christians." Though many African religious practices were denounced to the Inquisition, especially in Brazil, very few cases were actually turned into *processos* and brought to a full trial. Torture and coercion were rarely a part of the equation in Inquisition cases in which Africans were named.

I should stress that this is not a study of the Inquisition or of other institutions of the Catholic Church. Nor is it a study of any of the other prominent players in the Portuguese world during this period—Native Americans, East Indians, Gypsies, Moors, New Christians, etc. These are important topics, to be sure, but they are not my primary concern here. I discuss the Inquisition and the church insofar as they impact the lives of Africans and their immediate descendants, but I am more interested in the religious practices of Africans themselves. I examine other people's practices where they intersected with those of Africans, but only through an African lens. The reader should not take my neglect of these Western institutions and other peoples to be a statement on their inferior place in the formation of the colonial world. I am simply trying to tell the story of my subjects, as far as possible, from an African perspective, revealing their joys, their pains, and their fears through their own very distinct cultural prisms.

PART ONE

Living and Dying in
the African-Portuguese
Diaspora

CHAPTER ONE

Demography, Distribution, and Diasporic Streams

In the late 1720s, a young girl was enslaved in the interior of Angola. There, she was separated from her father, Catumbuque, her mother, Matte, and her two sisters, Quilome and Capaco. By the time she was marched to the Atlantic Coast and loaded onto a Brazilian-bound slave ship in 1728, she was ten years old. The young girl arrived in Rio de Janeiro, where she was purchased by a soldier named Manuel Henrique. Henrique took the girl to his local parish church, where she was baptized and given the Christian name, Caterina Maria. Caterina Maria worked in the soldier's home for only a brief time before he sold her to one Francisco Martinho. The girl spent three years in Martinho's service, before being sold yet again, this time to a man named José Machado. Machado carried Caterina Maria to Lisbon, where, at the age of fifteen, she was brought before the Portuguese Inquisition to answer witchcraft charges.

Machado testified that when he bought Caterina Maria in Rio, he was told that she had been baptized a Christian, but, he claimed, "she shows herself not to be." Indeed, Caterina Maria admitted that she "never had feeling or devotion" for the church. She consistently slept through mass. She threw her rosary beads "out the window." And she never confessed "well and truly." Nevertheless, Caterina Maria still had a strong belief in the powers of the African spirit world. In her confession before the Inquisition, she revealed that her Angolan father, Catumbuque, "taught her some words in order to do evil to whomever she might want, and the words were—Carinsca, Casundeque, Carisca." While the rendering in the Portuguese document does not lend itself to pre-

13

cise translation, a rough interpretation of the words might be: "May you be charmed; may you be overcome; may you be eaten."[1] The effects of the curse certainly reflected this interpretation. In Rio de Janeiro, Caterina Maria used the curse to injure her master Francisco Martinho. On one occasion, she said the words to make him fall down and split his head open. Other times, she claimed that the words made him so ill that he was "not able to get out of bed." In Lisbon, the oration resulted in a wound on the leg of her master, José Machado. The young Angolan also used these spells to attack rival servants in the home of her Lisbon master. Caterina Maria could spontaneously cause "toothaches, [and] pains in the nose, eyes and ears" of the assistants, Maria Caetana and Barbara Joachina. Then, just as suddenly, she could remove the pains by saying a single word in her language, "Cazamficar."[2]

Caterina Maria also claimed that during the night she traveled back to her Angolan homeland, where she spoke with various people, including "the daughter of her master, who had actually been exiled to that state."[3] In many Central African societies, it was believed that the spirit left the body at night and wandered freely. The events of the spirit world ("dreams" in Western parlance) were then interpreted to better understand the person's real-life experiences.[4] In the case of Caterina Maria, the people she encountered in her "night flying" to Angola instructed her that she "should make as much evil as she could" in the house of José Machado. Caterina Maria probably took these directives as an affirmation of her persistent attacks against her master and his other servants.[5]

The case of Caterina Maria is a convenient starting point for our study of African kinship, culture, and religion in the African-Portuguese world, because it reveals many of the conflicts and tensions that permeated the lives of African slaves in the broader diaspora. Caterina Maria no doubt felt the deep loss of her family when she was separated from them in the Angolan hinterlands. But their cultural legacy lived on, as Caterina Maria traversed the African-Portuguese diaspora, both literally and spiritually, from Angola, to Brazil, to Portugal, and back to Angola.

As we will see, Caterina Maria's journeys across the Portuguese world were far from extraordinary; nor was her tenacious hold on her Angolan past. Africans crisscrossed the Portuguese empire with their masters, carrying with them many of the ideas and beliefs that sustained them in their homelands. These specific values often were nourished by contacts with Africans from the same broad cultural/linguistic regions, if not the same "ethnic" groups. And these values were utilized, both individually and collectively, to challenge the power of slaveholders.

But before we delve more deeply into the cosmological and religious worlds of African slaves, we first need a better understanding of who these Africans were. In this chapter, we will examine the demographic contours of the slave trade in the Portuguese colonial world between 1441 and 1770, with a particular emphasis on the ethnic backgrounds of those Africans who contributed to the slave communities of Brazil. Portuguese and Brazilian slavers concentrated their trade on particular African regions for sustained periods of time, resulting in diasporic slave populations that often shared similar cultural backgrounds. While the statistical quantification of the slave trade will play an important role in our analysis, the "numbers" tell us little about how Africans themselves understood ethnicity once they arrived as slaves in the Portuguese world. As we will show, the slave trade itself contributed to important transformations in African understandings of identity and ethnicity.

The Slave Trade in the Portuguese Colonial World, 1441–1770

During the period under study, there were four distinct phases of the slave trade that shaped African culture in the Portuguese colonial world. Each coincided roughly with the turn of a new century. During the initial phases of the Portuguese slave trade, from 1441 to 1521, scholars now suggest that as many as 156,000 slaves were exported from the African coast to Iberia and the Atlantic islands.[6] The trade experienced a remarkable growth during the period, with the annual volume more than doubling between 1450–1465 and 1480–1499, from 900 slaves per year to around 2,200. The volume doubled yet again in the first decades of the sixteenth century. During the first twenty-five years of the trade the majority of the slaves came from Mauritania, but by around 1465, Mauritania was overtaken by the Upper Guinea coast as the primary source of Portuguese slave labor.[7]

The second phase of the slave trade commenced around 1518, when the trade began to shift from Europe and the Atlantic islands to the Americas. In August 1518, the king of Spain granted Lorenzo de Gomenot the right to transport 4,000 Africans to Hispaniola, Cuba, Jamaica, and Puerto Rico "direct from the isles of Guinea and other regions from which they are wont to bring the said Negroes."[8] Prior to this time, slaves were required to pass through Spain or Portugal to be taxed and "seasoned" before being sent to the Americas. Though the Portuguese would not begin shipping large numbers of Africans to their colony in Brazil until the second half of the sixteenth century, this shift in trade directly to the Americas represented a profitable new focus in the trade in human cargoes, one which would see more than 150,000 slaves arriving in Spanish America before 1600.[9]

Paralleling the rise of slavery in Spanish America was the growth of the slave population on the Portuguese island of São Tomé. Curtin has estimated that more than 75,000 slaves were imported into São Tomé during the sixteenth century.[10] But unlike the slaves arriving in Spanish America, the overwhelming majority of those arriving in São Tomé were from Central Africa. Though slaves from Senegambia and the Upper Guinea coast continued to be prominent in the slave populations of the Portuguese world, increasing numbers of Central Africans also began making their way to Portugal and Brazil. By the last decades of the sixteenth century, Central Africa had overtaken Upper Guinea as the primary source of Portuguese slave labor, especially in Brazil.

This third phase of the Portuguese slave trade, dominated by Central Africans, began as early as the first quarter of the sixteenth century, but took off in the 1580s, continuing well into the eighteenth century (see Map 2). The shift to Central African slaves can be attributed primarily to a series of wars in that region that were first initiated by the Portuguese army and its allies. The first large wave of slave exports from Angola came during Portuguese battles with the Ndongo in 1579–1580, a series of skirmishes that nearly drove the Portuguese out of the region. As the Portuguese established a foothold over the Ndongo around the turn of the century, these wars expanded to the east and eventually included the participation of various combinations of Portuguese, Matamba, Kasanje, Ndembu, Kisama, and Benguela soldiers. Warfare produced large numbers of prisoners of war who were sold into slavery. This eastward expansion continued through the 1680s and eventually included Lunda slaves by the 1700s. In addition to those slaves captured in the Angolan wars, the Kongo civil wars (1665–1718) also contributed large numbers of captives who were shipped to the Americas.[11]

The impact of these captives on Brazilian society was immeasurable. During the seventeenth century scholars now estimate that 560,000 slaves arrived in Brazil, the vast majority coming from Central Africa, especially through the port of Luanda. Until around 1680, more than 90 percent of Brazil's slave arrivals came from Central Africa.[12] It was during this time that Brazil emerged as the world's largest sugar producer. Indeed, the colony's association with sugar and Central African slavery was memorialized in the common expression, "Whoever says sugar says Brazil and whoever says Brazil says Angola."[13] Angolan primacy in the Brazilian slave trade was not threatened until the 1680s and 1690s when the supply of slaves reaching the port of Luanda was slowed by an unusually severe period of drought, famine, and disease.[14] Brazilian merchants from Bahia and Pernambuco reacted by shifting the focus of their trade to the so-called Costa da Mina, centered at present-day Benin. There, they initiated a trade in Bahian tobacco that brought large numbers

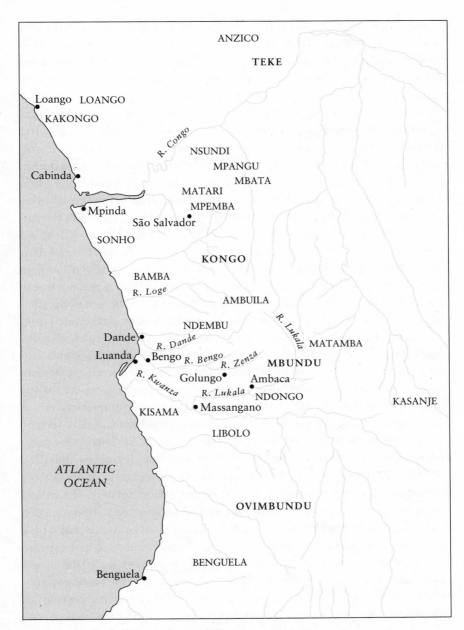

Map 2. Central Africa, Seventeenth and Eighteenth Centuries

of Mina slaves to Bahia. This trade became more regular through the first decades of the eighteenth century, as gold was discovered at Minas Gerais and captives were needed to mine the ore. Mina slaves continued to be the preferred labor force in the northeast of Brazil until well into the eighteenth century.

The introduction of significant numbers of Mina slaves to northeast Brazil beginning in the latter part of the seventeenth century constitutes the fourth phase of the trade and marks an important watershed in the history of Brazilian slavery. Until this time, with the exception of a brief period in the sixteenth century, slaves from Central Africa dominated the servile population in Brazil. During the first two decades of the eighteenth century, imports of Mina slaves outnumbered Central African slaves 153,000 to 129,000, with the majority of Minas destined for Pernambuco, Bahia, and Minas Gerais.[15] In terms of overall numbers of Africans in the Brazilian slave population, Central Africans continued to dominate through 1770 and beyond, especially in southern cities like Rio de Janeiro. Even in northeastern Brazil during the eighteenth century, better than one-quarter of slave imports continued to come from Central Africa.[16] Nevertheless, the Mina stream of the African slave trade would leave an indelible cultural imprint on the Brazilian landscape, quickening the process of creating an "African" (as opposed to Central African) population. Not until around 1770 would the Mina trade shift further down the African coast toward Lagos and the Niger Delta in present-day Nigeria. Increasing numbers of Yoruba (Mina-Nagô) were enslaved as a result of the civil wars in Yorubaland, introducing yet another cultural stream to Brazilian slave society.

In summary, the history of the African slave trade in the Portuguese colonial world through 1770 can be broken down into four distinct periods. The first, from 1441 to 1518, was characterized by the importation of slaves from Senegambia and Upper Guinea to Iberia and the Atlantic islands. The second period, beginning in 1518 and ending in the 1580s, continued to be dominated by slaves from Senegambia and the Upper Guinea coast of Africa, but with a rapid shift of destination toward the Americas. In addition, the Guinea stream was joined by a pronounced stream of Central Africans to the island of São Tomé, and later, to Brazil. The third period, beginning in the 1580s and continuing until the 1690s, was characterized by the overwhelming presence of Central Africans in the Brazilian slave population. During the final period, from the 1690s until around 1770, parallel streams of slaves from Central Africa and the Mina coast contributed to the social and cultural landscapes of slave society in Brazil.

Having defined these demographic watersheds, we should post several words of caution. First, the markers outlined here should not be viewed as fixed. Since we are most interested in measuring the processes of social and cultural change over time, we must recognize that most of these processes took place gradually, defying any neat chronological compartmentalization. A second cautionary note applies to the terms employed to describe various African ethnic groups. While I am keenly aware of the enormous diversity in African languages and cultures in the slave populations of the African diaspora, I do not view these differences as barriers, or even major obstacles, in the re-creation of African cultural forms.

Despite the dozens of ethnic groups that make up West and West Central Africa, the Atlantic coast of the continent can be divided into just three distinct cultural zones with shared linguistic and cultural understandings. The first of these cultural zones, the Upper Guinea, stretches from the Senegal River down to an area just south of Cape Mount in present-day Liberia, and includes, among other ethnic groups, the Wolof, Fula, Mandingo, and Biafada—precisely those ethnic groups that dominated the slave populations of sixteenth-century Portugal and Brazil. The second zone, Lower Guinea, extends roughly from Cape Palmas to the Bight of Biafra. This zone can be further split into two subgroups: the Akan, in the west, and the Aja, in the east. The majority of slaves from the Lower Guinea region who arrived in Brazil and Portugal in the early eighteenth century came from the Aja group. Finally, the third zone was Central Africa, the area from which the largest number of Brazilian slaves originated. Thornton stresses that the cultural and linguistic similarities within this region were greater than in any other part of Africa from which slaves were drawn. Indeed, one sixteenth-century observer noted that the differences between the major languages spoken in the region, Kikongo and Kimbundu, were no greater than those between Spanish and Portuguese, or Venetian and Calabrian.[17] By the seventeenth century, it was reported that the "Angola" language (probably Kimbundu) operated as the lingua franca of the entire region, even among interior peoples like the Angico, Monxiolo, and Malemba.[18] As we will see, this shared language, along with broadly shared understandings of religion and aesthetics, formed the basis for the "Bantu proto-nation" that emerged in the slave population of colonial Brazil.[19]

On the Luso-Brazilian side, the most commonly cited African groupings, or *nações* (nations), closely mirrored the regions suggested by Thornton. Prior to 1600, almost all African slaves in the Portuguese world were described as "Guinea" slaves, reflecting the dominance of the Upper Guinea coast in the Portuguese slave trade. The term "Guinea" continued to have currency until the end of the slave trade, but it had lost much of its precision by the beginning of the seventeenth century, as the Portuguese often used the term to describe

3 broad regions w/ mor specific grups within them

any African, regardless of his or her place of origin. The term "Guinea" essentially became a synonym for "African," often obscuring more precise identities.[20] Nevertheless, by around 1600, large numbers of "Angola" slaves also began appearing in the records. These so-called "Angolas" could come from any part of Central Africa, but most often came through the port of Luanda. After 1700, one finds numerous references to so-called "Mina" slaves, a reflection of the increase in slaves arriving from Lower Guinea, especially to the Brazilian northeast.

Cascading below each of these broad African "nations" or regional zones were dozens of more specific "ethnic" identities (see Map 3). Many of these were renderings made by the slaves themselves. While we should respect these self identities as accurate expressions of the way Africans saw themselves in Brazil, we also must recognize that the terms for collective identity in Africa were constantly changing, especially during the era of the slave trade. For example, the ethnic "Ndembu" (Dembo in Brazil) were actually a community of Kikongo- and Kimbundu-speaking strangers who had fled from early seventeenth-century Central African slave raids, forming a "new people" in the mountainous regions near the watersheds of the Nkisi, Loje, Dande, and Lukala Rivers (see Map 2).[21] Similarly, the ethnic term "Ngangela" (Ganguela in Brazil), while referring to peoples from the sandy plains east of the upper Kwanza River, was also a term of derision, imposed from the outside to designate "others" of marginal, enslavable status.[22] Thus, while "Dembo" and "Ganguela" probably came to have certain social, political, and cultural salience in the slave communities of Brazil, their African meanings were forged largely through the crucible of the slave trade. The collective identities of African slaves in the diaspora were often the end result of a process of uprooting, forced migration, and enslavement, rather than an indication of some stable ethnic stereotypes that persisted in "traditional" form.[23]

Other "ethnic" signifiers of the African-Portuguese world were even more highly problematic. In some cases, "ethnicity" reflected nothing more than the African port through which a slave passed on the way to Portugal or Brazil.[24] In other cases, African ethonyms might have been inventions of Europeans, rather than meaningful terms of African self-identity.[25] And in yet other cases, the ethnonyms were reflective of the African ethnic group from which the slave was purchased, not necessarily the ethnic group from which the slave derived. Still, even where these specific identities are problematic, we can be reasonably certain that these Africans came from the broader regions into which their more narrow ethnic identities fell. In Brazil, while these more narrow identities never completely lost their salience, African slaves increasingly iden-

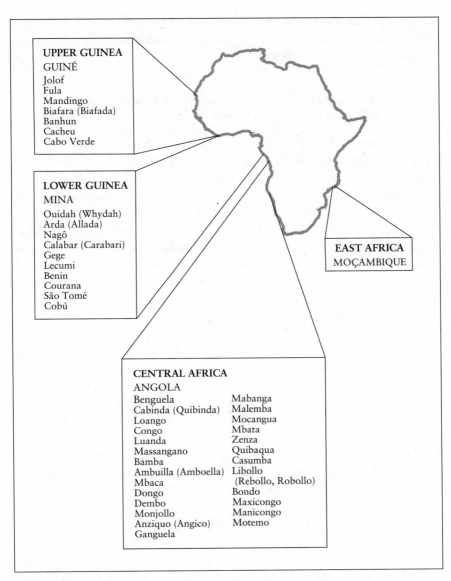

UPPER GUINEA
GUINÉ
Jolof
Fula
Mandingo
Biafara (Biafada)
Banhun
Cacheu
Cabo Verde

LOWER GUINEA
MINA
Ouidah (Whydah)
Arda (Allada)
Nagô
Calabar (Carabari)
Gege
Lecumi
Benin
Courana
São Tomé
Cobú

EAST AFRICA
MOÇAMBIQUE

CENTRAL AFRICA
ANGOLA
Benguela
Cabinda (Quibinda)
Loango
Congo
Luanda
Massangano
Bamba
Ambuilla (Amboella)
Mbaca
Dongo
Dembo
Monjollo
Anziquo (Angico)
Ganguela
Mabanga
Malemba
Mocangua
Mbata
Zenza
Quibaqua
Casumba
Libollo
 (Rebollo, Robollo)
Bondo
Maxicongo
Manicongo
Motemo

Map 3. African Nations and Ethnicities as They Appear in Brazilian Documents

Slave trade influenced more specific identities, not always accurate. Slaves looked at themselves as from the broader areas

tified themselves in broader regional terms like Angola and Mina. And it was these regional identities that often formed the foundation of the cultures that emerged in slave communities.[26]

The Creation of Slave Communities in Brazil: Origins and Ethnicities

While the broad contours of the slave trade to Brazil are clear enough, the impacts of these trends on particular properties were much more complex. Using inventories of individual properties over the course of several generations, we are able to get some sense of how the composition of slave society changed over time. Unfortunately, there survive very few series of inventories that allow us to trace the evolution of slaveholdings on individual properties over time, especially for the early colonial period. Among the most assiduous record keepers of the colonial period were the members of the various religious orders residing in Brazil, particularly the Jesuits and the Benedictines. Unlike those of most secular property holders, their records survive in several European archives.

Required to submit regular reports to their superiors in Rome and Portugal, the Jesuits and the Benedictines have left us with the most complete series of accounts of the everyday activities—economic, social, and cultural—of their various estates. These include frequent slave inventories, daily accounting records, and a wide range of letters and reports. These records are by no means complete for the entire period of this study; nor are they consistent in the kind or quality of information that they reveal. In addition, because the records come from peculiarly large, corporate, religious holdings, they are sometimes less than representative examples of what was going on in the broader secular society. Where differences with secular properties arise, I will point these out, and where possible, I will corroborate my microlevel findings on the religious properties with those from the broader secular world.

The number of slave inventories that have survived from the sixteenth century is indeed quite small, but even during this period we can already see a diverse slave population emerging. In 1572, the slave force of the Jesuit property, Engenho de Santana in Bahia, consisted of only 5.3 percent Guinea slaves, with the remainder being enslaved Indians.[27] Similarly, on the Jesuit estate, Engenho de Sergipe, Guinea slaves represented just 6.3 percent of the labor force.[28] But African slave labor gradually overtook Indian labor in the last years of the sixteenth century, as large segments of the Indian labor pool were wiped out by European diseases and as the Portuguese began to perceive Africans as superior workers.[29] By 1591, Engenho Sergipe's population of African descent was greater than 26 percent, with Angolas, Congos, Mocanguas, and Anziquos—all Central Africans—well represented in the cohort.[30] And by the 1630s, the Africanization of Sergipe was complete, with the estate's slave population being entirely African or of African descent.[31]

Though it appears that most properties shifted from Indian to African labor only gradually, there is sparse evidence that the pace of change was quicker in some places. As early as 1585, the *fazenda* (farm) of Bahian planter Vicente Monteiro was nearly 70 percent African.[32] And unlike its sister property of Sergipe, which became completely Africanized only some time between 1623 and 1638, the Jesuit sugar plantation Engenho Santana was entirely African and Afro-Brazilian by 1616, with Angolas, Calabars, and Ardas listed in the inventory.[33] In the 1580s, most observers agreed that the population of Bahia included around 3,000 Guinea slaves and 8,000 "Christian" Indians, indicating the still gradual shift to African labor.[34] But in Pernambuco for the same period, several observers believed that Africans outnumbered Indians by a ratio of 5:1.[35] Relying upon the smaller numbers of Africans counted by Father Fernão Cardim and Gabriel Soares de Sousa, scholars have long discounted Father Joseph de Anchieta's figure of 10,000 slaves from Guinea and Angola as being overly inflated for a Pernambuco which had, at the most, only 66 *engenhos* (sugar plantations).[36] But Jesuit Father Cristóvão Gouveia, writing in 1583, two years before Father Anchieta's estimates, found "46 sugar *ingenios* [sugar plantations] and each one of them with a great population, and for the service of these and more haciendas they have almost 15,000 slaves from Angola and Guinea, and almost 3000 Indians."[37] Certainly all of these slaves were not employed on the sugar plantations, and it seems likely that the numbers are inflated; however, both Anchieta and Gouveia found that Pernambuco's slave population was dominated by Africans as early as the 1580s, findings that merit closer scrutiny in future studies of Brazil's transition from Indian to African labor.

While the pace of change from Indian to African slavery is not altogether certain, there is no doubt that Brazil's slave labor force was thoroughly Africanized in most places by the first decades of the seventeenth century. The ethnic flavorings of particular properties varied, but the overall landscape was clearly dominated by Central Africans. Engenho Santana, whose 1616 African population was a mix of Angolas from Central Africa, and Calabars and Ardas from the Bight of Benin, apparently shifted to an African population composed entirely of Central Africans by 1674.[38] And at Engenho Sergipe, of twenty-three identifiable Africans in the inventory of 1638, nineteen were from Central Africa, while there were two Mandingos from Upper Guinea, and an Arda and a Lecumi from the Bight of Benin.[39] In order to maintain a steady supply of slave labor during the Dutch occupation of Angola (1641–1648), it appears that Sergipe was forced to rely primarily on Guinea and Mina slaves. For instance, during the *safra* (sugar harvest) of 1643–1644 sixteen *peças* (prime slaves) from Cape Verde were purchased for use on the *engenho*, as well as twelve other *peças* from "guine."[40] But the reliance on Guinea slaves was short-lived. By the *safra* of 1669–1670, Sergipe purchased twenty adult Africans, all but one of them from Central Africa.[41] It was during the period after 1654, when Portuguese and Brazilian buyers freed themselves from Spanish rule (1580–1640) and regained control of Angola and the Brazilian northeast (1654), that the Central Africa trade went practically unchallenged in its supremacy of slave shipments to Brazil, a trend that went unbroken until around 1690.

Beginning in the 1690s and extending over the first three decades of the eighteenth century, large numbers of Mina slaves arrived in the northeast of Brazil. Many of these were transported to the interior to work at Minas Gerais, where they formed the majority among African slaves until around 1750.[42] This Mina stream also had profound effects on the makeup of slaveholdings in the agricultural areas around Bahia, as is clearly reflected in the records of slave purchases and plantation inventories from the region. From 1704 to 1716 on Engenho Sergipe, 83 percent of the African slaves purchased were either Mina or Arda, while just 17 percent are listed as Angolas.[43] Schwartz's examination of inventories from nine Bahian *engenhos* in 1739 finds similar Mina dominance, with 82 percent Minas and 18 percent Angolas on these properties.[44] The 1730 inventory from Engenho Santana reveals a balanced mix of Minas (Gejes) and Central Africans (Angolas, Congos, Ganguelas).[45]

Even as large numbers of slaves from the Bight of Benin were arriving in Bahia during the first decades of the eighteenth century, Brazil's southern ports continued to draw an overwhelming majority of their slaves from Central Africa (see Map 4). Though the records remain largely incomplete, it appears that at least two-thirds of the slaves arriving into Rio de Janeiro during the early 1700s were of Central African origin. Table 1 shows the national and ethnic makeup of Africans named in the last testaments of slaveholders in two parishes in Rio de Janeiro from 1737 to 1740. During this period, two-thirds of the slaves were from Central Africa, and the trade from Central Africa to Rio de Janeiro only grew in subsequent years.[46] By the 1750s, Central Africans made up the majority on even the smallest slave properties in Rio. A typical *olaria*, or brickmaking facility, had five Central Africans and three Minas, as well as two creoles in its workforce.[47] An *engenhoca* (small sugar mill), which produced *aguardente* (rum), had six Central Africans and three creoles residing on the property.[48] And finally, a *fábrica de rede*, or hammock/net manu-

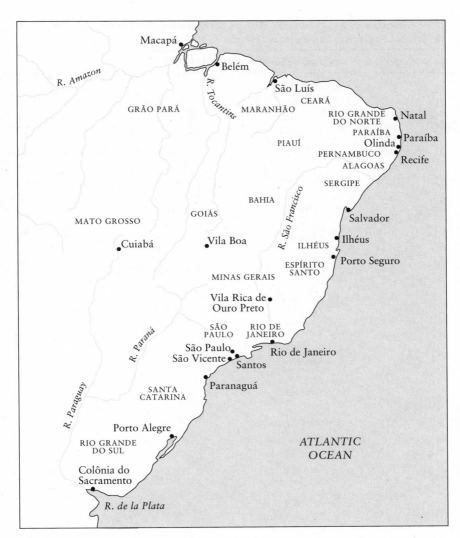

Map 4. Colonial Brazil

facturer, had a total of thirteen slaves in its employ, all of whom were males from Central Africa.[49]

Another notable trend in the makeup of Brazil's slave population by the eighteenth century was the increasing numbers of *crioulos* (Brazilian-born slaves) in some communities. Using inventories from Engenho Santana, Dauril Alden recently has argued that the overwhelming majority of slaves on Jesuit properties were Brazilian-born by the second half of the seventeenth century.[50] While there is no doubt that there was a significant trend toward a more "cre-

Table 1. Ethnicities and Nations of African Slaves Listed in the Wills and Testaments of Slaveholders in Rio de Janeiro, 1737–1740

Nation/Ethnicity	Number (% of Total)
Central Africa	
Angola	88
Benguela	41
Ganguela	21
Congo	9
Monjollo	5
Massangano	2
Bamba	2
Libollo	1
Maxicongo	1
Mbaca	1
Loango	1
Subtotal	172 (66.7)
Lower Guinea	
Mina	67
Carabari	2
Benin	1
São Tomé	1
Cobú	1
Subtotal	72 (27.9)
Upper Guinea	
Fula	2
Cape Verde	9
Subtotal	11 (4.3)
East Africa	
Moçambique	3
Subtotal	3 (1.1)
Total	258 (100.0)

Source: ACMRJ, Nossa Senhora de Candelaria and Santíssimo Sacramento, Óbitos, 1737–1740. This sample includes only those slaves for which some degree of regional accuracy can be determined. Hence, slaves identified simply as "Guinea" are not included.

ole" slave community on many of the ecclesiastical estates, African slaves remained an important part of the slave population on Jesuit properties, even into the eighteenth century. Of 28 adult slaves who are readily identified as either "creole" or African on Engenho Sergipe in 1623, 9 were creoles and 19 were Africans.[51] On Engenho Santana in 1674, there were 10 creoles and 12 Africans among the identifiable adult slaves.[52] And on Engenho Santana in 1730, of 178 slaves listed in the inventory, only 44 adults are readily identified; 38 were creoles or mulattoes, and 6 were Africans.[53] Thus, we can see the slow movement toward a more Brazilian-born population, but nothing approaching the level that Alden seems to suggest.

Although one can glean important data from the inventories, they sometimes obscure more than they reveal.[54] As a result of his findings, Alden suggests that by the 1670s Jesuit managers preferred to purchase "creole" and "mulatto" slaves rather than Africans.[55] But an examination of the actual purchase records of slaves indicates otherwise. Between 1704 and 1716 on Engenho Sergipe ninety-five new slaves were purchased. Of these, only forty-three are clearly identified in terms of their backgrounds. Twenty-nine are Africans, thirteen are *ladinos* (acculturated Africans), and only one is listed as "creole." No mulattoes appear to have been purchased.[56]

Another indicator of the number of Africans who were bought for the estate is the purchase price of slaves. Since recently arrived Africans usually cost significantly less than Brazilian-born slaves and *ladinos*, we can estimate the number of Africans versus Brazilian-born based on their purchase prices. While these numbers are admittedly uncertain, even the most conservative estimate suggests that more than 70 percent of the total slaves purchased for Engenho Sergipe between 1704 and 1716 were African born.[57] The records for Engenho Santana appear to confirm similarly large numbers of Africans purchased during the eighteenth century. Even as late as the 1750s, the Jesuit estates of Petinga and Sergipe were still purchasing only Africans in the years for which we have records.[58]

One significant way that large ecclesiastical estates did become more "creole" was through the inheritance of Brazilian-born slaves. Unlike the case of most secular properties, the religious orders were named as beneficiaries in the wills of various property holders, receiving slaves as well as other property. The orders also received slaves as alms. While these bequests are mostly obscured in the Jesuit records, we know that they occurred. For instance, in 1700, Padre Manuel Fernandes, sixty-five years old and ailing, donated twelve slaves to the Jesuit College of Rio de Janeiro.[59]

On the Benedictine estates, the evidence shows more clearly that inheritance and alms represented a significant proportion of slave acquisitions over long

Table 2. Slave Acquisitions of the Benedictine Monastery Our Lady of Monserrate, Rio de Janeiro, 1620–1772

Dates	Slaves Purchased	Slaves Inherited or Received as Alms
1620–1623	9	—
1648–1652	57	—
1652–1657	41	2
1657–1660	55	1
1663–1666	27	30
1720–1723	37	1
1726–1731	12	—
1733–1736	—	34
1737–1739	17	2
1739–1743	23	7
1743–1746	30	60+[a]
1747–1748	10	—
1748–1750	16	—
1760–1763	25	—
1763–1766	24	—
1766–1770	28	17
1770–1772	15	39
Totals	426	193

Source: ADB/UM, CSB 134 and 135.

[a] For the years 1743–1746, the documentary evidence clearly shows 60 slaves inherited. In addition, on one of the properties, Fazenda da Ilha, the documents report that "various slaves were . . . inherited." Thus, the total number was greater than 60.

stretches of time. Between 1620 and 1772, the Benedictine monastery of Our Lady of Monserrate in Rio de Janeiro inherited at least 193 slaves, a remarkable 31 percent of all slave acquisitions (see Table 2). Similarly, between 1660 and 1749, inheritances represented 33 percent of slave acquisitions at the monastery in Olinda.[60] Sketchier evidence for the monasteries at Bahia and Brotas reveals similar trends.

A number of these inherited slaves were probably African born, but because the slaves usually represented the legacies of well-established Brazilian slaveholders, there were probably fair numbers of creoles and even larger numbers of *ladinos* (acculturated Africans) who were also parts of the bequests. Though the fathers had little control over the quantity or quality of the slaves that they received through inheritance and alms, they clearly maximized the opportunities presented by these windfalls. Slaves that they did not want or need could be sold. In their trade in slaves, the Benedictines proved to be shrewd businessmen. To cite just one example, during the 1736–1739 triennial, the fathers of the monastery in Olinda bought eight slaves from the proceeds of five who were sold, and they still had 120 mil-réis left over with which they intended to purchase two more slaves.[61] While some slaves were sold for large profits, certain creoles and skilled Africans, like the two master carpenters inherited by the monastery in Rio de Janeiro between 1737 and 1739, were considered indispensable and were maintained for use on the order's own properties.[62]

As a result of the constant stream of human gifts bestowed upon the monasteries, the Benedictines had access to an artificial supply of slaves that most secular property holders did not have. The priests had the luxury of manipulating these slave gifts to their maximum benefit, selling difficult or unwanted slaves and keeping those who met their most pressing needs. From an economic standpoint, the Benedictines not only received large numbers of slaves at zero cost, but they also were able to stock their properties with slave artisans and technicians in positions that otherwise would have required salaried employees.[63] Yet, as Table 2 clearly shows, in spite of these economic windfalls, the Benedictines still had to rely on the vulgarity of the slave market. In the end, the Benedictines faced the same dilemmas as secular slave owners; properties remained functional only if they were replenished with more Africans.

Though we can speak broadly about shifts in the slave trade from Senegambia slaves, to Angola slaves, and finally to Mina slaves, the demographic reality on Brazilian properties was much more complex. In the earliest years, native Brazilians were the primary source of slave labor on most properties, but they were quickly replaced by a variety of "Guinea" slaves. These undifferentiated Guinea slaves, many from the Senegambia region, gave way to the first waves of Central Africans, beginning in the latter part of the sixteenth century. The slave populations on Brazilian properties remained overwhelmingly Central African throughout the end of the 1600s. Nevertheless, beginning in the last quarter of the century, the ethnic composition of some properties gradually became more heterogeneous and more "creole." This was especially true in the northeast of Brazil, where increasing numbers of Mina slaves began replacing their Central African predecessors, a trend that lasted roughly three decades.

Even as we acknowledge these important shifts, we must not lose sight of the overall ethnic terrain. Central Africans formed the foundation of most Brazilian slave communities, constituting more than 90 percent of slave imports to Brazil until the last decades of the seventeenth century. When some slave communities slowly began to increase their numbers naturally, the "creole" children born into these communities were most often born to Central African parents. Similarly, when slaves from the Bight of Benin and other parts of Africa began to arrive in significant numbers in the 1690s, they entered a cultural milieu that was decidedly Central African. Thus, early Central Africans had a profound impact on the slave cultures and societies that emerged in Brazil over the course of the eighteenth century and beyond. How these Central Africans, Minas, and "creoles" came together to form families, kinship groups, and communities is the subject of Chapter 2.

Kinship, Family, and Household Formation

On August 30, 1751, Father João Rodrigues Pina accepted payment of 110 mil-réis in exchange for the freedom of his Angolan slave, Lucrécia de André. At first glance, Lucrécia's manumission did not seem out of the ordinary. After more than twenty years as a slave, it seemed quite reasonable that her master would allow her to purchase her freedom. It also seemed plausible that, with the help of relatives or friends in the freed community, Lucrécia would have been able to collect the money for her *carta de alforria* (letter of manumission). But Lucrécia did not purchase her own freedom, and neither did anyone else in Brazil. The money for Lucrécia's freedom was paid by a ship's captain arriving from Luanda, Captain Manuel Rodrigues de Freitas Silva. The captain declared that he had been ordered to pay this money by Captain Félix José Nogueira, resident of the city of Luanda. Nogueira, in turn, had remitted the money to Father Pina on behalf of Manuel da Costa Perico, the brother of Lucrécia de André.[1]

Thus, after more than twenty years of separation, Manuel da Costa Perico was able to locate his enslaved sister, save the money for her freedom, and pass it in a four-man relay across the Atlantic Ocean, from Angola to Brazil. Whether Lucrécia de André made it back to Angola (or whether she would have had any desire to return after so many years away) is uncertain from the records, but her brother's dogged determination to free her from bondage is a testament to the importance of real kin and the attendant obligations of such ties in African societies. By purchasing his sister's freedom, Manuel da Costa Perico not only freed her from the rigors of servitude, but he rescued her from the oblivion of kinlessness. Across lifetimes and oceans, real kin could never be erased from one another's consciousnesses.

While Lucrécia's liberation by her Angolan brother represents an exemplary case of kinship and memory, other Africans were able to maintain ancestral relationships in a more direct fashion in the Americas. Indeed, there is sparse evidence from across the diaspora that some Africans made the Atlantic crossing with members of their natal kin group. For example, in Mexico City in 1629, Isabel Biafada appeared as a witness at the marriage of her creole nephew, Juan de Lomas, whom she claimed to have known since his birth. Thus, Isabel was in Mexico with one of her brothers or sisters. Similarly, Juan Angola maintained a close relationship with his sister Angelina, despite the fact that they were owned by different masters in Mexico City.[2] In 1669, four new slaves were purchased for the Bahian *engenho* of Sergipe do Conde: Miguel Bambaambuilla, his brother Pedro Bambaambuilla, their cousin Esperança Bambaambuilla, and her sister Maria Bambaambuilla.[3] And in the late 1680s, the Remire plantation in French Guyana owned discrete groups of Kalabari, Allada, and Whydah slaves. Evidence suggests that individuals from each of these nations probably "either knew each other before their sale in America or at the very least had common friends and family."[4]

Manumission records of slaves in Rio de Janeiro in the eighteenth century show similar trends. In 1751, Miguel Barbara, a freed black whose ethnic and national backgrounds are unclear from the records, purchased the freedom of Joanna Benguella for 128 mil-réis. Five months later he purchased the freedom of Ventura Benguella for 166$400. Though Miguel Barbara's relationship to the two slaves he freed is not explicitly stated, the fact that the two shared the same African "nation" suggests that Barbara acted upon some ethnic/kinship imperative, whether fictive or real.[5] More certain is the case of Caterina Mina who in 1754 was purchased for 200 mil-réis by the freed black Antônio de Basto Maia, who "declared that he gave the said quantity for the love of God, the said *preta* [black woman] being his sister."[6]

Despite this handful of examples of ancestral relationships surviving the Middle Passage, the painful reality of slavery in the Americas was that the natal lineages of most Africans were forever broken. And no matter how successful an individual was at creating new webs of kinship, these fictive or corporate webs of kinlike relationships could never replace what was lost in the break from the natal kinship unit. To be removed from the kinship network was to alter the life cycle in ways that are unimaginable for most Westerners. The meanings of the markers that define the human life span—birth, childhood, adolescence, marriage, child-rearing, old age, and dying—were all radically transformed. To face these challenges alone, without the collective support and shared understandings of the natal network of kin, was tantamount to social death.[7] And in spite of the re-creation of a variety of kinship forms in the Americas, the loss of natal kin must have loomed large in the lives of those who were enslaved and in the lives of those blood relatives who were left behind in Africa.

Even as the memory of real kin continued to burn in many enslaved Africans, they were confronted with the stark reality of their new isolation and solitude. Not to be vanquished, these Africans immediately began formulating new alliances and kinship groupings based, in part, on the shared experiences of enslavement and the Middle Passage. It must be stressed that for many Africans who entered the Atlantic slave trade, natal kinship ties had already been broken by war, drought, disease, forced migration, and enslavement in Africa. The creation of new kinlike ties was a phenomenon that was already occurring prior to embarkation for the Americas. Still, arrival at the Atlantic coast and subsequent European chattel slavery represented a stark departure, thrusting most slaves into a strange and unfamiliar world. Not only were these slaves facing new horrors at the hands of their European captors, but they were thrown together with a new cohort of African and African-descended strangers. Because of the extreme liminality that each individual faced as he or she was ripped from his or her homeland, solitude soon gave way to the reality of collective suffering. As such, friendships were made, alliances were forged, and new networks of kin were constructed, even as these Africans were making the dreadful crossing of the Atlantic.

Conscious of their isolation and the uncertain prospects for their futures, some enslaved shipmates called one another "*malungo*," a term that in Brazil came to be understood as "comrade," "relative," or perhaps "brother."[8] Though this term of adoptive kinship might simply be representative of the shared horror and triumph of surviving the Middle Passage, we should not lose sight of the broader symbolic meaning that such a title might suggest. The Portuguese translations of the Kimbundu-derived word *malunga* apparently did not capture the full meaning of the term. According to Joseph Miller, the *malunga* was a Mbundu symbol of authority, brought from the sea by the original ancestors, which could establish a new hierarchy of lineages in a given territory.[9] Because of the *malunga*'s close association with the sea, one can easily see why those who shared the misery and death of the Middle Passage would embrace such a term, but one should also recognize that by adopting "*malungo*," the newly enslaved were aware of their role in establishing new sets of kinship groups that reflected the vital social structures that had sustained them in Africa. Whether these new kinship groupings were patterned after African corporate structures or based upon the belief that they were creating altogether new natal lineages, the fact remains that many enslaved Africans began reconstituting themselves as members of larger kinship collectives capable of affirming their place in the world.

In some places, these new kinship communities would resemble those of the Portuguese, as slaves slowly adopted Western and Christian conceptions of marriage and nuclear families. But in many other places, slave communities remained thoroughly Africanized, with the majority eschewing Christian marriage for a variety of arrangements with African resonances. In this chapter we will examine more closely the complexion of family and kinship development among slaves in colonial Brazil. First, we will demonstrate that most slave families were built upon a wide range of male/female arrangements that were not sanctioned by the Catholic Church. We will then interrogate the meaning of Christian marriage in slave society, showing how the Western marriage ritual was variously rejected, adopted, and transformed by peoples of African descent. We will also look at patterns of household formation in a single Brazilian slave community, suggesting that even where a significant creole population was emerging, African kinship patterns continued to predominate. Finally, we will examine "homosexual" variations on kinship formation in African slave communities. While some of these relationships were probably born of unfavorable sex ratios, others were expressions of African institutional forms that survived in Brazilian slave communities.

Rites of Passage: Adulthood, Marriage, and Childbirth

One of the important markers in the lifetimes of most Africans was the rite of passage from childhood to adulthood. Across Africa, this transition was recognized through a series of ceremonies that prepared the young man or woman to become a productive member of society. While the ceremonies varied slightly from society to society, their meanings and impacts were remarkably similar. During adolescence, boys and girls were taken away from their communities and taught the duties of their respective sexes. Among the many mysteries that were unraveled for these young people were the joys of sex. In parts of Angola, young women were sequestered in a house built specifically for the occasion. After a number of days of instruction, they emerged as "grown" women able to sleep with men for the first time.[10] Father Girolamo Merolla, a Capuchin priest, noted the widespread belief that "if they did not do this, they would never be able to procreate."[11]

For young men, the process was similar, but was memorialized by the permanent mark of circumcision. Across Central Africa, "masters of circumcision" were called upon to initiate boys into young men. The ceremony was attended by the young man's family and culminated with grand celebrations of feasting and dancing. Well into the seventeenth century, Portuguese officials demonstrated their ignorance of Angolan ritual by questioning whether Africans were circumcising their male children because they were Jews.[12] The reality was that without circumcision, Angolan males were thought to lack virility and were rejected as social pariahs. The Portuguese soldier Antônio Cadornega, writing in 1680, reported: "All the pagans of these reigns use circumcision, even many of those who are baptized . . . and one is not considered a perfect man who is not."[13] The scar of circumcision was an indelible marker of one's manhood, and a requirement for marriage.[14] At the beginning of the eighteenth century, even in Brazil, it was reported that Angolan slave women refused to have sex with slave men who were uncircumcised.[15]

These preparations for sexual life were not only an affirmation and celebration of the reproductive capacity; they were also a way for adults to reveal the secrets of sexual pleasure to their adolescent children. Upon reaching adulthood, sexual activity was celebrated and encouraged, with little social stigma attached to what Westerners would call "promiscuity." Even in "marriage," sexual monogamy was not always practiced. Describing the sexual habits of Central Africans in the late seventeenth century, Father Giovanni Antônio Cavazzi wrote:

> To maintain a great number of concubines, which is an idea to which many conform, is not contrary to the inviolability of the sacrament, nor a discredit to the nobility and good fame of man, and they say that they maintain them, not incited by lasciviousness, but by the decorum of their very greatness. They understand that the honor of a woman is not obfuscated by the variety of her loves, nor by the number of her lovers, as long as she recognizes her husband as her principal lover.[16]

The code of Christian morality that the Portuguese applied to their own sexual relationships was absent in many African societies, where there was a distinction drawn between the communal obligations of marriage and individual carnal desires. For those who were sent to the Americas as slaves, the demographic landscape was so radically transformed that we cannot draw strong parallels between African and American sexual behaviors. Nonetheless, many of the same attitudes and African-type arrangements would persist, inspiring a wide array of negative commentary and attempts on the part of European clergymen to correct this "illicit" behavior by imposing Christian marriage.

Perhaps the clearest measure of the fact that slaves did not marry according to the custom of the Catholic Church was the high rate of out-of-wedlock births in the slave community. Reviewing the baptismal records from several Brazilian parishes makes it clear that the vast majority of slaves rejected Christian marriage as a way of affirming their relationships. For example, between 1691 and 1701, in the rural parish of Jacarepaguá in Rio de Janeiro 61.5 percent of slave children were born to parents whose unions were not recognized by Christian authorities.[17] Though the rate of out-of-wedlock births was high in all communities in colonial Brazil, it was almost always far higher in the slave community. Between 1723 and 1724, in the parish of Saubara in the Recôncavo of Bahia, 29.4 percent of babies born into the free population were born out of Christian wedlock, while 90.3 percent of the slave children were born to unmarried mothers.[18] Similarly, between 1751 and 1758, in the urban parish of São José in Rio de Janeiro, 85.6 percent of slave children were born out of wedlock, with nearly a third of these births being to "Angolan" mothers.[19] For the free population during this period, only 24.7 percent of newborns were conceived out of Christian wedlock.[20]

We should stress that even though the majority of slave women gave birth out of Christian wedlock, this does not mean that they were not involved in stable relationships. In some cases, the identity of the father is listed in the baptismal record as "*pai incognito*," but in other cases, both parents appeared for the baptism of their child. For instance, Luís and Antônia, both "Guiné" slaves, appeared for the baptism of their twins, Manuel and Maria, on June 26, 1691, even though both parents were listed as "single" slaves.[21] Similarly, in 1752, an Angolan-born slave named João da Silva readily acknowledged his fifteen-year-old daughter, Luísa, as well as the child's mother, Guiomar da Silva, even though João and Guiomar had never married in the Catholic Church.[22]

In some parishes, the baptizing priests allowed African mothers to name the fathers of their "natural" born children, even in cases where the couples were not "legally" married.[23] For example, between 1709 and 1714 in the urban parish of Santíssimo Sacramento in Rio de Janeiro, 93.4 percent of children born to African slave mothers were born out of Christian wedlock. Nevertheless, 35.7 percent of these African women provided the name of their child's father, acknowledging their relationships with these men and suggesting the probability of enduring bonds.[24] Indeed, during the five-year period, several unmarried African couples had sustained relationships that produced more than one child. For instance, Teresa Mina named Antônio Masangano as the father of her two sons Felipe (baptized on May 1, 1711) and Francisco (baptized October 11, 1713), indicating a relationship of at least three years. While Teresa and Antônio were the property of a single master (Domingos

Álvares Cazado), others maintained relationships even as they worked and lived with different masters. Maria Mina, slave of Josepha Duarte, named Antônio Mina, slave of King João V, as the father of her two daughters, Anastacia (baptized August 27, 1710) and Geralda (baptized March 2, 1713). Despite not marrying in accordance with the Catholic Church, Maria and Antônio forged a union that almost certainly had lasting social and cultural impacts on their daughters.

We can be sure that a number of enduring relationships remain obscured in the records, but at the same time, we should not assume that "single-parent" births were part and parcel of some broader pathology. As we have already noted, many African societies celebrated a sexual freedom that was rare in the West. The offspring of these relationships were by no means marginalized. Indeed, they were readily accommodated into existing family and kinship arrangements. Commenting on the status of "illegitimate" children in Angola, Father Cavazzi wrote: "The importance of being a legitimate child, so appreciated in Europe and in other parts, still seems to be completely unknown to many Ethiopes. They give as much equal consideration to the legitimate child as they do the illegitimate. Rather it seems, at times, they appreciate more the children that they procreate in the effervescence of illegal ardors than those who are the delicate fruit of Christian matrimony."[25] The reality, of course, is that many Africans forged bonds of kinship that were culturally sanctioned by their communities, not by the Catholic Church. Likewise, for African slaves and their descendants in the Americas, there was apparently little distinction made between those children born of "illegal ardors" and those born in "Christian matrimony." Catholic marriage was an institution that had little resonance in the worldview of most Africans. In the Americas, slaves created a variety of arrangements in accordance with their more pliant attitudes toward human sexuality and extended kinship. That the majority were not easily swayed by the preachings of Catholic priests should come as no surprise.

Despite the difficulty in convincing African slaves that they should embrace Christian marriage, from as early as the sixteenth century and extending until the end of our study in the 1770s, many Catholic missionaries fought the uphill battle of trying to reconcile slave couples with the Catholic Church. As early as 1583, Father Cristóvão Gouveia reported that around 100 Indian and Guinea slaves were married in Bahia, "removing them from their evil state."[26] Between 1617 and 1619, mission priests in the Recôncavo of Bahia reported marrying 112 slave couples, despite there being few priests who could speak the necessary African languages.[27] And again in 1702, missionaries in the Recôncavo reported marrying 46 slave couples who "were put on the path to salvation by means of Holy Matrimony" and saved from "the evil state that they were in."[28]

Although these missions bore many fruits, the fathers confronted a number of obstacles in their attempts to introduce slaves to the sacrament of marriage. The most formidable of these was the disparity in the number of slave men to slave women. Since African suppliers often were reluctant to part with female slaves of childbearing age and Brazilian buyers preferred strong, young males, the Brazilian slave population remained overwhelmingly male throughout the colonial period. Sex ratios (calculated by dividing the number of males by the number of females and multiplying by 100) on Bahian *engenhos* in the seventeenth century ranged between 115 and 336, with the average falling somewhere around 200.[29] Even on the Benedictine properties, where balance was carefully monitored, the sex ratio in the 1660s ranged from 114 at Engenho Guaguasú in Rio de Janeiro to 149 at Engenho Musurepe in Pernambuco.[30]

On the large secular *engenhos* the sex ratio hovered around 200 well into the eighteenth century, and the ratio was often higher outside of the sugar industry.[31] In 1738, a Rio blacksmith owned fourteen men and only three women.[32] During the same period, a typical manioc farm in Rio had seven men, one woman, and two young children; another manioc farm in the 1750s had ten men and only four women.[33] The sex ratio on three *olarias* (tile-making facilities) in Rio de Janeiro in the 1750s was three males to every female.[34] In Maranhão, the Jesuits presided over five different cattle ranches in the middle of the eighteenth century, which were staffed by a total of eighteen slaves — seventeen males and only one female.[35] And in the major mining cities of Minas Gerais in 1718, males represented more than 90 percent of the servile population.[36]

This overwhelmingly African, overwhelmingly male slave population had a major impact on kinship formation in Brazil. For African men, the extreme sex imbalance must have transformed many of their understandings of family and sexuality. Many male slaves came from African societies where women were increasingly dominant in the population. For instance, by the late eighteenth century, women outnumbered men two-to-one in parts of Angola, nearly the same ratio as men to women in the slave population of Brazil.[37] Angolans could adapt to this imbalance by relying on a well-established tradition of polygyny; men simply took additional wives. But the exact opposite was occurring in Brazil. Those men who might expect to have more than one wife in Africa, especially those who were put to work on small holdings where there were few women in close proximity, were now faced with the likelihood that they would not find female partners at all. And without female partners, they could not procreate. The sex imbalance certainly stifled the prospects of creating new natal lineages in Brazil and no doubt reinforced the Africans' sense of having suffered a social death. In short, cultural expectations regarding marriage and kinship were turned upside down.

By 1619, it was clear that the sex imbalance among Angola slaves was already taking its toll on the stability of slave relationships. On their mission to the Recôncavo of Bahia, two Jesuit fathers reported that Angolan men poisoned other male slaves because these men carried on "illicit" relationships with their wives.[38] With such high male to female sex ratios, it could only be expected that some women would attract the attention of more than one man. But the violence that resulted from these affairs was a function of false expectations. Angolan men came from societies where they increasingly had access to numerous wives; when the situation was reversed, their sense of masculinity was threatened. Some masters tried to remedy this situation by purchasing female slaves. In 1747–1748, on Engenho da Ilha in Rio de Janeiro, the Benedictines purchased seven Mina women "in order that they marry with the slave men of the same *fazenda*."[39] But the majority of masters remained indifferent to sex imbalances. The reality was that most masters viewed their slaves as beasts of burden; interpersonal and human relationships in the slave community were only a distant concern.

Another obstacle that stood in the way of clergymen in their quest to have slaves marry were the slave masters. For a variety of reasons, most masters were not quick to endorse church marriages for their bondsmen. In their 1619 mission to the Recôncavo, the Jesuit fathers reported that "for some reasons and inconveniences by the Devil's art," masters refused to order their slaves to marry.[40] One of the most obvious reasons that masters objected to church-sanctioned marriages was that these marriages often complicated economic decisions. The relocation or selling away of a slave who was a member of a church-recognized family destroyed the integrity of that family, and separation was widely recognized in Brazil as one of the primary reasons that slaves ran away. To make matters worse for the masters, canon law compelled them not to separate members of slave families. The masters' solution to this conundrum was to discourage church marriages and leave the slaves to their own devices in the relationships that they forged.[41] Of course, given the divergent cultural meanings of marriage in Africa and the West, slaves probably welcomed this lack of intervention.

Masters sometimes attempted to use the gulf between Christian and African understandings of marriage to their advantage. In arguments against sanctioning unions between slaves, masters claimed that Africans, unacquainted with the notion of permanent unions and unable to procure divorces, often resorted to killing their spouses with poison or "witchcraft" when they tired of the marriage.[42] Though probably apocryphal, this argument illustrates the master's awareness of the incongruence of Catholic morality and the types of arrangements that Africans created.

At times, even priests had difficulty reconciling the problem of slaves as property and slaves as members of Christian families. For the most part, priests cajoled, coerced, and even forced their slaves to marry. In 1584, Father Anchieta wrote that the slaves of the Jesuit College of Bahia were "separate[d] . . . from their concubines and subject . . . to the laws of matrimony."[43] But fifty years later, on Engenho Sergipe, Father Sebastião Vaz complained that the majority of the *engenho*'s slaves were single and living in sin. The situation remained unchanged at Sergipe in 1733, when Father Jerónimo da Gama lamented that most of the property's slaves were still unmarried. In the same year, on Engenho Santana, Father Pedro Teixeira exhorted the *engenho*'s slaves "to give up their evil state and marry," but to little avail.[44] The rhetoric of encouraging slave marriage was one thing, but the real-life difficulties of supporting slave families offered little incentive for the Jesuits actually to force the issue of family formation.

The fact was that fostering slave families could be exasperatingly expensive, not to mention socially disruptive for the masters. We have already mentioned the social difficulties arising from marriages in areas where the gender imbalance was extreme. This type of unrest and its associated violence were apparently rather common and became the pretext for some priests to actually ban slave marriages. Indeed, in 1745, the Franciscans took the radical step of prohibiting their slaves from marrying, "in order to avoid some disorders that have followed" such marriages.[45] Difficult pregnancies often incapacitated able-bodied female slaves for extended periods of time. According to the slave inventory of Engenho Santana in 1674, Antônia Criolla was out of work for eight months as a result of an illness that arose from a difficult childbirth.[46] If mother and child lived through the birth, there was no guarantee that the child would survive exposure to the numerous diseases that plagued slave communities. And finally, the cost of raising children to productive adulthood simply did not pay off in the same way that purchasing new adult Africans did.

Despite the potential disruptions caused by slave families, at least one group of priests zealously pressured their slaves to marry and encouraged them to form families. The Benedictines were widely regarded as among the finest plantation administrators in colonial Brazil. From as early as the seventeenth century their properties were relatively balanced in terms of sex ratios, and they owned few unmarried slaves. But for the slaves, coerced marriages came at a price. In 1751, Padre Antônio de Jesus Maria reported that he found a number of slaves living in concubinage at the monastery in Bahia. Among the women, there was one who was "most scandalous," who told the father that she did not want to marry, this after the father had already ordered that a *senzala* (slave quarter) be built for her and her prospective husband. When the father asked her why she did not want to marry, she replied that she was still a young girl. The father rebuked her, telling her that "for that very reason she should want to marry and that she should open her eyes." He then proceeded to threaten her, warning that "the monastery did not want a single and scandalous female slave and that she should choose a husband from the eight unmarried male slaves that the monastery owned. Otherwise, she should search for someone to purchase her, because poorly behaved and scandalous slaves did not serve the priests." In the days that followed, the woman acquiesced and was married to the man to whom she was originally betrothed, all to the great satisfaction of Father de Jesus Maria, who claimed that the slaves "do not cease in thanking me for removing them from the path of doom and putting them on that of salvation."[47]

The Benedictines were not alone in pressuring their slaves to marry. As early as 1707, official church policy required that masters deliver their slaves from "concubinage, . . . it being everywhere normal and almost common to permit them to go about in a state of damnation." Those masters who did "not take steps to turn [slaves] away from their wayward activities and ruinous condition" could see their slaves banished or imprisoned "without any regard for the loss which the said masters may incur."[48] Most slave masters ignored the church's orders. However, those who took the admonitions seriously were often quick to make marriage choices for their slaves. Father Antonil wrote that some masters would matter-of-factly tell their slaves, "You so-and-so, in your time will marry so-and-so," and the slaves were forced to obey.[49] Marriage records seem to affirm Antonil's claim, as it was not unusual for a master to have three or even four pairs of his slaves married in the same ceremony. In some cases the slaves may have chosen to marry in this communal fashion, but in others the master was almost surely in control. For instance, it seems unlikely that four females from the Mina coast of Africa would have chosen to marry three Angola males and one creole male, let alone all in the same ceremony. But this was the case when their master, João de Figueiredo, sent them forth to be married in Rio de Janeiro in the middle of the eighteenth century.[50]

The negative impacts of these unwanted interventions could present great difficulties for the slaves. Forced marriages were a recipe for a wide range of adulterous "crimes." Slaves simply ignored the hollow wedding vows that were forced upon them and carried on with relationships that were meaningful to them. Most masters turned a blind eye toward the "extramarital" affairs that resulted from coerced marriages, affairs that provided extra ammunition for their arguments that Africans were lascivious heathens. The consciences of the masters were clear because they had met their Christian duty by joining their slaves in holy matrimony, and they were free from the harassment of missionaries and church officials. But when these adulterous crimes came to the attention of the church, the slaves themselves were forced to pay for their masters' sins.

In January 1746, Lourença Correia da Lapa, the thirty-year-old slave of Sargento-Mor Antônio de Figueiredo de Almeida, was incarcerated for the crime of bigamy. A resident of Rio de Janeiro, Lourença was remitted to Lisbon for questioning by the Portuguese Holy Office. There, she confessed that it had been seven years since she worked in the house of her master, whose wife, Dona Isabel, forced her to marry an elderly slave named Pedro Banguer. The marriage was only "celebrated at the will of their masters," and the two slaves never consummated the marriage. Because Dona Isabel "punished her with supreme rigor," Lourença's master gave her permission to leave his house, and she went to the village of São João de Meritim. There, she served for some time in the house of one Estevão Rodrigues, where she determined to marry again. Uncertain how to deal with her first marriage, Lourença consulted a widowed friend named Clara Gata. Clara advised Lourença that she "could marry again since the first marriage was not a true one."

In accordance with Lourença's wishes, Clara organized her second wedding. First, she introduced Lourença to a suitable mate, 50-year-old Amaro de França Cordeiro, slave of Estevão Rodrigues. Next, Clara found four witnesses who were prepared to testify that they knew Lourença to be single and fit to marry. Two of these witnesses were unaware of her first marriage, but the other two knew that she was already married. All four apparently were persuaded by the cash bribe given to them by Clara Gata. On the strength of these four witnesses, Lourença and Amaro were married and lived together happily for four years before Lourença was jailed for bigamy.

Under examination by the inquisitors, Lourença was asked why, if she was so certain that her first marriage was not valid, she did not declare this fact to the priest who married her the second time. Lourença said that she wanted to speak the truth, but that her friend Clara Gata told her "to keep her mouth shut because it was not necessary to speak." Unimpressed by her pleas for mercy, the inquisitors ultimately sentenced Lourença to be publicly humiliated in the auto da fé, whipped in the streets *citra sanguinis effusionem*, and exiled to Castro-Marim for five years.[51]

The case of Lourença Correia has multiple layers, some of which raise questions that cannot be easily answered by the available evidence. For instance, why did Dona Isabel insist on the marriage between Lourença and Amaro? And why did she continue to abuse her slave? Was Dona Isabel jealous because her husband was having an affair with his slave, Lourença? One must also question why Lourença felt compelled to validate her "true" marriage with the Catholic Church. Though lacking a thorough understanding of church doctrine, she still embraced Christian marriage as a way of affirming her relationship with Amaro. Perhaps she believed that by marrying for a second time, she could erase the horrible experience of her first marriage.

Another interesting aspect of this case is the part played by Clara Gata. Her role as the wise, older matchmaker has strong African resonances. Older slaves, both male and female, were accorded a great deal of respect and authority in their communities, and Lourença seems to have relied upon Clara as a trusted, older "family" member, one who knew how to negotiate the minefields of Christian customs and laws. Clara's ability to rally other slaves around an "illegal" marriage was ingenious, but not unusual. From as early as 1616 in Lisbon, a priest noted that the "*preto* [black]" witnesses to the marriage of Francisco and Maria, pretos, "deceived me because none of them were from my parish." [52] Africans and their descendants found numerous ways to circumvent the bureaucratic obstacles that were placed in their paths, especially when these hurdles interfered with how they wanted to arrange their interior lives.

In short, peoples of African descent sometimes manipulated the loopholes in the marriage contract to suit their own needs, ignoring Christian strictures in order to marry multiple times. On the one hand, multiple marriages affirmed the growing cultural importance of Christian marriage; but on the other hand, these marriages indicated an unwillingness on the part of blacks to accept the requirements of Christian monogamy. Some Africans and their descendants transformed the marriage contract so that it was more aligned to their own cultural understandings.

This is not to suggest that polygyny was a widespread phenomenon among Africans in the diaspora. [53] As we have already noted, the dearth of females tempered any desire that slaves may have had to replicate African patterns of behavior. Indeed, the jealousies and disorders among male slaves that were caused by female infidelity suggest that polyandry may have been as prevalent as polygyny. But where possible, some African men carried on relationships with multiple female partners, sometimes even going through the trouble of having these relationships endorsed by the church.

In the mid-1620s, Francisco da Fonseca, a Mina slave in the city of Seville, Spain, married a slave woman named Joana Morena. He was married to her for eleven years, during which time he fathered two daughters with another Sevillian slave woman, named Francisca. Francisco gained his freedom, and eventually left for Lisbon, leaving behind his wife, his mistress, and two daughters. He was in Lisbon for eighteen years before marrying a free woman, Antônia Nogueira. In order to effect this marriage, Francisco convinced three other free blacks to swear that he was single and born in Lisbon. Francisco was married to Antônia for eight years, and they had a daughter together before Francisco was denounced to the Inquisition in 1660.[54]

Similarly, Manuel de Souza, a Benguela slave who resided in Pernambuco, was married on his master's *engenho* to Maria Cardosa, an Arda woman, in 1732. Shortly after his marriage, Manuel struck up a relationship with another slave named Maria Correia, a Mina woman who was the property of one of the *engenho*'s tenant sharecroppers. Because of "the great love that he had for . . . Maria Correia," Manuel also wanted to marry her. Consulting some Gypsy friends, Manuel was told that he should leave his first wife and marry Maria Correia. The Gypsies persuaded Manuel that his first marriage was of no concern and that "he would not be the first person to marry for a second time." In 1738, only six years after his first marriage, Manuel married Maria Correia, with one of the Gypsies appearing as a witness to lie that Manuel was single. Manuel's ruse was soon discovered, and he was jailed on the order of the Bishop of Pernambuco. Eventually, Manuel was forced to pay the ultimate price for his "sin." In addition to being sentenced to appear before the auto da fé and being publicly whipped "until blood flowed," Manuel was banished to the king's galleys for five years. He went to the galleys on November 20, 1742, but died less than three years later on April 25, 1745.[55]

While the great majority of African slaves chose to join together in a diversity of unions that the Portuguese labeled sinful, others voluntarily embraced the sacrament of holy matrimony and married in the Catholic Church. Yet even in the rare instances where this occurred, we should not assume that all of these slaves were adopting the Christian notion of marriage. And we certainly should not conclude that these marriages reinforced the institution of slavery. Indeed, the evidence from the parish records suggests that "marriage" was just one more way of crystallizing African ethnic and national alliances, perpetuating shared understandings of kinship, child rearing, and so on.[56]

An examination of eighteenth-century parish records from Rio de Janeiro gives us some insight into the importance of African regional identities in the forging of slave communities.[57] In a sample of marriages from the urban parish of Nossa Senhora da Candelária between 1751 and 1761, a total of 222 Africans were joined in holy matrimony (Table 3). Of these 222 individuals, 186 married other Africans. In other words, 84 percent of the Africans in the sam-

Table 3. Marriages Involving Africans in the Parish of Nossa Senhora da Candelária, Rio de Janeiro, 1751–1761

Type of Marriage	Number of Marriages	Number of Africans (% of Total)
Africans Married to Other Africans		
Married to Partners from Same Cultural Area		
Guiné with Guiné	47	94
Mina with Mina	15	30
Angola with Angola	4	8
Benguela with Benguela	2	4
Ganguela with Ganguela	1	2
Benguela with Ganguela	1	2
Benguela with Angola	1	2
Mina with Cabo Verde	1	2
Mina with São Tomé	1	2
	73	146 (66)
Married to Partners from Different Cultural Area		
Angola with Mina	5	10
Benguela with Mina	2	4
Angola with Cabo Verde	1	2
Massangano with Mina	1	2
Monjollo with Cabo Verde	1	2
Guiné with Cabo Verde	4	8
Guiné with Mina	6	12
	20	40 (18)
Subtotal		186 (84)
Africans Married to Non-Africans		
Mina with Crioulo	14	14
Mina with Pardo	4	4
Mina with White	1	1
Guiné with Crioulo	11	11
Guiné with Pardo	4	4
Cabo Verde with Crioulo	1	1
Congo with Crioulo	1	1
	36	36 (16)
Total	129	222 (100)

Source: ACMRJ, Nossa Senhora da Candelária, Casamentos de pessoas livres e escravos, 1751–1761.

Table 4. Marriages Involving Africans in the Parish of São Salvador do Mundo de Guaratiba, Rio de Janeiro, 1763–1770

Type of Marriage	Number of Marriages	Number of Africans (% of Total)
Africans Married to Partners from Same Cultural Area		
Guiné with Guiné	10	20
Angola with Angola	3	6
Benguela with Benguela	2	4
Benguela with Angola	2	4
Benguela with Bambambuira	1	2
Cabo Verde with Guiné	1	2
	19	38 (93)
Africans Married to Non-Africans		
Guiné with Crioulo	2	2
Motema with Crioulo	1	1
	3	3 (7)
Total	22	41 (100)

Source: ACMRJ, Freguesia de S. Salvador do Mundo de Guaratiba, Casamentos de Escravos (1763–1794).

ple married other Africans. In addition, 66 percent of the Africans in the sample married partners who came from the same broad cultural areas of Africa. Thirty-six Africans married crioulos, pardos, and whites, representing just 16 percent of all Africans who were married.

In the rural parish of Guaratiba, Africans were even more likely to marry partners from the same African region (Table 4). In a sample of forty-one Africans who married in that parish between 1763 and 1770, thirty-eight married other Africans (93 percent). Of these thirty-eight, all were married to people of the same or similar regional background. The remaining three Africans married crioulos.

Although the marriage registers provide us with a snapshot of African marriage patterns, they tell us little about the nature of the family arrangements that grew out of these marriages. In fact, one must remember that at least some of the marriages between Africans were probably unions coerced by the master. One way of peering beyond the marriage ceremony itself is to give a close reading to the baptismal records. Africans who brought their children to the baptismal font were also identified by their regional backgrounds. Thus, we not only get a glimpse of the social and cultural alliances that were forged by these marriages, but we begin to see how marriages between Africans were cemented through the celebration of child birth.

The sample taken in Table 5 confirms the patterns of African regional endogamy demonstrated in the earlier samples. Of 142 Africans who brought their children to be baptized in São José between 1751 and 1758, 128 (90 percent) married other Africans, and 110 (77 percent) of these married partners with similar ethnic, or national, affinity. The children of these unions were born "creoles" and were baptized in the Catholic Church, but their childhoods were lived mostly in the worlds of their African parents. The decision of these parents to marry a partner from the same African region was not a random or abstract choice. Africans who shared similar cultural understandings gravitated toward one another in the Americas and found ways to reconstitute common cultural ground through language, religion, child-rearing practices, and so on. In this respect, Africans were not unlike migrants in any other diaspora who sought to maintain social and cultural relations within ethnic boundaries. Endogamous marriage, whether endorsed by the church or not, was a first step in the attempt to recreate specific social and cultural forms in the Americas. Where the demographic situation allowed, Africans built upon these alliances, forming distinct groups of slaves who shared cultural understandings, built broad kinship units, and passed on knowledge to their creole offspring.

Unfortunately, the sources for colonial Brazil provide us with precious little material with which to reconstruct specific household and community arrangements for Africans and their descendants over time. There are only a few time-lapse series of slave inventories that survive for individual properties, and the majority of these lack information on household arrangements that can be traced across time. One set of exceptions are two slave inventories for the Jesuit Engenho Santana, one compiled in 1731, and the other in 1752.[58] Each of these inventories divides Santana's slaves into household groupings, with the social relationships of each person and their approximate ages also included. From these two documents, we get a brief glimpse of the shifting nature of household arrangements and kinship formation on a large sugar *engenho*.

The 1731 inventory from Engenho Santana is an outstanding example of African-type kinship structures being replicated in a predominantly creole society. Engenho Santana, which began to produce a self-sustaining core of creole slaves in the 1670s, was a mature creole environment by the 1730s. Though African imports continued to be necessary as a result of mortality, a solid creole core always survived, with the Africans being integrated and slowly socialized into the core.[59] Because the administrators of Santana supposedly took a

Table 5. Marriages Involving Africans Represented in the Baptismal Records of the Parish of São José, Rio de Janeiro, 1751–1758

Type of Marriage	Number of Marriages	Number of Africans (% of Total)
Africans Married to Other Africans		
Married to Partners from Same Cultural Area		
Angola with Angola	36	72
Guiné with Guiné	11	22
Benguela with Benguela	1	2
Mina with Mina	1	2
Congo with Congo	1	2
Cobú with Cobú	1	2
Guiné with Cabo Verde	1	2
Ganguela with Angola	1	2
Congo with Benguela	1	2
Benguela with Congo	1	2
	55	110 (77)
Married to Partners from Different Cultural Area		
Angola with Mina	3	6
Mina with Angola	1	2
Angola with Cabo Verde	1	2
Cabo Verde with Angola	3	6
Angola with São Tomé	1	2
	9	18 (13)
Subtotal		128 (90)
Africans Married to Non-Africans		
Crioulo with Angola	6	6
Pardo with Angola	1	1
Crioulo with Guiné	1	1
Cabra with Guiné	1	1
Angola with Crioula	3	3
Angola with Parda	1	1
Mina with Crioula	1	1
	14	14 (10)
Total	78	142 (100)

Source: ACMRJ, Paroquia de São José, Batismos de Escravos (1751–1790). Each of the marriages listed represents only one couple, even though that couple may have brought several children to be baptized during the eight-year period. For instance, even though Antônio and Gracia Angola appeared at the baptismal font three times, they are counted only once in the above table. Of the 78 couples represented in the sample, only 17 baptized more than one child.

benign, if not hostile, attitude toward marriage in the thirty years before 1730, the households were ones made by the slaves, with little interference from their masters.[60] And these households reflected a variety of arrangements that defy any neat summary or categorization.

Of fifty-seven distinct households, only ten were ones in which a male, a female, and their shared children lived together alone. The residents of these ten households represented 26 percent of the property's entire slave population. There were five households where a couple lived with a child who belonged to only one of the partners. Thus, the child was either born out of wedlock or born of a previous relationship. Such was the case with Antônio, his wife Joana Geje, and her "illegitimate" son Ignácio. Several households included a married couple with the siblings of one of the married partners. There were also several households composed of old women and single young men. Another household included the widower, seventy-year-old Antônio Congo, his adult children Martinho and Josepha, and the mulatta children of his deceased wife, Jerónima and Antônia. Finally, there were other units that were apparently made up of diverse unrelated individuals. For example, Manuel, age fifty, and his wife, Severina Geje (thirty), lived together with five single slaves—Mariana (twenty-four), Rosa Geje (twenty-five), Marcella Angola (fifty), Agostinho (sixty-five), and Maria (thirty).[61]

The willingness of households to adopt non-kin "outsiders" was a prominent feature of some African societies and allowed for the development of a mixed web of kinship on certain large Brazilian properties like Santana. This does not mean that core relationships between males and females—or marriages, if you will—were unimportant. Indeed, it was these enduring relationships that were the bulwark of the community and the mechanism that drove creolization. It was no coincidence that Joseph Passube, who was the father of seven living children on Engenho Santana in 1731, was celebrated as "the honor of the married men." By 1752, significant numbers of children from the 1731 inventory appear "married," in cross-cutting relationships that knit the community together even more tightly. In addition, despite the twenty-one years between the two inventories, nine of the twenty-six married couples who were living together in 1731 were still together in 1752.

Even though there is evidence that marriages cemented the creole core of Santana, we must bear in mind that Christian marriage was not the primary impetus for reproduction and expansion of kinship units on most secular properties in Brazil. As has been well illustrated by the baptismal records, the majority of slave women gave birth outside the boundaries of Christian marriage. And some of these births were to couples in long-standing relationships. In addition, new African imports arrived with frequency on most properties, thereby requiring the regular integration of strangers into communities. In the end, kinship formation in Brazilian slave society was a fluid process that included a variety of arrangements, and the webs of kinship that resulted from these multitude of arrangements were the essence of slave family and community.

Same-Sex Relationships among African Slaves

The foregoing account assumes that kinship structures based on heterosexual relationships were the norm in Brazilian slave communities; however, there is a great deal of evidence to suggest that kinship formation was much more complex. Given the unfavorable sex balance in Brazil, we must recognize that "normal" kinlike relations in Brazilian slave communities may have been those that were forged between males, rather than between males and females. In addition to the kinlike networks that were created during the Middle Passage among *malungos*, Africans developed other corporate webs of kinship that sustained them in Brazil. Perhaps the best-known examples were the runaway slave communities that came to be known as *quilombos*. In Central Africa, the *ki-lombo* referred to a merit-based, male warrior society that not only cut across lineage boundaries, but actually erased lineage ties based on natal descent. These lineageless warrior societies were a practical solution to the ruptures in natal kinship that were created by war, famine, and forced migration in Central Africa during the era of the slave trade.[62] In Brazil, isolated, lineageless, mostly male, runaway slaves sometimes reconstituted themselves in a similar hierarchical, kinlike fashion. For example, Brazil's most famous runaway slave community, Palmares, was clearly influenced in both real and symbolic ways by the Central African *ki-lombo*.[63] In the absence of real kin and with limited possibilities for creating new natal lineages, many African men likely found these corporate bonds an attractive means of (re)creating group identity in the Americas.[64]

While some of the kinlike structures created by African slaves in Brazil were of the corporate, hierarchical variety, others reflected relationships that we might today define as "homosexual." One way in which African men sought emotional sustenance under conditions of extreme social dislocation was to seek out intimate relationships with other men. Scholars, including those who study the slave family, have long recognized the sex imbalance in almost all American slave regimes, but very few have explored the possibility that same-sex relationships might have been fostered in slave communities where there were few women. Nor have they investigated the extent to which "homosexual" men might have made the crossing from Africa to Europe and the Americas.[65] In the Portuguese colonial world, there is evidence of at least two types of consensual same-sex relationships involving African slaves, one born of the unfavorable sex ratios in the slave setting and the other arising from institutional gender inversion in Africa.[66]

In areas where sex ratios among slaves ran as high as ten men to every woman, it should not surprise us that male slaves sought out other males to satisfy their sexual impulses. Since the personal and private lives of slaves remained largely hidden from the master class, few of these encounters were ever recorded; yet we should not let the silence of the records keep us from asking how gender-isolated men either maintained or reformulated their sexual and gender identities. Some no doubt remained exclusively "heterosexual," perhaps resorting to celibacy and/or self gratification.[67] Others became so desperate in their quest for sexual satisfaction that they resorted to bestiality.[68] But I would suggest that, because their isolation was so acute, some male slaves recast their sexual identities as they reached out to their male peers for a combination of sexual and emotional sustenance.

Inquisition records from the sixteenth and seventeenth centuries reveal several instances of same-sex behavior on the part of slaves in the Portuguese world. We should concede from the outset that the records of these behaviors are rather meager. For Brazil, of the eighty-five "sodomites" who appeared before the visits of the Inquisition in the years 1591–1769, only twenty-three were Africans.[69] And of these twenty-three, only a few of the cases provide us with enough information to make any tentative conclusions regarding same-sex behaviors among Africans in Brazil. However, by also utilizing cases from the tribunals of Lisbon and Évora, as well as chronicles of Portuguese priests and soldiers along the Angolan coast, we can at least begin to gain a fuller understanding of African perceptions of same-sex relationships in the sixteenth and seventeenth centuries.

The most common types of sodomy cases involving men of African descent were those in which the men were apparently seeking emotional and sexual satisfaction that was absent in many slave settings. While some of these men may have been predisposed to same-sex behaviors in Africa, others were probably reaching out, searching for companionship in a lonely and violent world. There is sparse evidence that male slaves were having sexual liaisons with one another as early as the 1580s. In 1583, Father Cristóvão Gouveia lamented the gender imbalance at the Jesuit College of Bahia. In describing the conditions of slave men, he noted that "it is necessary to buy them women so that they not live in an evil state."[70] This "evil state" might have been polyandry, but Father

Gouveia was most likely referring to same-sex practices among the slaves. Indeed, one of the first recorded cases of same-sex practices among slaves in Brazil occurred at the same Jesuit College only eight years later.

On August 21, 1591, Matias Moreira appeared before the visitation of the Portuguese Holy Office in Bahia to denounce the African, Joane, a "Negro" slave from "Guiné." Matias, a resident laborer in the Jesuit College of Bahia, saw Joane de Guiné and another "negro de Guiné" as they entered his place of work in the middle of the night. Matias could not identify the second "negro de Guiné" but described him as having a grossly swollen leg. The African with the swollen leg told Matias that Joane brought him to the college to sodomize him. Joane responded to the man's charge by calling him a liar in an African language that Matias claimed to understand.[71]

Though Matias did not actually discover Joane and his friend in the act of committing the *pecado nefando*, or "nefarious sin," it seems that Joane had a long history of sexual relations with other men. Prior to his encounter with the man with the swollen leg, Joane at one time had been the property of the Jesuit College. When the fathers discovered that Joane had committed sodomy on numerous occasions with an Angolan named Duarte, "without Duarte's consent," they sold Joane to one Bastião de Faria. On the basis of his familiarity with the setting, Joane no doubt thought that the Jesuit College would be a safe haven for his rendezvous with the man with the swollen leg.

While it appears from Matias's testimony that Joane was forcing his partners to have sex with him, a closer reading reveals that both the swollen-leg man and Duarte were probably consensual partners. There is no suggestion of how Joane forced the swollen-leg man to enter the college with him in the middle of the night. Since the man knew he was being brought there to have sex with Joane and since it appears that he willingly entered the college with Joane, we must conclude that he was complicit. As for Duarte, he claimed that Joane was the passive partner in their sexual encounters.[72] If this was the case, Duarte clearly did not resist Joane's advances, and, given their numerous encounters, Duarte probably welcomed Joane's invitations. It seems clear that all of the parties involved in these trysts were consenting partners.

Similar cases of consensual same-sex behavior among peoples of African descent were recorded across the Portuguese world. In Rio de Janeiro in the 1620s, a "Negro from Angola and the other from Brazil," were denounced by two witnesses who claimed that they saw the Angolan mounting the Brazilian from behind.[73] Similarly, in Bahia in 1645, the slaves Jerónimo Soares and Bugio were denounced when it became publicly known that they performed oral sex on one another.[74] In Lisbon in 1647, Doctor Francisco Vaz de Gouveia overheard two slaves, Antônio and Francisco, discussing their sexual relationship, and he subsequently denounced them to the Inquisition. In his confession, made on October 14, 1647, Antônio described how he and Francisco met. He stated that around June of 1647 Francisco propositioned him, asking if he wanted to spend the night with him. Antônio accepted his offer and the two had sex with one another. According to the record, this relationship continued, with the two men having sex on several occasions. It appears that their relationship ended only when the Inquisition intervened, ultimately sending Antônio away to the king's galleys for two years.[75]

Even though some same-sex relationships were clearly enduring emotional attachments, others had less to do with loneliness and the search for affection than with flexible gender categories that apparently existed in various parts of Africa. One noteworthy case occurred in the middle of the sixteenth century in the Azores and in Lisbon. Antônio, slave of Paulo Manriques, arrived on Ilha Terceira from his homeland of Benin some time in 1556. Upon his arrival, he immediately assumed the uncertain gender identity that he maintained in Benin. Refusing to wear the clothes that his master gave him, Antônio instead chose to dress in a white waist jacket buttoned down the front, with a vest made from an old woolen cloth that he found in his master's stables. On his head, he wore a tightly wrapped white linen, topped off by a hat. To all who saw him, he appeared to be a woman.

By profession, Antônio worked as a prostitute who went by the name Vitória. In order to lure men, Vitória made a variety of winks and gestures "like a woman." But he was also observed removing his hat and bowing "like a man." He apparently had a thriving business, since seven or eight men could sometimes be seen waiting outside of the little house where he worked. But within a year of his arrival in the Azores, Antônio's ambiguous gender identity became widely known, and the scandal of his transvestism gained the attention of the Inquisition.

During his interrogation before the Inquisitors in Lisbon, an interpreter was needed to translate, since Antônio/Vitória had not yet mastered Portuguese. He admitted to "sinning" with five men, three in Lisbon and two in the Azores. When the Inquisitors asked him whether many people believed that he was a woman, he responded that he *was* a woman and that men gave him money for his services. Antônio also claimed that he had the orifice (*buraco*) of a woman. The Inquisitors asked him if he created this orifice or if it was the result of some sickness, but Antônio claimed that he was born with it. Indeed, he stated that "there were many in his country who had the same *buracos* who were born with them." Antônio ultimately was subjected to a medical inspection to determine whether he was "man or woman or hermaphrodite." The examination showed clearly that Antônio "had the physical character of a man, without having any *buraco* nor other physical characteristic of woman." For committing the "abominable sin of sodomy against nature," Antônio was sentenced to spend the rest of his life in the king's galleys.[76]

Antônio's admission that there were many in his country who were anatomically endowed with *buracos* is an indication that there were others who also took on the dress and mannerisms of women. The role of these transvested individuals in sixteenth-century Benin is difficult to discern from the records, but they seemingly constituted a third gender category that was completely unfamiliar to the Portuguese.[77] Antônio's gender and sexual choices were apparently an accepted part of Benin society, an integral part of Antônio's identity which the Portuguese sought to erase because he was a "sodomite." Acts of sodomy had long been punishable by death in Portugal, but the Portuguese reserved their greatest contempt for passive partners like Antônio, the rationale being that male penetration was a "natural" act, while male reception was not.[78] These social and cultural vacuums in the Western mentality affected Africans and their descendants in profound ways, confining them to sexual, gender, and family categories that were, in many cases, completely alien to them.

The narrowness of Western gender constructions is brought into even sharper focus when we examine another third-gender category, this one from Central Africa. In the same 1591 denunciation of Joane de Guiné in Bahia, Matias Moreira also denounced a man named Francisco Manicongo to the Portuguese Holy Office.[79] Moreira stated that he had seen Francisco walking the streets of Bahia dressed as a woman and that Francisco was renowned among blacks as a "sodomite." Moreira went on to claim that he had traveled for a long period of time in the lands of Angola and Congo. During these travels, he had witnessed some of the "pagan Negroes" dressing like women. According to Moreira, these cross-dressing men performed the role of the woman in acts of sodomy. In fact, these cross-dressers were so prevalent in Central African society that there was even a word for them in the "language of Angola and Congo," *jinbandaa*.

Unbeknownst to Moreira, the term *jinbandaa* in Central Africa did not carry the same negative moral connotations that the terms "sodomite" or "nefarious sinner" carried in Christian Europe. Instead, the significance of *jinbandaa* was to be found in Central African religious beliefs. According to Malcolm Guthrie, the word stem *mbándá* means "medicine man," and throughout Central Africa words similar to *jinbandaa* implied religious power.[80] In fact, several revealing descriptions from the Angolan coast in the seventeenth century suggest that *quimbanda* sodomites were a discrete and powerful caste in Angolan society. As early as 1606, the Jesuits in Angola described "*chibados*,"

A *quimbanda* in Central Africa, seventeenth century. Spiritually and politically powerful in Africa, the *quimbandas'* ritual expertise waned in Brazil's slave communities, as the Portuguese prosecuted these men for transvestism and sodomy. Watercolor by Giovanni Antonio Cavazzi, "Missione evangelica al regno de Congo, 1665–1668"; courtesy Manoscritti Araldi, Papers of the Araldi Family, Modena, Italy.

who were "extremely great fetishers, and being men went around dressed as women and they had by great offense called themselves men; they had husbands like the other women, and in the sin of sodomy they are just like devils."[81] Writing in 1681, Captain Antônio de Oliveira Cadornega commented at length on the status of "sodomites" along the Angolan coast:

There is also among the Angolan pagan much sodomy, sharing one with the other their dirtiness and filth, dressing as women. And they call them by the name of the land, *quimbandas*, [and] in the district or lands where they are, they have communication with each other. And some of these are fine *feiticeiros* (sorcerers), for they beget everything bad. And all of the pagans respect them and they are not offended by them and these sodomites happen to live together in bands, meeting most often to give burial services. . . . This caste of people is who dresses the body for burial and performs the burial ceremony.[82]

Cadornega reveals three important points regarding the Angolan *quimbandas*. First, he suggests that they were a discrete social group that lived together in "bands." Second, the *quimbandas* were respected by others in the community. In fact, the Capuchin priest, Antônio Cavazzi, who was a resident of Angola from 1654 to 1667, wrote that "there is not a Jaga [Imbangala], whether captain in war, or peaceful *aldeia* [village] chief, who does not try to keep some of them [the *quimbandas*] to watch over him, without the counsel and approval of such, he will not dare to exercise any act of jurisdiction, nor take any resolution."[83] The *quimbandas* were apparently the final spiritual arbiters in political and military decisions. Finally, the *quimbandas* were not only considered "fine *feiticeiros*," but they performed traditional burial ceremonies, thereby exercising a wide range of spiritual roles. Taken together, these three points produce a compelling argument for the religious power and respectability of Angola's transvested "homosexual" community, a community that clearly set itself apart from the rest of society, apparently as one of the many kinlike divining and healing societies that were prevalent in seventeenth-century Central Africa.[84]

How transvested homosexuals became powerful religious figures in Central Africa is an interesting question, but that is not our primary concern here.[85] More important for us is the question of the *jinbandaa*'s transition to slave life in the Americas. Sixteenth- and seventeenth-century sources suggest that in Central Africa the *jinbandaas* were a group of religious leaders who carved out their own "third-sex" (gender defined) living space in the society. But the spiritual capacity of the transvested homosexual was so universally known that they were referred to not by their patterns of dress or by their sexual behavior, but by their roles as religious leaders. Only when these Africans encounter the Western world do we begin to see the breakdown of the gender-defined organization of this kinlike, transvestite, religious society.

This disjuncture between the gendered, religious space in Central Africa and the lack of such a space in the diaspora indicates several sobering things. First, those transvested homosexuals who were brought to Europe and its colonies as slaves were isolated not only according to race, but also according to their gender and their sexuality. Given the evidently small numbers of *jinbandaas* in the diaspora, there was no way for them to replicate their gender-defined communities in their new surroundings. Second, Western/Christian prejudice and repression against the feminine and against the passive homosexual contributed to the attrition of a seemingly well-defined African gender category that defied Western norms. And finally, the institutional foundation that gave this collection of transvested homosexuals religious power all but disappeared. Because they could no longer meet collectively to share knowledge and affirm their religious power, their powers were effectively diluted. Indeed, in Brazil, the very meaning of the term *jinbandaa* was transformed, at least within the white community. Rather than referring to an individual with religious power, the term *jinbandaa* became synonymous with the passive "sodomite."

Despite the powerful forces of Western cultural hegemony, we should still recognize the lens through which someone like Francisco Manicongo, or Antônio from Benin, addressed their individual gender and sexual identities. Even against the riptides of Western gender, sexual, and religious norms, Francisco and Antônio continued to see themselves in much the same ways that they had seen themselves in their homelands. Just as most Westerners could not conceive of identifying themselves as anything other than either man or woman, Francisco could not conceive of identifying himself as anything other than the transvested *jinbandaa*. And Antônio could not conceive of himself as anything other than one of the many from Benin who had *buracos* like his. Thus, they each shed the clothing given to them by their masters and continued to dress and act as women, seeking out male partners with little, if any, regard for the fact that they were committing mortal sins. Though their individual identities may have endured for some time, the kinlike groupings that sustained and affirmed them in their ethnic homelands were obliterated, leaving them as isolated and alone as those who left behind their natal kin.

Despite fragments of information on same-sex relationships, polygynous/ polyandrous relationships, and corporate, kinlike structures, as well as more ample information on out-of-wedlock births and Christian marriages in the slave communities, we are still able to make only tentative conclusions regarding family and kinship among African slaves in early colonial Brazil. Unfortunately, the family patterns that Africans and their descendants established in the colonial Portuguese world remain mostly obscured to us. Clearly there was a variety of arrangements, which were shaped as much by the temporal and demographic conditions of the slave community as by African survivals. We know that two out of every three slaves who arrived in Brazil were men. When we also take into account that only around one in four slave women was considered "married" when she gave birth, we can estimate that between 80 and 90 percent of all African slaves remained unmarried, at least in the Christian sense of the term. This vast group of "unmarried" slaves created family and kinship groups where they could, with many of these arrangements resonating with their African pasts. We must stress that these arrangements were the norm in most Brazilian slave communities; church marriages remained the alternative model for Africans throughout the colonial period. Even when they sought the endorsement of the Catholic Church, Africans aligned themselves with their ethnic/national peers more often than not, with some no doubt viewing marriage as a facade behind which to carry on with a variety of African-inspired kinship arrangements. Marriage, both in Africa and the Americas, was gloss for a diversity of male/female alliances—temporary and permanent relations, single and multiple partners—all aimed at building broader kinship units. But in spite of constant efforts to maintain and recreate links to their African pasts, the burdens of slavery, demographic decline, and abuse by masters all took their toll on slave families and kinship formation in the Portuguese world. It is to these subjects that we now turn.

CHAPTER THREE

Disease, Mortality, and Master Power

I n 1749, a slave named Gaspar Gonçalves ran away from the Jesuit Engenho Santana to the town of Rio das Contas in order to be with his lover, a slave woman named Jacinta Ramos. Gaspar was captured in Rio das Contas and held in the jail there for nine days before he was reclaimed by the Jesuits. Since most slave owners did not recognize the unions that their slaves created outside of Christian marriage, flight to visit loved ones or kin in faraway places was viewed by masters as both a loss of valuable labor and a possible threat to public safety. Punishment was a common response, especially for habitual offenders. But instead of punishing Gaspar for his attempt to flee Santana, the Jesuits made the extraordinary gesture of purchasing Jacinta Ramos at auction in Rio das Contas "in order to marry with the said slave [Gaspar], who ran away because of her."[1] The union between Gaspar and Jacinta was quickly sanctioned by the Jesuits, and the married couple established their own household on Santana.[2] Gaspar's resistance to the forced separation from his lover paid off in a fashion that was uncommon on most slaveholdings.[3]

Yet despite Gaspar and Jacinta's apparent triumph in carving out a small space of love and happiness in their lives, their relationship was doomed by an institution that was never lacking in ways to maim and torture its victims. Almost immediately upon her arrival at Santana, Jacinta encountered hardship. In 1750, she was bitten by a venomous snake.[4] Even though she survived this initial scare, the ravages of disease and the unhealthy work environment ultimately took their toll. By Lent of 1753, Gaspar Gonçalves was listed as a widower on an inventory of the *engenho*'s slaves.[5] During the four months between November 1752 and March 1753, Jacinta Ramos died, leaving behind a husband who had only four years earlier risked punishment, and even his own life, when he ran away to be with her.

The tragic story of Gaspar and Jacinta is merely one incident in a broader demographic calamity that claimed the lives of thousands of slaves in Brazil. No matter how successful Africans and their descendants were at creating new families and kinship networks, they were still subject to the rigors of disease, hunger, and physical abuse that were characteristic of Brazilian slave society. All of these maladies severely circumscribed the formation of stable family and kinship units. In this chapter we will examine more closely how demography, disease, and intervention by masters adversely affected the formation of slave families. We will also look at the violence that characterized Brazilian slave society and its profound effects on Africans and their descendants. Finally, we will raise the question of how enslaved Africans responded to the constant physical and psychological assaults that were waged against them and their loved ones.

Disease, Malnutrition, and Mortality among Brazilian Slaves

For the majority of those who were enslaved in Africa and bound for Brazil, slavery meant one thing—death. Despite the overwhelming emphasis in scholarly literature on the institution of slavery in the Americas, the fact is that in the late eighteenth century, as many as half of those who were enslaved in the interior of Central Africa never set foot on American soil. During the earlier periods, mortality rates were even higher.[6] Thus, the real story of African slavery ends long before most slaves even caught sight of the Americas. Of course, our concern here is with those who survived the journey to the Americas. Nevertheless, we must recognize that even for the survivors, death was a pervasive shadow that followed them and their loved ones even in the Americas.

To become a slave in the interior of Africa was to enter a world teeming with disease, starvation, and death. If the march to the African coast, incarceration in the coastal barracoons, or the Middle Passage did not claim one's life, disease would.[7] For an African-born slave to arrive in Brazil and live for more than three years was a remarkable achievement indeed. In the late eighteenth century, during this three-year window known as the "seasoning" period, more than 40 percent of the Africans who had survived the Middle Passage succumbed to various diseases in Brazil.[8] Smallpox and measles were the most efficient killers, wiping out large numbers of slaves in single out-breaks.[9] More pernicious were various intestinal disorders, including dysentery and parasites. Slaves also suffered from tuberculosis, malaria, tetanus, and pulmonary disorders. Perhaps the most offensive illness commonly acquired by African slaves was an intestinal disorder known as *mal de bicho*. Literally meaning "evil of the small beast," the sickness began with a bout of strong diarrhea, but the afflicted rapidly developed "in the anal orifice, both internally and externally . . . little ulcers containing maggots." The disease was characterized by an inability to control the bowels. Gangrene soon set in and the sufferer quickly died.[10]

Hunger and malnutrition were also aggravating factors in the poor health and physical deterioration of slaves. Beginning in the early seventeenth century, there were reports that Brazilian slaves were dying of hunger. By the end of the century, it was common practice among many planters to allow their slaves one day per week to cultivate their own foodstuffs. Still, in times of drought or economic hardship, slaves could not produce enough to feed themselves, and their rations were among the first expenditures that masters cut.[11] Commenting on the obligations of masters to feed their slaves, in the 1760s, the Benedictine Father Superior commented, "Gravely sins the master who avoids spending by not feeding the slave; there must be established in him the necessity of breaking this belief."[12]

Young children were particularly vulnerable to hunger and malnutrition, since they were incapable of planting their own subsistence crops. In times of famine, slave parents took extraordinary measures to ensure that their children were fed. In the 1760s, slave mothers on the Benedictine properties were so desperate that they apparently prostituted themselves in order to meet their children's needs.[13] Children also engaged in the practice of "dirt eating," sometimes with lethal consequences. Slave masters and commentators on Brazilian slavery believed that this practice stemmed from some sort of self-destructive habit of Africans and their descendants. Writing in the second decade of the nineteenth century, Englishman Henry Koster noted that masters believed that slaves ate lime and dirt "for the purpose of destroying themselves." Koster went on: "it is strange that the habit of eating lime and earth should be contracted in some instances by African and likewise by Creole children, and as frequently by free children as by those who are in slavery. This practice is not created as if it were a disorder, but it is accounted a habit, which, by attention from those who have charge of the children—in watching and punishing them, may be conquered without the aid of medicine. I know some instances in which no medical treatment was deemed necessary: but the individual recovered by means of chastisement and constant vigilance."[14]

We now know that dirt eating is one of the primary symptoms of the disease known as pica, an illness that results from deficiencies in potassium, iron, calcium, and magnesium.[15] In other words, childhood dirt eating was a symptom of extreme malnutrition, a desperate biological response to a lack of essential minerals. The child who survived bouts of dirt eating likely soon succumbed to starvation or some other vitamin or mineral deficiency.

Mission reports and plantation-level data confirm that large numbers of Africans succumbed to hunger and disease in Brazil, especially in the sixteenth and seventeenth centuries. As early as 1582, the Jesuit Engenho Santana was forced to cease operations for five months due to an epidemic that killed eighty-three "Guiné and Indian *peças*," more than half of the estate's entire workforce. Only the leasing of African slaves from Bahian merchant Francisco da Costa salvaged the sugar crop, but even with this stopgap measure, the cost of the leased slaves exceeded the profits from the harvested sugar.[16] Plagues continued to devastate the nonwhite population through the end of the sixteenth century. In 1597, Padre Ignátio Tholosa reported that between May and August of that year, 2,000 Indians, Africans, and creoles died in Bahia. Protected from the overwork, undernourishment, and pestilent conditions that killed Africans and Indians, Europeans also had built up immunity to diseases like smallpox and measles. Thus, Africans died at rates far in excess of Europeans.[17]

By the seventeenth century, Brazil's slave population was overwhelmingly African, and the death toll continued to mount. In a mission report from the Bahian Recôncavo in 1617, the priests noted that "almost all of the people who are put on the *fazendas* and *engenhos* are new, and the majority of the *ladinos* (acculturated slaves) and old ones are dead from smallpox and measles, which like a branch of plague prevails with great fury."[18] Statistical evidence bears out the mission's findings. Between 1617 and 1638 on the Jesuit Engenho Sergipe, more than 250 "Guiné" slaves were purchased, but more than 150 of these died, leaving the *engenho* with fewer than 100 slaves in 1638.[19] At this rate of loss, the *engenho*'s slave population was replaced almost twice over during the 21-year period. In Rio de Janeiro, the rector of the Jesuit College, Antônio Rodrigues, reported that more than 150 slaves died on Jesuit *fazendas* between 1646 and 1649. He went on to note that the deaths occurred "during the time that Angola was occupied by the rebel Dutch and it was not possible to put others in their place."[20] But even after the slave trade from Angola resumed, newly arrived Africans continued to perish at a staggering rate. The Benedictine monastery at Rio de Janeiro acquired fifty-seven slaves during the 1663–1666 triennial, thirty by inheritance and the remaining twenty-seven through purchase. Of these fifty-seven, fifteen were already dead by the end of the tri-

Table 6. Crude Death and Birth Rates on Various Brazilian Properties, 1617–1778

Location	Dates	Crude Death Rate	Crude Birth Rate
1. Engenho Sergipe (Bahia)	1617–1638	70–80	—
2. Jesuit College (Rio de Janeiro)	1646–1649	83.3	—
3. Engenho Guaguasú (Rio de Janeiro)	1648–1652	70.5	—
4. Benedictine Monastery (Olinda)	1663–1666	105.3	—
5. Engenho Santana (Bahia)	1674–1676	40	53.3
6. Engenho Musurepe (Olinda)	1726–1730	26.9	—
7. Engenho Santana	1730–1731	39	—
8. Engenho Sergipe	1730–1733	66.6	—
9. Engenho Petinga (Bahia)	1744–1745	115	—
10. Engenho Santana	1748–1752	27	28
11. Fazenda Saubara (Bahia)	1750–1760	115 (males) 81 (females)	17–26
12. Engenhos Musurepe, São Bernardo, Goitá (Olinda)	1766–1769	7.5	19.6
13. Engenhos Musurepe, São Bernardo, Goitá	1772–1778	18.7	—
14. Central Africa	1700s	90	—

Sources: (1) ANTT, CSJ, Maço 14, No. 1; (2) ARSI, Brasilia 3 (I)/VFL Roll 161, ff. 273–74; (3) ADB/UM, CSB 134; (4) ADB/UM, CSB 138; (5) ANTT, CSJ, Maço 54, No. 7; (6) ADB/UM, CSB 138, f. 170; (7) ANTT, CSJ, Maço 15, No. 24; (8) ANTT, CSJ, Maço 70, No. 431; (9) ANTT, CSJ, Maço 15, No. 25; (10) ANTT, CSJ, Maço 54, No. 52; (11) S. B. Schwartz, *Sugar Plantations*, 366; (12) ADB/UM, CSB 139; (13) ADB/UM, CSB 139; (14) Miller, *Way of Death*, 381–82.

ennial.[21] During the same triennial, the slave population of the Benedictine monastery at Olinda declined 19 percent. In 1663, the monastery reportedly possessed 126 slaves; by 1666, this number dropped to 102, despite the acquisition of 16 new *peças* during the three-year period.[22]

There was no apparent drop in slave mortality levels in Brazil until the last quarter of the seventeenth century. Plantation-level data are relatively scarce, and crude mortality rates (calculated as the number of deaths per 1,000 slaves in a given year) are an imperfect measure of overall mortality, since stillbirths and the deaths of small babies were not included in most plantation reports. Still, Table 6 demonstrates that crude mortality rates of slaves on ecclesiastical properties were greater than 70 per 1,000 during the first half of the seventeenth century, a rate very near the 90 per 1,000 that has been estimated for war-torn, slave-producing regions of eighteenth-century Central Africa.[23]

A steady improvement in the mortality rates of slaves can be seen beginning in the 1670s, particularly on Engenho Santana, where we have already noted a significant pattern of creole births beginning in this period (see Chapter 2). But just fifteen years earlier, in 1659, Father Filipe Franco complained that Santana was in dire need of more slaves, "because, of those that I have on the *engenho*, some die; others are of no service because of incurable diseases, and of those I bought, there are also some who died."[24] Father Franco's prayers were answered the following year when Salvador de Sá, a fellow Jesuit and former Angolan governor, arranged to send 40 *peças* directly to Santana at only minimal cost to the Jesuits.[25] Relieved, Father Franco gave thanks to God, commenting that "in Brazil one cannot make a *fazenda* without Negroes."[26] From this cargo of Angolan slaves that arrived at Santana in 1660 emerged the Brazilian-born creole core that began to appear in the inventories of the 1670s.

Despite the slow emergence of a creole population in some places, in the middle of the eighteenth century disease still wiped out significant portions of many slave populations. The first three years of the 1730s were especially difficult on Engenho Sergipe, where thirty-six slaves died. In 1731, Father Mateus de Sousa complained that "this *engenho* is very much lacking in slaves; some have died and others are very old and just not able to work. Many little creoles have been born but many also die."[27] Epidemics also continued to take their toll on Brazil's slave population. The high mortality rate at Petinga in 1744–1745 was symptomatic of one such outbreak. It was reported that "there was generally on all of the *engenhos* and slaveholdings of Brazil a great ruin with a universal epidemic that arrived in a ship of Negroes from the Mina Coast . . . many with measles, causing a great deal of damage, losses, and expense to these *engenhos*."[28]

To make matters worse, the infirmaries of large *engenhos* served as a breeding ground for the numerous contagions that slaves passed to one another. On Engenho Sergipe, surrounding houses blocked fresh air from passing through the infirmary, and the building had no windows for ventilation. Commenting on the dangerous and dilapidated conditions, Father Jerónimo da Gama wrote that "it is not enough to make a great amount of sugar; to save the *fazenda* is a better way to have sugar."[29] The Jesuits were not alone in their neglect of the living conditions of their ailing slaves. The houses that comprised the infirmary of the Benedictine monastery in Rio de Janeiro were so overcrowded in the 1740s that the slaves were forced to build a subordinate house for the overflow.[30] Thirty years later, it was reported that the same houses were "little apt for the cure of the sick," because they had earthen floors and open roofs that exposed sick slaves to the elements.[31]

Slaves who survived the brutalities of disease, overwork, and malnutrition had an extremely difficult time reproducing themselves during the period of our study. During the eighteenth century the Brazilian-born population increased on ecclesiastical properties, as mortality rates fell below birth rates, but birth rates were still quite low. Prior to the regular use of birth control, crude birth rates usually ranged between 35 and 55 per 1,000 in most stable populations.[32] The birth rates of slaves on the Jesuit and Benedictine estates hovered below 28 for most of our period (see Table 6). The 53.3 birth rate on Santana between 1674 and 1676, though truly exceptional for Brazil's slave population, was merely average when compared to levels of procreation in other societies. Disease was clearly one factor in keeping the birth rate so low. Malnutrition and overwork also contributed to low levels of fertility among women. Finally, extended lactation and postpartum sexual abstinence among certain African ethnic groups also may have contributed to the low number of births among slave women.[33]

While statistics on mortality and birth rates give us some insight into general trends in the demography of Brazil's slave population, we should not lose sight of the personal tragedies that arose from demographic decline. Even on an apparently "stable" *engenho* like Santana, which was becoming more creole in the 1670s, death and disease were pervasive. Over the course of this period, Santana had a total of around eighty-five slaves who worked on the plantation. Even though "only" six slaves died during the two years between 1674 and 1676, fifteen others suffered from debilitating illnesses or injuries. Thus, in those three years nearly one quarter of Santana's slaves faced assaults on their health. Among the illnesses was that of Antônia Criolla, who was idle for more than eight months after a difficult childbirth. Her newborn did not live to see her recover. Also afflicted was Pedro Mobanga, who received twenty bleedings and three purges as treatment for his "difficult sickness." Vitória had a wound on her leg that incapacitated her for more than five years. Antônio Criollo fell "crippled" between 1674 and 1676. And Duarte Tacheiro had a deep wound on his leg. Nevertheless, he continued to work.

Young children were particularly vulnerable to the ravages of death and disease in the slave environment. As we have already noted, gender imbalances and negative health factors militated against normal birth rates. Thus, live births were generally a rare phenomenon, and there were few children to be found on most properties, especially prior to 1650.[34] As early as 1586 the Jesuits expressed concern over the high mortality rates among children on their Brazilian properties. In that year, it was ordered that female slaves with children not be allowed to work more than four or five hours per day, "because one has seen that many die because they are not able to raise them well, walking with them in the airs . . . working for long periods of time."[35] Whether plantation administrators complied with these orders is uncertain, but child mortality rates remained high.

Even where the slave population included relatively large numbers of children, these children suffered the effects of death, disease, and dislocation more acutely than any other sector of the slave population. Of the seventy-three slaves on Santana in 1674, twenty-nine were children under the age of sixteen, a solid 40 percent of the *engenho*'s slave force. Four of these children were dead by 1676, meaning that the annual mortality rate among children under sixteen was a disturbing 69 per 1,000, more than one and a half times the rate of the *engenho*'s overall population.[36] Three more children lived with relatives or adopted kin because their birth parents were dead.[37] And three more were young Africans whose parents were apparently left behind in their homelands.[38] Thus, in 1674, 34 percent of Santana's children were either orphans or soon to be dead themselves.[39]

The Impacts of Slavery on Children

The physical and psychological effects of childhood slavery have been grossly understudied aspects of the slave experience, especially from the developmental perspective.[40] In a brief but provocative passage of *The Masters and the Slaves*, Brazilian anthropologist Gilberto Freyre was one of the first scholars to suggest ways in which the institution of slavery warped people from a very tender age. Freyre contended that the young slave was both "a playmate and a whipping-boy" for his young master. "His functions were those of an obliging puppet, manipulated at will by the infant son of the family; he was squeezed, mistreated, tormented just as if he had been made of sawdust on the inside—of cloth and sawdust . . . rather than of flesh and blood like white children."[41] In their games, white children pretended that slave children were their beasts of burden—"cart-oxen, saddle-horses, beasts for turning the millstone, and burros for carrying litters and heavy burdens. But especially cart-horses. . . . A bit of packing-twine serve[d] as the reins and a shoot of the guava tree as a whip."[42] Freyre suggested that "the psychic repercussion upon [white] adults of such a type of childish relationship should be favorable to the development of sadistic and masochistic tendencies." But he ultimately concluded that it was mostly white women who "displayed this sadistic bent, owing to the greater fixity and monotony in the relations of mistress and slave girl."[43] The adult relationship between male masters and their slaves was supposedly more benevolent and paternal.

Though many of his arguments on the subject were not fully developed,

Freyre's assessment of childhood experiences under slavery in Brazil endures as one of the fullest treatments of the subject. Freyre's halcyon views of Brazilian slavery as a benign institution have long since been refuted, but his emphasis on the damaging psychological impact that slavery had on children—white and black—is an area of slave studies that deserves to be revisited. The ways in which children were coded to understand their place in the world are sometimes difficult to grasp in historical documents, but attempting to decipher the psychological damage that occurred at various stages of childhood development can be particularly revealing for those engaged in slave studies.

Childbirth and its cultural meanings were radically transformed as African slave women shifted from African natal kinship member to Brazilian slave. As natal kinship structures disintegrated and freedom of movement disappeared in Brazil, women could no longer expect to share their children with their fathers and brothers in accordance with matrilineal practices. Where fertility and childbirth were once viewed as causes for communal celebration, enslavement threw many African practices into question. This extreme break from past understandings led to a variety of responses on the parts of slave women in the treatment of their children in Brazil. As we have seen, some created new kinship structures, replicating as much as possible what they had known in their homelands. Indeed, slave births on Jesuit properties were celebrated with food and drink in much the same manner that births were celebrated in Africa. The custom became so entrenched among slaves on Jesuit properties that slave fathers would threaten the overseers with running away if their demands for chickens and wine were not met on those occasions.[44]

While some slave mothers celebrated the appearance of a baby, others could not cope with the perceived kinlessness and physical abuse that awaited their newborns under slavery. Although evidence is slim and the practice would have been out of keeping with African celebrations of fertility, abortions were not unheard of either in Africa or in Brazil. Under certain dire circumstances, it was apparently acceptable for an African woman to abort her fetus. In December 1730, a widow named Mariana Fernandes was jailed in Luanda for practicing "witchcraft." Pregnant, she drank an unnamed mixture to effect an abortion.[45] Similarly, on Engenho Sergipe in 1623, slave women who were impregnated by white men, rather than facing the wrath of the slave men, drank "some things" that resulted in abortions.[46] In both of these circumstances, the facts dictated that the children of these women would have been born into marginal, kinless situations. Communal support was clearly an important prerequisite for a socially acceptable birth among Africans and their descendants across the African-Portuguese diaspora.

For slave women who had little communal support in raising their children, or who recognized the likelihood that their babies would succumb to disease and malnutrition, abandonment of their newborns was also an option. Alice Scheper-Hughes has argued forcefully that in areas of extremely high infant mortality, women reject the "motherly instinct" to nurture and protect their young. With survival of the children unlikely, attachment to the newborn is viewed as a futile, psychically costly endeavor.[47] Though there is little direct evidence to support the argument that Brazilian slave women adopted such attitudes, the conditions of Brazilian slavery sometimes encouraged the abandonment of young children, particularly among those slave mothers who had run away from their masters. Baptismal records are dotted with references to *exposto* (abandoned) slave children who were left to the care of white "patrons." For instance, in 1692, a newborn baby emerged from the *mato* (forest) of Jacarepaguá in the arms of a "Negro" runaway. The runaway was returning to Jacarepaguá after having spent a year and a half in the *mato*. The baby's mother, who had also fled to the *mato*, gave up her child to the man and told him to return the baby to town, perhaps believing that her daughter's chances for survival would be greater in the town rather than in the dangerous and uncertain world of the fugitive slave. Upon arriving in the town, the child was baptized and given the name Jacinta, but the rest of her life remains a mystery.[48]

Similarly, in 1739, Antônia Criolla had been a runaway for two years when her master made his last will and testament in Rio de Janeiro. The master, Manuel da Silva, claimed that Antônia secretly returned to his property and gave birth to two children during her extended absence. According to da Silva, Antônia abandoned the newborns in some houses where she knew that da Silva's wife would discover them and raise them.[49] Whether these children were being "abandoned" by their mothers, being given a chance for survival, or some combination of the two, is certainly subject to debate. Still, unless their mothers returned to claim them, these children joined the legions of other uprooted, orphaned, and abandoned children who grew into adulthood without knowledge of their natal kin.

Orphanage and abandonment of slave children occurred in a multiplicity of ways. Parents fell ill and died. Parents ran away, leaving behind their young. And children were stolen away from their families and kinship communities in Africa. The number of enslaved African children increased steadily over the history of the trade, as supplies of prime male slaves became scarcer and scarcer on the African coast. By the eighteenth century, slaves boarding ships at Luanda included significant numbers of younger males.[50] Though precise figures are difficult to come by, in part because of underreporting of the numbers of slave children packed onto slave ships, it now appears that more than

20 percent of the slaves departing from West Central Africa in the late seventeenth and early eighteenth centuries were children.[51]

We must keep in mind the ages of these children when we attempt to measure the impact of their orphanage. In general, the younger the child was orphaned, the less likely he would remember his natal kin, cultures, and so on, once he reached adulthood. There are a number of Inquisition cases in which African-born slaves who were taken from their parents as very young children stated that they did not have any memories of their parents.[52] As children reached the age of reason and understanding, though, the homeland became indelibly etched in their consciousness. And Africa would arrive with them at their various destinations across the diaspora. Those who were taken from Africa as children between the ages of eight and twelve were perhaps the hardest hit by the institution of slavery. Almost simultaneously these children were faced with the loss of their parents, dislocation from their kinship unit, enslavement, and the difficulties of adjusting to a new social and cultural milieu—not to mention the dangers of a new disease environment. The miseries of those who survived defy explanation, but it is clear that memories of Africa shaped the social and cultural identities of many well into adulthood.

Once children became a part of the slave community, they were confronted with a new set of bitter realities. As toddlers, they were already becoming aware of the harshness of slave life. Instead of passing their days in the comfort of their mothers' care, young children often were supervised by elderly slaves who could no longer perform more strenuous labor.[53] Only when the children's mothers returned from their daily labors would they be reunited with their young ones.

Toddlers also began to experience the crushing physical and psychological control that their masters exerted over them. Not only were young children forced to witness the daily humiliation and degradation that their parents received at the hands of their masters, but they were themselves sometimes the victims of the master's sadistic whims. In the middle of the eighteenth century, Garcia de Avila Pereira Aragão, one of Bahia's wealthiest residents, committed a series of atrocities against dozens of his slaves, including young children. The youngest was a three-year-old girl named Leonarda. Aragão "called her and ordered that she should be lowered, placing the little face of the poor little girl over a fire of hot coals . . . putting his hand on her face so that she would not be able to turn away from the fire, and he began to fan the fire with his other hand." On another occasion, he ordered a four-year-old boy named Archileu to guard a fig tree so that birds would not make off with the fruit. When Aragão found a fig bitten by the birds, he stripped the boy naked and "whipped him rigorously with a horse whip about the shoulders, legs, and all the body." Finally, he tortured a six-year-old boy by dripping hot candle wax on him, "such that the pain from the fire made him jump up in the air, accompanied by a scream of pain . . . and [Aragão] laughed at this with great glee."[54]

As children entered adolescence, their labor burdens and the extravagance of their tortures increased. By the ages of twelve to fourteen, slaves already were considered adults by many masters, and were therefore assigned the tasks of full-grown workers.[55] Sometimes this premature leap to adulthood led to horrific workplace accidents. Inexperience was no doubt a contributing factor in the death of a young mulatta on Engenho Musurepe in Olinda, "who being obliged to crush cane without having the age or the strength became stuck in the crusher (moenda) and the crusher milled her with the very cane."[56] Other young girls were forced into prostitution, with all the earnings going to their masters. It was not unusual to see slave girls ten and twelve years old walking the streets of Brazil's biggest cities.[57] The mostly male frontier of Minas Gerais was a particularly popular destination for Brazil's enslaved prostitutes. In 1733, fourteen-year-old Rosa Egipcíaca, a Courana slave born on the Mina coast, began to sell her body in Minas Gerais. There, she prostituted for fifteen years before being converted to Christianity, eventually becoming a spiritual sage to dozens of followers.[58]

Reaching adolescence not only meant exposure to the rigors of adult labor, but the teenage years also marked the introduction of slaves to the vilest of sexual abuse and tortures. Among the many slaves tormented by Garcia de Avila Pereira Aragão was sixteen-year-old Hipólito. During one brutal session, Hipólito was whipped for three hours by two other slaves. He was then bound by his wrists and raised about nine feet above the floor. A cord was tied around his testicles with a 7.5 kilogram weight tied to the end of it, pulling the boy's scrotum toward the floor "such that the miserable one gave screams."[59]

Adolescent slaves, male and female, were also the targets of rapists.[60] Rosa Egipcíaca was repeatedly raped by her first master in Rio de Janeiro, all prior to her fourteenth birthday.[61] Similarly, in 1618, Pêro Garcia, the owner of four engenhos in Bahia and master of hundreds of slaves, was denounced for repeatedly raping two of his slaves, fourteen-year-old Joseph and fifteen-year-old Bento.[62] Other rapes occurred more spontaneously. In the 1720s, a pardo soldier named Manuel de Faria attacked a twelve-year-old boy on the streets of Rio da Prata in Minas Gerais. The slave boy was selling sweets on the streets when Faria threw him "violently to the ground . . . laid over him and copulated with him from behind." Both the soldier and the boy were imprisoned for some time, but the boy was eventually released to the custody of his master.[63]

Priests were also guilty of taking sexual liberties with slave boys. In 1626, a priest known simply as Father Antônio, was making the Atlantic crossing from Rio de Janeiro to Lisbon. Also on board was a fourteen-year-old Angolan-born slave named Cristóvão. Father Antônio repeatedly attempted to seduce the boy, offering him clothes, candy, and other enticements, but Cristóvão refused the father's advances, telling him flatly that "he was a Negro and he did not want to sleep with a white man in his bed." But Father Antônio would not give up. One night he entered the boy's bed and attempted to penetrate him as he slept. The boy awoke screaming. As he kicked Father Antônio to the floor, two other young slaves awoke and also began screaming. This commotion drew the attention of the ship's captain, who had Father Antônio bound in chains for the remainder of the journey.[64]

In 1646, a similar case occurred in Bahia, where Father Antônio de Serisa sexually assaulted a *moleque* named Domingos, or Banyo by his Angolan name. One night as they were preparing to sleep, the Father grabbed Banyo's private parts and asked him to show them to him. The priest also pulled out his own penis, placing it in the hand of the boy. Banyo threatened to scream if the priest did not immediately open the door. Fleeing the room, the boy told one Manuel Faya that Father Antônio "was not a priest but a devil."[65] During the same year, a number of priests in the Benedictine monastery in Bahia were accused of raping young male slaves. Like new prisoners arriving at a penitentiary, young, freshly arrived Africans apparently were the favorite targets of rapists.[66] Antônio de Vasconcelos, a student at the Benedictine monastery, confessed that one priest ordered him to bring a newly arrived *boçal* slave to him. Vasconcelos, "suspected that the priest, whose name is Frei Domingos, took the Negro away in order to sin with him since he was bought on that day."[67]

The journey from childhood to adulthood was painfully quick for most slaves, and childhood innocence was too often corrupted by death, disease, hunger, rape, and torture. We now know that traumatic childhood episodes can lead to irreversible psychological damage that persists into adulthood.[68] For many slave children, their lives were a series of traumatic episodes that were tantamount to the worst forms of child abuse. To deny that some slave children sustained permanent psychological damage would be to deny their very humanity. Unfortunately, maturing to adulthood did not result in an escape from these traumas. All of the fears that haunted slaves as children continued to loom large well into their adult lives. On a purely physical level, adult slaves were better equipped to endure the assaults of disease, hunger, and physical abuse, but the repressive power of the master continued to take a steep psychological toll on them. As slaves matured and attempted to create families, masters constantly intervened, threatening to erode or dissolve their most intimate relationships.

Physical and Sexual Abuse and Its Effects on the Slave Family

So far, we have discussed the demographic difficulties faced by slaves in attempting to form families and communities. Gender imbalance, death, and disease militated against the creation of stable family units across the African diaspora. Nonetheless, where possible, slaves succeeded in creating a variety of long-term relationships that resulted in the formation of slave families. Yet even under the best of circumstances, slave families could be fractured by sexual abuse, manumission, and the sale of family members. No matter how successful slaves were at creating spaces in their interior lives, they were never completely outside the reach of their masters. Masters regularly intervened in the lives of their slaves in ways that could be both personally disruptive and psychologically devastating. Sexual abuse of women by masters and free men was one of the major disruptive forces in the slave quarters, and slave families were deeply affected by these unwanted intrusions. Many slave masters believed that their right to slave ownership included the right to sexual exploitation. Manuel Nunes Pelouro, who was accused of forcing his slave, Clara, to commit acts of sodomy in Rio das Mortes in 1755, summed up this sentiment when he told Clara that "being his slave, she had to serve him in everything."[69] Throughout the Portuguese diaspora, many whites acted on this assumption. In Bahia in 1623, white men were apparently raiding the slave quarters of Engenho Sergipe at night in order to rape slave women, including some women who were married.[70] One year later in 1624, a São Toméan planter, Francisco de Almeida, was accused of carrying on "illicit relationships" with a slave mother and her two daughters. As a result of these forced sexual encounters, one of the daughters, Pascoela, ran away from her master, leaving her mother and sister behind.[71] In 1702, it was reported that Carmelite priests in Goiana, Pernambuco, were impregnating slave women who were married. The husband of one of the women complained bitterly about the mulatta daughter his wife bore, fathered by Padre Manuel de São Gonçalo. In order to pacify the angry man, the mulatta baby was sold away to a surgeon.[72] Finally, in 1741 on the Benedictine Engenho São Bernardo in Olinda, it was reported that one Father Vitoriano was hiding an "illicit relationship" that he was having with a slave woman. When the male slaves on the *engenho* heard about this relationship, they apparently became quite agitated. It was rumored that some of them armed themselves with knives in order to stab the man "presumed to have had a relationship with a negra." [73]

While some cases of forced sexual relations between masters and slaves were clear disruptions to family and community, other sexual encounters could be a threat to the slave's very life. Some of these "relationships" were consummated literally at the end of a whip or the barrel of a gun. For example, in 1703, João Carvalho de Barros, a resident of the Bahian Recôncavo, was accused of sexually assaulting a number of his slaves. Among them was a woman named Domingas, who confessed that when she refused to submit to anal sex with Carvalho, she was severely whipped.[74] Similarly, a Benguelan slave named Joseph claimed that he always resisted the acts of sodomy that were imposed on him by Carvalho. Carvalho responded by threatening, and at times, giving "rigorous punishments" to his slave. In addition to Domingas and Joseph, at least three other male slaves suffered sexual assaults at the hands of Carvalho.

Carvalho's favored method of assault was to force himself on a male and a female slave at the same time. According to Joseph, on four or five occasions, his master came looking for him and took him to the bed of the female slave, Domingas. There, with all three in the bed, Carvalho told Joseph that he should have intercourse with Domingas. According to Joseph, he always resisted his master's orders but acquiesced when he was threatened with punishment. As Joseph was having sex with Domingas, his master entered him from behind, "wounding him with the force with which he penetrated him." Under questioning by the Inquisitors, Joseph said that he knew that sodomy was an "abominable sin," and that "in his land [Benguela] that sin is punished with penalty of blood and fire." Despite his pain and suffering at the hands of his master, as well as his candid confession, Joseph was eventually sentenced to public whipping and five years in the king's galleys.[75]

The fact that Joseph was punished, after being repeatedly victimized by his master, was one of the cruel ironies of Portuguese custom and law. As noted earlier, the passive partner in acts of sodomy was assumed to be the criminal. Thus, slaves who were anally raped could be subject to prosecution by the Inquisition. The sexual objectification of male and female slaves was, therefore, unwittingly reinforced by canon and civil law. Worse still, masters could confess to sodomizing large numbers of slaves and be absolved. They could then go on raping their slaves with little fear of reprisals.

This was the case in 1739 when Manuel Álvares Cabral confessed to sodomizing six of his male slaves in Minas Gerais. When the slaves were questioned about the incidents, the majority said that they did not resist for fear that their master would punish them, although one Angolan slave pleaded ignorance, stating that he was "without knowledge of the ugliness of that sin."[76] Cabral's confession "cleansed" him of his sin, but his slaves continued to suffer. Four years later in 1743, Manuel Álvares Cabral had relocated to the village of Boavista in Pernambuco. There, a Mina slave named Luís da Costa, confessed that one day while he and his master were out in the woods, his master forced him to submit to anal sex. Cabral threatened to shoot his slave if he did not comply. Luís unwillingly surrendered to his master on this one occasion, but claimed that it never happened again because he fought against his master's continued advances.[77]

Perhaps the most violent sexual assaults of slaves occurred in Pará in the late 1750s and early 1760s. Francisco Serrão de Castro, heir to a large sugar *engenho*, was denounced for sodomy and rape by no less than nineteen male slaves, all Africans. Among those who were assaulted were teenage boys and married men. As a result of these sexual attacks, a number of the victims suffered from "swelling and . . . bleeding from their anuses." Francisco Serrão de Castro apparently infected his slaves with a venereal disease that eventually took more than a quarter of his victims to their graves.[78]

The violence and coercion that characterized the rape of male slaves were symptoms of a broader pattern of violence aimed at forcing male slaves to submit to their masters' power. Slaves constantly challenged their roles as Brazil's beasts of burden by slowing the pace of their work, running away, and more rarely, violently rising against their masters. One of the many tools of pacification at the master's disposal was rape. To rape a male slave was to feminize him—to conquer him both physically and psychologically. Slaves were not unaware of their masters' attempts to emasculate them. One of Francisco Serrão de Castro's victims, João Marimba, a thirty-year-old Maxicongo, attempted to rebuff his master's advances, asserting that "he was not a negra for him to sin with, but a man."[79] In large sugar-producing areas where slaves often outnumbered whites, the sexual subordination of male slaves was not an unimportant instrument in maintaining social control. Only with some level of submission on the part of the male slave population could white patriarchal order be ensured.

Though sexual abuse was one method of subduing the adult slave population, the most common forms of slave control were beatings and physical torture. The whip was used liberally by many masters, so much so that in the seventeenth century an often-repeated refrain among slaveholders went as follows: "Whoever wants to reap benefit from his Negroes must maintain them, make them work well, and beat them even better; without this there will be no service nor any profit."[80] Confirming this axiom, one seventeenth-century observer in Paraíba noted that the majority of the slaves were from

Africa, "especially from Angola, and they do all of the agricultural service day and night, always maintained with many whippings."[81] In addition to beatings, slaves suffered other forms of physical torture including burning with hot wax, branding, castration, and the amputation of breasts, ears, and noses.[82] Attempting to rationalize such cruelty, one master claimed that the punishments were necessary because the slaves were "like devils."[83]

The frequency of excessive punishments compelled the king to issue laws protecting slaves from master brutalities. In 1688, the king extended to slaves the right to denounce cruel masters to civil or ecclesiastical authorities. Any master who was found guilty of excessive cruelty could be ordered to sell his slaves.[84] Despite this legal proscription, slaveowners continued to exert almost untrammeled physical power over their human chattel. The laws were rarely enforced.[85]

Poor whites, wealthy sugar planters, and even men of the cloth were known to beat and torture their slaves. In 1678, Francisco Jorge was incarcerated for whipping a slave to death in Bahia but was released when he pleaded that he was a poor man with a wife and children. In similar fashion, Pedro Pais Machado, the owner of Engenho Capanema in Bahia, was arrested in 1737 for killing two slaves and a freedman who allegedly injured one of his oxen. Machado murdered one of the men by hanging him by his testicles until he was dead. After a judicial inquiry, Machado was released, in part because he was "a noble person with family obligations."[86] For white Brazilians, maintaining the social and political order almost always took precedence over justice for slaves.

On the properties of the Jesuits and the Benedictines, slave punishments were no less harsh. In 1633, it was reported that the overseer on Engenho Sergipe governed the slaves "with the devil in his mouth and the stick on the backs of the poor creatures." Father Antônio Roiz, who submitted the report, concluded that the overseer "knows how to treat the bulls better than the Negroes."[87] In similar fashion, several priests testified against the cruelty of Father Salvador dos Santos, who was abbot of the Benedictine monastery in Olinda from 1746 to 1749. Various priests claimed that under the leadership of Father Salvador, many slaves ran away because of the beatings that they suffered. Among the slaves injured by Father Salvador was Pedro, who was in chains for so long that his foot became "mutilated" by infection. Another slave, Ventura, was so fearful of the whipping that he was due to receive that he cut his own throat while awaiting punishment in the *tronco* (stocks). Ventura was unsuccessful in his attempt to end his life. The Benedictines called a doctor who was able to stop the bleeding, "which cost a great deal." For the Benedictines, Ventura's humanity was not the concern. Rather, it was the

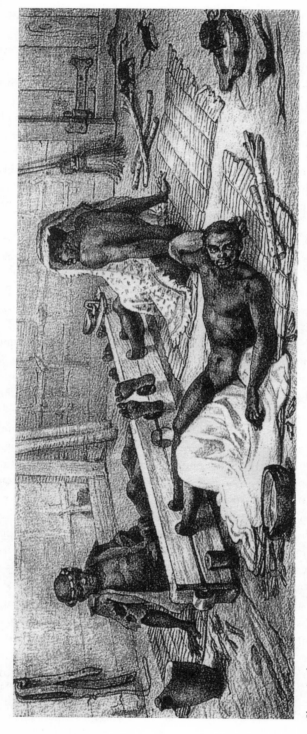

Slaves in the *tronco* (stocks), nineteenth century. Lithograph by Jean-Baptiste Debret, *Voyage pittoresque et historique au Brésil* (Paris, 1834).

prospect of losing a valuable piece of property that drove them to save his life. Even on the most fundamental question of human existence—whether to endure life miserably or end it mercifully—slaves sometimes had little control over their own bodies.[88]

Other Disruptions to Family and Community: Slave Sales and Manumission

The slave master's interventions into the lives of his slaves were not limited to overt physical intrusions like beatings, torture, and sexual abuse. More benign, but no less devastating, were interventions that underscored the slave's position as a piece of movable property. The separation of slaves from their families and communities was one of the many pernicious ways in which masters diminished the humanity of their bondsmen. Families were shattered as husbands, wives, and children were sold away to different masters. Africans and their descendants coped with these losses the best they could, sometimes creating new families in their new locales, but the memories of loved ones left behind must have endured.

On August 28, 1643, Antônio da Costa and Margarida de Sousa were married in Lisbon. Both were the slaves of Francisco de Sousa, and both were born in São Tomé. Antônio and Margarida lived together as man and wife for four years, during which time Margarida gave birth to a daughter. After the death of their master, the master's widow sold Antônio to Brazil, informing Margarida only after Antônio had already departed. Margarida tried to write letters to her husband, but she and her daughter never received any reply. For more than ten years Margarida waited patiently for some news of her husband. Finally, in the 1650s, two free blacks, who had recently returned from Brazil, reported that Antônio had died while serving on a sugar *engenho*.

Assuming that she was a widow, Margarida married a free black named Fernão Mendes, also born in São Tomé. Margarida and Fernão were married for six years, and they had two daughters before Margarida was informed that her first husband was still alive. A man arriving in Lisbon on a ship from Brazil told her that Antônio da Costa had sent him to call on her and that Antônio was working on an *engenho* in Rio de Janeiro. Margarida, who likely never saw Antônio again, was compelled to immediately separate from her second husband, Fernão Mendes. The Catholic Church maintained that her second marriage was invalid since her first husband was still alive.[89]

From this single case, we can see three generations of Margarida's family being permanently altered, all with bitter effects. First, we know from the Inquisition record that Margarida was taken away from her parents in São

Tomé when she was eight years old. She was effectively orphaned in the same instance that she was enslaved. Then, each of her two marriages was dissolved, one because Antônio was sold away, and the other because the Catholic Church forbade her from marrying a second time. Finally, the three daughters, who were the products of Margarida's two marriages, were forced to suffer the difficult consequences of broken families.

For Margarida, and others like her, the Christian concepts of marriage and family were a cruel delusion. The sacrament of marriage raised a fundamental contradiction between slaves as thinking, feeling human beings and slaves as partible property. Supposedly unbreakable bonds between husband and wife were routinely broken by the laws governing property. No matter how much slaves tried to adhere to canon law, their relationships were undermined by the larger society's belief that they were nothing more than chattel.

As we think about masters' interference in the slave family, we must bear in mind that the majority of slaves created family structures that were not in keeping with European norms. Still, the deep meanings of family and community were no less real among those who created their own arrangements than among those who were married in the Catholic Church. Thus, the removal of a slave from any community likely had wider implications for friends, family, and kin. Even in those cases where families were sold away intact, we must take into account the strong kinlike ties that were broken by removing a family from the larger slave community. The web of kinship ties that defined the slave community was permanently transformed. And the sense of loss was keenly felt, not only by the family removed, but by all in the community.

Slave families and communities were not divided only by the sales of kinsmen; they could also be broken apart by manumission. Though manumission was clearly seen as a blessing by most slaves, the tensions that arose when one family member was freed and others remained enslaved were extremely difficult to overcome. Freedom completely transformed one's life chances, opening new opportunities to move, to earn, and to love. For a newly freed person to remain tied to an enslaved loved one required a level of commitment that not all were willing to make. The flush of freedom and its attendant temptations were often too great to resist.

To cite just one example, in 1767, Pedro de Oliveira Lima (Angola) and Juliana Maria (Creole), both servants in the Carmelite Convent of Rio de Janeiro, were joined in holy matrimony. They already shared a young son, João, who was born prior to their marriage. When Juliana was three months pregnant with their second child, Pedro took advantage of his recent manumission and departed for Lisbon. Perhaps he was fleeing the horrors of his slave past, or perhaps he was merely seeking new opportunities. In any case,

Pedro cut all ties to his Brazilian past and started a new life in Lisbon. There, he married for a second time to a Cape Verdean woman named Domingas do Amor Divino. Juliana anxiously awaited her husband's return to Rio, but fourteen years passed before she learned of his new life in Portugal. Pedro eventually was sentenced to seven years in the king's galleys for the crime of bigamy.[90]

Manumission could also force freed persons to choose between one of the several families they had created during their servitude. In the middle of the eighteenth century, Isabel Angola and José Angola, slaves of Estevão Pais, were married. Isabel, who gained her freedom, left her master's *engenho* to live with her slave daughter, Águeda, who was born before she met José. Isabel lived with her daughter for several years before hearing rumors that José was dead. Wanting to substantiate the rumors, Isabel returned to the *engenho* of Estevão Pais to learn the truth about her husband. There, Pai Antônio, a Congolese slave, confirmed that her husband was dead. Isabel then returned to the *engenho* where her daughter lived and married a slave named Antônio Ribeiro.[91]

Using manumission as an incentive, some masters even coerced their slaves to become masters of their own children. This was the case in 1751, when João Rodrigues Álvares, resident of Carahí, outside of Rio de Janeiro, freed his Angolan slave, Maria de Ramos. João freed Maria because she was his wife "and it was not just that his wife should be under subjection of slavery." Apparently, Maria's son was not deserving of the same familial consideration. In Maria's *carta de alforria* (letter of manumission), João noted that when she came into his power, Maria brought with her a son named Francisco Rodrigues, a "crioullo from Angola who is today ten years old." Rather than freeing Maria's son, João Rodrigues required that the boy "serve them as their slave for as long as they are alive." Only upon both of their deaths would the boy gain his freedom.[92]

Of course, many slaves remained loyal to their families after gaining their freedom, and some even went to extraordinary lengths in raising funds to free family members. Masters were not hesitant in exploiting a freed person's obvious affections for one of their slaves, and the master would often demand well above market value in exchange for the loved one's freedom. In 1749 in Rio de Janeiro, Maria de Encarnação traded two houses and a small tract of land for her husband's freedom. These were apparently the only properties that Maria owned, since it was stipulated in the *carta de alforria* that as long as Maria continued to stay in the houses, she would be "obliged to pay . . . the rate of 800 réis per month."[93] Similarly, in 1753, Rita da Silva purchased the freedom of her husband, Antônio Mina. Antônio, who was a barber by trade, was probably worth no more than the 350 mil-réis that his wife paid for him. But in addition to the 350 mil-réis, paid over two years, Rita also had to give Antônio's master an Angolan *moleque* named Mateus. Thus, she paid at least twice her husband's market value.[94]

For African slaves who lived to old age or who came down with life-threatening illnesses, manumission was no longer the aspiration that it was in their youth. Rather, manumission loomed ominously, threatening to cut off their food supply, evict them from their shelters, and remove them from the loved ones who cared for them in their waning years. One way for the master to rid himself of economic liabilities was to free old and emaciated slaves. No longer economically productive, these slaves were a drag on the profitability of the master's business. In 1728, the Bahian writer Nuno Marques Pereira noted that rather than incur the cost of curing their sick slaves, many masters simply threw them off the property when they fell ill.[95] Further evidence from manumission records bears out Pereira's claim. Of 180 Africans who were manumitted in Rio de Janeiro between 1749 and 1754, eighteen were listed as "already very old" and/or "with various ailments."[96] The majority of these old and infirm slaves, with few resources and no place to go, were essentially put out to die.[97]

Thus, like so much else in the slave's life, even the joy of manumission was tempered by the reality that freedom was earned under the master's terms. Broken families, ownership of children, economic insolvency, and even death were among the many compromises of freedom. Whether within the institution of slavery or on the way out, Africans and their descendants could not escape the transformative power of their masters. Slaves were subjects, property, units of production; and if their human concerns were acknowledged at all, they always remained only a distant concern.

The foregoing descriptions of the horrors of slavery are by no means exhaustive. Nor do they take into account the daily rigors of work on Brazil's sugar plantations, mines, cattle ranches, and so on. Rather, these descriptions are meant to demonstrate the impotence of slaves in controlling many facets of their day-to-day lives. At every stage of the human life cycle, death and disease were very real threats. From early childhood until death, the slave master exerted an enormous amount of power over his human chattel, often times disrupting the slaves' most intimate family and kinship bonds. Slaveholders also believed that in order to maintain the white, male-dominated social and political order, mental, physical, and sexual abuse were acceptable tools of repression. Though the experiences of slaves no doubt differed, and some suffered more than others, it seems almost inconceivable to suggest that there were slaves who went untouched by these damaging forces.

For those who grew into slavery from childhood, these assaults were particularly acute, sapping their innocence at a very tender age. As these young slaves grew into mature adults, they reacted to their childhood traumas in a variety of ways. Some were most certainly broken by the accumulation of suffering that they were forced to endure. We can never know the rate of psychological disorder among slaves, but it must have been high. Notations of "crazy" (louco/a) slaves in property inventories are not unusual. For scholars to acknowledge that some slaves were psychologically damaged by their experiences under slavery is not to suggest that slaves, writ large, were vanquished by the institution. Rather, it is an acknowledgement that slaves suffered the same human frailties as those in the larger society. By embracing the notion that Africans and their descendants were impervious to the slings and arrows of slavery, there is a grave danger of reifying the slaveholders' beliefs that slaves were inhuman savages who could endure almost any assault on their persons.[98]

On the other end of the psychological spectrum, there were also slaves who, as adults, repeated the patterns of violence and abuse that were carried out against them as children. Violence begot violence, as slaves struck out physically against their masters, overseers, and especially their fellow slaves. During the early colonial era, there are only sporadic references to individuals or small groups of slaves rising against masters or overseers. Most of these were quick strikes made in the heat of anger; they were not larger attempts to overthrow the institution of slavery. The two slaves who killed the overseer on the Benedictine Engenho Guaguasú in Rio de Janeiro between 1711 and 1714 are a typical case. The administrators of the *fazenda* commented that the two perpetrators "deserve[d] to be well punished for their brazenness." Recognizing the dire consequences of their actions, the two slaves immediately ran away from the *engenho*.[99] The overwhelming threats of master and societal retribution were usually enough to prevent overt challenges to the plantation hierarchy. Therefore, overt physical challenges were rare.

Slaves were far more likely to strike out in violence against their fellow slaves. Scattered throughout the colonial records are references to slaves maiming and killing one another. Some of the rivalries were rooted in jealousies between lovers. This was the case in 1731 on Engenho Santana in Bahia when a male slave found his wife in the company of another man. The man beat his wife, prompting her to stab him fatally in the chest.[100] The motives for other acts of slave violence remain largely hidden. But, not wanting to lose their labor, masters always tried to protect their slave property from prosecution. In Rio de Janeiro in 1678, Bento de Araujo ordered two of his African slaves to deliver a message to the Island of Flamengo, owned by Anna Bernaldes and her son Nicolão Soares. When the slaves arrived at the island in their canoe, they were assaulted with knives and swords. Both of Araujo's slaves were killed, and nobody was ever prosecuted for the crime. Araujo was certain that Anna Bernaldes and her slaves were responsible for the murders. He claimed that Bernaldes induced her slaves to lie to the judicial inquiry in order to cover up their involvement.[101] Similarly, in the 1740s in the Bahian township of Santo Amaro, Jesuit priests were forced to pay a surgeon to cure a slave who was stabbed in the chest by one of Engenho Sergipe's slaves. Included in the 24 mil-réis expenditure was the promise that the "aggressor of this libel" would not be remitted to justice.[102] When slaves were prosecuted for their crimes in Portugal, masters could make a donation to the crown in order to receive a royal pardon. Such was the case in Lisbon in 1633, when Gonçalo de Paiva paid the crown a thousand réis to pardon his slave Manuel Alguão, who had nearly killed another slave named Domingos.[103]

While some slaves were broken by the institution of slavery and others fought back with violence, the majority of Africans who made up the Brazilian slave population in the early colonial period fell between these two extremes, responding to the violence and uncertainty of slavery with more subtle forms of resistance. Many Africans ran away to join their brethren in the runaway communities in the heavily forested areas around Brazil's largest cities, but life in the *quilombos* could sometimes be as uncertain as on the master's property.[104] Food and provisions were always in short supply. And the frequent raids on the masters' villages usually invited the firepower of military and mercenary groups. Slaves also negotiated small spaces within the confines of the institution—gifts for newborns, provision grounds on which they could raise their own crops, and so on. To some extent they were also able to control the nature and pace of their work, breaking tools or slowing down their work pace when masters demanded too much of them. But even with these small pin pricks to the hard exterior of the institution, slaves still could not escape the death, disease, and violence that were at the core of Brazilian slavery.

Despite their inability to escape these pernicious forces, slaves as a group still never gave in to their masters' desire that they become pliant and docile. Breaks in lineage, stolen childhood, death, disease, hunger, low fertility, and physical abuse could not be overcome on a temporal level, and overt physical violence was an impractical solution to these difficulties. The tenuous and uncertain nature of the slave's existence in the Portuguese world necessitated different kinds of responses. As we will see in the chapters that follow, Africans and their descendants often addressed the institution of slavery and the attendant threats to life with the most powerful weapons at their disposal, weapons far stronger and seemingly more effective than physical resistance. The great leaveners of power in the slave societies of the African-Portuguese world were not muscle and might, but rather, African forms of religion and spirituality.

Argues that they created new kinship bonds, were trying to maintain old ways, sometimes adapting to slavery (marriage) but kept elements of their cultures too (3rd gender) but also very controlled by disease, malnutrition, high mortality, extensive master control + abuse. w/ all of these circumstances, the most powerful form of resistence was Religious + spiritual expressions

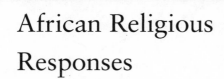

PART TWO

African Religious Responses

CHAPTER FOUR

Catholic vs. "Other"
in the World of Believers

Across the Portuguese empire during the sixteenth, seventeenth, and eighteenth centuries, Africans were thrust into a religious world that was dominated by the Catholic Church. In spite of apparent Catholic hegemony, however, the church and many of its adherents perceived themselves to be under constant assault by a variety of religious groups, including Muslims, Jews, Anglicans, and Lutherans. Looking through the prism of Muslim and Anglican slaves in Portugal, in this chapter we will examine the complex and contradictory defense of Portuguese Catholicism put forth by the church and its Holy Office of the Inquisition. As we will see, these contradictions had profound effects on Africans in their attempts to forge temporal and spiritual pathways to freedom.

Islamic Jolof Slaves in Portugal

The first waves of African slaves began arriving in Portugal in the second half of the fifteenth century, many of them Muslims from Senegambia. As early as the tenth century, there was a Muslim presence on the northern fringes of the Senegal River. By the thirteenth century, the Jolof Confederation was firmly established, extending Islamic beliefs across a vast geographic area from the Senegal River in the north to the Gambia River in the south. Included in the confederation were the Mandingo, Fula, Jolof, and Tukulor peoples. The Portuguese first made contact with the peoples of Senegambia in the 1440s and soon recognized Islam as the dominant religion of the region.

Map 5. People and States of Senegambia, Sixteenth to Eighteenth Centuries

In 1455, Alvise da Cadamosto, a Venetian merchant-trader in the hire of the Portuguese, wrote that the religion of the Jolof kingdom of Senegal was "Muhammadanism," adding, "they are not, however, as are the white Moors, very resolute in this faith, especially the common people."[1] Despite their conversion to Islam, many Jolofs continued to adhere to a variety of pre-Islamic beliefs. Though Cadamosto viewed these traditional beliefs as a break in Islamic orthodoxy, the two belief systems probably existed simultaneously, fulfilling different spiritual needs as the context warranted.[2]

The arrival of Portuguese traders along the Senegambia coast had a profound impact on the Jolof Confederation. The coastal provinces of Kayor, Waalo, and Bawol had direct contact with the burgeoning Atlantic trade, while the Jolof remained landlocked. The economic prosperity of the coastal provinces transformed the balance of power in the confederation. No longer willing to subject themselves to Jolof rule, the coastal provinces began to break away. During the middle of the sixteenth century, a series of wars wracked the Jolof territories, as the coastal provinces began asserting their independence (see Map 5). The disintegration of the Jolof Confederation produced large numbers of Muslim slaves, who were funneled toward the coast and sold to Portuguese traders.[3] Many of these Muslim captives ended up serving as slaves in Spain, Portugal, and the Americas, where they continued to worship Allah. Not surprisingly, these Islamic slaves from Senegambia drew the attention of the Portuguese Inquisition. Between 1549 and 1554, at least eight Africans—seven Jolofs and one Fulani—were accused of practicing Islam near Lisbon. The majority of these Africans simply asserted the superiority of Islam over the religion of their Catholic masters, pointing out, among other things, that Christians did not bathe before prayers. Several others expressed the belief that God had no son and that Jesus was the servant of Mohammed.[4]

Islamic practices among Senegambian slaves continued well into the latter half of the century. In 1566, a Jolof named Zambo (before being baptized Antônio), attempted to run away from his master in Lisbon. When he was caught, Zambo declared that he originally was enslaved by the "Moors," who captured him in the wars that they carried out against the Jolofs.[5] The Moors later sold him and other enslaved Jolofs to a Portuguese merchant on the coast of Senegal. The group of Jolof slaves was then taken to Lisbon, where they were "sold to diverse parts." Zambo confessed that prior to his enslavement, he was an adherent of Islam, often reciting the *shahada* and performing other Islamic ceremonies.[6] Even after being baptized in Lisbon, Zambo claimed that he re-committed himself to Islam. He also continued to carry out various Islamic ceremonies.[7]

Not only did Jolof slaves continue practicing their religion, but many transformed their African military expertise into a sustained challenge to their servitude. In the 1540s, runaway communities of Jolofs in the Spanish Caribbean battled against their former masters, using the same cavalry skills that they had learned in the wars of Senegambia.[8] In urban areas like Lisbon, horsemanship was not so useful, but the organizational and planning skills of Jolof soldiers no doubt helped them in their plots to hire and steal boats in order to return to Africa. Throughout the sixteenth century, many small groups of Muslims challenged their enslavement by attempting to flee to Islamic Africa, a less than 200-mile journey from the southern coast of Portugal. A number of these attempts were unsuccessful, but they demonstrate the refusal of Jolof slaves to submit to Christian servitude.

The failed attempts at flight can be attributed to a number of logistical problems, including navigational errors. In 1516, a group of four Africans from the fishing village of Peniche stole a boat and attempted to sail for Africa. After traveling only a hundred miles, the four men went ashore, certain that they had arrived in their homeland. In fact, they were still in Portugal. After walking inland, the four runaways were quickly captured.[9]

Other runaway plots were foiled during the planning stages. In 1554, two "Turkish" slaves, Antônio and Pedro, determined that they were going to run away to "the land of the Moors." In order to achieve this end, the two men met with a Jolof slave named Francisco, a fishing boat operator in Setúbal. Francisco decided that he too would like to escape and agreed to guide the men to freedom in his master's boat. The three men decided that the best day to leave was on a Sunday during the *festa dos negros* (party of the Negroes). Presumably, the attention of the authorities would have been diverted during the weekly gathering of the city's blacks.[10] But after some reflection, Francisco changed his mind. At forty years of age, Francisco believed that he was "too old to find work in a new land" and that he would "not be able to eat as a free man." For Francisco, pragmatism ultimately won out over the lure of freedom.[11]

Another plot that fell apart in the planning stages occurred in 1564 when a Jolof slave named Antônio joined two "Turks" in attempting to return to "the land of the Moors." Despite being baptized, Antônio declared that he never truly became a Christian, and that it was his desire to return to a Muslim nation. He procured a boat for their passage, but the plot was discovered before the three men could set sail.[12]

Still other Jolof slaves were caught just as they were making their departure. In 1565, two Jolofs, the aforementioned Zambo and a slave named Antônio, discussed the possibility of escaping to "the land of the Moors." The two men had numerous conversations, with Antônio trying to convince Zambo that their condition was too miserable to endure. Antônio complained that his master did not give him clothing, food, or shoes. Finally persuaded that they should abandon their suffering, Zambo responded to Antônio, "Brother, let's go." Antônio told Zambo that he would steal something of value from his master and sell it in order to pay a boatman. The two slaves spoke to a boatman named Antônio Francisco, who agreed that he would drop them off on any beach in "the land of the Moors." Zambo paid Antônio Francisco 500 réis for himself and a thirteen-year-old Jolof girl named Antônia. Antônia had arrived in Lisbon the same year as Zambo, and he apparently felt some kin-like responsibility for the young girl, because he later claimed that he forced her to come with him. Another Jolof named Pedro gave Zambo nine vintéis

(180 réis) to pay the boatman so that he might also make the crossing. It was agreed that all of the parties would meet at the boatman's house on a Saturday night and depart from there. Zambo, Antônia, and Pedro arrived at the house on the appointed night. There, they waited for Antônio until nine o'clock, but he never showed up. Finally, the three Jolof slaves left without their comrade. Just as they entered the boat to make their departure, they were captured by two *alcaides* (justice officials), who immediately took them to jail.[13]

Since the majority of the extant records describe failed escape attempts, we can never be sure how many Jolofs succeeded in gaining their freedom in Muslim territories. But the ceaseless efforts of these Islamic slaves to shed the chains of bondage and return to their homelands reminds us that they willingly accepted neither their servitude nor Christianity. The rituals and beliefs that sustained these Africans in their Senegambia homelands were not erased when they arrived in Lisbon as slaves. On the contrary, these beliefs were so deeply held and so fundamentally different from the beliefs of their masters that they could not be easily abandoned or transformed. As the cases demonstrate, ethnic and religious solidarity compelled Jolofs and their Muslim compatriots to seek one another out, continue practicing their faith, and hatch escape plots, even in the face of slavery and virulent Christian hostility.[14]

Testing the Bonds of Faith: Forced Conversions of Slaves to Islam

Not all slaves accused of practicing Islam were born into the religion. Some were Christians who were forced to convert to Islam when they were captured and enslaved by North African Muslims. One such case was that of Domingos, a 32-year-old slave who was the son of a Gujerat Indian man and an Angolan woman. In 1587, Domingos appeared at the Portuguese fort in the village of Arzilla (Asila) in Morocco (see Map 6). He was dressed in the "clothing of the Moors" and was called by his Muslim name, Mansor. Before the vicar general of the village, Domingos recounted a seventeen-year odyssey in which he was sold to North Africa, converted to Islam, and "forced" to live as a Muslim.

Domingos grew up in Lisbon in the house of Governor Diogo Lopes de Sousa. His married parents were also servants of the governor, and they all lived together until Domingos was sold at the age of fifteen. His new master, Diogo Pires, carried Domingos away from his family to the city of Ceuta in North Africa. Domingos suffered a difficult life at the hands of Pires and decided that he would run away to Spain. But before he could put his plan

Map 6. Portugal and North Africa, Sixteenth Century

into action, Pires sold him to a Moor. The Moor continued to treat Domingos poorly, and Portuguese officials eventually ordered him to sell Domingos away from Ceuta, presumably to a Portuguese Christian.

Rather than return Domingos to a Christian master, the Moor took him to the countryside and abandoned him at a Moorish settlement near the village of Tituão. There, Domingos encountered a group of Moors who asked him who he was. He replied that he was a Christian. The Moors then asked if they could convert Domingos to Islam. Domingos answered affirmatively. Domingos was taken to Tituão, where he consented to a variety of Muslim conversion ceremonies, including circumcision. He lived in Tituão for two years but claimed that he never set foot in a mosque and never practiced Muslim rituals. Instead, he went around in the company of Christians and renegade Muslims (*Elches*).

After his time in Tituão, Domingos left for Fez, where he volunteered to join the army of the Moroccan king, Ahmad Al-Mansur (1578–1603). Al-Mansur became king of Morocco in the aftermath of the Islamic victory at the battle of Alcazarquivir, a decisive campaign that thwarted the Portuguese king Don Sebastião's attempts to conquer the Maghreb and saw the Portuguese king lose his life. Al-Mansur consolidated this victory and set out to liberate those Moroccan towns that were still under European rule—Arzilla, Ceuta, Mazagão, and Tangier. Domingos served in Al-Mansur's army for some time, presumably fighting against Morocco's Christian enemies, the Spanish and the Portuguese. But "yearning for the milk of his Mother Church, and sick of that life," Domingos ran away with six *Elches*, destined for the Portuguese settlement at Mazagão. As the seven men fled, they were chased by Moors. Three of the runaways were captured and killed, while Domingos and the others hid in the woods. Unable to continue on their path to Mazagão, the four survivors remained in Islamic Morocco. Despite his attempts to flee, Domingos received a pardon from the Moroccan king and rejoined the army. He eventually returned to Fez and married a Muslim woman. He lived with the woman for three years, during which time they had a daughter together. Becoming "sicker and sicker of that vile [Muslim] life," Domingos abandoned his family and once again set off for Christian lands. He traveled only by night, taking shelter in thickets during daylight hours. Along the path, Christian captives directed him toward the Portuguese fort.

When Domingos finally arrived in Arzilla, he confessed his sins to the vicar general, who took it upon himself to reacquaint Domingos with Christian doctrine. Despite his many years in Muslim lands, Domingos still remembered most of the Christian teachings of his youth. He even claimed that while in Morocco, he often said the Lord's Prayer and Hail Marys. Though Domingos spent nearly twenty years in "hostile" Muslim territory, he never abandoned the religious core that he developed in his formative years in Lisbon. Domingos was thoroughly Christianized by the time he was sold to his Muslim master at the age of fifteen, and no matter how much a practitioner of Islam he appeared to be on the exterior, his Christian faith was never broken. The church recognized the depths of his devotion. On March 1, 1587, Domingos stood before parishioners at the Catholic Church in Arzilla where he was reconciled to the church and absolved of all sins.[15]

It was not at all uncommon for Christianized slaves to be caught in the vortex of religious struggles between Catholics and Muslims in the Mediterranean and Atlantic during the late sixteenth and early seventeenth centuries. Like Domingos, most of the Christian slaves who were forced to convert to Islam never completely accepted their new faith. In 1615, a 20-year-old slave named Diogo gave his confession to the Portuguese Holy Office in Lisbon. Diogo, who was born in Bahia to African parents, was taken to Lisbon at a very young age. When he was twelve years old, Diogo was ordered to return to Brazil to work on the *fazenda* of his master's brother. During the Atlantic crossing, Diogo's ship encountered a pirate vessel near the Canary Islands. The crew of the pirate ship, a mixture of English and North Africans, boarded the Portuguese vessel and kidnapped Diogo. Diogo was taken to Algiers, where he was sold to a Moor named Camarit. Camarit forced Diogo to convert to Islam, threatening him with a variety of punishments. Fearing for his life, Diogo acquiesced to his master's wishes, was circumcised, and took the Islamic name Tombos. Diogo lived with Camarit for seven or eight years, working as a mariner on Camarit's pirate ship, plundering other seafaring vessels.

Eventually, Diogo found himself working on the ship of a renegade English captain. Diogo labored on the pirate ship for four months before the captain decided to return to England. Upon arrival there, the captain requested a royal pardon for betraying the crown of King James I. The king granted the captain's pardon, and the crew was allowed to disembark. Diogo lived free in England "because in that reign nobody is a slave." While in London, Diogo met some Portuguese Catholics who encouraged him to confess his sins, which he did. After four months in England, Diogo boarded a ship bound for Portugal. Diogo disembarked in Lisbon and enjoyed six days of freedom before turning himself in to his original master, Francisco de Paiva. Diogo again confessed his sins, stating that all the time he was in Barbary, he never truly became a Moor. Nor did he leave the Catholic Church. He claimed that he became a Moor, only on the exterior, out of fear for his master. And he understood that in Islam he could never have salvation.[16]

The loyalty that Diogo displayed in returning to his master might seem remarkable if not for the fact that he was thrust into the unfamiliar and inhospitable environment of North Africa at such a young age. The removal from his master's home and the forced conversion to Islam at the age of twelve no doubt isolated him in a way that made him yearn for the relative stability of his Lisbon childhood. With very few black faces to greet him, London was probably no more inviting than Algiers, despite the sweet taste of freedom.

Diogo returned to his master's home because he could find social and spiritual salvation there. Diogo's world view was decisively shaped during his early childhood, and his tenacious grasp of Christianity was only one symptom of that relatively "stable" past.

Domingos and Diogo were not alone in holding on to the beliefs and values of their slave childhoods, especially vis-à-vis North African Muslims. Around 1618, a five-year-old boy was taken from his parents, enslaved, and sold to Dutch traders in the Angolan city of Luanda. The young boy was then taken to Holland, where he was baptized and given the Christian name Antônio. Antônio's master, Gaspar Afonso Martel, taught him to recite the Lord's Prayer and the Hail Mary. He also took Antônio to mass regularly. After about a year in Holland, Antônio left with his master for Brazil. There, he continued to attend mass and say his prayers. Two years later, at the age of eight years, Antônio left Pernambuco with his master, bound for Porto. While at sea, their ship was overtaken by North African pirates, and Antônio was stolen away to Algiers, where he was sold to a Moor named Mahmet. Through a variety of torments, Antônio was forced to convert to Islam and given the name Monas, his third name in only eight years. Despite being "obliged to renounce God in an exterior fashion," Antônio claimed that "in his heart he was truly Catholic and [always] guarded the faith."

Antônio's master ordered him and other slaves to go out to sea and pillage Christian ships. One day in 1631, after ten years in the employ of his Islamic master, Antônio and the other Christian captives rose against the Moors aboard his master's ship, killing many of them. Those Moors who survived the rebellion were thrown into the sea and left to drown. After wresting control of the ship, the Christian slaves guided the boat into the city of Porto, where they turned themselves in to Portuguese authorities. There, Antônio revealed his familiarity with Christian doctrine. He knew that the Virgin Mary was the mother of Christ and that Christ was in Heaven and on earth. Antônio also stated that his original master taught him that "Christ died in order to save us" and that "outside of his law there was no salvation." Even though he was kidnapped and "converted" to Islam at the tender age of eight, ten years later Antônio still remembered his master's teachings, teachings that no doubt were nourished by his interactions with other Christian slaves and their combined opposition to their Islamic masters. The Inquisitors required Antônio to undergo further instruction in the faith, but they were convinced that he was truly a Christian and readily accepted him back into the Catholic fold.[17]

In all of these cases, the Portuguese believed that Christian slaves were forced to convert to Islam. The Portuguese also believed that these Chris-

Believed that forced Conversions to Christianity
Worked but not other religions.
Ironic

tians maintained their faith, despite their forced conversions. They were probably correct in assuming the religious devotion of these slaves, but Portuguese officials failed to see the inherent contradictions in such a formulation. It was assumed that the "conversion" of slaves from Christianity to Islam was somehow fundamentally different from the "conversion" of Africans to Christianity. Ironically, Africans were expected to abandon the religious and cultural beliefs of their youths and adopt the Christianity of their Portuguese masters; however, the same was not true of Christians who were enslaved by Muslims. Religious chauvinism led Portuguese Catholics to conclude that Christian slaves would not voluntarily abandon the faith and convert to Islam, but that newly arrived Africans would quickly adopt Catholicism. What the Portuguese failed to note was that religious chauvinism was a widespread phenomenon. All forced conversions, including those to Christianity, were extremely problematic. It was unlikely that any person would readily abandon the religious beliefs that gave structure and meaning to their everyday lives, especially when those beliefs could be used as a tool against the oppression of slavery.

Africans and the Anglican Threat in the Portuguese World

While black slaves were often caught in the crossfire between Christians and Muslims during the sixteenth and seventeenth centuries, by the eighteenth century another religious option emerged for some slaves in Portugal—Anglicanism. And the Portuguese once again exhibited their contempt for other religions in a confounding series of contradictory Inquisition cases. But before examining these cases we must provide a brief background on the origins of the Anglican "threat" in Portugal.

After the discovery of large deposits of gold in Brazil at the end of the seventeenth century, Portugal had an abundance of cash that it sought to spend in the world market. Beginning in 1703, the Portuguese signed a series of commercial treaties with England, exchanging Brazilian gold for English goods. Portuguese domestic industry was largely neglected, and by the middle of the century, Portugal was dependent upon England as its primary supplier of vital consumer goods. As a result, English merchants and traders were a prominent presence in Portugal's port cities, and many of these Englishmen brought their human chattel with them as they traveled to Portugal and beyond.

The Anglican Church had been a primary concern for Catholics since the Council of Trent in 1545, but it was only in the 1700s that Anglican practices appear to have drawn notice from the Portuguese Inquisition. During the first

years of the eighteenth century, the Portuguese tolerated the religious practices of many of the Englishmen who resided in their country. But as Portugal's
dependency on Britain became more pronounced, resentment toward English
merchants grew. Though the Inquisition could not take action against the merchants themselves, they did hear the complaints of English slaves residing in
Portugal.

In 1734, a fifteen-year-old Cape Verdean named Thomas, the slave of an
Englishman who lived in Lisbon, expressed his desire to become a Roman
Catholic. Thomas's master had not indoctrinated his slaves in any faith. He
had instead chosen to ignore their religious desires. Yearning to be like the majority of his fellow slaves, Thomas asked another Englishman why his master
had not ordered him to be baptized like the other Catholic slaves. The Englishman responded that Thomas's master "would not want [him] to live under the
[Catholic] law." Thomas also reported that he and another "Christian" slave
were given meat to eat on Fridays, Saturdays, and during Lent. Though the
inquisitors were clearly displeased that Thomas's master prevented his slaves
from freely practicing their desired faith, they apparently did nothing to facilitate Thomas's conversion to Catholicism. The case never came to full trial.[18]

During the same year that Thomas attempted to become a Catholic, another
slave claimed that his English master "forced" him to practice Anglicanism
against his will. Carlos, a sixteen-year-old Guinean slave of the English consul
in Lisbon, stated that he was kidnapped from his home in Cacheu, Guinea,
when he was ten or twelve years old. After passing through Cape Verde and the
Azores, Carlos was sold in Lisbon. He had been living with the English consul
for three and a half years when he recounted his ordeal to the Inquisition.

After serving in the English consul's house for a year and a half, Carlos was
baptized by an Anglican minister, even though he secretly desired to join the
Catholic faith. Like the aforementioned Thomas, Carlos wanted to worship
in the same way as his fellow slaves. Carlos had already witnessed his master beating slaves who tried to adhere to Catholic dietary restrictions, and he
claimed that he did not voice his wishes to become a Catholic for fear of similar reprisals. Even though he was baptized in the Anglican Church, Carlos
continued to try to practice Catholicism. He was educated in the mysteries of
the Catholic faith by the other servants in the consul's house. He learned the
doctrines and the orations by memorizing a card that they made up for him.
And he claimed that he awoke very early on saints' days to go to a convent to
hear mass.

One night, an Anglican page in the house noticed that Carlos wore some
rosary beads and two veronicas around his neck.[19] The page dutifully reported
Carlos to the wife of the English consul, who told Carlos that if he wanted to

practice Catholicism, she would sell him to another master. The consul's wife then told her husband about Carlos's transgression. Wanting to discover who had persuaded Carlos to wear the rosary and the veronicas, the consul beat him with a whip and locked him in a house for four days, providing him with only a small ration of food. Carlos refused to incriminate the other Catholic slaves in the house. After four days of incarceration, Carlos dreamt that he heard a voice that told him to get up and escape out the open window. The voice also told him that he was favored by the angels. Awakening from his dream, Carlos went to the window and found his way out. He fled to the beach, where he slept until morning. At dawn, he returned to his master's house, collected his card of orations, and went straight to the Convento do Corpo Santo, where he declared his intent to become Catholic.

Remarkably, the Portuguese Holy Office not only allowed Carlos to convert to Catholicism, but they freed him from bondage. Citing his attendance at mass, his oration card, and his abstinence from meat on prohibited days, the inquisitors concluded that the English consul had to relinquish Carlos with no financial compensation "because the right of religion is stronger than that of servitude and paternal power." On March 29, 1734, Carlos walked away from his master a free man.[20]

Of course, "the right of religion" applied only to those slaves who wanted to be Catholics. Portuguese slaves who wished to practice religions other than Catholicism were subject to swift prosecution. In this respect, the Inquisition functioned as a tool of spiritual repression, not unlike the whippings and beatings that Muslim and Anglican masters meted out to their spiritually wayward slaves. This stark contradiction on "the right of religion" was brought into even sharper focus by a case that arose only three years after Carlos was set free.

In 1737, an eighteen-year-old Angolan-born slave named Cesário was brought before the Inquisition for heresy. When Cesário was a very young child, he was taken from Angola to London. He was then moved from London to Porto, where he was sold to a Portuguese man named Guilherme Anuil. Cesário was baptized, educated in the Catholic doctrine, and confessed his sins on a regular basis. After some time, Cesário accompanied his Portuguese master back to London. While they were there, a man named João approached Cesário and tried to convince him that he should convert to Anglicanism. João told Cesário that if he were baptized by an Anglican priest, he would immediately be free from his master. João added that, as a free man, Cesário might earn as much as 30 mil-réis working in the house of a wealthy nobleman (fidalgo). Initially, Cesário rejected João's offer, noting that he had already been baptized in Portugal. But João told him that his first baptism was unimportant and that "he could be baptized four or five times." Finally persuaded, Cesário consented to the baptism. João took him to a cleric who baptized him in the manner of the Anglican Church.

The next day, Cesário's master learned what his slave had done, and he set off to punish him. But the master's son requested that he should pardon Cesário because he was young and did not know what he was doing. Giving in to his son's requests, Guilherme Anuil locked Cesário in a room and ordered him to be put aboard the first ship bound for Porto. When Cesário appeared before the Inquisition one year after returning to Porto, he attributed his Anglican baptism to "ignorance and young age." He claimed that he never set foot in the Church of England and that he continued to say the rosary. The only reason he went through with the baptism was "because of that man who harassed him, promising him his freedom."

Ultimately, the inquisitors found Cesário guilty of formal heresy. Nevertheless, they argued that he was "a boy of very few years, born and raised among pagans." They also noted that he "was still so reserved, that he barely understands the Portuguese language and speaks poorly." The Holy Office concluded that Cesário merely lacked proper instruction in the Catholic faith. He was ordered to undergo instruction in Church doctrine and the mysteries of the faith.[21]

The Portuguese Holy Office was quick to excuse Cesário's Anglican baptism as nothing more than a youthful indiscretion, swiftly returning him to his master; but just three years earlier, they ruled that Carlos was perfectly rational when he rejected Anglicanism in favor of Catholicism. Ironically, Carlos was several years *younger* than Cesário when he made his decision to convert to Catholicism. Carlos was also only four years out of his African homeland, while Cesário had been raised in the Catholic faith since he was a child. Despite Carlos's youth and recent arrival from Africa, the Inquisitors ruled that his "right to religion" outweighed his English master's property interest. The same was not true for Cesário. Clearly, the "right to religion" meant only one thing—the "right to Catholicism." In the eyes of the Portuguese Inquisition, slaves like Cesário never had the "right" to choose other religious options, especially if Portuguese masters might be threatened with the loss of their human property.

These apparent contradictions are easily understood if we remember that the Inquisition was both a religious and a political institution. The inquisitors were driven largely by their own deep religious faith and their contempt for other belief systems. They were also not unaware of the economic and political tensions that existed between Portugal and England. As was the case with Muslims and Jews, religious, economic, and political imperatives led the

Portuguese Holy Office to rule consistently in favor of Catholics in their disputes with Anglicans. Carlos was an extraordinarily fortunate beneficiary of these policies, gaining his freedom from his Lisbon-based Anglican master. But Cesário and others like him remained trapped, unable to escape the coercion of their bondage or the coercion of the Catholic faith.

From the slave's perspective, forced religious conversions were always imperfect. Muslim slaves from Senegambia rarely abandoned Islam, despite being baptized as Catholics throughout the Portuguese world. Similarly, among black Christian slaves who were forced to convert to Islam, few actually abandoned the Catholic faith, despite their lowly status under Portuguese Catholicism. Remarkably, all of the Christian slaves in our sample who appeared before the Inquisition were under the age of fifteen when they were forced to convert to Islam, yet they still held tightly to the Christian faith of their childhood years. Finally, the "Anglican" slaves who converted to Catholicism were all African-born boys who were exposed to some form of indigenous African religion before being taken to Europe. They were then converted to Anglicanism, even as they were thrust into an environment where their social peers were predominantly Catholic. It was from the influences of these slave peers that they developed a Catholic identity. In short, their religious beliefs were being shaped by the environment in which they were growing up.

Few people would question the allegiance of Christian and Muslim slaves to their respective faiths, even in the face of extreme torture and duress. And it would not surprise most people to learn that very young, culturally isolated Africans were most likely to embrace the Catholicism of their social and racial peers. But scholars have had a difficult time embracing the notion that many African slaves, even those who arrived at destinations where Africans constituted the majority of the slave population, continued to adhere primarily to the religious beliefs of their African homelands. These scholars have made the same assumption that the Portuguese made: since most Africans were not members of one of the recognized monotheistic faiths, they were religious tabula rasa and were quickly converted to Christianity. But Africans who adhered to "traditional" beliefs, even after being "converted" to Christianity, were no different from African Muslims who were "converted" to Christianity. They continued to see the world through the religious prism of their African pasts. Since most Africans entered into slavery as young adults, they were even more fixed in their beliefs than were those very young Christian slaves who were "forced" to convert to Islam. We certainly cannot claim that mature Africans abandoned their core beliefs, while young Portuguese slaves of African descent held onto Christianity in the face of Muslim assaults. In the next chapter we look more closely at the complexion of Central African religious beliefs. We will also provide a more thorough critique of those scholars who adhere to a "devout" Judeo-Christian approach in assessing African religious principles, both in Africa and in the broader diaspora.

CHAPTER FIVE

Theory and Praxis
in the Study of
African Religions

As the number of Muslim slaves arriving in the ports of the Portuguese colonial world began diminishing in the second half of the sixteenth century, there arrived new waves of Africans whose religious beliefs were unlike those of most slaves the Portuguese had previously encountered. The overwhelming majority of these slaves were from the Central African areas of present-day Angola, Congo, Gabon, and Cabinda. These Africans brought with them to the Americas certain core beliefs and practices that were undeniable products of their indigenous pasts. When we discuss core beliefs and practices, we must attempt to distinguish those cultural beliefs that were central to one's sense of personhood from those that were secondary and thus more malleable. In the case of Central Africa, these core beliefs and practices included a religious cosmology based on the division between the world of the living and the world of the spirits, with a particular emphasis on the importance of ancestral spirits. My primary focus in the chapters that follow are those indigenous religious beliefs and practices that were transferred throughout the African-Portuguese diaspora. By comparing the ritual practices and beliefs of Central Africans in Africa with the beliefs and practices of their brethren in the Americas, we can demonstrate that certain core beliefs were not destroyed by the influences of Western Christianity.

Central African Cosmology

Before looking at the religious practices of Africans in the broader diaspora, we must first have some understanding of the belief systems that sustained them in the lands of their birth. There was a great deal of variation in religious practices from ethnic group to ethnic group and even from kinship group to kinship group; however, there appear to have been broad religious understandings that were shared by nearly all Central African peoples. One of the distinguishing features of Central African cosmologies was the belief that secular structures were intimately bound to religious ideas. Political, social, economic, and cultural ideologies were all animated by a tightly woven cosmology that explained the origins of the universe, the constitution of the person, and the connections between the worlds of the living and the dead. This broad cosmology dictated codes of behavior and ritual practices; explained the sources of illness, infertility, or other malevolence; and delineated the relationships between human beings and the various deities.

In more specific terms, the universe was conceived as divided between the world of the living and the world of the dead. These two worlds were separated by a large body of water through which the dead had to pass in order to reach the other world.[1] Though the souls of the dead moved on to the other realm to join the souls of deceased ancestors, they never completely abandoned the world of the living.[2] There was a fluidity between the two worlds that allowed ancestral spirits to remain engaged in the everyday lives of their surviving kinsmen. Indeed, ancestral spirits were believed to be among the most powerful influences in shaping the fortunes of their surviving kin. Ancestors witnessed village disputes, sometimes intervening to uphold moral codes and community standards. They watched over hunters in the forests, protected women during childbirth, and insured bountiful harvests. In return, the ancestors expected to be loved and remembered. They required food at communal feasts, expected to be consulted in important family decisions, and demanded proper burials and frequent offerings at their graves. In this way, the living and the dead formed a single community, with social and moral obligations flowing in both directions.[3]

The Central African conception of humanity was closely related to the model of the divided world. Human beings were considered "double beings," consisting of a visible outer shell and an inner, invisible entity that was the actual or essential person. The "soul" was an eternal force that could act independently of the outer being. When the outer person slept, the soul flew off to pursue its own labors and adventures, thereby explaining what Westerners understood to be dreams.[4]

On earth, the most powerful people were thought to possess whole and complete souls. To maintain the well-being of the soul, humans relied on the dead to protect them from evil. These appeals occurred at grave sites or in other ritual settings where the living made offerings to the dead in exchange for power and protection of the life force.[5] When illness, misfortune, or other signs of weakness occurred, it was interpreted to mean that the spiritual protection of the soul was no longer effective. Because good health was viewed as a sign of social and spiritual power, sickness was interpreted as a symbol of a much broader and more general social failure. Sometimes, ancestral spirits invoked illness as punishment for those who failed in their obligations to their kin. At other times, the weakening of the soul was attributed to witches and evil spirits who separated the soul from its body by stealing it, often while the person was sleeping. The longer the soul was away from its shell, the risk of illness and death increased, as the witches continued to "eat" away at the soul.[6]

To counteract the depletion of the life force by disgruntled ancestors and witches, individuals might rely on ritual healers or diviners to intervene on their behalf. The diviners, in addition to being able to predict past and future occurrences, were able to determine which spirits were plaguing the body of an individual. After determining the cause of the "illness," the healer prescribed a variety of remedies, including treatment of the witchcraft through natural medicines (roots, herbs, etc.), appeasement of ancestral spirits with feasts in their honor, or ritual judgments of the suspected living witches. These judgments usually consisted of a trial, or ordeal, that had to be endured by the suspected witches. To determine the guilty party, suspects had to undergo a rigorous physical test (often drinking poisons). The innocent always survived unharmed, while the guilty succumbed, revealing their identity as witches.[7]

Some healers, usually "normal" men and women, were chosen by the water and earth spirits to cure specific diseases or illnesses or to protect from malevolent forces. The spirit revealed itself to the chosen individual through an unusually shaped object of the natural world—a shell, a stone, or a piece of wood. These objects were thought to contain the essence of the spirit. By manipulating the object in a ritual manner, the healer could be possessed by the spirit and be endowed with its power. Some of these fetish objects were embellished with "medicine" pockets that supplemented the power of the spirit. In other cases, the fetish object was a manufactured statuette with medicine put into a hole in its stomach or in a container such as a bag or a calabash. The medicine consisted of various power-saturated substances from the natural world—plants, minerals, hair, sweat, blood, and so on. These fetishes and medicines were also sold by the healers to protect against wild animals, to protect the foundations of houses, to kill thieves, to protect crops, to ensure fertility, and so on. By using the proper medicines and engaging in carefully choreographed rituals, individuals could protect themselves from a wide array of malevolent forces.[8]

The Limitations of Western Outlooks on African Culture

Broadly speaking, this was the cosmological world of Central Africans in the seventeenth century. Though this is admittedly only a thumbnail sketch of a broadly conceived Central African cosmology, the reader should be able to discern some of the differences between European and African cosmologies. The transfer of Central African ideas and their associated rituals across the Portuguese world is clearly shown in the Inquisition records and in the writings of various travelers, clerics, and merchants who resided in those areas, but reading these accounts presents difficulties. One must recognize and filter out Western biases that flaw these otherwise useful documentary sources. Descriptions of African practices, both in Africa and in the African-Portuguese diaspora, were not only condemned and marginalized as "sin" and "idolatry," they also were misinterpreted as the work of the Devil, thereby distorting and omitting important elements crucial to understanding ritual processes. Despite the biases inherent in the sources, if one sets aside the pejorative descriptions they provide, one can clearly identify the unmistakable religious imprint of Central Africa, in some cases, in almost exactly the same forms that existed in Africa.

Unfortunately, the Portuguese were not the only ones who misinterpreted the meanings and significance of African religious forms. Even in the present day, histories of Africa and the African diaspora suffer from the inability of many "devout" Christian scholars to shed the dominant paradigms of Judeo-Christian thought.[9] As such, the interpretation of African religions has been difficult for many Western scholars. Though most scholars engage their subjects with the best of intentions, the essence of African religious meaning has been diluted by the tacit assumption of Christian superiority. In their attempts to reconcile progressive, antiracist agendas with their certainty that African religions are inferior to Christianity, "devout" scholars have used a Christian template in their analyses of African rituals and beliefs, often attempting to find Christianity where it did not exist. Unfortunately, this Christian paradigm only distorts and obscures our understanding of African religious principles. Many of these devout thinkers have operated on the unconscious assumption that if they can demonstrate Christian elements in African thought, they can somehow redeem Africans' humanity. Ironically, these analyses not only misrepresent African religious beliefs, but they reify the same sorts of patronizing and ethnocentric attitudes that the original European colonizers exhibited toward Africans.

Among the many preconceived notions that scholars bring to the study of African religions are at least three important misconceptions that derive from Judeo-Christian theology. The first is the belief in a single, omnipotent, fixed God. This assumption has led some scholars to search for the Christian God in Africa, filtering African supreme beings through their own understandings of the Christian divinity. But there are important differences between the Christian God and the African creators. In most African societies, the supreme being was not conceived as a universal creator, but rather as the creator of a particular people. This "original ancestor" was concerned only with the well-being of his descendants; not with all of humanity. Many Africans also believed that the creator could be transformed in accordance with political, economic, or social change. As we have already noted, religious beliefs and everyday secular activities were intimately connected. Thus, change in the secular world often impacted religious beliefs and practices, including humans' relationship with the supreme being.

For example, in Kongo, the arrival of the Portuguese resulted in a correlation between *nzambi mpungu* (the creator of all things) and the Christian God. Gradually, *nzambi mpungu* became more involved in the everyday affairs of many Kongolese, especially those who identified themselves as Christians. No longer remote and inaccessible, *nzambi mpungu* was now the subject of frequent worship for Kongolese Christians.[10] In other African societies, changing historical conditions initiated the complete reinvention of the supreme being. For example, among the Ewe and Fon peoples of the so-called Mina Coast, historical change resulted in a variety of different supreme beings over time.[11] This volatility in the nature of the supreme being illustrates not only the futility of attempting to find the "true" Christian God in Africa but also shows that African cosmologies were not constructed around a supreme being in the same way that Christianity was. Instead, a variety of separate and distinct ancestral spirits and deities were the spiritual arbiters of the temporal world.

While most scholars acknowledge the importance of these "lesser" spirits, many have suggested that these spirits were direct manifestations of the supreme being, which supposedly served as intermediaries between the worshiper and the one true God, similar to Catholic saints. Insofar as the lesser spirits were often understood to be the lineal offspring of the creator, there was indeed a hierarchy of kinship and respect. But the lesser spirits were not necessarily considered an extension of the supreme being's will.[12] As with all families, each member had his or her own characteristics and earthly utilities and was worshipped in accordance with specific human needs. Indeed, across Central Africa, it was the spirits of the most recently deceased ancestors who often took the most prominent roles in the lives of the living. The supreme being had no role in these relationships between man and the other spiritual beings. Thus, rather than seeking to reveal the Christian God in Africa, studies of African religions should attempt to understand the specific utility of ancestral spirits and their relationship to man.

The second questionable assumption made by many Christian scholars is that God is a mysterious and unknowable entity from the paradise known as Heaven. In Africa, this assumption fails on at least two counts. First, as we have already suggested, most African deities were well-known to their adherents—by name, by where they lived, by their personal characteristics, by what illnesses they might cause, and so on. Second, the notion of Heaven, in the Judeo-Christian sense, was unknown in African religions. There was no belief in Africa analogous to the Christian belief that life on earth was inferior to that which would be enjoyed in the "other world." As Ugandan anthropologist Okot p'Bitek succinctly states, "African ethics is not grounded on a promise or threat by some god that the good people will, in the future, enjoy life in heaven, while the bad will cook in a great fire."[13] Instead of moving on to heaven or hell at death, African souls moved on to the world of the ancestors, where they joined the souls of their "dead" kinsmen, but they were still capable of occupying the same temporal space that they occupied when they were "alive," influencing the fortunes of their living relatives and friends.

Finally, and perhaps most importantly, many Christian scholars assume that the ultimate goal of religion is communion with and worship of the one inscrutable God. Most Africans, on the other hand, viewed their religions as a way of explaining, predicting, and controlling events in the world around them. African rituals and beliefs were designed to deal directly with the fortunes and the dangers of the temporal realm—disease, drought, hunger, sterility, and so on. As such, religion provided many of the explanations for what Westerners call "science."[14] In the Western world, religion and science evolved into two separate spheres of thought, with science being the preferred method of explaining and controlling the temporal world. The religious domain became a preserve for metaphysical communion with God. But in Africa, religion and science were inextricably bound.

Let me cite one example to illustrate the potential similarities between African religion and Western science. In most African cosmologies, an herbal cure whose efficacy was proven time and again was regarded as a "strong" spiritual remedy, affirming the ritual knowledge of the diviners and curers who proffered the cure. For Westerners, a near perfect rate of herbal/medicinal success would be regarded as a scientific truth, with the cure being attributed to the chemical properties of the herbs. Both cures operated in the same manner, but the Africans attributed the cure to the spirits, while Westerners attributed it to a supposedly more rational science.

One might argue that the distinctions between Western science and African religion were mere semantic differences. The African interpretation might simply be called the science of religion, since the outcomes ultimately were the same as in the Western world. Indeed, scholars have demonstrated that many African spiritual cures can withstand the challenges of Western science. But this approach completely ignores the religious interpretation of the remedy and implicitly reduces to the level of superstition all those African beliefs and practices that do not meet the threshold of scientific certainty. By privileging Western science as the only valid explanation for African cures and healing rituals, scholars ignore the essential character of many African religious forms. The only way for scholars to interpret African cosmologies with any degree of accuracy is to take African beliefs and practices on their own terms.

Though African and European cosmologies were largely incompatible, some scholars are now suggesting that the key to religious exchange had little to do with replacing one belief system in favor of another. Rather, religious exchange between Africans and Europeans depended upon a series of shared revelations, revelations that resonated within both the African and European spiritual traditions. These shared revelations occurred as early as the late fifteenth century, when the Portuguese began their efforts to convert the Kongolese to Christianity. For instance, soon after the first Catholic priests arrived in Kongo, two Kongo noblemen dreamed simultaneously that a beautiful woman implored the Kongo to convert to Christianity. The Kongo noblemen consulted the Catholic priests to interpret this strange coincidence. The priests explained that the woman in the dreams was the Virgin Mary and that the dreams were "miracles and revelations." [15] For the Kongolese, dreams had long been understood to be important sources of revelations. The Catholic endorsement only served to reinforce the dream's meaning. Thus, the dream functioned as an important revelation in both systems of thought.

The recent work of John Thornton has been most persuasive in arguing for the importance of revelation in the formation of African Christianity.[16] Thornton's explanations for the ways in which African revelations were integrated into Catholic thought are convincing to a point. Where Catholic priests were willing to make spiritual concessions and admit the validity of certain African revelations, some Kongolese were drawn into the Christian fold. In fact, one of Thornton's most important contributions is the notion of a thoroughly

Africanized version of Christianity arising in Kongo in the sixteenth century.[17] But the Catholic priests validated only a very small number of Kongolese revelations, declaring all other revelations to be the work of the Devil. While the Catholic Church considered revelations to be extraordinarily rare and miraculous expressions of God's will on earth, the Kongolese depended upon continuous revelation for their daily survival.

By emphasizing revelation over the broader cosmology, Thornton downplays the real essence of Central African religious thought. The cosmology of Central Africa was *built* upon the necessity of continuous revelation, while Christianity increasingly was becoming a religion based on communion with the one "true" God.[18] In the Christian context, sources of revelation were finite, limited to God, Jesus, the Virgin Mary, and various saints. The revelations that were proffered by this limited cast were so rare and extraordinary that when they did occur, they were judged to be miraculous. When the Catholic saints revealed themselves, the validity of the revelation had to be confirmed by the Catholic clergy, an irritating obstacle that had no precedent in African thought. Central African revelation, on the other hand, was ordinary, continuous, and included a variety of local deities and ancestral spirits whose function was to intervene from the other world on behalf of those in the temporal world. This constant dialogue between laypeople and the spirit world was the linchpin of African cosmology and became the primary target of Catholic extirpation campaigns.

As Thornton readily admits, Europeans saw "a considerable part of African religious life as being of diabolical nature."[19] Everyday forms of curing, healing, and divination were often considered the work of the Devil. Even so-called African "Christians" continued to practice these rituals, prompting commentary from Catholic clergymen. In a 1612 letter to the King of Portugal, the Bishop of Congo, Manuel Baptista, wrote that the people of Kongo were "incapable" of serving God "because the vices are so old and the barbarism is so great that they cannot be cured."[20] Some years later, Father Cavazzi wrote that there were "bad Christians" from Kongo who were "apparently avowed to our religion, but, hidden, they protect the *feiticeiros*, the foundation and support of all the idolatry."[21] As Cavazzi makes clear, those Kongolese who embraced the Catholic faith clearly did so on their own terms, persisting in their beliefs in indigenous African forms.

Catholic priests had little tolerance for African rituals and practices. Across Central Africa, priests burned "idol houses" and "fetish objects" in grand public displays meant to demonstrate the impotence of African spirits and religious leaders (*nganga*).[22] In 1716, Father Lorenzo da Lucca, who had been in Kongo for over ten years as a missionary, complained bitterly about the pro-

Capuchin priest burning an idol house in Kongo, ca. 1750. Watercolor by Father Bernardino Ignazio da Vezza, "Missione in prattica [dei] Padri cappuccinni ne' Regni di Congo, Angola, et adiacenti," Biblioteca civica centrale di Torino, MS 457.

liferation of "diabolical witchcraft" in the region around Luanda. He argued that if the African healers were not punished, the city would be "boiling over in a few years swollen from the assembly [of witches]." Father da Lucca went on to complain that he alone could not "remedy these disorders" without the power to punish, and that "with the exception of a violent remedy, this open wound is almost incurable—*extremis malis, extrema remedia*. And if this precept was given to remedy the wound, there would be many more believers." Father da Lucca predicted that there would be dire consequences if African practices were not curtailed. He wrote that there was not only the "fear of losing the law of God, but moreover of His Majesty losing the Reign, because if these witches (*feiticeiros*) multiply themselves they can corrupt all of these people."[23] The attempts to crush traditional practices and reduce the number of African revelations to acceptable levels illustrates the narrowness of the European Catholic conversion project in Central Africa.[24] Despite a growing indigenous Catholic priesthood, and even millenarian challengers like Dona Beatriz Kimpa Vita,[25] interpretation of Christian doctrine ultimately rested in the hands of European priests and missionaries. While Europeans embraced some African revelations as valid in the Catholic tradition, the vast majority were rejected as being the Devil's work. Thus, the core of African religious belief—continuous, everyday forms of revelation used to explain, predict, and control the temporal world—was viewed by European priests as a "diabolical" oppositional threat.[26]

Despite the rejection of traditional African practices and beliefs by most Catholic priests, some Kongolese still embraced a Catholic identity, especially vis-à-vis their "heathen" neighbors to the north and east. As noted earlier, this was a distinct brand of African Christianity, with strong influences from traditional Kongolese cosmology. Some of the Kongolese elite became well-versed in the commandments, prayers, and sacraments of the church. Others were Christians "only in name." At the very least, many Kongolese were familiar with the "broad outlines of the Faith" and readily added these elements of Catholicism to their arsenal of spiritual beliefs.[27] But to argue that the Kongolese were Christians, and leave it at that, is to strip them of their spiritual core. Catholicism simply could not meet the here-and-now needs of most Kongolese, even into the eighteenth century, after more than two centuries of practice as the official state religion.

Catholicism and traditional Kongolese beliefs remained discrete cosmologies because their ends were vastly different. Christian revelations, when they occurred, demonstrated and validated the power of a largely unknowable, mysterious, otherworldly God. And this most often required blind faith—communion with an idealized apparition dwelling in the heavens. Kongolese revelation, on the other hand, was a dialogue between the living and the world of the spirits, including the spirits of ancestors, whose powers and foibles were familiar and well known, in real life as well as in death. Faith in a particular deity was verified by the bounty, or lack thereof, that was offered by the deity. If the deity was not producing, then those in the temporal world were failing to accede to his or her wishes. The followers of the deity could either acquiesce to the demands required by the spirit, or they could seek sustenance in another spirit. In this way, African cosmology was based upon an intimate, dynamic relationship between the living and those in the other world.

Though Thornton provides a nuanced assessment of the complexities and contradictions of African Christianity, he still insists on labeling the Kongolese primarily Christians. Unfortunately, Thornton's emphasis on Kongolese Christianity pushes him dangerously close to the arguments made by the "devout" scholars mentioned earlier. While I do not contest Thornton's argument that the Kongolese adopted Christianity as a fundamental part of their individual and collective identity, I do question the extent to which Christian identity trumped other religious identities among the Kongolese. Indeed, if Christianity was naturalized, as Thornton argues, it must have been naturalized into some body of religious thought that already existed. The problem is that we do not have a ready-made set of conceptual terms to delineate the system of Kongolese belief that continued, even as Christianity was naturalized by that belief system. Thus, a label like "African Christianity" becomes a convenient way of describing Kongolese religion, writ large.

The danger in this formulation is that it dilutes the Kongolese cosmological core. Against some of his best arguments for the complex nature of Christianity in Africa, Thornton forsakes the Kongolese spiritual core and replaces it with a Catholic one.[28] Certainly Thornton would not assert that the Europeans who "adopted the revelations of African diviners and mediums" were adherents *only* of African beliefs.[29] Yet this is precisely the type of suggestion he makes when he labels the Kongolese Christians.

I am not arguing that there were no Kongolese Christians. There were. But they were not *just* Christians. A more plausible theoretical explanation for Kongolese beliefs is that Christianity and indigenous Kongolese religion operated in *parallel* fashion, with the broad Central African cosmology still being the dominant religious paradigm for most Kongolese, especially in the process of conversion to Christianity.[30] Without doubt, there was some overlap in these traditions, especially at the symbolic level. The Kongolese were quick to recognize the Christian God as *nzambi mpungu*, the creator of all things. They also drew parallels between the Catholic saints and their ancestral deities. The Catholic priests and their superiors in Rome accepted these spiritual convergences as expressions of Catholic orthodoxy.[31] But despite what the priests believed, the Kongolese were likely using Christian symbols to represent their own deities, and they continued to worship them as they always had. In one of his earliest works, even Thornton acknowledged that "the Christian faith in seventeenth-century Kongo was in all its essentials simply Kongo's own religious system renamed."[32]

In the initial stages of conversion, just as the Europeans believed that the Kongolese were embracing God and the Catholic saints, the Kongolese probably believed that the Europeans were embracing their deities. Wyatt Mac-Gaffey has quite accurately called this stage of Kongolese-Portuguese interaction "dialogues of the deaf."[33] The worldviews of Africans and Europeans were so radically different that religious meanings probably were misinterpreted on both sides. Over the course of several generations, the blending of various aspects of the two traditions eventually led to the development of a distinctly Africanized form of Christianity that began to be seen as a religious movement independent of traditional Kongolese cosmology.[34] Nonetheless, the *core* elements of Kongolese cosmology, even for those who were

Funeral mass in Kongo with offerings of food for the dead, ca. 1750. Watercolor by Father Bernardino Ignazio da Vezza, "Missione in prattica [dei] Padri cappuccinni ne' Regni di Congo, Angola, et adiacenti," Biblioteca civica centrale di Torino, MS 457.

self-identified "Christians," remained explanation, prediction, and control. Christian faith was, at best, a parallel system of belief that served to complement Kongolese worldviews.

Conversion to this Africanized form of Christianity did not render the Kongolese solely Christian; Christian and Kongolese spheres continued to operate separately, with most adherents being "bi-religious." As historian Sandra Barnes has put it, "The essential point about religious systems that parallel one another is that each of them is like an arena: participants come and go. People ordinarily assign one religious label to themselves, but there are no sanctions levied on those who move among several arenas simultaneously."[35] Kongolese Christians and practitioners of traditional beliefs were often one and the same, sliding seamlessly from one belief system to another, a process that was informed by a common core cosmology that emphasized earth-bound pragmatism over faith.

The phenomenon of parallel religious practices and shifting arenas is perhaps best illustrated in a case from a late seventeenth-century mission in

Kongo. Capuchin priest Andrea da Pavia was losing patience with his parishioners, who persisted in visiting indigenous diviners and healers. The priest confronted his flock, demanding to know if they "wished to observe the Laws of God or their superstitious ceremonies." In a telling response, the majority responded that "they firmly believed in God and everything that was taught to them [by missionaries] but that they also believed in their ceremonies and . . . observances."[36] Clearly, this was an indication that the Kongolese were practicing Christianity as well as their indigenous religious beliefs. The two were discrete systems of belief, but they were not necessarily incompatible.

We should emphasize that Europeans also practiced parallel beliefs, especially when Christian cosmology ceased to be an effective remedy to temporal concerns. When Portuguese Christians exhausted all possibilities of prayer and faith in their attempts to control their environments, they were quick to turn to African diviners and curers. Nevertheless, the core of their belief system remained communion with God. Ultimately, the differences in Christian and African cosmologies boiled down to a conflict over the hierarchy of worship, particularly when addressing temporal concerns beyond human control. Africans worshipped multiple deities (including Christian ones in some cases) in an effort to control their daily environments, while Christians depended upon the mercy of the one true God and a finite group of saints to aid them in their daily travails.

African Culture and the Creolization School: A Critique

The religious conflicts discussed so far in this chapter were never limited to the African context. They applied equally to the broader diaspora. Enslaved Africans carried their religious beliefs with them wherever they were dispersed across the globe, and their beliefs and rituals consistently clashed with those of their captors. Few scholars have challenged the notion that slaves carried elements of Africa with them to their various destinations, but the depth and extent of African cultural and religious diffusion has persisted as a matter of scholarly dispute.

The reigning contention is that the pain and cruelty of the Middle Passage and slave life, coupled with separation from their familiar ethnic cultural milieu, forced slaves to abandon most elements of their specific African pasts and to create entirely new creolized "slave societies." According to this perspective, the diversity of African languages, cultural beliefs, and social structures in the slave populations of the Americas necessitated the creation of these so-called "new" communities. African "survivals" might have been important at the symbolic level, but they had limited relevance to the institutions that were forged in response to the uncertainties of slave life. Creolization is therefore rendered largely as a reaction to enslavement—an American-born defense mechanism, with little consideration of specific elements from the African past.[37]

Other scholars have argued for a more sustained connection between Africa and the Americas, showing how African cultural and religious forms "survived" in the African diaspora.[38] Unfortunately, these survivals have tended to be broadly conceived and detached from specific African historical contexts. In these renderings, Africa often becomes static and homogenized. But as we will see, some African beliefs and practices were more than diluted, culturally detached survivals. As Thornton has cogently stated, "the fact is that in the eighteenth century African culture was not surviving [in the Americas]: It was arriving."[39] Indeed, evidence from previous chapters on family, kinship, and Islam, as well as from chapters on religion that follow, suggests that the cultural and religious values of specific African peoples were transferred to the Americas.

Neither the creolization nor the survivals approach suffice to explain the complex religious experiences of enslaved Africans in the diaspora. New data on the slave trade demonstrate that Africans were not always arriving in the Americas in heterogeneous "crowds." Rather, many were arriving in coherent cultural groupings that shared much in common—language, kinship, religion, and so on. To be sure, European chattel slavery and the Middle Passage altered African understandings of malevolence, but the ways of addressing these new forms of evil often remained the same. The functional and structural integrity of specific African rituals and beliefs was sustained from Africa to the Americas. Just as in Africa, religious practices in the diaspora were a tool for addressing a variety of social ills, including slavery. The challenge is to trace these specific survivals in their various historical contexts, from Africa to the Americas.

By subjecting specific survivals to historical scrutiny, we will show how Central African religion emerged as a counter-hegemonic force that constantly chipped away at the foundation of Brazilian slave society. Examining the evolution of African religious beliefs and practices in Brazil across almost two centuries, we will also see how so-called "Mina" slaves, as well as "Guineas" and "Mozambiques," joined with their "Angolan" counterparts to challenge their servitude through religious means. When significant "creolization" did occur among Africans, beginning in the eighteenth century, the process of cultural exchange was most salient among Gangthe and Minas, or Ndembos and Ardas, not between Africans and Portuguese. The broad cosmological core (explanation, prediction, control) shared by the majority of these African peoples allowed them to forge common understandings and to continue challenging their servitude. Thus, Angolas, Ganguelas, Minas, and Ardas also became "Africans."[40]

If the process of becoming "African" was essentially an American phenomenon, we must pay careful attention to the very specific ideas, beliefs, and rituals that ultimately contributed to this collective identity. We also must recognize that the pace of change was dependent on the ability (or inability) of African peoples to reconstruct specific institutions. In Brazil, sustained Central African domination in the slave trade resulted in the proliferation of Central African cultural forms and religious institutions during the seventeenth and eighteenth centuries. In this chapter, we have suggested that most Central Africans shared broad cultural and religious understandings. While these core beliefs give us some idea of how Central Africans understood their worlds, they only begin to suggest how Central Africans addressed the maladies and tribulations that were directly associated with their enslavement. In the next chapter, we begin our analysis of specific African rituals, examining Central African forms of divination in slave communities. We will also show how the form and function of Central African divinations were strikingly similar to those of Africans from the so-called Mina coast, as well as other parts of Africa. Finally, we will demonstrate how African forms of divination were used as tools of resistance against the institution of slavery.

CHAPTER SIX

African Divination
in the Diaspora

During the seventeenth and eighteenth centuries, one of the most common ways that Africans explained, predicted, and controlled the world around them was through divination. At its most basic level, divination involved communication between the world of the living and the world of the spirits. Diviners performed a variety of ritual activities to invoke these spirits and learn their intentions for those living on earth. Mediating between the two worlds, the diviner could predict past and future events, uncover the guilt or innocence of suspected criminals, and determine the cause of illness or other misfortunes.

Across Africa, one of the diviner's primary roles was to determine the cause of social fissure in society, most often leaving the restoration of balance and harmony to others, particularly village or family elders. The spirit world revealed certain truths to the diviner and his clients, but the diviner usually did not pass judgment on the revelation. The interpretation of the revelation was left to the broader community. In this respect, the office of diviner was generally a conservative social phenomenon, reinforcing the public's opinions and broader sense of morality. At the same time, the diviner often acted as a balance against the power of elders, safeguarding the community against any compromise of the collective well-being. Diviners also acted as mediators or translators for societies that were undergoing rapid social and political transformations, bridging the gap between tradition and change. In short, the diviner acted as the fulcrum for a balanced and peaceful society, but his or her

119

findings were never completely sacrosanct, in that they required affirmation and interpretation from the larger society.[1]

Once Africans became human property and were no longer the masters of their own social and political fates, the African imperatives of divination shifted to accommodate their new condition as slaves in the Western world. On the one hand, social disruption was a common feature of chattel slavery and no doubt provoked an outpouring of appeals by African diviners seeking explanations from the spirit world. The misfortune of enslavement itself begged a spiritual explanation, as did the brutalities, famine, and disease that accompanied the institution. Within the nascent slave communities of the diaspora, Africans utilized diviners in attempts to forge the same types of communal balance that diviners had helped create in their homelands.

On the other hand, the master class often accepted the power of African divination and attempted to co-opt it as a way of maintaining and legitimizing white rule. Recognizing the widespread embrace of divination in the slave community, masters often used their African slaves to divine who had stolen a particular object, who had "bewitched" whom, or the whereabouts of runaway slaves. Because divination rituals resonated with most slaves, the divinations were almost always accepted as valid within the slave community, even though peoples of African descent were often implicated. In one respect, this reinforced the institution of slavery, aiding the master in determining the guilt of those rebelling against the institution. But it was also an indication of the master class's embracing the institution of divination as a way of mediating social unrest. African diviners always maintained control of the outcome of the divination and were ultimately accountable to the slave community. Thus, in some instances, Africans were able to seize control of social and judicial inquiries that directly impacted the slave community.

Central African Divinations in the Diaspora

Central African diviners were particularly adept at seizing control of criminal investigations in the slave community, searching for remedies that took into account the interests of both masters and slaves. These investigations usually took the form of ordeals or trials, in which the diviner invoked the spirit world to reveal the guilt or innocence of suspected criminals. For instance, in Bahia in 1685, a freed "Congo" named Simão was accused of murdering fifteen slaves through the use of witchcraft. The majority of his alleged victims were the slaves of André Gomes de Medina, a wealthy planter in the parish of Santo Amaro de Pitanga. The only evidence of Simão's guilt was the discovery of pans full of herbs, claws, teeth, and hairs of various animals in his house. To discover the true identity of the murderer, Medina ordered that a trial be conducted by a Congo diviner named Gracia.

Gracia, who was a slave in the parish of Cotegipe, arrived at Medina's property and began the divination ritual. She put three large sticks on the ground and set a large pot of water on top of them. Setting a fire underneath the pot, the water soon began boiling. Gracia threw a rock into the pot and "chanted some words in her language."[2] With the water now at a full boil, through the interpreters that she brought with her, Gracia ordered each person who was present to put a hand inside the pot and remove the rock, assuring them that if they were innocent they would not be harmed. One by one, whites as well as blacks submerged their hands in the boiling cauldron, with each one walking away without so much as a burn. Finally, when it was Simão's turn, he removed his hand from the boiling water, only to find that his hand and arm were completely ulcerated from the burns. For the gathered multitude, Gracia's divination "confirmed the opinion that [Simão] was a witch (*feiticeiro*)."[3]

Simão vociferously denied the charges against him. In his defense, he stated that the "powders" that were found in his house were made from the heads of snakes. The powders were used as antivenom for the bites of other poisonous snakes. Simão claimed that he was taught this remedy by his first master and that many other blacks used these powders for the same effect. Simão also asserted that the witchcraft charges were leveled against him by slaves who were "jealous of his freedom." Simão had recently gained his freedom from the daughter of André Gomes de Medina and was now a manioc farmer (*lavrador de mandioca*).

Simão's case is a clear example of how African divination operated to achieve balance and harmony in the slave community, from the perspective of both slaves and the master. First, just as in Africa, the divination process was utilized to affirm opinions that were already widely held. Even before the trial, Simão was the primary suspect in the murders of the fifteen slaves. Gracia's divination merely confirmed his guilt. Second, by finding a freed person guilty of the crimes, slaves were assured that one of their own would not be found guilty. Finally, Gracia's ritual affirmed the likely widely held belief that Simão's freedom and economic strivings were the result of some otherworldly force, perhaps even "witchcraft."[4] Simão was keenly aware that there were slaves who were "jealous" of his freedom. From the African perspective, his rapid rise from slavery to economic self-sufficiency was not easily explained. How else could he gain his liberty and become a *lavrador*, if not by some strong spiritual power? Certainly Simão was manipulating the spirit world for his own benefit, so why wouldn't he also seek revenge against the master class?

As for André Gomes de Medina, the man who had lost fifteen of his slaves to "witchcraft," he too benefited from Simão's guilt. He could rest easily with the knowledge that none of his slaves were attempting to undermine his prosperity. Rather, the murders of his bondsmen were the work of a person who was a member of a particularly insidious class of people—freed blacks. Throughout the colonial period, freed blacks were seen as a threat to the economic and social power of whites, competing with them in business and commerce, as well as stoking the flames of revolt against white rule.[5] Simão's acts of malice came as little surprise to André Gomes de Medina and probably confirmed preexisting stereotypes about the dangers lurking in the freed black community. Thus, in one deft stroke, Gracia's divination ceremony satisfied the behavioral ideals of both the African and the Portuguese communities, revealing a sort of "résumé of [the] whole social order."[6] The outcome of Gracia's ritual reinforced both African religious beliefs (by revealing the malevolent source of Simão's successes) and Portuguese colonial order (by protecting the master's source of economic power—his slaves—and prosecuting a known "danger"—a freed black).

In spite of this mutually satisfying remedy, Gracia's divination ritual should not be viewed as African capitulation to the colonial order. There clearly was an element of acquiescence in meeting certain Portuguese ideals, but this acquiescence was a pragmatic response to the Brazilian slave setting. As we have already noted, African diviners were mediators during periods of social transformation, and the oppression of chattel slavery in Brazil demanded new divination strategies. Gracia created an ingenious synthesis from the differing Portuguese and Central African sociocultural imperatives. By finding a mutually satisfying solution for both master and slaves, Gracia was able to reassert the importance of African divination, even under hostile circumstances. From the African perspective, this ability to adapt to changing social conditions was the hallmark of a good diviner. In the final analysis, Central African divination continued to function in Brazil just as it had in Africa—as a "dynamic reassessment of customs and values in the face of an ever-changing world."[7]

The recasting of Gracia's divination ceremony to address new social circumstances also should not obscure the fact that the instrument of justice used in this case was distinctly African. In fact, the ceremony conducted by Gracia was quite common across Central Africa during the seventeenth century. At almost exactly the same time that Gracia was performing her ceremony in Bahia, Father Cavazzi described the Central African divination, called *jaji*, in the following manner: "The *feiticeiro* lays a rock in a pan of water. . . . When the water boils, the accused is obliged to remove the rock with his hand. If he is burned, he is judged as guilty; if he does not receive harm, each one of those present acclaims him innocent, without any more inquiry."[8] Similarly, Father Girolamo Merolla recalled that the "witch" took the rock out of the boiling water "with his bare hand, ordering the others to do the same; those that take it out without being scalded are presumed innocent, whereas the contrary exposes their guilt."[9]

By comparing the descriptions of Cavazzi, Merolla, and others with the description of Gracia's ritual in Bahia, we can see quite clearly that the religious/judicial apparatus known in Central Africa as the trial of *jaji* made its way across the Atlantic in a nearly pure structural form. The transfer of rituals like *jaji* complicates simplistic arguments about African survivals versus African creolization in the Americas. Clearly, African rituals and practices conformed to new social conventions in the Americas, just as they had done when changes occurred in Africa, but this should not divert our attention away from the fact that the rituals themselves remained essentially the same. Form and function were retained, even as temporal imperatives changed. As Wyatt MacGaffey has succinctly argued, "Change must be change in something that itself continues."[10] In Brazil, distinctly Central African rituals and practices continued, even as adaptations were made to meet the needs of the slave society.

Another Central African divination ordeal, similar to the trial of *jaji*, occurred in Bahia on a small island near Ilha de Maré in 1646. To discover who had stolen some cloth on the *fazenda* of Duarte Roiz Ulhoa, a slave named Gunza[11] prepared a balm, which he mixed in a dish. When he had finished preparing the balm, he rubbed some on the arm of each person who was gathered to witness the ordeal. After each person's arm was anointed, Gunza took a needle and passed it through the arm. He promised that if the person were not the one who had stolen the cloth, he would not be harmed. Only the guilty party would bleed. After exonerating all of the suspects who were gathered for the ordeal, including a number of whites, Gunza began conducting the ritual on himself, naming potential suspects who were absent from the gathering. He inserted the needle in his arm over and over, saying "in the name of so-and-so . . . if he stole the cloth then my arm will put forth blood." After sitting through most of the ceremony, our only witness, a thirty-year-old carpenter named Miguel Fernandes, became disturbed with the proceedings and left. As he made his departure, he scolded his white peers, telling them that the ceremony "was not a thing for white men to see." While many whites believed in the "supernatural" powers of their African slaves, they were some-

In a divination ritual known as *jaji*, Central Africans attempt to remove a rock from a boiling cauldron, seventeenth century. Used to divine the identity of a guilty person, a trial by *jaji* left the innocent unscathed and absolved. Watercolor by Giovanni Antonio Cavazzi, "Missione evangelica al regno de Congo, 1665–1668"; courtesy Manoscritti Araldi, Papers of the Araldi Family, Modena, Italy.

times too squeamish to remain complicit in ceremonies that seemed to be the very workings of the Devil.[12]

Not all of the divination ceremonies were so offensive to the devout or the faint of heart. Another Central African ritual simply involved the use of a cord and a ball. In 1634, Francisco Dembo (Ndembu), a slave on Itaparica Island in Bahia, was called to the house of Roque Antônio Barbeiro to divine who pilfered a dish. Standing up, Francisco took a cord and put it under his foot. He threaded the cord through a ball, which dropped to his feet. Holding the cord near his face, Francisco ordered each person to pull the ball up. As the suspects pulled the ball, Francisco asked aloud if that person had taken the dish. If the answer was "no," then the person was able to pull the ball up to Francisco's face. After some time, a slave from a neighboring property entered. Francisco asked if she had stolen the dish. Unable to move the ball from its position at Francisco's feet, the woman was revealed to be the thief, and she immediately confessed to the crime. Like many other Central African "trials" in Brazil, someone from outside the immediate slave community (in this case, a neighboring slave) was ultimately judged to be the guilty party, reinforcing the ritual as a satisfying remedy that balanced the interests of both slaves and masters.[13]

Not all Central African divinations operated as communal trials or ordeals. Some simply functioned as revelations aimed at uncovering the cause of individual misfortune. Sometimes, these divinations revealed the most intimate and embarrassing details of people's private lives. In 1721, Barbara Morais, a white woman living in the city of Olinda, had exhausted all pharmaceutical remedies in trying to find a cure for her bed-ridden husband, who had been suffering from a mysterious illness for more than eight years. Determining that her husband must be suffering from *feitiços* (witchcraft), Morais summoned an "Angolan" named Domingos João Pereira to divine the cause of her husband's illness. Domingos began his divination by drawing a cross in the dirt with his finger. On top of the cross, he put a calabash with various objects inside of it. Domingos tapped on the calabash with his finger and cast some blessings on top of it "in the language of Angola." He then emptied several objects from the mouth of the calabash into the palm of his hand. These objects included "some things like roots" and "a silver coin."

Reading the objects that emerged from the calabash, Domingos informed the sick man that his ailments were "*feitiços* that were given to you by a woman who you had a relationship with before marrying this one; and the cause that she had for this was because she wanted to marry you, and since you left her and married with another, she made this for you to suffer." Skeptical of

Domingos's divination, the man wanted further proof that what Domingos said was true. So Domingos prepared a dance with three little bottles: "grabbing one, he danced with it and he showed the bottle suspended in the air." Inside the bottle "appeared a very old black man with a red belt fastened around his stomach and a shepherd's staff on his shoulder, with some roots in one hand and some coins in the other." The roots and the coin were precisely what had spilled out of Domingos's calabash. When the sick man saw them in the hands of the man inside the bottle, he understood that "that *preto* was who gave the *feitiços*, and the roots the material from which they were composed, and the coins the payment that he received for the evil." Domingos then reached for another bottle, and again displaying it suspended in the air, there appeared inside of the bottle the mulatta, "who ordered that the *feitiços* be made for the sick man because he rejected her."[14]

All of the elements of Domingos's divination ritual were classically Central African, and more specifically Kongolese. First, the drawing of the cross in the dirt was probably not the Christian crucifix, but rather, a Kongo cosmogram. Wyatt MacGaffey has stated that these cosmograms were representative of "God [*nzambi mpungu*] and man, God and the dead, and the living and the dead. The person taking the oath stands upon the cross, situating himself between life and death, and invokes the judgment of God and the dead upon himself."[15] When Domingos set his calabash over the cross, he was invoking the spirits of the dead to reveal the origins of his client's illness. They did so by spilling out only two objects from the array of objects that Domingos had in his calabash.[16] Domingos then "read" the two objects according to their prescribed meanings, determining that the man was bewitched by his former lover.

The bottles that Domingos "danced" with were also very much a part of Kongo cosmology. Various commentators in the eighteenth century noted that the Kongolese and their descendants in the diaspora used bottles to lure and trap evil spirits.[17] Most of these bottles were hung from trees and were used to protect homes and crops from malevolent spirits, but Domingos used his bottles to reveal the evil spirits that were the source of his client's illness. The two evil spirits, the old African *feiticeiro* and the mulatta, revealed themselves inside the bottles, proving their malevolence and their guilt.

Other divinations of Central African origin proliferated in seventeenth- and early eighteenth-century Brazil.[18] In addition to the ordeals and revelations already mentioned, Brazilian slaves conducted others, including the ordeal of Golungo, which was commonly used "to find out who committed some crime."[19] Central African slaves were also known to divine future occurrences.

Johan Nieuhof, a Dutchman who visited Brazil between 1640 and 1649, commented that it was common for Africans "to predict when the ships would arrive that had left from Holland for Brazil."[20] These, and other forms of divination, demonstrate that a wide range of Central African beliefs were re-created in Brazil, always maintaining their essential form and meaning but adjusting to accommodate the imperatives of the colonial slave environment.

Perhaps the most widespread "Angolan" divination ritual was the *quibando*, a ritual that, as it turns out, was not even of African origin, let alone Angolan. The term *quibando* comes from the Kimbundu word *kibandu*, which means "sieve."[21] But what came to be known as the *quibando* in the African-Portuguese diaspora in the late seventeenth century had its origins in Europe, at least as far back as the sixteenth century. In sixteenth-century England, the ritual was carried out in the following manner: "Stick a pair of shears in the rind of a sieve and let two persons set the top of each of their forefingers upon the upper part of the shears holding it with the sieve up from the ground steadily; and ask Peter and Paul whether A, B, and C hath stolen the thing lost; and at the nomination of the guilty person the sieve will turn around."[22] The ritual made its way to Portugal by at least the seventeenth century and was one of several forms of divination practiced in the country during the period. The ritual was most commonly called "the scissor and sieve" divination.[23]

One of the earliest descriptions of the *quibando* ritual in Brazil appears in several Inquisitorial confessions made in 1687 in Bahia. In one of these confessions, Sebastião de Prado Pereira, an infantry captain, stated that some time around 1683 he saw a woman named Mariana Pinheiro and one of her young slaves perform the *quibando* divination.[24] Pereira described the ceremony in the following manner: "holding a scissor, [Maria Pinheiro] attached the points of it on the *quibando* with the hand of the black girl (*negrinha*) on one ring of the scissor and the hand of the woman on the other. And the woman [Maria Pinheiro] said these words: For S. Pedro and S. Paulo and for the Apostle Santiago, that so-and-so stole this. . . . And the *quibando* gave a turn when they arrived at the name of a person who now he does not remember."[25] As one can clearly discern, the *quibando* divination is almost exactly the same as the divination of the scissor and sieve from sixteenth-century England and seventeenth-century Portugal.

The Portuguese were not unaware of the Angolan identity they were imposing on the age-old European ritual. In a 1721 Inquisition case from Recife, it was noted that in Portugal, the *quibando* was called *peneira*.[26] Both words mean "sieve." Nevertheless, those in the Portuguese colonial world persisted in calling this divination ritual by its Kimbundu name. From Brazil, all the way to the colony of Goa, in western India, the Portuguese used the Kimbundu signifier to identify what was clearly a European ritual.[27] The question is why the ritual took on an African identity in the Portuguese world in the latter part of the seventeenth century.

The common denominator in all of the *quibando* cases that I examined was the judgment that a slave was the guilty party. Also, unlike other cases of African divination, whites almost always conducted the *quibando* ritual. The Portuguese most likely gave the scissor and sieve divination an African veneer because it fit well with the widely accepted idiom of "dangerous" and "exotic" African divination. Despite its European origins, by the late seventeenth century, many Portuguese Catholics recognized the ritual as fitting into the same category as African divination rituals, all of which were considered "diabolical" or "superstitious." The scissor and sieve ritual was, after all, remarkably similar to many of the Central African trials and ordeals we have already described.

By giving the familiar an African identity, the Portuguese colonists benefited in several ways. First, they transformed a European superstition into an African one, deflecting attention away from their own deviation from Catholic orthodoxy and reinforcing the correlation between Africa and the diabolical world. At the same time, by renaming the ceremony *quibando*, whites gained some modicum of control over the "superstitious" and "diabolical" world that was normally controlled by Africans. Africans probably understood and embraced the meaning of the ritual since it resonated with their core understandings of divination. This enabled the Portuguese to divine "like Africans," at least during this one ceremony. Ultimately, the shift from *peneira* to *quibando* was more than a simple linguistic turn; it was an acknowledgement that Central African forms of divination were stronger and more effective than those of the Portuguese.

Divination among Slaves from West Africa and the Mina Coast

Slaves from other parts of Africa also engaged in divination in the Portuguese colonial world, performing rituals comparable to those of slaves from Central Africa. Like Central African slaves, these slaves received messages from the spirit world, which were mediated by the diviner and his clients in order to address temporal concerns. Even though broad understandings of the meanings of divination were shared by almost all Africans, the nature of the ceremonies varied widely among different African ethnic groups. The rituals and symbols used to instigate the divination process and invoke the spirits differed in accordance with very specific historical and cultural resonances. Many of these deeper meanings remain hidden from view, but we should still recognize that divination ceremonies were the products of very specific African cultural backgrounds and were a manifestation of the broader social history of the various peoples.

Specific cultural meanings and divination trends are particularly difficult to discern in the ceremonies of those slaves who were not well represented in the slave populations during the seventeenth and eighteenth centuries. We get isolated snapshots of particular rituals that were carried out in the diaspora, but there is no indication of how deeply etched these rituals might have become in the slave communities. Nor is there any sense of how long these rituals might have been sustained.

For instance, in 1591, André Buçal, a recently arrived slave from "Guiné,"[28] divined using a pan in Bahia. André put the pan on the floor, and standing a short distance away from it, began reciting orations "in his language." The pan began moving furiously along the floor, and André touched it in order to feel the force emitted by it. The nature of the force revealed to André that one of Gaspar Pereira's slaves had run away to join "the band of Maré." As a result of André's divination, Gaspar Pereira was able to recover his missing slave.[29] In 1693, in Maranhão, a slave named Sebastião Mandingo divined who stole a knife. Sebastião did this by taking some herbs and rubbing them inside a cup of water. He began naming different people as he continued mixing the herbs in the water. When the herbs suddenly turned the water into a thick sauce, he knew he had arrived at the name of the thief.[30] Finally, in 1726, on the island of São Tomé, Francisco Benin divined using pieces of calabash and kola nuts, over which he proffered "certain words in the language of his land."[31]

The introduction of large numbers of Mina slaves to Brazil at the beginning of the eighteenth century led to further variations in the types of divination ceremonies being practiced by Africans. But with the Minas, we have a clearer notion of the deeper symbolic meanings of certain divination ceremonies, since we know that many of them came from the area around the Gulf of Benin. Perhaps the most common form of Mina divination involved divining in a pan of water, symbolic of the riverine bodies of water that the souls of many Mina slaves crossed as they passed from the world of the living to the world of the ancestors.[32] It was believed that spirits could be invoked to enter water and proffer divinatory messages. In 1734, Joseph Mina, a slave in the town of Poincepe, outside of Rio de Janeiro, divined by putting a plate of water inside a circle that he drew on the ground. Looking into the water,

Joseph put a small stick in his mouth and asked the plate various questions. At this invocation, a slight voice could be heard, giving Joseph the answers to his queries.[33]

Many years later in 1799, José Mina was in jail in Paraíba when he used water to divine his own fate. While still in prison, José took a coin and laid it in a plate of water. After some time passed, José looked into the water and announced that he would not be sent to the jail in Rio de Janeiro, as he had feared. In fact, José predicted that he would be freed in Paraíba on a Wednesday. In the end, everything happened just as José divined.[34]

Africans from the Guinea and Mina coasts also were known to divine using snakes. Among certain Mina peoples—for instance the Ewe, Fon, and Yoruba —snakes were idolized as deities.[35] And in Upper Guinea, it was not unusual for diviners and healers to carry snakes with them to help them divine.[36] Across West Africa serpents were believed to be endowed with the power to bring great riches and wealth, or alternatively, terrible misfortunes. Some of these beliefs apparently carried over to Brazil. In 1725, a slave named Francisco carried a calabash with a snake in it through the streets of Olinda, Pernambuco. When called upon to divine, Francisco removed the snake from the calabash and coiled him on top of his head. The snake then "spoke" in Francisco's ear, telling him the information that was to be divined. When the divination was complete, Francisco put the snake back in the calabash and collected money from his clients.[37]

Whether divinations were Central African, Mina, or Guinea, we still cannot ignore the fact that many whites manipulated African divination rituals to suit their own needs. As we have shown, whites used African diviners to find thieves, suspected murderers, and runaway slaves. Despite the apparent contradiction in African slaves divining the guilt of other people of African descent, we must recognize the complexity of these exchanges. On many occasions, diviners found blacks from outside the immediate slave community guilty of wrongdoing, thereby meeting the collective "communal" expectations of both slaves and masters. In other instances, the transaction was strictly a financial one, with the divination being exchanged for cash, cattle, or other valuable goods. In this way, some slaves and freed Africans probably were able to earn some degree of financial independence for themselves or, at the very least, earn a favored place with their masters because of the financial rewards that their divination services provided.[38] In all of these cases, Africans used the widespread recognition of their divination powers to seize a moment of power from their masters, using the opportunity to carve financial or judicial spaces for themselves in a community that was otherwise hostile to their individual autonomy.

African Creolization in Africa and the Diaspora

Even though Africans practiced distinct forms of divination based on very specific cultural resonances—various "ordeals" in Central Africa, water ceremonies along the Mina coast, etc.—there were also a number of rituals that were similar to one another, transcending ethnic groups and wide geographic spaces in Africa. These widely practiced rituals probably facilitated the process of creolization among Africans from various ethnic backgrounds, leading to the creation of distinctly "African" forms of slave culture. One example of these shared rituals is the Central African ordeal of *jaji*, which was described by Cavazzi in seventeenth-century Central Africa and replicated in seventeenth-century Bahia. It seems that *jaji*, or the ordeal of the hand in boiling water, was also prevalent in Dahomey during its early history. According to Melville Herskovits, this ritual was called *amízoka* in Dahomey. Unlike in Central Africa, the object that was to be pulled from the boiling water was not a rock but rather a "seed," which was used in playing a game called *adjí*, similar to the English game of draughts, or checkers. Except for this one difference, the divination of *jaji/amízoka* appears to have been the same.[39]

Clearly, the use of varying implements of divination was culturally important, but the broad contours of the ceremony were remarkably similar across a vast geographic area in Africa. Although I can find no direct evidence that the ordeal of *jaji/amízoka* spread from one area of Africa to another, it seems more than coincidence that the two ceremonies would be practiced in almost exactly the same fashion in both Central Africa and Dahomey. It also seems more than coincidental that the primary difference in the Central African and Mina rituals—the use of the *adjí*—sounds strikingly similar to the name of the Central African ritual—*jaji*. Might there have been a process of cultural exchange in Africa that preceded or coincided with the rise of the Atlantic slave trade, one in which *jaji* and *adjí* became conflated? Although sound answers to this question remain elusive, it is clear that by the eighteenth century Mina and Central African slaves in Brazil probably shared broad core beliefs about the meanings and significance of divination. And in some cases, their respective divination rituals were almost mirror images of one another.

Another category of shared divination beliefs among Africans that likely made its way throughout the diaspora was augury, or divination through omens. These beliefs were extraordinarily diverse in nature. In Central Africa, Father Cavazzi noted that bad omens included the barking of dogs, the singing of birds at night, the crow of a rooster outside of the normal hour, and the flight of crows overhead. A bee flying around somebody indicated the imminent arrival of strangers. And the list went on. In Cavazzi's view, "any little occurrence is motive for those unfortunate souls to believe in a thousand strange follies and to fall on superstitions."[40] Among the Ewe-speaking peoples of the Mina coast, many of these "signs" from the natural world operated in the same way that they did in Central Africa. Just as in Central Africa, the crow of the rooster in the middle of the night was a bad omen. The gathering of crows indicated the onset of war. And sneezing was a warning that the inner spirit might be preparing to leave the body, opening the way for malevolent spirits to take over and bring illness.[41]

The most important lesson to be learned in examining the "shared" divination rituals and beliefs of various African peoples is that many Africans, despite being separated by thousands of miles on the African continent, shared certain broad religious understandings. Though the means of divination sometimes varied, the ends were consistently the same—the restoration of temporal balance through spiritual intervention. When Africans were enslaved and brought together in the diaspora, they encountered other Africans who spoke different languages and who came from varying cultural and social traditions, but whose core religious beliefs were remarkably similar to their own. Language and other social structures were sometimes obstacles in the early creation of a cohesive slave community, but religion served as a common idiom for a variety of African peoples, allowing them to communicate across these other boundaries. Where possible, African slaves almost always gravitated toward those of their own ethnic group, but we should recognize that spiritual affinities facilitated a process of "Africanization" among various ethnic groups. The essential "African" religious core that emerged from these shared beliefs stood as a direct challenge to Portuguese religious and cultural hegemony.

The process of Africanization took place mostly within the slave community. If African slaves used familiar rituals in the presence of the Portuguese, then they certainly were guided by these ceremonies in constructing their interior lives. Unfortunately, our lens on the interior practices of Africans is limited by the scarcity of sources. Most Africans did not write, and Portuguese commentators simply did not have access to the most intimate affairs of Africans. Nonetheless, there are several instances where the Portuguese stumbled upon gatherings of Africans conducting their rituals. From these glimpses, it is clear that Africans and their immediate descendants utilized the talents of diviners as a matter of course.

In the city of Salvador, in 1646, João Luís, a thirty-year-old white soldier, confessed that he witnessed his neighbor, Domingos Umbáta (Mbata), conducting various divination rituals for other Africans during the night. João claimed that Domingos threw some leaves and manioc flour into a bowl of water. He then made a cross and a circle around the bowl and threw some powders on top of it. Finally, he mixed it all up with a knife, and the contents of the bowl began boiling as if they were on fire, despite the fact that there were neither "hot coals nor fire." According to João, Domingos looked into the bowl and spoke with the other Africans "in his language . . . such that he [João Luís] could not understand him."[42]

Other interior African practices were revealed by curious "spies," both whites and free people of color. In 1634, Mateus de Matos, a free mulatto who lived on Itaparica Island in Bahia, was one of several people who denounced Francisco Dembo (Ndembu). Mateus stated that one night he and a friend were trying to spy on the activities of Francisco as he was divining for other Africans on the sugar plantation of Francisco de Abreu. When Mateus and his friend arrived at the door of the house where Francisco was divining, they heard Francisco announce their presence, even though they never entered the house. Mateus attributed Francisco's knowledge to the "art of the devil," because it was dark and there was no way Francisco could have seen them hiding outside.

Similarly, on another night, a twenty-two-year-old white man named Francisco Ribeiro crept up to the house where Francisco Dembo was divining. Ribeiro claimed that while hiding near the house, he heard a hoarse voice that sounded as if it were coming from the roof. The voice said, "Look there, Francisco Ribeiro, you will pay us for what you bring. I wanted to rest and the whites come to watch." Ribeiro immediately blessed himself and retreated to a safer spot, farther away from the house of divination. Later, he saw Francisco Dembo and "other Negroes" leave the house.[43]

The nighttime divinations of Domingos Mbata and Francisco Dembo for "other Negroes" demonstrate the depth and resilience of African religious practices in Brazil. Even after toiling all day for their masters, rather than sleeping or trying to alleviate their physical exhaustion, African slaves sometimes passed their free time engaging the spirit world with their fellow slaves. These gatherings were always viewed with suspicion and trepidation by the master class. Not only were masters fearful of the "diabolical" rituals that their slaves might be practicing, but they worried that these gatherings were precursors for rebellion. Given the acknowledged strength of the African spiritual world, it is difficult to discern which they feared more.

African Divination and Slave Resistance

No matter how the functions and outcomes of many African divination ceremonies were expanded to accommodate the needs and expectations of the master class, we must remember that Africans always maintained control of the divination process itself, whether within their own communities, or in the broader colonial world. Sometimes the outcomes of African divinations did not affirm the expectations of white clients, working instead in favor of the slaves. For instance, in 1728, many slaves were dying on the property of Domingos Alves da Costa in Minas Gerais. These deaths were believed to be the work of a *feiticeiro*, who was infecting the other slaves on the property. In order to identify the *feiticeiro*, a slave named José Mina was called to divine. José arrived one evening at da Costa's house and told him that he would make his investigation on the following day. Anxious to discover the identity of the *feiticeiro*, da Costa woke José at the crack of dawn so that he could begin his divination. José requested a candle and a plate of water, both of which he laid on the floor. Later, he put a metal cross and a ring into the water, where they laid for some time. Then, he took a small calabash and took it to his mouth, speaking to it three times in his own language. After speaking into the calabash, he laid it on the floor next to the plate of water and covered it with his hat. With all of the implements in place, José looked at the plate of water and then removed his hat from the top of the calabash. The calabash remained still. José again stared into the plate of water and again removed his hat from the top of the calabash. And again nothing happened. Finally, after looking into the plate of water for a third time, José uncovered the calabash, and it gave a half turn without anybody touching it.

Once the calabash made its turn, José Mina told Domingos Alves da Costa that he did not have a *feiticeiro* in his house. Furthermore, José told him that he should order the release of the four slaves that he had jailed as suspects for the crimes, and that he should order his other slaves back to work. According to Domingos Alves da Costa, José had no way of knowing that he had incarcerated four suspects. Domingos had his other thirty-five to forty slaves locked up so that they could not speak with José. Based on José's revelations, Domingos was convinced that José was an agent of the Devil and denounced him to the Inquisition. Whether he obeyed José's request to free the suspected *feiticeiros* remains unclear.[44]

While some African diviners made revelations in favor of their enslaved brethren, others took advantage of their master's respect for their divining powers, manipulating the master's ignorance of the rituals to their own advantage. For example, in Salvador, Bahia, in 1687, two sisters, Mariana de

Mendonça and Julia de Carvalho, had an object of great value stolen from their house. To try to recover the item, they brought in a slave diviner from a neighboring property. The women told the slave that they would pay him very well "if he made the stolen thing appear." The unnamed slave scratched some wood shavings from the door of the house and from the stairs. After taking the scratchings, the slave requested some money (two *patacas*) from the women so that he could make the mixtures needed to divine. The women were uncertain exactly what the slave was requesting of them since they could not understand "the crude (*boçais*) words of the said Negro."[45] Nonetheless, they acquiesced and gave the slave his two *patacas*. After receiving his money, the slave left the house and was never heard from again.[46]

In still other instances, African diviners delivered bad news to their masters, informing them that they or their loved ones were complicit in a criminal act. In 1618, Antônio, a "Guinea" slave in Bahia, looked into a bowl of water in order to divine who had stolen some money and a silver cross. After peering into the water, Antônio determined that the youngest son of his master had stolen the money and the cross. He also revealed that the boy had hidden the cross in a certain box. When the box was opened, the cross was there, just as Antônio had predicted.[47] Similarly, in the 1730s, an Angolan diviner named Luzia Pinta determined that two female slaves were the thieves who had stolen some money from their master in Minas Gerais. However, Luzia also revealed that one of the women was apparently owed the money. The woman stole the money because her master had slept with her without paying for her services.[48]

That African diviners sometimes implicated the master class in their cere-monies demonstrates quite clearly that the majority of these rituals did not simply become another tool of the white power structure. On the contrary, white adoption of African forms of divination can be understood as an impor-tant concession of juridical and spiritual power.[49] On one level, just by adopt-ing the Central African forms of divination, whites diminished the power of their own judicial structures. Some whites obviously found the African judg-ments more convincing or more efficacious than pursuing potential suspects through the colonial legal system, which was a relatively weak institution in Brazil, especially in rural agricultural areas with large numbers of slaves.[50] As long as Africans were finding only other Africans guilty in these judgment ceremonies, the rituals could be viewed simply as African forms of justice, "separate from the master's institutions."[51] But as soon as whites accepted the guilt of their own relatives and friends, the power structure was turned upside down, turning divination into a potent form of resistance, as whites became the objects of African institutional control. Even though these cases may have been rare, and though whites could always resort to rejecting African religious forms as the work of the Devil, the cases demonstrate the extent to which religious and temporal power were contested in Brazil.

African forms of divination were re-created in the Portuguese world in a variety of forms. Very specific rituals that resonated with particular African ethnic groups were replicated, particularly in Brazil. Central Africans—Kongos, Ndembus, and Mbatas—brought various divination rituals with them from their homelands during the seventeenth century. Though other ethnic groups made contributions to the field of divination, it was not until the eighteenth century that Central African dominance was contested. Beginning around the last decade of the seventeenth century, so-called Mina slaves, mostly from the Slave Coast of present-day Togo and Benin, brought new forms of divination to Brazil, particularly to Bahia and Minas Gerais. While there were differences in the symbolism used in Mina divinations, many of the rituals were remarkably similar to those of Central African slaves, probably facilitating the process of "Africanization" in the slave communities.

The institution of divination changed very little from Africa to the Americas, but the condition of slavery did transform the imperatives of many divination rituals. As we have shown, divination rituals within the slave community probably remained similar to those that were practiced in Africa. But where whites attempted to co-opt the powers of African divination, diviners were often forced to adapt ceremonies to the slave culture, balancing the communal needs of masters and slaves. This adaptation should not be viewed as a fundamental transformation forced by the white colonial power structure. Rather, it was an adjustment that was in keeping with African traditions. African divination was constantly changing in accordance with the ebb and flow of temporal conditions. The acclimation to American slavery was made in much the same way that acclimations were made for wars, droughts, and famines that periodically occurred in African societies. In all cases, the driving force behind divination was the restoration of communal balance and harmony. In Brazil, African diviners almost always factored slave interests into this communal equation, often finding "outsiders" guilty of various crimes. By protecting those in their immediate slave communities, African diviners reclaimed a bit of religious and juridical power from their masters.

Finally, there were cases of African divination in which slaves seized outright control of the divination process and its outcome. Some slaves took economic advantage of their masters by accepting payment without performing the divination. Others divined against the master's expectations, finding slave suspects innocent of the crimes of which they were accused. And still other African diviners determined that the masters themselves were to blame for particular crimes. In all of these cases, the master class ceded judicial power to their slaves and provided space for slaves to resist their condition.

Indeed, in every instance that whites consulted African slaves to divine for them, Africans were given the opportunity to transform religious power into resistance to their enslavement. Some diviners were able to grab more temporal power than others, but the very act of consulting Africans was an admission of African spiritual potency, resulting in small cracks in colonial power and the slave regime. The next chapter discusses yet other ways in which Africans used their divination and religious powers to address their condition, particularly in the realms of healing and medicine.

CHAPTER SEVEN

Calundús, Curing, and Medicine in the Colonial World

Throughout Central Africa, illness, misfortune, and physical weakness were rarely understood to be naturally occurring circumstances. Instead, physical decline and death most often were believed to be caused by destructive spiritual forces. These forces could come from the world of the living or the world of the dead, and were indicative of some breach between the individual and his community or between the individual and his ancestors. To counteract these spirits and restore the balance and harmony that were integral to individual and communal well-being, Africans consulted a variety of diviner/healers, who determined the cause of the malady and prescribed the appropriate remedy.

In Central Africa, one of the most common forms of "medicinal" intervention was spirit possession. Unlike the divination practices described in the previous chapter, the possession of human beings, usually by ancestral spirits, was a more direct and spectacular form of divination. Instead of the diviner acting as a mediator for public rituals that were interpreted by both the diviner and his clients, the diviner literally received a spirit from the other world, giving the spirit a human form and allowing the client to converse directly with the other world. Once the spirit entered the body of the diviner/medium, even the medium's voice·was transformed into that of the spirit. The spirit then could be questioned and engaged in conversation, with the medium's body merely serving as the vessel for communication. In this way, clients could learn not only the sources of their discontent, but the remedies needed to correct them.

Contemporary descriptions from Angola and Kongo indicate that spirit mediumship functioned in much the same fashion across Central Africa, with clients directly contacting the spirit world to learn the roots of their worldly problems. In his travels across Angola in the seventeenth century, the Capuchin priest Antônio Cavazzi, described the possession rituals of the *xinguila* (spirit mediums) in some detail. He explained that these "riffraff" were extremely numerous and very much esteemed among the Imbangala (Jaga), as well as other peoples of the region. Cavazzi described the possession ritual of the Imbangala as follows:

> The man or woman puts himself in the middle of the multitude and orders that all obey him, since the function is promoted not by his caprice, but by the interior impulse of the consulted spirit. Meanwhile, the musicians play their instruments and excite those present with appropriate songs and shouting, capable of frightening even the wild beasts. They sing some diabolical songs with invocations, judged efficacious for persuading the Devil to enter into the body of the person. The person, for his part, swears an oath to the Devil and invites him to take possession of him. At the sound of these supplicants, the Devil gives himself to the intervention. . . . Then the *feiticeiro* (witch) gets up with much seriousness, and remaining still for several moments, immediately begins to agitate, moving his eyes in their sockets, laying himself on the ground, contorting furiously, bending all of his members. . . . The *feiticeiro* then begins proffering extravagant words, confused and metaphoric, not without previously having forewarned those present that they are not his words, but of the spirit of such deceased Jaga, whose name he then assumes, conserving [that name] until the end of the function. . . . The Jagas go to this possessed person because they judge that he knows everything that happens in the other life, and they use the forms of respect and reverence that they would use with a demigod, interrogating him and receiving answers as if he were the consulted spirit. The possessed threatens misfortune, predicts misadventure, curses, reprimands the avarice of relatives, requests new sustenance, new foods, new human blood and new victims.[1]

Luca da Caltanissetta, another Italian priest who traveled throughout Central Africa at the end of the seventeenth century, described spirit possession in Kongo. Caltanissetta noted that when the Kongolese wanted to know the cause of "death or sickness or a lost item and who was the author of such

Angolan *xinguilas* possessed by spirits of the deceased, seventeenth century. In the original watercolor, both *xinguilas* have red taffeta tied around their waists and are marked with white clay (*mpemba*) above their waists and on their arms and legs. Also note the axe in the right hand of the *xinguila* in the background. Upon being possessed, the *xinguila* took the axe as a visual representation identifying the spirit that had entered his body. Since the client in this case is a soldier (kneeling), the *xinguila* is probably acting as a medium for a powerful warrior. Watercolor by Giovanni Antonio Cavazzi, "Missione evangelica al regno de Congo, 1665–1668"; courtesy Manoscritti Araldi, Papers of the Araldi Family. Modena, Italy.

evil," they went to the *nganga ngombo* (spirit medium). The onlookers circled around the *nganga ngombo*, singing and praying "for the Devil to enter the head of that witch (*fatuciero*)," since it was believed that spirits entered their hosts through their heads. Once the spirit took possession of the diviner, the onlookers began asking questions about who poisoned whom, or how someone died, or the location of a lost object. The spirit responded to their queries, reciting "through the mouth of that witch a thousand lies, and if their desire is to have a sickness treated, he also knows the remedy for it."[2]

Father Cavazzi described the *ngombos* of Kongo in much the same way that Father Caltanissetta did, observing, "It is the custom of the devil to enter into him . . . turning him into a tireless speaker and saying through his mouth extraordinary things in diverse languages." Cavazzi added that "in order to augment the reputation of his excellency, he frequently walks turned upside down, with his hands on the ground and his feet in the air, making, in the manner of prestidigitators, extravagant things and great obscenities."[3]

While the terms "*xinguila*" and "*ngombo*" never appear explicitly in any of the documents that I examined for colonial Brazil, there is evidence suggesting that these specific religious figures continued their practices in the Brazilian slave setting. For instance, a 1694 Inquisition case from the parish of São Gonçalo in Bahia describes a freed black named João who called "his children . . . to his head to speak to him to make the cures that he wanted." Witnesses explained that prior to being possessed, João "walked on one foot, throwing the other one violently over his shoulder." Once possessed by the spirits of his deceased children, João offered his cures "in a raspy voice, like something from another world."[4] Similarly, in the early 1780s, a freed black in the parish of Iraruama, Rio de Janeiro, was accused of various acts of "witchcraft," including spirit possession. In one of the denunciations, the freed black is described as walking through the streets "with his head toward the ground and his feet in the air, jumping . . . in the air and speaking in the language of his land."[5]

If we accept that these were the workings of the *xinguila* or the *nganga ngombo* in Brazil, we should also look very carefully at the physical descriptions in the cases. One might speculate that the physical acts of throwing one's foot over a shoulder and walking on one's hands are an early form of the Afro-Brazilian martial art that came to be known as *capoeira*. The Central African derivation of *capoeira* has been long known, but scholars of *capoeira* have struggled to trace its deeper religious meanings. T. J. Desch-Obi has suggested that Central African martial artists assumed an upside-down position as a mirror image of *kalunga*, the inverted world of the ancestors. This ritual inver-

Man assumes inverted position as he leads the funeral procession of a Congolese king's son in Rio de Janeiro, nineteenth century. Lithograph by Jean-Baptiste Debret, *Voyage pittoresque et historique au Brésil* (Paris, 1834).

sion allowed the individual to draw strength from the spirit world.[6] Perhaps Brazilian *capoeira* emerged, in part, from the behaviors of spiritually powerful diviners and healers, who also walked on their hands to draw strength from *kalunga*.[7]

While we can only speculate about the connections between spirit possession and its impact on certain aspects of Brazilian slave culture, we can be certain that the transfer of Central African forms of spirit mediumship to Brazil was frequent and sustained during the colonial period. The first clear reference to African spirit mediums occurs in Bahia in 1618, when a denunciation was made describing the "Negroes from Guiné" who "call[ed] the dead to hear them." These slaves were alleged to have used animal blood to help invoke the spirits of their ancestors. They also played musical instruments, sang, ate, and drank "with much excess."[8] Central African forms of spirit possession remained a common feature of Brazilian slave life even past the end of our study in 1770, but there was a dramatic increase in the documentation of possession cases between 1685 and 1740. During this period, one can find dozens of references to Central African possession rituals in Inquisition cases, letters from missionaries, and even in popular poetry and literature. It is during this period that we will concentrate our examination of spirit possession in Brazil.

Central African Forms of Human Possession: *Calundús*

Divination ceremonies that involved human possession most often were referred to in Brazil by the corrupted Kimbundu word *calundú*. In Angola, *quilundo* was a generic name for any spirit that possessed the living.[9] These spirits of deceased ancestors possessed the living for a variety of reasons, but usually as punishment for a lack of proper veneration and respect. The punishment was believed to manifest itself in any number of illnesses that could debilitate and even kill the person who was possessed, eating away at his soul until he was dead. In an early eighteenth-century document from Central Africa describing the "pagan rites and superstitions observed by the Negroes from the Reign of Angola," an anonymous priest (perhaps Bishop D. Luiz Simões Brandão) described *quilundos* in the following manner:

> When somebody suffers an infirmity . . . , he is understood to have *Quilundos*; in order to cure these they consult a surgeon called *Nganga* of *Quilundos*, who orders that the ill one be put in a dark house at night, accompanied by various of his assistants; and the surgeon goes into another room without any person, where he invokes the Devil, with whom he consults about the illness and results in the *Nganga* saying that he [the ill person] does not have to fear his lost health, since he will restore it for him, and he reprimands him for not recognizing him immediately as the Author of his life, and that as punishment, he allowed him to come down with such an illness in order to reduce him to his obedience; and . . . he promises him his health through the hand of his *Nganga*, who will give him the cure if he makes a pact; he may have his health if he makes a feast (*festa*) for the *Quilundo*, who is the idol invoked, with many demonstrations of gratitude.[10]

Because the term *quilundo* had a universal meaning, describing *any* ancestral spirit who possessed the living, it probably became a widely recognized term for spirit possession across all of Central Africa. Certainly this generic quality made it a recognizable term for Central Africans in Brazil, as *calundú* quickly became the shared idiom for spirit possession in the slave and free black communities.

Once *calundú* took root in Brazil, around the middle of the seventeenth century, its Central African meaning was broadened somewhat. Not only did *calundú* describe the actual spirits that possessed the ill person, but it became the preferred way of describing the ceremonies and dances that preceded possession and divination. Despite these cosmetic changes, Brazilian *calundú* ceremonies were scripted in much the same manner as possession rituals in

Central Africa, with the medium invoking the spirit to enter his or her body, followed by a direct conversation between the spirit and the client. Contrary to the claims of some historians, *calundú* was not a syncretic practice in Brazil, at least not until the mid-eighteenth century.[11] As we will see, very specific ceremonies and implements of divination were transported from Central Africa to Brazil.

The vast majority of *calundú* ceremonies were conducted in order to determine the cause of illness. As we have already noted in Chapter 3, African slaves suffered tremendous losses to disease, malnutrition, and overwork in Brazil. Since most Central Africans did not believe in any "natural" causes of physical deterioration outside of old age, these slaves often turned to spirit mediums to learn the origin of their maladies. In the first part of the seventeenth century, it appears that most of these possession ceremonies were confined to the black community. In a 1618 denunciation, it was noted that witchcraft and human possession "serve[d] all of the Guiné slaves in Bahia."[12] There is no mention of whites taking part in African possession rituals during this period.

Yet over time, whites too began to adopt Central African forms of curing, seeking out *calundeiros* (practitioners of *calundú*) to heal their illnesses. The process of white acknowledgement of the power of African cures was a gradual one. At first, whites used Central African diviner/curers only to cure their slaves. In the 1630s, Francisco Dembo cured a number of "sick Negroes" in Bahia, apparently only on Wednesdays. During these meetings, "the souls of the little children . . . from his land" would possess him and give remedies to the gathered slaves. Many of these slaves and freed Africans went to Francisco on their own accord. Whether they paid him is unclear. But other slaves were taken to Francisco by their masters, who paid him for his services. For example, Cosme da Costa paid Francisco six *patacas* to cure his slave Juliana, who "they said was sick from poison."[13] The practice of whites using African healers to cure other blacks apparently became widespread by the second half of the seventeenth century. In the 1660s, even the Benedictine monastery at Olinda paid "Negro curers" to heal their ailing slaves.[14]

Whites sought out African curers to heal their sick slaves, perhaps because they believed that African "witchcraft" would respond only to African cures. In the late 1730s, several slave masters in Bahia took their ailing slaves to a Carmelite priest named Luís da Nazaret. The slave masters hoped that Father Luís would be able to exorcise the demons that were making their slaves ill. Father Luís examined the slaves and determined that they were infected with *calundús*. Instead of trying to cure the slaves in the manner prescribed by the Catholic Church, Father Luís ordered the masters to take their slaves to African *calundeiros*. He admitted that "exorcisms did not remove that caste of *feitiços* because they were a diabolical thing," and that "only the Negroes were able to remedy" the *calundús*.[15]

This admission by a Catholic priest was revealing. Not only was an official of the church acknowledging the power of African spirits, but he conceded that the church's most powerful weapon against witchcraft—exorcism—was impotent against the strength and power of "diabolical" African spirits. As the reputation for African spiritual strength grew, some whites became impatient with the ineffectiveness of exorcisms, as well as with the bleedings and purgings that were the common medicinal remedies for most ailments in the Western world. Looking for stronger remedies, whites began to tap the strength of African healing powers, especially *calundús*.

Despite the occasional acknowledgment of African spiritual powers by Catholic clergymen, most priests viewed the white embrace of *calundú* with a great deal of scorn. In 1685, the Bahian priest, Father Domingos das Chagas, wrote to the Holy Office stating that "many white persons cure themselves with [*calundús*] with such little unease of conscience as if they worked a very moral thing."[16] In January 1715, Father Antônio Pires wrote from Bahia complaining about the proliferation of "Lundus."[17] Seven months later, Father João Calmon noted that the Lisbon Tribunal was "very distant from this Bahia, where the witchcraft and merriment that the Negroes make, which they call Lundus or Calundus, are scandalous and superstitious, without it being easy to avoid them, since even many whites can be found in them."[18] And finally, in 1720, an anonymous report from Rio de Janeiro complained about "various Ambunda [Mbundu] cures, which are not effective except by art of magic, to which the whites give great credit, [and] they consult the Negroes."[19] In the view of many Catholic priests, the "great credit" that whites gave to Central African *calundeiros* was an indication that some whites were not only conceding medical superiority to Africans, but they were also acknowledging the religious power of their African slaves.

Knowledge of Angolan *calundús* was widespread among the Portuguese in Brazil by the end of the seventeenth century, provoking negative commentary from a variety of observers. Even poets were compelled to comment on the "satanic" rituals of the Angolans. Gregório de Mattos, perhaps the most famous poet of colonial Brazil, wrote the following verse describing the white adherents to *calundú*:

> All these quilombos,
> With peerless masters,
> Teaching by night
> Calundus and fetishism

Thousands of women
Attend them faithfully.
So does many a bearded man [a Portuguese]
Who thinks himself a new Narcissus.

This much I know: in these dances
Satan's an active partner.
Only the jovial master
Can teach such ecstasy.[20]

Perhaps the most famous description of *calundú* comes from the travel narrative of a pious "pilgrim" on his way from Bahia to Minas Gerais in the 1720s. The pilgrim was sleeping one night on the property of a certain slave master when he was awakened by what he described as "a horrendous clamor . . . that seemed to be the confusion of hell." The next morning the pilgrim lodged a complaint with the master, who assured him that he would order his slaves not to perform their *calundús* that evening. The pilgrim asked the master, "What are *calundús*?" And the master answered that "they are entertainment or divinations that the slaves are accustomed to making in their lands . . . for learning various things, like from where illnesses arise; and for divining some lost things; and also for having luck in their hunts and agriculture; and for many other things." The pilgrim, shocked at this revelation, reprimanded the master for consenting to his slaves' performance of such "superstitious" rituals. The pilgrim also accused the master of having mortally sinned by breaking the First Commandment (Thou shalt have no other gods before me).

Wanting to set himself right with the church, the master called for his slaves to gather and meet with the pilgrim. The pilgrim immediately challenged the Master of the Calundús (*Mestre dos Calundús*). The pilgrim describes the following exchange:

I asked the Master of the Calundús: Tell me, son, (better to call him [son] than father of evil) what are Calundús? He said to me with great embarrassment and shame that they were used in his lands when having parties, recreation, and divination. You don't know (I said to him) what this word "Calundús" means in Portuguese? The slave told me that he did not. Then I want to explain to you (I said to him) the etymology of the name, what it signifies. Explained in Portuguese and Latin, it is the following: that it hides the two: *Calo duo*. You know who these two are that are hidden? It is only you all and the devil. The devil hides and you all hide the great sin that you make by the pact that you have made with the devil; and you all are teaching it to others and making them sin in order to carry them to hell when they die.[21]

Having sufficiently frightened the master and his slaves, the pilgrim repeated the Catholic orations and litanies with his new converts. He also ordered the master to burn all of the musical instruments—*canzás* (scrapers), *tabaques* (cylindrical, conical drums, usually played between the legs), tambourines, castanets, and so on—used in the *calundús* so that there could be a full "restoration" of their collective souls.

Brazilian *calundú* ceremonies varied somewhat from curer to curer, but the broad contours were the same for all practitioners. And despite the fact that some of the cures were made for whites, all of the ceremonies remained distinctly Central African in form and philosophy. For instance, on August 12, 1701, Felícia Pires, a forty-year-old white woman from Rio Real, Bahia, appeared before an official of the Inquisition to confess her sins. Felícia declared that she had been stricken with blindness for a number of years, when one day, her husband, Mateus Nunes, told her that he knew of a man named Pedro de Sequeira who owned a slave who could restore her vision. Felícia sought out Pedro de Sequeira, who told her that she would have to give a cow for the cure that his slave Branca would perform for her. Felícia agreed to these terms, and a time was scheduled for her cure.

On the appointed night, Felícia was accompanied by a young mulatta, who guided her by the hand to the house of Pedro de Sequeira. When they arrived at the house, they were led to a smaller auxiliary house on the same property, where they were greeted by a large group of slaves, as well as by Pedro de Sequeira. Some of the gathered slaves began playing instruments—*canzás* and *tabaques*—while Branca danced and sang in "the language of Angola." She wore only a white loincloth, and on her torso were stripes of white clay that she called "*pemba*." After a great deal of dancing and singing, Branca gave a great leap and suddenly fell to the ground as if she were asleep. One witness, João da Cunha, claimed that when Branca fell unconscious two "negra" assistants outfitted her with a "painted cat skin" that was hung around her waist, a band of red taffeta, also around her waist, a white cloth on her chest, as well as a "naked dagger" and a little hoop, one held in each of her hands. Soon, she rose, and in a voice that the others said was that of *nganga*, she called for the spirit of her deceased eldest son. Branca claimed that the spirit would not appear to her because he was "ashamed" by the great number of people who were witnessing the invocation. In order to sate the spirit's hunger and earn his respect, a table had been arranged with food and drink, including a drink called "*aluá*." Apparently pleased with the offerings, the spirit finally appeared and offered an herbal remedy for Felícia's blindness, a remedy that ultimately did nothing to alleviate her lack of sight.[22]

Though the broad outline of this case may be clear, it might be helpful if we provide a little background and explanation for some parts of the ceremony. Felícia Pires consulted Branca in the hopes that Branca could remove the *calundús* that were causing her blindness. When Felícia entered the room, she heard the musical instruments of spiritual invocation—*canzás* and *tabaques* —both instruments of Central African origin.[23] As Branca danced, the music and her Kimbundu orations were designed to invoke the spirits of her children to enter her body. The white clay, or *mpemba*, with which Branca anointed herself was to make her more accessible to the spirit world. It was believed that the spirits of the dead went to *mpemba*, or the underground world of the white clay, when they left their coffins.[24] White clay came to be understood as a symbol of the "good" dead and was used widely in Central Africa as a protective balm against malevolence.

When the spirit finally entered Branca's body, she fell to the floor motionless. As she recovered, she was no longer Branca, but took on the identity and the voice of her deceased son, a transformation that was signified by the addition of the "cat skin" wrap and other implements. Hearing the altered voice and speech pattern of Branca, the other Africans immediately knew that she had been possessed, fulfilling her role as the *nganga*. In this case, the *nganga* (Branca) was possessed by her deceased son. In order to facilitate the ceremony, offerings of food and drink were made to the spirit, who, through Branca's body, ate and drank the offerings, including the *ualuá*, a Kimbundu word for an alcoholic beverage made from fermented rice flour, corn meal, or pineapple husks.[25] Food and drink were a common way of placating angry or uncooperative ancestral spirits. Branca's son ultimately offered a remedy for Felícia's blindness, a remedy of herbs and roots that Branca later retrieved from the woods.

Other Brazilian *calundú* rituals varied somewhat in the types of materials used for invocation of the spirits, but they still conformed with Central African practices. For instance, in the 1680s, an Angolan slave named Lucrécia performed *calundús* in Bahia, wearing ribbons and a crest of feathers on her head. After singing and dancing, she fell to the ground motionless, and flour was sprinkled on her face. Like the white clay that Branca used to invoke the spirits, the ribbons, feathers, and flour invoked the spirits for Lucrécia.[26] Once Lucrécia finally divined the cause of her client's illness, she applied medicinal herbs to achieve the cure.[27]

In other cases, the blood of chickens, cows, or other animals also was used to induce the spirits to possess the curer. For instance, in 1712, a freed An-

A *calundú* in northeast Brazil, seventeenth century. Dancing to the sounds of *tabaques* and *canzás*, several of the Africans appear to have already been possessed by ancestral spirits. In particular, note the man with the crest of feathers on his head and the woman at the center of the painting. The feathers indicated possession by a powerful ancestral figure, perhaps a former chief or king. Also note the man on the far left, imbibing what may be the ceremonial drink *aluá* from a clay jar. Painting by Zacharias Wagener (1614–1668), "Negertanz," *Thier Buch*, pl. 105; courtesy Staatliche Kunstsammlungen, Kupferstich-Kabinett, Dresden, Germany.

golan woman named Angela Vieira was denounced for performing *calundús* in Bahia. To invoke the spirits, Angela anointed herself with the blood of a calf, which had been slaughtered by those gathered in her house. The calf was given to Angela by the cattle trader, Dionizio Soares, and his "*parda* concubine," Josepha. Angela later divined various illnesses and used roots to cure them.[28]

Similarly, in the 1680s, a slave named Caterina cured with *calundús* in Rio Real, Bahia. Dressed in the skins of "wild animals" and anointed with white clay on her face, Caterina sang and danced to the playing of the *canzás*. In the language of her homeland (Angola), she spoke in the voices of her deceased relatives, who provided her clients with explanations for their illnesses. Later, Caterina went to the woods to search for roots and herbs to cure her clients.[29]

Still other *calundús* resonated more clearly with the slaves' specific African regional pasts. In 1721, in the town of Rodeio, Minas Gerais, whites and blacks gathered at seven o'clock every Saturday night to consult a Central African woman named Gracia. Accompanied by three other African dancers, Gracia invoked the ancestral spirit to enter her body. But Gracia did not invoke just any spirit. She invoked Dom Filipe, who the denouncing priest "suppose[d] was a King of Kongo." There was no Dom Filipe among the many people contesting the Kongolese crown during the early eighteenth century. Nor was there a Dom Filipe who was King of Kongo in earlier years. There was, however, a Dom Filipe who was King of Ndongo from 1626 to 1664. Perhaps Gracia was being possessed by the former Ndongo king, or perhaps Dom Filipe was some other venerated ancestor. Either way, once Gracia was possessed, some of her clients fell to their knees in front of her, "speaking to her as if she were Dom Filipe, giving her lordship [and] making great reverence to her." Among other things, Gracia/Dom Filipe attempted to cure blindness and divine the location of runaway slaves.[30]

While it is important to note that specific ethnic rituals, like Gracia's invocation, were replicated in Brazil, it is more vital that we recognize the deeper meanings of these rituals. Just like the divination rituals discussed in the previous chapter, *calundú* was Central African religion in action. It was not the "diabolical superstition" or "witchcraft" that some Portuguese observers would have us believe that it was. Central Africans utilized familiar rituals and cures like *calundú* to address illness and social conflict, just as they had done in Central Africa. The setting and context changed, but the applicability of ritual and belief did not. If anything, the unexplainable pain and suffering associated with slavery only reinforced the need for the kinds of temporal remedies that ancestral spirits provided.

This emphasis on ancestor worship and spirit possession remained strong in Brazil, even as large numbers of whites began embracing elements of a Central African worldview, seeking African spiritual remedies to their everyday problems. In the face of Catholic, and even secular, persecution, Central African religious forms maintained their resiliency, catering to the medical and spiritual needs of African slaves, while at the same time offering an alternative for whites seeking remedies to their worldly ills. Though white adherents to African beliefs sometimes had different temporal imperatives than Africans (i.e., finding runaway slaves), they were nonetheless embracing a worldview in which the powers of Africans and their ancestors were predominant. In these ritual settings, white adherents became dependent upon the religious power of diviners and curers who were often their slaves. By endowing Africans with this power, *calundú* and other Central African religious forms posed themselves as direct challenges to white Portuguese Catholic hegemony.

Calundú and the Forging of Economic Passageways

While *calundú* clearly had entered the consciousness of most Brazilians by the beginning of the eighteenth century, its actual practice remained the preserve of Central Africans, who used its powers to improve their daily conditions, not only from a divining/curing perspective but also from an economic perspective. Among economic historians of Brazil, there has been a great deal of debate over the degree to which slaves were able to negotiate economic spaces within the slave regime. Some scholars have argued that master exploitation and social control left little room for slaves to create their own economic passageways, while others have suggested that slaves grew and sold their own crops, resulting in a "peasant breach" of Portuguese economic control.[31] In addition to earning money by selling various foodstuffs, a small number of slaves and freed Africans also were able to create economic inroads for themselves by selling their religious services, requiring whites to pay for their divinations and cures, as well as for those of their slaves.

For instance, in the 1630s, Francisco Dembo was called to diagnose the illness of a slave named Caterina, who belonged to Francisco da Almeida. Almeida wanted to know if Caterina was truly ill or whether she was just pregnant. Francisco confirmed Caterina's suspicion that she was sick with *feitiços* (witchcraft), and he subsequently removed some powders from under her arm that were the source of her illness. Francisco de Almeida paid Francisco one and a half *patacas* for his cure but was later angry to learn that Caterina was indeed pregnant and probably would have healed "without [Francisco] curing her." Since Caterina would have been forced to work through her pain had she been diagnosed as pregnant, Francisco's divination not only paid off for him financially but it relieved Caterina of some toil and hardship, at least in the short term. Again, we see slaves using their religious power to ameliorate their collective condition, undermining the dominant social and economic order.[32]

Francisco certainly was not alone in using his religious gifts to earn a living. In 1698, Gracia, a slave on Ilha de Maré in Bahia, performed *calundús* to divine various things. In addition to curing a number of people, Gracia divined the location of a stolen canoe and determined whether a woman's husband was being faithful to her. Despite the fact that Gracia was a slave, witnesses said that she "had fame as a diviner and that this was how she earned her living."[33] Whether Gracia kept all of her earnings or whether she was a *negra de ganho* (slave for hire)[34] who split her earnings with her master is unclear from the record. Either way, she was probably able to build a modicum of economic independence with her religious skills.

Other slaves clearly worked as *negros de ganho*, performing divinations and cures for a variety of clients and then splitting their earnings with their masters. In 1705, a man named Domingos Coelho was accused of hiring out his slave Domingos to divine and cure "in the houses of many white men" in Bahia. Several people testified that Domingos "cured and divined with the favor of his master and he split with him his earnings."[35] Using the proceeds from their cures, slaves like Domingos, Francisco, and Gracia could begin to gain some degree of financial freedom, perhaps eventually earning enough money to purchase their way out of bondage.

Even though slaves made economic inroads using their religious powers, masters also profited handsomely. We have already seen how the Angolan slave, Branca, attempted to cure Felícia Pires of her blindness. Before Felícia was able to consult Branca, Branca's master, Pedro de Sequeira, required that Felícia give him a cow as payment for the cure. Apparently, Pedro de Sequeira made quite a handsome profit from the African curers that he owned. Several years earlier in 1694, he received payments for the cures of yet another of his slaves, a woman named Luzia, who also performed *calundús*.[36]

Whites even went so far as to purchase slaves for the explicit purpose of earning money from their cures. In the 1680s, in Bahia, Pedro Coelho Pimentel admitted that he purchased the married couple Lucrécia and André "because they would always give him some earnings from their cures." Pimental knew their reputation because Lucrécia had been owned by several other masters who had named her as a curer. Just as Pimentel planned, both slaves earned money for him with their divination and healing skills.[37] That masters were confident enough to purchase slaves solely on the premise that they would earn money from their cures demonstrates that there was a high "market" demand for African diviners and healers, providing us with further evidence of the widespread embrace of Central African religious power.

Some masters probably did not share the earnings of their diviner/curer slaves, but these slaves still benefited from their religious powers. Because they were such valuable moneymakers for their masters, they likely were treated differently than other slaves. At the very least, *calundeiros* reaped the benefits of the offerings that were made to the spirits—foods and wines that the majority of undernourished slaves could only hope to have. The *calundeiros* also opened up culturally resonant moments of "freedom" for their enslaved brethren. Every *calundú* ceremony included a small entourage of helpers who aided the *calundeiro* in his or her invocations—dancers, musicians, and so on. By including other slaves in the proceedings, the *calundeiro* ingratiated himself or herself to others in the community, reinforcing not only the religious importance of *calundú*, but also the social "freedoms"—music, dance, and food—that came along with it.

Other Forms of Medicine and Curing

In addition to the various generic *calundús* that were performed in Brazil, there were several specific types of *nganga* who divined with possession rituals. The *nganga nzambi* was a "priest of the spirits" whose specialty was the treatment of illness, particularly illnesses due to the retributions and punishments made by the forgotten spirits of the dead.[38] In 1721, a Portuguese priest, Father Joseph de Modena, returned to Lisbon from Angola and was questioned about his mission in Central Africa. In the process of his interrogation, he was asked what *Zumbi* was. The priest responded:

> *Zumbi* is an illness that comes naturally [but which] the witch (*feiticeiro*) attributes to diabolical arts, saying that the sick person is suffering from the soul of one of his dead relatives. The sick person gives many edible things to the *feiticeiro*, who says that the soul of the dead person requests these things and that because he was not given the referred things, the dead person entered the body of the sick person and caused him this illness. And the *feiticeiro* is called in order to cure from the *Zumbi*, and they give him banquets and parties with the food he requests.[39]

The *nganga nzambi* sated the hunger of angry spirits all over Central Africa, from Angola to Benguela, curing numerous people of illnesses caused by their dead ancestors.[40] Given the prevalence of disease and illness in the slave communities of Brazil, it is not surprising that Central Africans continued curing in this fashion even after they were enslaved. The *nganga nzambi* apparently was not uncommon across Brazil during the early eighteenth century. A 1720 report from Rio de Janeiro noted that there were "various witches whom they all call *Ganganzambes* [who] kill or give life . . . and in this there enter many Brazilian-born whites (*brancos filhos da terra*)."[41] Though we have no specific descriptions of the *nganga nzambi* at work in seventeenth- or eighteenth-century Brazil, we know that they were practicing their art, most likely hidden behind the more generic term for those who practiced spirit possession — *calundeiros*.

The second specific *nganga* who operated in Brazil was the *nganga wisa*. *Nganga wisa* literally means "priest of power." I can find no description of how the *nganga wisa* operated in Central Africa, but there is one tantalizing description from Brazil. In the 1690s, a slave named Luzia cured various people in a "public house" in Rio Real. Luzia called for her assistants to play *canzás* and sing to her in the language of Angola. She emerged dancing and carrying animal skins in her hands. Luzia began to tremble and then suddenly leaped into the air. Just as she made her leap, the doors to the little house were closed and the candles were blown out. As the crowd waited silently in the darkness, a rattling noise could be heard on top of the roof. Without warning, something fell from the ceiling and there was a loud smack on the table in the middle of the room. Then a voice announced, "I am gangahuiza." Subsequently, through *nganga wisa*, Luzia was able to effect her cures.[42]

Human possession was not the only Central African form of divining/curing that made its way across the Atlantic. The Kongolese influence, in particular, contributed other cures to Brazilian slave communities. For instance, in 1789, a slave named Antônio Congo was denounced for "making *calundús* with two dolls" on Fazenda Santa Guiteria in the town of Itatiayo. Using his two dolls to divine and cure, Antônio healed many patients who could not be cured by Portuguese surgeons or herbalists. Some of Antônio's clients paid as much as ten *oitavas* (twelve mil-réis) for their cures, more than one-tenth the cost of a prime male slave in Brazil's mining region.[43]

The two dolls referred to in Antônio's denunciation were probably *kitekes*, wooden statues that served as representations of the ancestors among the Kongolese. These "dolls" were apparently common in eighteenth-century Brazil. Seventy years earlier in 1720, a Catholic priest in Rio de Janeiro reported that Central Africans possessed "various images that they call *Quitecles* to which they give cult, saying, this is my son; this is my father; this is my brother. And just as though [the image] were alive, they offer it sustenance."[44] As in the case with human possession, the spirits of deceased ancestors could be invoked to possess the *kiteke* and proffer advice, remedies, and so on. In order to facilitate the possession, the diviner made offerings of food and liquor to the spirit. The *kitekes* were apparently not as common in colonial Brazil as the more generic *calundús*, but the *kitekes* were prevalent enough to draw the attention of church authorities, and their mere presence in Brazil demonstrates the tenacity of certain Kongolese beliefs.

By the end of the seventeenth century, Mina slaves were also beginning to make medical/religious contributions in the Portuguese world. The cures of Mina slaves differed somewhat from those of Central Africans. Instead of relying primarily on human possession to determine the cause of illness, Mina slaves used other rituals, divinations, and herbal cures to heal the ill. One of the more common implements of Mina divining and curing was a large basket, which might contain powders, shells, bones, hair, teeth, feathers, and other powerful substances from the natural world, all of which might be endowed with spiritual power. Using the basket and its contents, the diviner could perform various rituals to determine the cause of illnesses.

For example, in 1692, a freed Mina named Mateus carried his basket with him when he went to cure a white man named Manuel Pacheco de Araujo in Moribeca, Pernambuco. Mateus removed a basin from inside his basket and put it on top of his head. Speaking to the basin "in his language," he then removed a small stick from the basket. He took the stick and licked it with his tongue. Still reciting orations, he ran the stick from his left hand to his forehead. Finally, he told Manuel Pacheco de Araujo that he did not have *feitiços* (witchcraft), but that "a woman had made something to make him want her." This spell that the woman manufactured was making him ill. To free Manuel from the ailment, Mateus gave him some roots and powders. He told Manuel that he should take the medicines to the river and lie backwards, against the current. With equal amounts of the substances in each hand, he was to utter certain words and scatter the powders. Presumably, the symbolic gesture of letting the substances wash down the river would also wash away his ailment.[45]

Another case of a Mina slave using a basket to carry his instruments of divination occurred in Recife in 1692. A slave named Gonçalo went to the house of Joana de Souza, promising that he could cure her ailment. Gonçalo entered Joana's house and, removing the top from his basket, began speaking to it. To Joana's great surprise, "some voices like little birds responded to [Gonçalo]." Fearing that this was "an evil thing," Joana quickly fled from the scene. Gonçalo tried to calm her down, assuring her that the ceremony was to determine the cause of her illness and to help her find a cure. But Joana could not be convinced. Ultimately, she refused to consent to the divination.[46]

Instead of baskets, some Minas carried their medicines in calabashes. Domingos Álvares, who was born in Nangô on the Mina Coast, was denounced in the 1740s for, among other things, making various cures for people in Pernambuco and Rio de Janeiro. Using purgatives, enemas, and ointments, in various ritual fashions, Domingos cured many people, including whites and *pardos* (mixed race), but "mostly Negroes." Domingos carried his roots, herbs, powders, and leaves in a large calabash. After drinking a mixture made by Domingos, one *parda* woman "ran to her house . . . and vomited up some hairs, and [expelled] from her rectum some bones that seemed to be from chickens and the talons of a hawk." Once the woman expelled the malevolent substances, she was relieved from her suffering, "which was like pin pricks" all over her body. Domingos also was reputed to cure colic, cancer, and paralysis with his arsenal of medicines.

In his confession and examination, Domingos admitted that "he was publicly procured by various persons in order to remove diverse maladies that they understood to be *feitiços*." He claimed that his remedies were "natural" and that they were taught to him by various people in his homeland. Familiar with the virtues of various roots and herbs (fennel, juniper, rosemary, and so on), Domingos said that if he applied a cure and it was ineffective, he would continue using others until the sick person recovered from his or her illness. The inquisitors, convinced that Domingos's cures were the result of a pact that he had made with the Devil, wanted him to admit that his cures were the work of Satan. But Domingos would not confess. He maintained that his cures were "natural" and that this was "the way they heal" in his country. Refusing to concede that he was in league with the Devil, Domingos was tortured on the *potro*, a device used to inflict excruciating pain, pulling the body's joints, slowly dislocating shoulders, elbows, knees, etc. Ultimately, Domingos was sentenced to appear before the Auto da Fé and exiled to the Portuguese Algarve for four years.[47]

On the surface, the differences between Central African and Mina healing rituals that we have outlined here may seem fairly stark. In order to divine the source of illness, Central Africans in Brazil relied heavily on human possession, while Minas most often utilized objects that captured and harnessed spiritual power (baskets, calabashes, pans of water, etc.). This is not to say that there was not overlap in ritual understandings. As we have already shown, Minas and Central Africans shared broad understandings regarding a variety of symbols and rituals. But the common denominator in all of these cases was the ultimate treatment of the disease or illness. Using powerful substances from the natural world — such as roots, herbs, leaves, and so on — Africans of all ethnic stripes attempted to influence the spirits that were believed to be racking their bodies. Despite differences in forms of divination, Minas and

Central Africans found common ground and began to weave together distinctly "African" forms of curing in Brazil.

One example of these "hybrid" African forms of healing occurred in Olinda in 1770. On the evening of August 30, the priests of the Convento de Nossa Senhora do Carmo were busily removing floodwaters that had inundated their convent. As they were taking buckets of water to the woods, the priests found two Africans engaged in what was apparently a healing ritual. The Africans, a Mina slave named Isabel and a freed Angolan named Francisco, were both nude. When the priests walked up on the two Africans, Francisco was beating Isabel on the shoulder blades with several live chickens, reciting some orations after each stroke of the chickens.[48] Isabel then laid in a tub of water. Beside the tub was a large stone jug that Isabel claimed was full of holy water. But the priests concluded that the jug could not contain holy water because of the "bad smell which emanated from it." Near the river's edge, the priests found two baskets, one large and one small. Inside the baskets were roots, a candle, a strip of red cloth with a rattle attached to it, a ribbon with more rattles attached to it, and the "rib of a dead person." Finally, Francisco carried a sack that contained a variety of substances—anise, lavender, black pepper, malaguetta pepper (*pimenta da costa*)[49], ginger, orange peels, lime navels, pits of the African palm fruit, cumin, brazilwood, a pig's tooth, a tanning needle with a cotton thread, and various beans, some from Brazil and others from Angola.[50]

Though it is difficult to discern exactly what was taking place between these two Africans, the mixture of Mina and Central African healing traditions is evident. The rituals themselves were apparently Mina rituals. The flagellation with chickens was very much in the tradition of Vodun. In Haiti, this practice became known as *passer poulet* and was used literally to sweep away bad luck. When the ritual was complete, the chickens were supposed to be shaken "like dusty feather-dusters" in order to remove the evil spirits.[51] The bath that Isabel took also appears similar to the curative baths of herbs, plants, and alcohol that were common among *Vodouisants* in the broader diaspora, but one can also find herbal baths being administered to cure illnesses in Central Africa during this same period.[52] Finally, the presence of the two baskets also suggests a strong Mina influence; but at the same time, Francisco's sack of various objects, including palm fruit and Angolan beans, point to Central African influences.[53] The internal dynamics of the process of Africanization in slave and freed African communities in colonial Brazil are very difficult to unravel, but we should recognize that as this process took place gradually over time, the broader core religious beliefs that were shared by most Africans were never abandoned. Indeed, this shared emphasis on controlling the temporal world was the mechanism that brought together Mina and Angola, especially in the inhospitable settings of colonial Brazil.

Predictably, the priests who found Isabel and Francisco in the woods judged that all of their healing implements were "against the honor of God." As a result, they apprehended the two Africans and confiscated "all of the composition of their evil" and carried them to jail. As they were making their way to the city lockup, Isabel refused to walk, so the priests commenced beating her with some pine branches. In a bold display of courage, Isabel told the priests that if they continued to beat her, she would "make something that would make them fall dead right there, and then she would retaliate against her master." The priests later learned that Isabel had been put out of her master's house on suspicion that she was using malevolent forms of witchcraft.

Isabel's acid response to the priests who were beating her, as well as the threat she made against her master, were the elements of African religious power that whites feared most—the malicious infliction of injury or illness by disgruntled or unhappy Africans. These were not idle threats. In 1745, Domingos Álvares, the Mina curer who was exiled to the Algarve for cures that he made in Rio de Janeiro and Pernambuco (see above), was denounced for "bewitching" a white couple in Castromarim, Portugal. Antônio Viegas called Domingos to cure the paralysis of his wife, Domingas de Andrade, who could not move from the waist down. Domingos determined that she was suffering from *feitiços* and provided her with a cure that led to her quick recovery.

Not satisfied with the payment he received for his cure, Domingos resorted to his religious powers to punish his delinquent clients. Less than a month after proffering his cure, Domingos placed a number of objects at the door of Antônio Viegas and his wife. Among the objects was a doll with 39 pins in it, hairs, bones, snake skin, pieces of glass, kernels of corn, and some grave dirt, all things intended to do harm to the couple. Domingos told Domingas de Andrade that the *feitiços* were for her and all the people in her house, as well as for their cattle. Domingos Álvares was denounced and again sentenced by the Inquisition. He was eventually ordered to appear before the Auto de Fé, was publicly whipped, and exiled for four years to the city of Bragança in the far north of Portugal.[54]

As is amply demonstrated by the case of Domingos Álvares, the line between the diviner/curer and the so-called "witch" was precariously thin. The same slave diviner who one day found runaway slaves or a cure to an illness could, on the following day, inflict injury and mayhem on the master, his family, and other slaves. The masters were acutely aware of the "diabolical" power of African religions, and many lived in constant fear of the "witchcraft" that their slaves might cast upon them. Some, like Isabel's master, responded by simply throwing suspected witches off their property. But others suffered the wrath of their slaves, slowly deteriorating away in painful deaths. From the perspective of the African slave, religious power became one of the fiercest tools of resistance, a stealthy, silent killer of the hated master, and a very real threat to the colonial status quo.

CHAPTER EIGHT

Witchcraft, Ritual, and Resistance in the African-Portuguese Diaspora

Any discussion of "witchcraft" in the seventeenth and eighteenth centuries must begin with several cautionary words on the deeper meanings of the term, especially as it applied to the African context. From the Western perspective, witchcraft was a relatively fixed set of concepts, implying evil, malevolence, and sin. Witchcraft was widely understood to be the Devil's work. In most of Africa, on the other hand, the terms used to describe what Westerners call witchcraft were much more ambiguous.[1] In many societies, there was no discrete term that distinguished good rituals from malevolent rituals. The practice of evil was just one component of what might better be understood as a bundle of hidden religious powers. As we have seen in the previous two chapters, these powers could be used in a variety of positive ways—divining, curing, and so on—that restored harmony and balance to both individuals and communities. But the special power to uncover malevolence and heal could also be used to harness malevolence and cause harm. Africans reasoned that if a diviner/curer had the power to see evil spirits and expel them with his/her powers, then certainly he/she was capable of controlling similar forms of evil for his/her own nefarious purposes. This circularity between the "bewitching," the divination, and the remedy demonstrates the extraordinarily ambiguous nature of religious discourse in African societies. Those endowed with religious powers could do both good and evil at the same time.[2]

Unfortunately, by using the pejorative term "witchcraft" to describe African religious practices, many Western observers implicitly have reduced African religious expressions to their potential for evil. The positive aspects of African religions often remain hidden behind this "evil" veneer. A more balanced assessment would recognize the ability to control evil as just one aspect of a complex set of religious powers. As noted in Chapter 5, Central African understandings of religious malevolence were tied to temporal misfortune, especially misfortune caused by hidden human powers. Those who used their religious powers to harm other people or to insure their own successes, rather than for the advancement of the common good, were deemed to be malevolent. One of the outcomes of malevolent religious behavior was a growing social and/or economic inequality between the spiritual tormentor and everyone else in the community. Thus, two of the classic symptoms of religious malevolence were unjust suffering on the part of the victims and rapid, unexplained social/economic wealth on the parts of the spiritual tormentors. From the African perspective, enslavement and economic exploitation by Europeans fit both of these criteria, but the impacts of these strong and unfamiliar new forms of malevolence radically transformed religious meanings in Africa and the diaspora.

Evidence of Portuguese spiritual malevolence was abundant all along the Central African coast. It was widely understood that Europeans carried away black bodies in order to "eat" them.[3] For Central Africans, crossing *kalunga* (the Atlantic Ocean) in slave ships represented a premature death at the hands of witches, who nourished themselves on black bodies in the land of the dead (the Americas). The "profits" from these black bodies were then returned to Africa in a variety of trade goods. Cooking oil was believed to be pressed from African flesh. The red wines that Portuguese traders sold were said to be the blood of their African victims.[4] European cheeses were African brains.[5] And gunpowder was thought to be the ashen residue of African bones that were burned by Europeans.[6] The evocative imagery conjured up by the emerging dialectic between the slave trade and European wealth demonstrates just how deeply the slave trade impacted African discourses on malevolence. Europeans used their hidden powers to enslave Africans and commodify their bodies for their own enrichment.

The arrival of Europeans in Africa thus marked a significant shift in the meaning of malevolence in Africa. Some scholars are now suggesting that African understandings of the Western concept of "witchcraft" were *products* of the slave trade, rather than the result of some timeless African "tradition."[7]

Prior to contact with Europeans, Africans viewed religious malevolence through a micropolitical prism that allowed for familiar religious antidotes. Good and Evil were part of the same cosmological continuum, and both could be controlled with familiar religious rituals and practices. Europeans introduced a new form of social and economic malevolence—the Atlantic slave trade—that transformed this cosmological balance. Wars, disease, forced migration, and other misfortunes instigated by Europe's appetite for slave labor —all were understood to be symptoms of this unprecedented misery.

If the slave trade and economic exploitation were the impetus for transforming certain forms of religious malevolence into "witchcraft" in Africa, then actual enslavement by Europeans must have been understood as the most virulent form of witchcraft, one that required a powerful religious counterattack in order to be freed from the curse.[8] Ironically, this defensive posture on the part of the enslaved thrust them to the forefront of witchcraft discourse in the Portuguese world. The Portuguese already had a well-established history of dealing with witchcraft and "fetishism" long before they encountered ethnic and racial "others" in their imperial ventures. During the Renaissance, Europeans of all stripes believed that devils and witches operated freely in the temporal realm. Numerous books and treatises dealt with the subjects of witchcraft and superstition. Indeed, witchcraft discourse became so detailed and refined that one scholar recently has labeled the phenomenon "the science of the devil."[9]

For the most part, the Portuguese were content to follow the philosophical and literary leads of English, Spanish, and Italian writers on the subject during most of the sixteenth century. Lacking an indigenous intellectual discourse on witchcraft, the Portuguese church adhered to the broad contours of European witchcraft constructions. It was widely understood that God used witches and the Devil to punish sinners and test man's faith. The use of diabolical power to counter diabolical power was prohibited by the church, because that necessarily meant invoking the Devil. Only prayer and faith in God could counteract the Devil's powers in a safe and Christian way.[10]

Not until the seventeenth century did Portuguese Inquisitorial theologians begin commenting at length on the nature of witchcraft.[11] In the view of Portuguese witchcraft philosophers and "scientists," rituals, orations, and symbols used to counteract evil all were evidence of a pact with the Devil. Even rituals that involved Christian prayers and the use of sacred objects were suspect, because they most often were applied by "profane" people who were "contrary" to the sanctity of the words or objects being used. In the Portuguese context, these profane people were generally understood to be "ignorant," "rustic" peoples, and particularly single women.[12] By the seventeenth century, Portuguese witchcraft discourse was becoming fused with an emerging discourse on social class, one in which a literate, educated, and "civilized" male elite tried to distance itself from the popular masses, who were allegedly mired in the vulgar world of superstition and magic.[13]

Predictably, Catholic clerics were not the only ones who believed that witches were agents of the Devil. Judges, doctors, and other Portuguese elites also believed in the power of the Devil through witches.[14] Yet, despite this widespread belief, the Portuguese never viewed witchcraft as a real threat to Christian order and reason. Since most Portuguese witches operated alone, rather than in groups, none of the witchcraft panic or terror that infected other European countries made its way to Portugal. The Portuguese were much more concerned with maintaining religious orthodoxy vis-à-vis Judaism, Islam, and Protestantism than they were with prosecuting witches. It was believed that by using God's remedies—baptism, confession, holy water, the sign of the cross, and exorcisms—individual witches could be reclaimed from the Devil's grasp.

The Portuguese carried these witchcraft beliefs with them when they encountered African religious practices on a sustained basis in Brazil beginning in the late sixteenth century. Just as class and gender were becoming fused with witchcraft discourse in Portugal, so too did race and ethnicity become fused with witchcraft discourse in Brazil. All African religious practices were suspected of being the work of the Devil. The major difference between the Portuguese and Brazilian settings was that the African "witches" were present in large numbers in Brazil and were capable of using their religious powers to physically harm their masters and threaten the Catholic faith.

Thus, the religious battle ground was set: "witch" versus "witch." Africans, who understood their enslavement to be the result of Portuguese religious malevolence, countered with their most powerful religious antidotes, which were recognized and feared by the Portuguese as "witchcraft." In their attempts to counter the slings and arrows of slavery—mistreatment, malnutrition, disease, kinship instability, and so on—African slaves (and freed Africans) mounted a steady religious assault against the white witches who were causing them such grave misfortune. In its most benign forms, African religious power was used simply to protect slaves from their master's assaults. For example, in 1646, a freed Angolan named Domingos Umbáta (Mbata) was denounced for helping two "negras" improve their relationships with their mistresses. To protect the slaves from the wrath of their mistresses, Domingos had them bathe themselves in a tub of water that contained crushed leaves, a rattle, and a jaguar tooth. Presumably, the bath would shield them from their mistresses' venom.[15]

Such attempts by slaves to insulate themselves from their masters' power were apparently widespread across Brazil. In a 1702 report on the Jesuit missions to the Recôncavo of Bahia, Father João Pereira noted that because Angolan slaves were not able "to endure the rigor with which [their masters] shackle them, they use many mixtures in order to make their masters (as they are accustomed to saying) have a good heart for them."[16] Slaves in Minas Gerais believed that wheat root taken from a swamp had the power to free them from punishments. Still others in Minas Gerais performed rituals with the scrapings from the soles of their master's shoes as a way of protecting themselves from beatings.[17] And in Alagoas, slaves chewed on roots and small sticks to prevent their masters from beating them.[18]

These practices were not confined to Brazil. In Lisbon, in 1688, a Mozambican slave named Antônio heard that there was a slave named Agostinho who could prescribe an herb that would "impede the ires and passions of his master." Antônio sought out Agostinho, who agreed to share his herb with Antônio. Agostinho told Antônio that in order for the herb to be effective, he needed to enter his master's house with the herb in his mouth. After chewing it, he should spit on the ground and rub the saliva with his foot. If he followed this prescription, Antônio's master would not punish him for his errors. Putting the herb to the test, Antônio left his master's house early one morning and did not return until late at night. Past experience told Antônio that his master was going to be angry that he had stayed away for the entire day. But, having used the herb, he found that "his master did not fight with him, nor offer him any harsh words, as on other days when he made these and other similar errors."[19]

Stronger forms of African religious power were aimed directly at the master or his family, sapping their physical strength or, in some instances, making them "crazy." For example, in 1704, an Angolan slave named Mai Caterina (Mother Catherine) was accused of bewitching her master, Capitão Luís Fernandes. Mai Caterina cast a spell on her Bahian master that made him have "such profound sleeps that in order to awaken him, it is necessary . . . to lift him up."[20] Similarly, in 1686, a Bahian slaveholder named Álvaro de Mattos called on an Angolan woman named Dona Maria to cure his wife, Isabel de Almeida. Mattos stated that his wife was "going crazy" because of some *feitiços* that one of his slaves had given her. Dona Maria prescribed some herbs that led to Isabel's rapid recovery.[21]

The most powerful forms of African religious antidotes were intended to maim or kill whites and their families. Whites were acutely aware of slave vengeance. Writing in the first decade of the eighteenth century, Father André João Antonil warned that masters who administered excessive punishments risked having the slave's relatives or friends "take revenge upon them, using either witchcraft or poison."[22] Such was the case in 1743, when an Angolan-born slave named Antônio Mascarenhas was charged with various crimes on the island of Madeira. Among those who denounced Antônio was Nicolão Soares, who testified that Antônio entered his locked house in the middle of the night "to commit some dishonesty" with his female slave named Teresa. Antônio and Teresa stole some gold, an emerald ring valued at 14,000 réis, a blue silk coat, a new skirt, and other clothes. They then fled to a cavern, where they hid for three days. Nicolão Soares received word of their where-abouts and was able to capture the two fugitive slaves. As punishment for their crimes, Antônio was placed in jail and Teresa was sold away to the Azores.

Soon after Antônio was jailed, various unsettling things began to happen to Soares and his family in their house. In particular, paper cuttings were found in the clothes of all the family members. These cuttings were in the shapes of circles, triangles, and crosses. Even visitors to their house began to find the cuttings in their clothes, "causing great fear among their neighbors and friends." Soares had his house exorcised and sprinkled with holy water, which resulted in a brief period of peace, but the cuttings soon resumed. Eventually, the cuttings appeared not only in his house, but also in the house of his mother, Mariana Mendes da Silva. Soares presumed that Antônio was "casting these spells upon him in hatred and vengeance for having sold away the slave [Teresa]."[23]

Though Nicolão Soares and his family apparently found Antônio's *feitiços* before they could take their intended physical effect, other whites were not so lucky. In 1646, a Bahian woman named Angela de Sequeira was suffering from a long-term illness that would not abate. One night she found in her pillows some packets that contained bird feathers, bird beaks, and sea shells. Her mulatta slave Beatriz confessed that she put the objects in her pillows "so that [her mistress] might love her." But even after the packets were removed from her pillows, Angela de Sequeira's condition continued to worsen.

A diviner/healer named Francisco Arda, who was the slave of Lieutenant Francisco Pereira do Lago, was called in to see whether there were more *feitiços*. The Arda slave made a ceremony, throwing a little river water into a plate with some scrapings from a little stick that he brought with him. Over the plate, he made some gesticulations, looking from one side to the other, and later announced that there were more *feitiços* buried in the yard. Francisco Arda took a green twig and used it to sprinkle the ground with the river water. At the place where the twig wilted, Francisco ordered the observers to dig. There, they found packets filled with fingernails, hairs, and powders. Francisco said that these were the *feitiços* that were making Angela de Sequeira ill and that they were placed there by her mulatta slave Beatriz. Beatriz denied having knowledge of this second set of *feitiços*, and even though they were also removed, Angela de Sequeira continued to suffer from her illness.[24]

Freed blacks also used their religious powers to express grievances with whites. In 1646, a freed black named Apolónia was accused of bewitching four children in Bahia, among them the grandson of Antônio Coelho Pinheiro. Pinheiro claimed that he witnessed Apolónia standing at his doorstep around midday on April 3. His grandson was inside the house sleeping. Several hours later, the child's father went to wake him but "found him bewitched." The child refused to breastfeed and his lips were blue, "a signal that they say is from bewitching." Within twenty-four hours, the child was dead. Because of her reputation as a witch and her close proximity to the child, Apolónia was accused of the crime. Whether she actually played a role in the boy's death remains uncertain.[25]

The depth of so-called "witchcraft" conspiracies in slave communities is demonstrated most clearly by a case from Recife in the early 1780s. For more than three years, a wealthy slaveowner named Manuel Rodrigues de Senna was bedridden, nearly paralyzed from an unexplained illness that doctors and pharmacists could not cure. After exhausting all worldly means of finding a cure, Senna opted to test the remedies of the Catholic Church. Father Fidélis de Partana, an Italian Capuchin priest, was called in to perform an exorcism. Father Fidélis began his ceremonies, and "in less than five minutes, [Senna] rose from the bed without any pain." As Father Fidélis continued the exorcism, Senna began expelling from his mouth various things that were impossible to swallow—a four-inch-long fish skeleton, pieces of coal, large amounts of sand, cockroaches, and other "beasts." As a result of Father Fidélis's exorcism, Senna quickly recovered from his illness.

Soon after the exorcism, Senna began to suspect that two of his slaves were responsible for his protracted illness. Over a period of years, Domingos Angola and Gonçalo Mina conspired to "cast various things of witchcraft in the food and drink that were destined for [their master] and also for various slaves of his." Senna slowly became aware that his two slaves were aiming to do him harm, even after he was cured of his paralysis. On one occasion, he overheard the two slaves plotting to poison his milk. He also suspected that the men were entering the kitchen and putting *feitiços* in his food. As a result, he prohibited them from climbing the stairs on the outside of the house that led directly to the kitchen.

Further evidence of the slaves' guilt arose from an unlikely source. One day while the mistress of the house was giving the cook, Maria Angola, some lashes for "carelessness in the service of the house," Maria began confessing. She cried, "My Senhora, do not punish me, because I promise that I did not throw anything else in the food of my master." Surprised by Maria's spontaneous confession, the mistress asked her what it was that she threw in her master's food. The cook responded that they were "*feitiços* ground into powder that the pretos Gonçalo and Domingos gave to her when she went to the stairs." Even after their master had prohibited the two men from climbing the stairs to the kitchen, Domingos and Gonçalo continued slipping the *feitiços* under the door, warning Maria that if she did not put them in their master's food, they would one day put the *feitiços* in her food. Maria confessed further that when her master arose from the dinner table screaming in pain, it was because of the *feitiços* that were put in his food. She also said that she put other *feitiços* in her master's sugar cane liquor (*garapa*) that pushed him "to the edge of death." Gonçalo, who was present during Maria's confession, did not deny his role.

Eventually, Maria admitted that she had thrown *feitiços* in her master's food on that very day. Sitting down to eat his meal, Manuel Rodrigues de Senna told his wife that he did not want to eat after hearing Maria's confession. But Senna's wife admonished her husband, telling him that she did not believe Maria's confession; nor did she believe in *feitiços*. She insisted that she and their children would eat the food if her husband would not. Soon after eating, the mistress and her children became violently ill with abdominal and chest pains. The family dispatched another house slave, Romana Mina, to find Father Fidélis, who later arrived with a colleague. The two priests exorcised the entire family and gave them holy water with various relics to drink. They all later recovered.

But this was not the end of the story. During her confession under the whip, Maria Angola told her mistress that she was terrified that Domingos and Gonçalo would seek vengeance against her for revealing their crimes. The two men had warned her that if she disclosed their role in trying to bewitch their master, they would kill her with the same *feitiços*. The two slaves had made similar threats against Romana Mina, who also put powders, little onions, peels, and "other filth" into the food of their master. Sure enough, soon after revealing the guilt of Domingos and Gonçalo, Maria Angola began to swell around her neck. Within six days she was dead, "screaming against Gonçalo that he killed her with *feitiços*." Domingos and Gonçalo were also suspected of killing five other slaves with witchcraft, including a newly arrived Mina slave who ate an apple full of *feitiços* that was given to her by Gonçalo Mina. The new slave "began screaming in pain, saying in her language that she would die of *feitiços* that he had given her." Within three days, the new slave was dead.[26]

The accusations against Domingos Angola and Gonçalo Mina reveal a great deal about broader understandings of African witchcraft in Brazil. Prior to

Maria Angola's confession, Manuel Rodrigues de Senna and his family clearly were among those whites who did not believe in the supernatural powers of their slaves. Senna did not consider his illness to be the result of witchcraft until he had exhausted all medical possibilities. He gradually began to consider the possibility that his slaves might be responsible for his illnesses, but his wife still refused to believe that there was such a thing as witchcraft. She even used herself and her children as human guinea pigs, eating food that they were warned was tainted with *feitiços*. Only after the entire family became ill did the gravity of the situation become apparent. Finally convinced that African witchcraft was a real and dangerous threat, Senna reported his two slaves to secular and religious authorities. Gonçalo was sold at public auction, while Domingos was remitted to the Holy Office in Lisbon.

The refusal of some whites to believe in African forms of witchcraft was a function of several factors, not the least of which was a confusion between poison and *feitiços*. By the 1780s, when Domingos and Gonçalo were accused, very few Portuguese were still being persecuted for witchcraft.[27] The rationalism of the Enlightenment had taken hold, and people were less likely to admit their belief in the supernatural. Many of the tools of African witchcraft were what the Portuguese would have called poison (*peçonha*). Had someone told Senna's wife that she was being poisoned by her slaves, rather than being bewitched, she probably would have been more likely to believe them. But because the majority of African malevolence still fell under the broad label of "witchcraft," poisonings often were subsumed under this banner. From the Portuguese perspective, poisoning became just another form of African *feitiços*.

The blurring of the lines between poisoning and witchcraft was probably due to African influences on witchcraft discourse in Brazil. From the African perspective, Portuguese poisons were natural substances endowed with the power to counter other forms of witchcraft, or malevolence. Thus, attempts to kill the master with poisons are probably better understood as attempts to eradicate witches. The master's witchcraft was being answered with an even more powerful form of African witchcraft. Powders and herbs that were endowed with the power to heal disease could also be used to heal the malevolence of Portuguese masters, sometimes maiming or killing them and their families in the process. In all cases, the power of the substances was attributed to the spirit world. Thus, to call poisons "*feitiços*" was very much in keeping with an African worldview and was just one more way in which Africans controlled certain spiritual discourses in Brazil.

That Domingos and Gonçalo were accused of killing as many as five African slaves with *feitiços* was not at all unusual. In fact, in the Inquisition cases, slaves were accused of killing other slaves just as often as they were accused of killing their masters. As early as 1639, the Bishop of Brazil, Pedro da Silva, noted that "the Negroes from Angola . . . [who] they call *feiticeiros* . . . kill with poison or other methods the other Negro men and women with great facility."[28] Similarly, in 1671, the municipal council of Salvador complained to the Crown that the white residents of Bahia were suffering great damage "because of the many slave deaths caused by the *feiticeiros*." The suspects could not be prosecuted because there was not enough evidence, but the accused were nevertheless exiled to far-away places "where they could not do so much damage."[29]

Though never approaching the epidemic levels of Renaissance Europe, Brazilian witchcraft accusations of the seventeenth and eighteenth centuries were certainly more pronounced and widespread than the Portuguese variant, with Africans being the prime suspects in the murders of their fellow slaves. In 1685, as described in Chapter 6, wealthy Bahian planter André Gomes de Medina accused Simão Congo of murdering fifteen slaves with witchcraft.[30] Similarly, in 1687, Bahian slaveowner Manuel Leite Feira "presumed that a Negro of a neighbor of his . . . whose name is Pedro Dongo (Ndongo) gave *feitiços* to some slaves of his, some dying and others becoming gravely ill."[31] Five years later in Pernambuco, a slave named Ventura was accused of killing three other slaves in a very short time. Ventura's master, it was reported, "out of fear, hides the Negro when they come for him [and] one presumes that he consents to what [Ventura] does."[32] In 1698, Jerónimo Álvares denounced four different slaves for killing other slaves in the parish of Matoim in Bahia.[33] One year later, in 1699, a slaveowner named Joseph Fernandes accused a neighboring slave of killing one of his slaves with *feitiços* in Rio São Francisco, Bahia.[34]

Finally, during the second decade of the eighteenth century, two slaves, Gaspar da Costa and Gonçalo de Cuna, were accused of various witchcraft murders across northern Brazil. The two slaves originally lived in Pernambuco, but were exiled to Bahia after their master determined that they were killing other slaves. In Bahia, they were again accused of killing with *feitiços* and were sold to Espírito Santo. When they arrived in Espírito Santo, Gaspar was thrown in jail for his "criminal" activity, but he escaped to his master's house where he continued "killing people as he was accustomed to doing before."[35]

The custom of selling away slaves suspected of witchcraft was not uncommon, since masters had real fears of their slaves' religious powers. But those whose slaves were the victims of witchcraft had little recourse. Some slaveowners tried to defend their economic interests by taking up their grievances with the master of the slave *feiticeiro*. In Rio de Janeiro in the early 1780s, a poor widow named Teresa Maria de Jesus discovered that one of her slaves, a man named José, was "full of *feitiços*." José knew that his illness was the work of a woman named Rosa, slave of Captain Vidal Rodrigues. Teresa Maria carried José with her to the house of the captain and demanded that Rosa cure José. Otherwise, she insisted, the captain should be prepared to purchase the dying José. Teresa Maria appealed to the captain, telling him that she was poor and alone and could not afford to lose José's labor. Captain Rodrigues responded by severely beating Rosa, who was unable to provide a cure for José. José was eventually healed by another slave.[36]

Although many African understandings of religious malevolence persisted in Brazil, one way in which this malevolence clearly was transformed was in the so-called "bewitching" of fellow Africans. Slaveholders' fears that Africans were destroying their human property made understandings of religious malevolence far more complex and multilayered in Brazil than they were in Africa. On the one hand, just as in Africa, Africans were using their religious powers in attempts to reconcile disruptions that arose within their own communities. Certainly, everyday misfortunes were still sometimes attributed to other Africans, especially where there were perceived social distinctions within slave communities.[37] On the other hand, an attack on another slave using African religious powers was always more than a personal attack; it was also a strike against the master's economic and social well-being. Every act of malevolent witchcraft against a slave became an act of resistance against the slave master. The depletion of slaves due to witchcraft—whether real or imagined—was a blow to the institution of slavery. Thus, African religious power operated on at least two overlapping levels in the African-Portuguese diaspora: one, the "traditional" community level; the other, a more global, antislavery level. No longer just a way of addressing local or "traditional" problems, African religious power posed a real and dangerous threat to Portuguese slaveowners in Brazil.

Witchcraft, Ritual, and Romance

African religious power was used not only to oppose the condition of slavery; it was also used to fight various misfortunes that were a result of the institution. The extreme gender imbalances that characterized many Brazilian slave communities, especially during the seventeenth century, certainly inspired religious responses by African men, who on average outnumbered women by a ratio of two to one. In 1638, Father Francisco Monteiro Soares, vicar of Ilhéus, reported that a "negro de Guiné" named Antônio "was a *feiticeiro* who separated wives from their husbands."[38] Presumably, Antônio made his *feitiços* so that other African men could cohabit with the scarce numbers of women. Antônio's so-called witchcraft also might be interpreted as a statement on the cultural inapplicability of Western conceptions of marriage in African slave communities, where, as we have already noted, Africans adhered to a variety of family and kinship patterns that were often not in keeping with Western norms.

While some Africans sought to remove potential sexual partners from the restrictions of Western marriage, others took out their sexual frustrations in more personal assaults on their fellow slaves. In 1699, a creole slave named Francisca was suffering from *feitiços* in Bahia. When she was administered an antidote, she vomited up "a ball of hairs with some black seeds." Francisca claimed that the *feitiços* were made for her by an African slave who was angry that she would not sleep with him.[39]

By the eighteenth century, as the gender ratios in some slave communities became more balanced, slave women also began using their religious powers against their female rivals. Around 1780, a slave named Rosa "had public fame for being a *feiticeira* who killed various slaves and cattle" in Rio de Janeiro. At one time, Rosa was married to a slave named Fellis. When she learned that Fellis was also married to another slave named Eva, Rosa killed Eva, and later Fellis, both with *feitiços*. Rosa was also "suspected of killing all of the babies that were being born to the slave women" of her master, Captain Vidal Rodrigues.[40]

In Portugal, the isolation of Africans and their descendants was even more acute than in Brazil, prompting some to take desperate measures to find a mate. In 1733, a free African couple, Manuel Pereira da Silva (Congo) and Bernarda de São Dionísio (Angola), were terrorized by a jealous seductress in Lisbon. Manuel confessed that he was attending the celebration of Nossa Senhora da Aracaya when he met a black woman named Antônia Maria do Rosário. Several days later, the woman sought out Manuel and asked him if he wanted anything from her. Manuel responded that he did not want anything from her because she had nothing to offer him. Angry that she had been spurned, Antônia told Manuel that he would pay for what he said.

Several weeks later, Manuel was in his house "when he came down with such a great perturbation in the head" that he grabbed his cloak and hat and went looking for Antônia. According to Manuel, when he arrived at Antônia's door, his "perturbation" calmed down. And when he spoke to her, it calmed even further. Manuel had sex with Antônia and returned home. Manuel claimed that when he was away from Antônia, he continued to suffer from her "evil": a constant fever, abdominal pains, and swelling on his face and stomach. Wanting to rid himself of this menace, Manuel stole a silk garment from his wife and carried it to Antônia. Manuel hoped that this gesture would buy her goodwill, but his act of desperation backfired. Shortly after Antônia received her gift from Manuel, Manuel's wife entered Antônia's house and reclaimed the stolen garment. Attached to the garment was a small package, containing a red rag, some little sticks, some bones, and four pieces of cane. Manuel's wife soon began suffering from neck and chest pains that kept her from sleeping, as well as headaches and stinging sensations all over her body.

Exhausted by his and his wife's suffering, Manuel summoned Antônia to his house and demanded that she remove the *feitiços* that she had given them. Antônia admitted that she had made the *feitiços* but said that she could not remove them without first speaking to her spiritual adviser, a slave named Maria de Jesus. Maria de Jesus arrived at the house and said that she made the *feitiços* at the request of Antônia. She confessed that Manuel's *feitiços* consisted of some water that Antônia dripped on him, water that she had used to wash her private parts. Maria de Jesus also confessed that in addition to the *feitiços* attached to her silk garment, Bernarda was also affected by a sack of woolen fabric that was attached to the head of her bed. Inside the sack was a doll with pins stuck through the head and a needle stuck through the body. A similar doll was also found under Bernarda's mattress.[41]

Not all of the attempts to find love were harmful or violent. Some remedies were more coercive in nature, designed to entice a potential lover to accede to the wishes of a suitor. For example, in 1688, the Mozambican slave, Antônio, used a small stick as a charm to attract women in Lisbon. Antônio paid another slave three cruzados for the red stick, which was about the size of a finger. Supposedly, if the stick were to touch "any white or black woman or single or married and of any condition or quality, she would immediately give herself up to the one who touched her on any part of her body and even on the clothes." Testing the stick's effectiveness, Antônio immediately carried it with him through the city. Antônio passed "a negra he had never seen before" and "touched her with the stick on the outside of her clothes . . . without saying a word to her." As Antônio moved away from her, the woman called for him two times. Antônio calmly walked over to meet the woman. After a short conversation, he walked her back to his living quarters and had sex with her. The woman then departed, and Antônio never saw her again.[42]

Slaves in Brazil used similar substances to draw the attentions of potential lovers. In 1725, two female slaves in Cabo Frio, near the city of Rio de Janeiro, used various "diabolical modes in order to get the men that they wanted." Francisca and Luzia, both "Guiné" slaves, washed their private parts, saving the water to give to men to drink. When the men drank the water, the women were able to achieve their "evil intents." Similarly, Francisca killed a vulture and, taking its brains, made a fine powder out of them. She threw the powder at "any person she wished to have illicit acts with," and within a few hours the man was in her clutches.[43]

Francisca and Luzia's use of powerful substances from the natural world was not unusual in either African or European traditions. Some of the most commonly used substances to attract members of the opposite sex were elements from the human body—blood, sperm, urine, hair, fingernails, and so on.[44] Because Portuguese and Africans had shared understandings of the power of these human elements, we find records of several cases in which whites prescribed remedies to blacks. This was especially the case in Portugal, where blacks were atomized in such a way that access to other blacks was often quite limited.

For instance, in 1671, in the small Portuguese town of Villanova de Anços, a Cape Verdean slave named Esperança confessed that she had had an affair with a young man named Manuel Francisco de Oliveira. Esperança learned that Manuel was preparing to marry another woman and, in order to stop the marriage, looked for some *feitiços*. She went to a white woman named Sebastiana de Carvalhal, who was esteemed for making *feitiços* for "diverse persons." Sebastiana told Esperança that in order to attach herself to Manuel, she needed to bring her some of his hairs and semen. Eight days passed before Esperança returned with specimens of Manuel's hair and semen. Sebastiana put them into a vase and assured Esperança that she could rest easily. As long as she was in possession of Manuel's hair and semen, he would always search for her, even if he married the other woman. Just as Sebastiana predicted, Manuel married the other woman, but he ran away from her, searching for Esperança.[45]

Slaves in Portugal also took love advice from Moors. In the 1730s, in Lisbon, a creole slave named Marcelina Maria received counsel from a Moorish slave named Antônia. Searching for ways to obtain and keep men, Marcelina got several remedies from Antônia. The first was designed to conquer the will of a man and make him want to have sex. Antônia told Marcelina that in order to get any man, she should cook an egg and sleep with it between her legs. She should then feed the egg to the man she desired. Antônia also taught Marcelina that in order to keep a man, she should moisten her finger in her vagina and make two crosses over the eyes of her man. If she did this, her man would never stray, nor leave her.[46]

Even though Africans and their descendants embraced some elements of European and Moorish traditions in Portugal, when Africans themselves proffered remedies, we can discern differences in the types of objects used to achieve the remedies. For example, in Lisbon, in 1737, a white man named Antônio went to a slave named João Angola to see if he could "make something that would make a woman want him very much, since he wanted to marry for fear that they would make him a soldier." João Angola told Antônio that he knew of no remedy, but that he was familiar with a man who might be able to help. João went to visit another slave, Domingos, who was locked up in the city jail for debts he owed to his master. Domingos gave João two small sticks. He instructed him to tell Antônio that he should put a part of the stick in his mouth before he went searching for a woman and that this would attract any woman he might want.[47] João carried the sticks to Antônio and collected a payment, which he split with Domingos.[48]

The sticks that were sold by Domingos and João were not unlike the stick used by Antônio Mozambique or the ground vulture's brain used by Francisca Guiné. All of these substances were utilized by Africans to help rectify the void in human contact and affection that was created by slavery. In Brazil, gender imbalances and instabilities caused by death, disease, and forced separations inspired male and female slaves to seek remedies that would give them access to members of the opposite sex. In Portugal, these same obstacles were exacerbated by the acute isolation and marginalization felt by peoples of African descent. Even though some of the objects and rituals used by Africans to address affairs of the heart dovetailed with Portuguese superstitions, we should not lose sight of the fact that these were still very African responses to misfortune. The sticks, powders, and rituals all were used in attempts to influence the temporal world and transform their condition. The everyday use of such charms, talismans, and rituals was a common feature of slave communities throughout the African-Portuguese world.

Central African Rituals and Beliefs in Controlling Everyday Affairs

Africans used a variety of charms, talismans, and rituals to bring themselves luck and to protect themselves from various maladies in their everyday lives. The earliest of these rituals to be noted in Brazilian slave communities were of Central African origin. Three rituals, in particular, stand out in the documents: the *quijila*, the *tambo*, and an unnamed ritual used to discover the whereabouts of a missing person.

The *quijila*, which in the Kimbundu language means "prohibition," were dietary restrictions that were followed by many Angolans during the seventeenth century. According to Father Cavazzi, the *quijila* were old Mbundu laws and customs that were reinstituted in Angola during the seventeenth century by Temba-Ndumba, who was the wife of Zimbo, chief of the Imbangala (Jaga). Cavazzi noted that these "ridiculous and superstitious" laws were traditions that were long followed by Mbundu ancestors. They included prohibitions against eating pigs, elephants, snakes, and other animals. These dietary taboos were believed to bring success in war, hunting, and agriculture.[49] Neglecting the *quijila* could bring dire consequences. Father Merolla noted that those who mistakenly ingested forbidden foods believed that they would die quickly unless they sought remedy from a magician (*Maghi*).[50]

In Brazil, some Angolan slaves continued to follow these strict dietary restrictions, abstaining from "meat, fish, seafood, and many other things."[51] In a 1720 report from Rio de Janeiro, it was noted that Angolans followed these "*quigillas*," fearing that if they broke the taboos, they would immediately fall dead or become crippled in the feet and hands.[52] Portuguese observers judged that the "*quigillas*" were "an explicit pact that these pagans make with the Devil . . . that passes by tradition to children, grandchildren, and many more descendants."[53] Though the negative Portuguese assessment is predictable, it also reveals the tenacity of certain Angolan beliefs in Brazil. Not only were Angolans adhering to their own systems of belief, but they were succeeding in passing these beliefs down through multiple generations, just one more indication of the resilience of Central African beliefs in seventeenth- and eighteenth-century Brazil.

The second Central African ritual practice to appear in Brazil, the *tambo*, was an elaborate funeral ceremony designed to insure the comfortable passage of the dead person's soul to the other world. In Angola, these ceremonies were preceded by eight days of mourning, during which the body was displayed and paid final respects by neighbors and family. At the end of the eighth day, the body was prepared with a ritual bath of roots and herbs "in order that the soul of the dead would not return [to earth] . . . and without this ceremony, they [Angolans] believed that the soul would appear and make them sick."[54] The next morning, the funeral party commenced. Father Cavazzi described it as follows:

> The party begins early in the morning, and during the time that that infernal mockery lasts, all of the surrounding environs for a distance of one mile remain giddy. The dancers, with the great admiration of those who see them, spin around on one foot like tops; afterward, entangled among [the dead], they quickly give turns, raising confusing voices, without anyone knowing if they speak, sing, cry, laugh, if they lament, or if they are happy about the death of that person.

Among such delirious ones, there was one elected *xinguila*, this is the

Temba-Ndumba, seventeenth-century Imbangala queen, known for having revived ancient Mbundu laws and dietary restrictions, which many Angolans observed both at home and abroad in the African-Portuguese diaspora. Watercolor by Giovanni Antonio Cavazzi, "Missione evangelica al regno de Congo, 1665–1668," Manoscritti Araldi, Papers of the Araldi Family. Modena, Italy.

priest or minister of the funeral, coming close to the face of the dead one, he asks him repeatedly what was the cause of his death. But as the dead cannot speak, the *xinguila* responds in the name of the dead one, and with an altered voice. . . .

Meanwhile, they do not forget themselves, eating in order to recharge their strength, nor the dead person, judging that he needs food just as they do. Then, with their stomachs filled, they throw the rest of the food and drink over the cadaver.[55]

Given the absolute necessity of proper ritual burials in most Central African societies, it should not surprise us that slaves continued these practices in Brazil, as well as in other locations in the diaspora.[56] The alternative was to be victimized and tortured by the disgruntled souls of the dead. In most locations, slave masters were not receptive to their slaves' wishes to provide proper burial ceremonies for their deceased brethren. Indeed, the corpses of dead slaves were often left to rot in shallow graves, where they could be dug up and eaten by dogs or wild animals. Others were dumped onto beaches and taken out to sea with the tide.[57] The appearance of human bones in the pastures worked by slaves understandably caused great fear and scandal among those who found them.[58]

Despite the disdain that most slave masters showed for their slaves' spiritual needs, some masters allowed their slaves to continue with the *tambo* rituals. During the 1630s, slaves in Pernambuco were reported to "bury their relatives and address them with a ridiculous, strange shouting. They sit around the grave and ask the dead person, singing as one: 'Hey, hey, hey, why have you died? Hey, hey, hey, did you lack bread, flour, tobacco, or pipe?' After all these multiple and useless questions, they throw pieces of tobacco and all sorts of roots into the grave, so that the deceased may continue to enjoy himself in his other life."[59] Similarly, at the beginning of the eighteenth century, an ecclesiastical report from Rio de Janeiro described the "*Tambes* of deceased Negroes of the city." The "*tambes*" of Rio de Janeiro were remarkably similar to the Imbangala *tambo* described by Cavazzi. The Brazilian variant took place in the slave quarters (*senzalas*) and consisted of large gatherings of slaves "with their *atabaques* (conical drums, played between the legs), *engomas* (large, standing drums), and other instruments." Just as in Angola, the slaves ate and drank, and the ceremony was presided over by a "*feiticeiro* who assumes various practices." The Catholic priest who lodged the report viewed the *tambes* through a sexual prism, noting that the slaves cohabited "indiscriminately" and that "one finds some licentious whites" at these affairs.[60]

Whether or not people had sexual liaisons at these funeral parties is probably unimportant. Certainly, the *tambes* provided a rare opportunity for slaves to socialize "freely," but the deeper meanings of the *tambes* should not be lost behind the priest's moralistic clamor. Central African slaves required these elaborate funeral ceremonies to appease the spirits of the deceased. Otherwise, angry spirits would return, spreading more of the death, disease, and suffering that were already rampant in most slave communities.

The third ritual, allegedly of Angolan origin, involved the recovery of missing persons. It was believed that if one tied certain cords or a piece of clothing of a missing person to the door through which he left, he would soon return.[61] This belief was very much in accordance with the Kongolese practice of *kanga*, the harnessing of power through symbolic binding or tying.[62] In Brazil, the ritual most often was used to recover runaway slaves. For example, in the 1690s, a slave of Captain Domingos Pinto Ferrás ran away from his home in Bahia. The captain's wife, Maria Pereira, moored a piece of cloth that belonged to the runaway slave to the back door of their house. Two days later, the slave returned to his master, who attributed the slave's speedy return to his wife's ritual.[63]

Bolsas, Mandingas, and Other Talismans from the "Guinea" Coast

By the end of the seventeenth century and well into the eighteenth century, the most popular and widely used talisman in the African-Portuguese diaspora was the *bolsa de mandinga. Bolsas* could be found in almost every corner of the African-Portuguese world, from Bahia to Madeira, from Mazagão, North Africa, to India.[64] Typically, the *bolsa* was a pouch made of cloth or leather that was worn around the neck or other parts of the body on a cord or string. Inside the pouch could be any number of substances, including folded pieces of paper with Christian orations written on them, rocks, sticks, roots, bones, hairs, animal skins, feathers, powders, consecrated particles, and so on. The various combinations of substances were prescriptions that were designed to help the wearers in their everyday affairs.

Each *bolsa* had its own virtues. Some protected the wearer from the master's beatings. Others assured victories in games. And still others had the power to help slaves escape from bondage.[65] But by far the most common form of *bolsa* was one that protected slaves in quarrels. These *bolsas* had the virtue not only of protecting from fistic blows, but they also made the wearer impervious to knives, swords, and even gunshots.

While similar pouches of substances were used by Europeans as far back as the Middle Ages, the proliferation of *bolsas* in the Portuguese world dur-

Fruit vendor with *bolsas de mandinga* around her neck and hanging from her belt, Rio de Janeiro, ca. 1776. *Bolsas* were small pouches, usually worn around the neck, that contained powerful substances from the natural world—leaves, hair, teeth, powders, and the like. Each *bolsa* had its own distinct powers, but the most common ones were believed to protect the wearer from bodily injury, even knife thrusts and bullets. Painting by Carlos Julião, *Riscos Iluminados de Figurinhos Brancos e Negros dos Uzos do Rio de Janeiro e Serro do Frio* (Rio de Janeiro: Biblioteca Nacional, 1960), pl. XXXIII.

ing the eighteenth century can be attributed primarily to Africans, particularly those from what the Portuguese called the "Guinea" and "Mina" coasts.[66] The use of the term *bolsa de mandinga* makes clear that African *bolsas* were to be distinguished from those that might be more familiar to the Portuguese. The first documented mention of Mandingo *bolsas* comes from the Jesuit Father Balthezar Barreira. In a long description of the Guinea coast written in 1606, Barreira related the practices of the Mandingos, including the use of *bolsas*: "They follow the sect of Mohammed . . . they have mosques and schools of reading and writing and many priests (*casizes*) who carry this plague to other reigns from the band in the south, tricking the people with *bolsas* that they make with metal and of very well-cured leather, in which they put writings full of lies, affirming that having these *bolsas* with you, neither in war, nor in peace, will anything bad happen [to you]."[67] Barreira's quote reveals that the Mandingo used *bolsas* in their attempts to proselytize among non-Muslims on the Guinea coast. The "lies" that were inside the *bolsas* were Islamic prayers and orations drawn from the Koran. These prayers likely were put inside *bolsas* that already contained other powerful substances. As Islamic scholars moved across the region, *bolsas* with Islamic prayers were spread "to other reigns," eventually becoming prevalent across much of West Africa.

By the middle of the seventeenth century, Mandingo remedies similar to the *bolsas* described by Father Barreira were already being used by the mixed-race Afro-Portuguese community around the port of Cacheu, Guinea. In 1656, Crispina Peres Banhu, a *parda* (mixed-race) woman, was having a difficult childbirth in Cacheu. To relieve her suffering and initiate the birth, Ambrósio Gomes, a white man, tied some cords of black and white cotton around her waist and arm. Reportedly, these cords were those that "the Negro Mandingas were accustomed to bringing . . . and they have them for their relics." Ambrósio told Crispina that "he used the same cords in order not to be injured in war." In addition to the cords, Ambrósio gave Crispina some powders with water, which she drank. The combination of the cords and the drink facilitated the birth of Crispina's baby. Once the child was born, Ambrósio removed the cords from one of Crispina's arms and tied them around her other arm. He told her that she should leave the cords attached until her baby walked. When the baby finally walked, Ambrósio returned and removed the cords, collecting a goat as payment for his remedies.[68]

One of the first recorded cases of a slave using a *bolsa* in the African-Portuguese diaspora occurred in Lisbon in 1673, but at this early juncture, the offending pouch was still called a *bolsa*, and not a *bolsa de mandinga*. A "negro" slave named Manuel was denounced by a cleric named Miguel Gomes da Rama. Gomes da Rama said that some time around May 1672, Manuel was collecting water at the public fountain when he got into a fight with a soldier who was on guard. The soldier tried to stab Manuel, but Manuel dodged the soldier's thrust. Manuel taunted the soldier, telling him that he should go ahead and stab him, but the soldier refused. Gomes da Rama, who witnessed the incident, later asked Manuel what he would have done if the soldier had actually stabbed him. Manuel responded that if he were stabbed, the dagger "would not do any damage because the dagger would bend and would not enter." Gomes da Rama asked him how this could be, and Manuel held up one of his arms. Tied to his wrist was "a sewn piece that appeared . . . to have something inside of it." Manuel said that the pouch protected him from harm, and that if Gomes da Rama wanted to bet on its effectiveness, he would gladly bet five or six *tostois*[69] that no knife could penetrate him. Gomes da Rama declined Manuel's offer and concluded that he must be a *feiticeiro*. As further evidence, Gomes da Rama testified that on the island of Madeira, where Manuel had worked before arriving in Lisbon, he was renowned for putting his sword on the ground with the blade facing upward. With the point of the sword against his chest, Manuel would throw himself on top of the sword, and the sword would double without entering his body.[70]

By the turn of the eighteenth century, the virtues of African *bolsas* were becoming well-known in Lisbon, and the African character of these pouches was beginning to be emphasized. Public demonstrations, like the one offered by Manuel, had become commonplace, and some slaves had a thriving business selling *bolsas* to blacks and whites alike.[71] For instance, in 1700, a Cape Verdean slave named Francisco sold a variety of *bolsas* to white men in Lisbon. Francisco's *bolsas* not only protected the wearer from injury in fights, but he could also make ones that ensured victory in games or guaranteed that the wearer could attract any woman he might want.[72]

In the letter to the Inquisitorial prosecutor (*promotor*) that was included with Francisco's denunciation, the priest who heard the denunciation made an explicit link between African beliefs and witchcraft. In describing Francisco's *bolsas*, the priest wrote: "One presumes the likelihood of a pact with the Devil, [since] the said *bolsas* come to him from his homeland [Cape Verde] . . . and it is quite safe to presume the frequency of *feitiçarias* that there are among that caste of people."[73] In other words, because Francisco was a black African, his *bolsas* and their powers were automatically assumed to be the work of the Devil. The *bolsas* that were well-known in medieval Europe were being transformed into the *bolsas de mandinga* that were the work of Africans, agents for the Devil.

During the first half of the eighteenth century, although *bolsas de mandinga* took on their own distinct "diabolical" character, they remained common among all castes of people in the Portuguese world. In Angola, a white soldier gave an Angolan soldier, Vicente de Morais, a *bolsa* that was to "free one from dangers." Doubting the authenticity of the *bolsa* that was given to him by the white man, Vicente decided to perform an experiment to see if it would work. He put the *bolsa* around the neck of a stray dog and shot him with his pistol. The dog was not injured, leading Vicente to conclude that "the *bolsa* was Mandinga."[74]

Perhaps the clearest indication of the proliferation of *bolsas de mandinga* in the African-Portuguese diaspora comes from a series of cases from the late 1720s and early 1730s. During this period, a number of well-traveled slaves were denounced for using *bolsas de mandinga* in both Portugal and Brazil. From just a handful of Inquisition cases, an intricate web of relationships and exchanges between dozens of African *mandingueiros* (manufacturers of *bolsas de mandinga*) emerges. In 1729, Luís de Lima, who was born on the Ouidah (Judá) coast in Dahomey, confessed to using *bolsas* in Brazil (Pernambuco) and Portugal (Porto). Luís proclaimed that he "never felt fear of anything" when wearing his *bolsa de mandinga*. He also said that he had been stabbed on numerous occasions and never been injured. In his confession, Luís named twenty-six other slaves, many of them also Africans from the Mina coast, who used *bolsas* or other "*mandingas*." The majority of those named in Luís's confession had spent some time in Brazil before going to Portugal with their masters.[75]

Among those named in Luís's confession was his friend Manuel de Piedade, a Bahian-born slave who was jailed in Lisbon in 1730. Manuel had run away from his ship-captain master in Porto. After five slaves denounced him before the tribunal in Coimbra, Manuel was jailed in Lisbon for being a *mandingueiro*. His most serious crime was selling the ingredients and materials needed to manufacture *bolsas de mandinga*. He was alleged to have prepared the ingredients in the countryside, outside of the cities in which he lived, in concert with the Devil.[76]

Only one year later, two more Africans, both from the Dahomean slave port at Ouidah, were processed for being *mandingueiros*. José Francisco Pedroso and José Francisco Pereira were the slaves of two brothers who lived in Lisbon. They were accused of manufacturing and selling *bolsas de mandinga* to various people in and around Lisbon, but both were suspected of bringing their knowledge of "witchcraft" from Brazil, "in whose state there is frequent use of *mandingas*." Like Luís de Lima in Coimbra, José Francisco Pedroso named five accomplices, all of whom had connections to Brazil. Pedroso himself had lived for some time in Rio de Janeiro and claimed that there were many other *mandingueiros* whose names he could not remember.[77]

The threads that tied all of these *mandingueiros* together, besides their personal connections, were their common origins and enslavement in Brazil. The majority departed from the Mina coast of Africa, and more specifically the Portuguese fort at Ouidah, which was established in 1721. It seems quite possible that some of these men knew each other even prior to their departure from the African coast, although there is no direct evidence to support such a connection. When they arrived in Brazil, they entered a colonial world that, in the view of metropolitan Portuguese, was teeming with human "savages" — Native Americans, Africans, and even colonial whites. Witchcraft was believed to be widespread, much of it of African origin. In 1714, Father Manuel Carvalho wrote that "generally in that land, one uses *feitiçarias*, *mandingas*, *cartas de tocar* ["touch letters"], and superstitious cures with words for many ailments, and in the *sertões* [hinterlands], to cure cattle. And the *quibangos* [are used] in order to divine who made thefts and some things of the future, everything done with publicity."[78] From the Portuguese perspective, Brazil truly was a dangerous place, populated by innumerable witches who were the very embodiment of the Devil.[79]

Once these Mina slaves arrived in Lisbon, they were suspected of witchcraft, not only by virtue of their blackness and Africanness, but also by their ties to Brazil. To some extent, Portuguese suspicions may have been correct, especially if "witchcraft" was understood as a sustained religious opposition to slavery. The common experiences of these Mina slaves, from Africa to Brazil to Portugal, forged a sense of oneness among them that transcended geographical boundaries. No matter where they were in the African-Portuguese diaspora, these slaves sought one another out and exchanged religious remedies that directly addressed the hardships that arose from their slavery.

We have already seen how *bolsas* worked as armor against knives and guns, but *bolsas* and other *mandingas*[80] were also used to escape the blows of slavery. Some slaves went to great lengths to avoid their master's abuses. In the 1720s, a slave named José bought a series of *mandingas* that were aimed at his violent master in Porto. First, he bought a tooth that would allow him to run away from his master. This remedy apparently failed. Later, he went to another slave, the aforementioned Luís de Lima, and bought a prescription that would compel his master to sell him. This remedy was highly effective, as José's master informed him that he indeed planned to sell him away. But fearing that his next master would be equally vicious, José again sought the help of the *mandingueiro* Luís de Lima. Using a string of shells, de Lima divined that José would have greater success in his new master's house, which he did.[81]

Other slaves used their *bolsas de mandinga* to protect themselves from the master's whip. In 1732, a Lisbon slave named Antônio de Sousa reacted with

contempt when his master punished him "very roughly." Antônio was protected by a blue cloth *bolsa* filled with red feathers "of some bird from Brazil,"
a piece of bull horn, and some little pieces of white paper.[82] Five years later,
also in Lisbon, a slave named Domingos offered João Angola a *mandinga* that
allowed its owner to open locked doors and exit through them without being
noticed. Using this *mandinga*, Domingos told João that he could run away
from his master.[83]

Similarly, around 1742, on the *fazenda* of Olho de Peixe in the *sertão* (hinterlands) of the village of Jacobina, Archbishopric of Bahia, an Angolan slave
named João da Silva aided a runaway slave named Manuel de Barros. Manuel
was on his way from the *sertão* to the city of Salvador, when he stopped over
at Olho de Peixe. João offered him some food to sustain him for the rest of
his journey. As a token of thanks, Manuel gave João a leather *bolsa* that had
the power to free him from his servitude. João never capitalized on the alleged power of the *bolsa*. In fact, he showed it to several white people, asking
them if it would be good to carry the *bolsa* around his neck. A cattle rancher
opened the *bolsa* and told João that it contained various ingredients, including the oration of San Marcos. Eventually, João was betrayed by a young girl
named Teresa. He was called before Padre João Mendes, vicar of the Freguesia
of Santo Antônio da Jacobina. The vicar opened the *bolsa*, revealing a square-
shaped rock, a piece of garlic, two pieces of lead, a piece of consecrated host,
and the oration of San Marcos. Ultimately, João was remitted to Lisbon, where
he was sentenced to appear before the auto da fé, publicly whipped, and exiled
for four years to the Portuguese Algarve.[84]

The presence of Christian orations inside many *bolsas de mandinga* should
not draw our attention away from the deeper meanings of the *bolsas*. Just as the
original *bolsas* used by Muslims on the Guinea coast contained Arabic scripts
from the Koran, many *bolsas de mandinga* in the Portuguese world had writings and orations from the Bible and Catholicism. This does not necessarily
indicate that the users of the *bolsas* were integrating Muslim or Christian theology into their spiritual world. We must remember that most non-Muslims in
Africa and most slaves in the Portuguese world were illiterate. If those carrying the *bolsas de mandinga* were even aware that the scrawl on the paper were
words to be read, the power of the orations was probably not in what they
said. Rather, the power most likely resided in the magic of the words themselves.

For many illiterate peoples, the written word literally seemed to "speak"
to those doing the reading. African slaves, many of whom did not speak the
languages of their captors, were astonished and amazed when they first encountered these papers and books that could "talk." In one of the first slave

narratives ever published, James Albert Ukawsaw Gronniosaw described his first encounters with the written word. Gronniosaw, who grew up in Bournou, the "chief city" of the Kingdom of Zaara, was first enslaved by the Dutch. He explained his understanding of the strange and magical texts that were read by his first master:

> [My master] used to read prayers in public to the ship's crew every Sabbath day; and when I first saw him read, I was never so surprised in my life, as when I saw the book talk to my master, for I thought it did, as I observed him to look upon it, and move his lips. I wished it would do so with me. As soon as my master had done reading, I followed him to the place where he put the book, being mightily delighted with it, and when nobody saw me, I opened it, and put my ear down close upon it, in great hopes that it would say something to me; but I was very sorry, and greatly disappointed, when I found that it would not speak.[85]

Gronniosaw was not the only African who believed that books could speak. Other Africans, including the well-known Olaudah Equiano, believed similarly.[86]

For the majority of African slaves, literacy remained elusive, and the written word probably maintained its mysterious and magical quality throughout their lives. The Christian orations that were placed in *bolsas de mandinga* can therefore be understood in much the same way that we understand other powerful objects that were put in *bolsas*. The written word was a magical talisman that provided powerful protection, perhaps drawing its power from Christ or the Catholic saints, but more likely getting its strength from the world of the dead. Inanimate objects (papers or books) that had the capacity to "talk" could get their "voice" only from the spirit world. To harness these voices and carry them in a pouch was powerful medicine indeed.

In the last three chapters, we have attempted to demonstrate the variety of religious responses by Africans and their descendants to the conditions of their enslavement. In the process, we have shown how African religious ideas were transformed as a result of these brutal conditions. This does not mean that the African lens was abandoned, or even that particular ethnic rituals were abandoned. To the contrary, many of the Kongolese, Mbata, Ndembu, Imbangala, Arda, and Mina remedies remained virtually the same from Africa to Europe and the Americas. But the symptoms of misfortune were radically changed with enslavement by the Portuguese. The obstacles to everyday survival grew, and the struggle to maintain one's sense of humanity intensified. These harsh new conditions required a more forceful response, an expanded assault on the new forms of evil that were enslaving so many Africans and carrying them to their deaths in the *tumbeiros* (floating tombs) of the Middle Passage, or in the mines and cane fields of Brazil. While the content of African religious practices remained remarkably similar in the Portuguese colonial world, the temporal goals of these rituals and beliefs shifted in accordance with the challenges presented by slavery.

Much of what the Portuguese called witchcraft were desperate attempts to resist the hardships of slavery that we discussed in the first three chapters — death, disease, illness, gender imbalance, community instability, and abuses by masters. Slaves used divination, medicine, and other forms of so-called witchcraft to address these new and unfamiliar social ills. African forms of divination shed light on those "malevolent" slaves and freedmen who challenged the social or economic norms of the slave community. Divinations also were used to free Africans from "guilt" and to hold whites responsible for certain crimes. African cures addressed the wide range of new diseases and social illnesses that were encountered in the diaspora. And finally, this so-called African witchcraft was utilized as a tool of outright resistance, as slaves maimed and killed the master, his loved ones, and his property (human and animal). In short, the mental horizon of African religion was necessarily expanded to meet the needs of a slave community that was constantly under siege.

If African religion was to some extent re-created and recast by the conditions of slavery, then the Portuguese were equally as adaptable in their re-creation of witchcraft as an archetypical African form. Rituals of witchcraft that had distinct European and Portuguese provenance were inexplicably transformed into African rituals. The Portuguese "*peneira*," the scissor-and-sieve divination, was converted to the Central African *quibando* divination ritual, just as Portuguese *bolsas* became *bolsas de mandinga*. It was not enough that the "heathen" practices of Africans already put them in alliance with the Devil. The Portuguese reinforced African "Otherness" by reinventing their own forms of "savagery" and giving them an African veneer. This dialectic between racism and witchcraft changed the meanings of Portuguese witchcraft and hardened racial attitudes. As Michael Taussig notes, in the colonial worlds, witchcraft and magic functioned as "a gathering point for Otherness in a series of racial and class differentiations embedded in the distinctions made between Church and magic, and science and magic . . . [an] Otherness in which savagery and racism [were] tightly knotted."[87] Race and culture became fused, as Africans became the receptacle for all things savage.

In spite of — or perhaps because of — the increased marginalization of Africans as dangerous, exotic savages, many Luso-Brazilians began affirming and even employing African forms of religious power. We have already shown how individual Portuguese used African divinations and cures to address their own temporal concerns. We have also shown how African witchcraft could wreak havoc in Brazilian slave communities. But African religious power transcended specific individuals and communities, penetrating into the deepest crevices of some of the most sacred Portuguese institutions, including the Catholic Church. In the next two chapters, we will look more closely at how African religions adapted to the challenges of Catholicism and examine, in turn, the impact of African religious culture on the Catholic Church in Brazil.

PART THREE

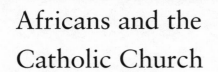

Africans and the
Catholic Church

CHAPTER NINE

African Catholicism
in the Portuguese World

Despite the tenacity of many African religious beliefs, Catholicism did make some headway in the African communities of the Portuguese colonial world. Still, we must be careful not to overstate the pace of conversion to a more creolized and Christianized population among Africans and their descendants. The embrace of Catholicism among Africans was slow and uneven. And even where we see apparent evidence of devout expressions of Christian faith, often we can still find elements of the African religious past operating alongside Christian practices. In this chapter, we examine the impact of Catholicism on the lives of Africans in the Portuguese colonial world, with particular attention given to the Brazilian context. Just as Africans gradually embraced certain elements of the Catholic faith, they also transformed the Brazilian Church, putting an indelible African mark on the religious landscape of colonial Brazil.

Becoming a Christian, Becoming a Slave:
The African Background

The earliest widespread conversions of sub-Saharan Africans in the Portuguese colonial world occurred in Kongo. From as early as the fifteenth century, a distinctly African form of Catholicism was practiced among the Kongolese elite. Over time, Catholic beliefs and practices spread to the common people of Kongo, as missionaries, indigenous clergy, and lay preachers fanned across the region, proselytizing in even the smallest villages. In rural

Catholic mass celebrated in Kongo, ca. 1750. Watercolor by Father Bernardino Ignazio da Vezza, "Missione prattica [dei] Padri cappuccinni ne' Regni di Congo, Angola, et adiacenti," Biblioteca civica centrale di Torino, MS 457.

areas, people might see a lay preacher only once a year. Nevertheless, many were familiar with the rudimentary practices and prayers of the faith and met regularly on Saturdays to say the rosary.[1]

Despite the Catholic veneer that many Kongolese displayed, the depth of their understanding of things Catholic remains unclear. As noted in Chapter 5, the cosmological worlds of the Kongolese and the Catholics were very different. As a result, most Kongolese viewed Catholicism through their own distinct spiritual and cultural prisms, only gradually grasping the meaning of the Christian cosmos. Where contact between clergy and laity was irregular, the tenets of Christianity probably remained only a peripheral concern. European priests frequently made references to Kongolese "errors" in their understanding of the Catholic faith. In some instances, not even the indigenous African clergy adhered to Catholic precepts, thereby raising questions about the form and function of Catholic beliefs and practices as they filtered down to ordinary parishioners.

For example, in 1718 a Capuchin missionary denounced Father Miguel da Silva, a Kongo-born priest, who "had great disregard for Our Holy Catholic

Faith and [who] abused the sacraments." Among other things, Father da Silva was accused of marrying couples who for many years had lived together outside of Holy Matrimony. Father da Silva's error was not that he married these couples but that he failed to make them confess the sins of their "illicit relationships" before performing the marriage ceremony. In the view of Father da Silva and the couples he was marrying, these relationships probably were not sinful. Therefore, confession was deemed unnecessary.

When Father da Silva heard confessions, he did so in his house, with "the penitents on one side and on the other . . . a quantity of people with whom the confessor [was] conversing." Because of the large gathering, the distractions, and the "confusion of voices," Father da Silva heard only two or three sins from each confessant, and "without more exam or attention," he absolved each person. As penance, the confessants gathered in a group and, taking turns with a large staff, each one publicly beat himself, reciting his sins — "I was at the place of the *feitiços*. I ate meat on Friday. I broke the sixth commandment," and so on.[2]

On the one hand, it is clear that the basic sacraments were administered by Father da Silva. As such, there is no doubt that his followers were Christians. On the other hand, we have no clear sense of how his flock interpreted the Christian ceremonies that they performed. Apparently, Father da Silva's sacraments were naturalized to adhere to Kongolese cultural understandings. At the very least, it appears that Catholic confession was integrated into a broader communal critique of individual transgressions. Father da Silva consulted others, perhaps even community elders, as he heard people confess their sins. And the penance was performed in a broad setting for all to see. Just like the meanings of God (*nzambi mpungu*), the saints (ancestors or *kitekes*), and the cross (cosmogram), the sacraments very likely were understood within the context of Kongolese cosmology.

For Angolans, religious beliefs operated in a similar fashion to those in Kongo. Some Angolans, like the slaves of the Jesuit College in Luanda, probably embraced elements of Catholicism, perhaps even grasping such abstract theological notions as the Trinity. Nevertheless, many of these slaves continued to worship ancestral spirits alongside the Christian God. For example, in 1698, a thirty-year-old slave named Gregório Pascoal, whose parents also had been the property of the Jesuit College, confessed that he assisted more than thirty other Angolans in the sacrifice of a goat. The sacrifice was made "in veneration of a deceased person." Similarly, Caterina Borges confessed that she and her two daughters bathed her deceased granddaughter in water fortified with a variety of herbs. The herbal bath was made to ensure "that the soul of the dead would not return . . . and without this ceremony, they believed that the soul would appear and make them sick." Both Gregório Pascoal and Caterina Borges continued to believe in the temporal power of ancestral spirits, even as they claimed that they "never had a pact with the devil, nor did [they] part with the Catholic faith."[3]

These confessions demonstrate two important points. On the one hand, Gregório and Caterina recognized the necessity of voluntarily confessing their "sins," indicating a clear understanding that the church viewed their behaviors as violations of the faith. On the other hand, there was no remorse or willingness to abandon these beliefs and practices. Gregório and Caterina both pointed out in their confessions that these rituals were "custom" among their people. Thus, these confessions stand as a statement of the duality of Angolan religious beliefs. Angolans continued to hold on to their traditional beliefs and practices, even as some of them proclaimed an allegiance to the Catholic faith.

Expressions of allegiance to Catholicism took a variety of forms in Angola, depending largely on the amount of exposure one had to Catholic teachings. In urban coastal areas like Luanda, where the permanent presence of the church and its missionaries ensured frequent reinforcement of Catholic instruction, Angolans probably gained a more thorough understanding of the Catholic faith and its principles, even though most refused to abandon their traditional beliefs. In the rural hinterlands, the understanding of Catholicism was far less complete. For example, in the mid-seventeenth century, Father Antônio Romano was on a mission in the province of Kisama, where he sought to deliver the *soba* (village headman) Malumba a Cambolo from his "paganism." Upon offering the *soba* baptism, Father Romano learned that the *soba* had already been baptized some years earlier. When Father Romano reminded the *soba* that it was his duty to protect the law of God and the church, the *soba* replied that he was not concerned about Christian salvation and that "he wanted to go where his ancestors were." To which Father Romano replied, "[They are] in hell, burning in the infernal fire with the demons for eternity." Unbowed by the threat of eternal damnation, and unwilling to surrender his ancestral ties, the *soba* responded that "thus, he wanted to go there where they were." For Malumba a Cambolo, going to hell with his ancestors was preferable to going to heaven with the Christian God.[4]

Other Central Africans simply integrated the Christian God into their own pantheon of deities, without acknowledging his supremacy. In 1752, Sebastião Fernandes Correa, also a native of the province of Kisama, was arrested and sent to Luanda for questioning. Correa was accused of maintaining an "idol house" in the hinterlands near Golungo, where he was apparently involved in the slave trade. Before burning the idol house in question, the arresting soldier ordered a search of its contents. Among the "idols" found inside, he reported, was an image of Jesus Christ that was "scratched up, not being very smooth from so much use, through being worn around the neck and through lasciviousness." Correa probably utilized this image of Jesus as an ancestral spirit, represented in the form of a *kiteke* idol and worshipped just like any other ancestral spirit, through a variety of offerings and rituals that made the idol appear worn. By integrating Jesus into the pantheon of venerated ancestors, Correa acknowledged the power of the Christian savior. But because the statue of Jesus was found among indigenous statues on Correa's altar, the Catholic Church judged him to be a heretic. According to Correa's worldview, his embrace of Jesus very likely made him a Christian. However, the Catholic Church simply could not recognize his faith.[5]

Among the many misinterpretations that plagued the relationship between Europeans and Central Africans, perhaps the most significant was the one involving the Catholic sacrament of baptism. There is a great deal of evidence that Central Africans equated baptism with the simple act of eating salt. As part of the baptismal ceremony, Catholic priests placed a piece of salt on the tongues of their African converts. Since baptism functioned as the initiation into the Christian fold, many Central Africans recognized taking salt as the primary symbol of their Christianity. Other sacraments like marriage, confession, and the administration of Last Rites were usually rare occurrences in Central Africa, since there were so few priests. But people demanded "to eat salt" with great fervor. As Catholic priests entered Kongolese towns, mobs of people would demand to be given salt. If there were delays, the Kongolese would become restless, threatening the priests with bodily harm and forcing them to perform the ceremony.[6]

When mission priests were slow to offer baptismal salt in Mbata in the mid-seventeenth century, some of the most impatient residents returned to their houses in disgust, spreading "false accusations" against the priests. Others complained that they did not understand the need for religious instruction, "as if the grace of baptism was an exterior and material thing." Still other residents directly interrogated the priests, asking, "Why so many cautions and so many exams about the seriousness of our purposes and about what we are obliged to believe? Did we not come voluntarily? Did we not arrive here to eat all the salt that you give us, like the other whites? Why and for what are there so many difficulties?"[7]

The priests probably said more than they knew when they accused the residents of Mbata of believing that baptism was an "exterior and material thing." In Kongolese traditional belief, salt was thought to be a repellent of evil people and spirits.[8] Thus, it was believed that evil could be avoided through Christian baptism, or eating salt. Whether salt was understood to ward off evil prior to contact with Christianity remains unclear. It very well may have been another creation of the instability and uncertainty that arose from contacts with the Portuguese. The Kongolese easily could have interpreted the baptismal salt as the essence of European witchcraft and spiritual power. To be "like the other whites," with their economic and social power, meant embracing their most potent religious ritual: baptism.[9]

Regardless the origins of Kongolese belief, it is clear that during the era of the slave trade, most Kongolese understood baptism simply as the taking of salt (*yadia mungwa*). European clergymen were very much aware of this fact, and they recognized that the "impropriety of language does not cease to be a danger." Father Cavazzi wrote, "to remove from the mind of the indigenous ones an error of such consequences, the Capuchins attempted to substitute the words '*cudia mungua*,' which means 'to eat salt,' with the words '*lusuculu-lunguisi*,' which means 'sacred bath,' and they took care to teach them not only the manner of administering, in case of necessity, this sacrament, but also of what its essence consists."[10] Despite attempts on the part of European Catholics to recast the meaning of baptism, some indigenous priests continued using *only* salt in their baptisms, omitting all of the other ceremonies. In the early 1700s, Father Miguel da Silva, the Kongolese priest accused of performing improper marriages and confessions, baptized hundreds of people in this fashion in the Kongolese territories of "Tumbi, Lemba, Sumbi, Guimenga, Boya, and Matari."[11] Thus, baptism continued to be associated with eating salt well into the eighteenth century.

The point of this discussion on the relationship between baptism, salt, and witchcraft is to demonstrate yet again how Central Africans interpreted Christian rituals through their own cosmological lens. Baptism (eating salt) was understood as an external protection against the evils that plagued Africans. It was very much a temporal remedy, not a prescription for eternal salvation and the washing away of sin. For those who were then or later enslaved, these were the so-called Christian beliefs that they carried with them to the African coast and on to the Americas. The rituals and practices of Christianity were often understood as just one more form of powerful medicine.

The links between witchcraft, spiritual power, and Christian ritual become even more clear when one examines the responses of Central African slaves to their mass baptisms on the coast of Luanda prior to embarkation for the Americas. During the early seventeenth century, slaves were gathered together in the church or main plaza one day before departing Luanda. As many as 700 slaves might be baptized in a matter of three or four hours. The priests did not catechize or even teach the slaves who the Christian God was. They instead followed a three-step process: first, they went to each slave and told him his Christian name, writing it down for him so that he would not "forget"; second, they put salt in the mouth of each slave; and finally, they put water on the heads of the slaves. Thus, the baptism was complete.[12]

When these slaves arrived in the Americas and were asked how they understood their baptisms and the washing of their heads, they responded in the language of witchcraft and power. Some slaves quite literally said that they thought of their baptism as a "thing of witchcraft" in order for the Europeans "to eat them." Others responded that the ceremonies were to prevent them from having sex with the slave women during the Middle Passage. Others believed that the water would protect them from illness. And still others thought that the water was to "enchant" them so that they would not rise against the whites on board the ship. None of the slaves understood their baptism as a washing away of sin.[13] Thus, for the majority of Central Africans, their first exposures to Christian rituals were seen through the prism of their temporal misfortunes. Enslavement was a pernicious form of witchcraft, and Christian rituals, particularly baptismal water, were understood as a means of further ensuring the European "enchantment" or power over Africans.

The Catholic Ministry in Brazil

Though some historians have shown how Kongolese slaves continued to practice Africanized forms of Christianity in the diaspora, I have found only scattered evidence that Central Africans brought Christian beliefs with them from Africa to Brazil.[14] Indeed, in all of my research, I have encountered only one short passage that suggests a strong connection between Central African Christianity and Brazilian slave Christianity. The passage comes from the chronicle of an Italian Capuchin missionary, Dionigio de Carli, who traveled from Europe to Brazil and then on to Central Africa in the 1660s. When de Carli arrived in Pernambuco in 1666, he described a black woman who knelt before him, beating her breast, and clapping the ground with her hands. Inquiring as to the reason for the woman's strange behavior, de Carli was told by a Portuguese observer: "Father . . . , she is of the kingdom of Congo, and was baptized by a Capuchin; and being informed you are going thither to baptize, she rejoices, and expresses her joy by those outward tokens."[15] How the Portuguese witness was able to interpret the Kongolese woman's behavior is not altogether clear in the source; however, even if we take his explanation at face value, we must balance this woman's expression of devotion against other, overwhelming evidence that suggests a more incomplete Christianization of Central African slaves in Brazil.

Although some African Christians were arriving in the Americas as slaves, evidence from Central Africa suggests that, in fact, many of them had a very limited understanding of the Christian faith. We have already shown that church policy on the African coast included mass baptisms for departing slaves, an implicit admission on the part of the Catholic clergy that the majority of these Africans had *not* been baptized previously. We have also shown that many slaves who arrived in the Americas understood neither the content nor the meaning of their baptism on the African coast, yet another indication that Christianity had not taken firm root. Finally, the Catholic Church in Central Africa had a standing policy of condemning suspected "witches" to slavery in Brazil. The Capuchin priests Father Cavazzi and Father Merolla each described instances in which they condemned Central African diviners and healers to slavery in Brazil.[16] In addition, Africans themselves were known to sell "witches" into the slave trade. Thus, a disproportionate number of African diviner/healers probably found their way into the slave population of Brazil, thereby exaggerating their influence among Brazil's slaves and diminishing the impact of African Christians. Indeed, throughout this period, Catholic priests and missionaries in Brazil noted glaring inadequacies in the religious instruction of most slaves. Not only did most Africans arrive in Brazil unfamiliar with the most basic Christian precepts, but many of them remained in that condition for many years.

During the earliest years of African slavery in Brazil, language was the most formidable obstacle to the effective proselytization of the slave population. Until around 1620, the language barrier prevented European priests from administering the sacraments in a fashion that was remotely comprehensible to the majority of African slaves. As early as 1583, Father Cristóvão Gouveia noted, "The Padres go on continuous missions to the *ingenios* (sugar plantations) . . . [around Olinda] where they catechize, baptize, and attend to other extreme necessities, not only for the Portuguese, but principally for the slaves from Guinea who are almost 15,000 and for the Indians who are almost 3,000 . . . and as the clerics do not understand, nor know their languages, they are not able to help them as they should."[17]

This situation persisted into the seventeenth century, when large numbers of Angolan slaves began arriving into the Brazilian northeast. In a 1617 report from the Jesuit missions to the Recôncavo of Bahia, the missionaries complained that the Angolans arrived with no religious instruction and that the Brazilian priests were ill-equipped to administer to the newly arrived slaves. The missionaries reported:

> Firstly, the people from Angola who come to these parts of Brazil are mostly unenlightened in the doctrine and the things that pertain to their salvation.

Because at present, almost all of the people are new who are put on the *fazendas* and *engenhos*, and the majority of *ladinos* [acculturated Africans] and old ones are dead from smallpox and measles. . . . And as there are no priests who know their language who can teach them and administer the sacraments of matrimony, confession, and communion . . . they receive a great lack in everything necessary for their salvation. And even if they were baptized in Angola . . . rarely or never does one find that one knows what he received in the baptism and to what he is obligated to God, and they are totally ignorant of everything that pertains to the substance of the mysteries of Our Holy Faith; and thus with this blindness they persevere after coming from Angola among the Christians, and in the face of the Church for a space of many years, after being 4, 5, and 6 years in the house of their masters, without knowing what is necessary for them for their salvation.[18]

The Jesuits did their best to help bridge the language gap. During the same 1617 report, it was noted that some of the Jesuit missionaries were "very intelligent in the language of Angola" and had some successes in administering the sacraments to the Angolan slaves of the Recôncavo. Two years later in 1619, the Jesuit missionaries reported that they catechized nearly 9,000 souls, who "because they did not know the language [Portuguese], had gone five and six years without confession." The missionaries judged that prior to their arrival to administer the sacraments, these slaves went around as nothing more than "brute animals."[19] One year later, in 1620, another Jesuit, Father Simão Pinheiro, remarked that the College of Bahia was awaiting the arrival of two more Jesuits who were proficient in the "language of Angola." The two young clergymen were dispatched to Brazil by the Father Superior of Angola for the specific purpose of helping the order minister to Angolan slaves.[20]

In their attempts to reach out to Angolan slaves, the Catholic Church faced another problem that ultimately proved even more daunting and more persistent than linguistic barriers. Throughout the colonial period, there was an acute shortage of priests who could minister to the growing slave population, especially outside of the major coastal cities. The resident priests and missionaries pleaded for reinforcements, but their calls for help usually fell on deaf ears. In 1592, the Jesuit Father Gabriel Soares de Sousa requested that the order send more priests to Pernambuco to minister to the "many pretos from Angola who do not have another remedy for their souls without the padres of the order."[21] Nearly a century later, in 1671, the Jesuits in Bahia complained that because of the lack of priests, "so many souls suffer . . . [and there is a] great need because in these parts there is a multitude of pagans who come from the Reign of Angola, all of them lacking the Christian doctrine."[22]

Finally, in 1720, an urgent appeal was sent from Rio de Janeiro to the Inquisitor General and the King of Portugal requesting more priests. The letter argued that the souls of the "Negroes from Angola" were "hurling toward hell," and "the principal root of such errors is the pagan barbarity in which they live, without having instructors . . . who show them the true path to salvation."[23]

Increasing the numbers of priests might have helped alleviate the burdens of the overworked priests and missionaries who were already struggling to proselytize the slave population of Brazil, but numbers alone could not guarantee that the slaves would understand the substance of their religious "conversion." The cosmological gap between Europeans and Africans was far too great. Writing in the early 1700s, Father André João Antonil lamented the fact that baptized slaves "do not know who their creator is, what they are to believe, what law they are to protect, how they are to commit themselves to God, why Christians go to Church, why they adore the consecrated host." He also said that when slaves knelt to pray, they wanted to know "to whose ears" they were speaking. In addition, slaves wondered where their souls went when they left their bodies.[24] In short, African slaves were searching for temporal answers that were absent from Christian doctrine. Abstract concepts of "faith" had no place in their worldview.[25]

Some priests were aware of the great care that was needed to overcome the cosmological gap between Europeans and Africans. Converting Africans to Christianity would take more than a simple understanding of the rituals and the orations. It would take a complete cosmological reorientation. Jesuit Father Jorge Benci warned parish priests that "there is no point in the slaves saying how many people are in the Holy Trinity and praying the Credo and the Commandments and the other orations; but it is necessary that they understand what they say, that they perceive the mysteries of believing, and that the precepts penetrate well enough that they retain them." Father Benci implored the parish priests to explain themselves thoroughly and make certain that the slaves understood what they were being taught.[26]

As if the obstacles of language, cosmology, and chronic understaffing were not already enough to overcome, the Catholic clergy also found their conversion attempts thwarted by slave masters, who were often little concerned with their slaves' spiritual well-being. In the minds of most masters, time spent on religious instruction amounted to lost profits. Missionaries and priests argued that slaves should have at least Sundays and saint's days free from work so they could attend mass. In the early seventeenth century, many planters blatantly disregarded the church's wishes. In 1624, São Tomé sugar planter Francisco de Almeida was denounced for not allowing his slaves to hear mass on Sundays and saint's days. Adding insult to injury, Almeida's slaves worked next to the main path that led to the parish church, causing "notable scandal" to all of the passers-by.[27] In Bahia, during the same period, Jesuit missionaries suggested ways that planters could gradually shut down the sugar mill on saint's days and then reopen it at sunset so as to minimize losses. Still, some planters were willing to "break the commandments of God," forcing their slaves to work to make just "four more *tarefas* [quotas] of cane."[28]

By the middle of the seventeenth century, many masters allowed their slaves to have Sundays free, but in return, the slaves were expected to provide their own food and clothing. Thus, slaves spent their Sundays cultivating the small garden plots (*roças*) that their masters provided for this purpose. Predictably, the church was not pleased with this arrangement. Jesuit missionaries recognized that the lack of food and clothing meant that rather than attending mass, "when [the slaves] are left free on saint's days, they take advantage of these days by going to work on their *roças*, searching . . . for what to eat and for what to buy in order to clothe themselves." Some slave women were even forced into prostitution in order to feed and clothe themselves. The Jesuits complained that the policy of forcing slaves to feed and clothe themselves was a "pernicious" one that "seems law among the Masters, and it does not give them any unease of conscience." The priests appealed to the masters to provide for their slaves' material and spiritual necessities, leaving Sundays free for Christian worship.[29]

While many planters set aside Sundays for slaves to tend to their own material needs, others continued to make their slaves work through the Sabbath. By the eighteenth century, these planters had refined their arguments against providing Sundays as free days. In response to suggestions that their slaves should attend church on Sundays, masters contended that slaves would not use their free time to worship the Christian God. Rather, they would party, carouse, and worship their own gods—all in great offense to the Catholic Church. One slave owner summed up these sentiments most succinctly. When asked why he forced his slaves to work on Sundays, he answered: "There are two reasons: The first, because there are slaves who are sent to hear mass who intrude on other *fazendas* . . . where they engage in these reprehensible *calundús* and *feitiçarias*. The second reason is because when I send them to mass, they get drunk and quarrel mindlessly and cause great mischief. . . . I resolve that it is better judgment to give them maintenance and clothing, and occupy them, because it is also certain that the idle slave ordinarily creates vices and these result in the major offenses to God."[30]

This slave master no doubt had his own economic agenda in mind when he forced his slaves to work through the Sabbath, and his comments reveal a deep patriarchal condescension. But at the same time, his observations probably were not far off the mark. Zacharias Wagener, who lived in Dutch Brazil from 1634 to 1641, made similar observations regarding the slaves' use of their free days. He wrote: "When the slaves have worked hard for a whole week, they are given Sunday off. They usually assemble in specially designated places and spend the day in wild dancing to the sound of flutes and drums—men and women, children and old people alike. This is accompanied by frequent libations . . . often until they are too deafened and drunk to recognize one another."[31] For slaves who were given a choice about how to spend the Sabbath, the Catholic Church apparently had little appeal. Many slaves who were allowed to go to mass declined to do so. Instead, they used this time to tend to their religious needs in ways that resonated with their African pasts, worshiping their ancestors and other deities. They also took advantage of the rare free time to share drinks with friends (and ancestral spirits) outside of their master's purview.

In the final analysis, one must conclude that most African slaves in Brazil remained largely unaffected by the Catholic Church. The comments of two Jesuit missionaries in Pernambuco sum up the effects of the church's benign neglect of Africans. In 1689, they visited the engenhos of Cabo de São Agostinho, outside of Olinda. There, they "removed many souls from the state of perdition in which they were for many years, and they removed many errors and abuses, principally in the Angolan slaves in which predominated, in some, so much ignorance that they did not have anything more than the name of Christians."[32] Slaves who were Christian "in name only" committed many of the "errors and abuses" that we have discussed in the previous chapters—divination, "witchcraft," and curing. Though Catholic priests lamented the spiritual condition of the slaves, most Africans were probably thankful for the lack of church intervention in their lives. Left to their own devices, they could recreate many of the religious structures that sustained them in their homelands.

Christianity in the Diaspora

Where Christianization did make inroads in the African-Portuguese diaspora, the process occurred slowly and unevenly. In places like Portugal, where the African presence was always rather small, African religious beliefs probably faded rather quickly, as peoples of African descent were immersed in the teachings of the church and Portuguese society. Similarly, among Africans who were enslaved at a very young age, some were effectively creolized and became ardent Christians.[33] In most of Brazil, however, large numbers of slaves and a constant influx of Africans, combined with an institutionally weak church, led to a much more gradual and incomplete embrace of Catholic teachings. Once Africans and their descendants did begin to accept certain elements of Catholicism, it was not at the expense of their own cosmologies. Just as the Kongolese had done for hundreds of years in Africa, Brazilian slaves naturalized Catholicism, integrating many of its elements that coincided with their own worldviews. Building upon these symbolic resonances, Africans and their descendants created unique forms of Afro-Brazilian Catholicism. These distinctly African forms of Catholicism continued to be practiced in parallel with the more familiar African religions, never vanquishing the more clearly discernible African practices during the colonial period.

We have already noted some of the transformations that Africans imposed on Catholic forms, transformations like the meanings of baptism and the cross. But these were not the only Catholic symbols that were reshaped in the African mind. Africans changed the meanings of a variety of sacred symbols and institutions of the Catholic Church to conform to very specific African understandings. One of the most potent symbols in the African-Catholic world was the *pedra d'ara*, a piece of marble with an internal compartment filled with the relics of martyred saints. The *pedra d'ara* was believed to possess a magical power that was essential in realizing the mystery of the Holy Eucharist. The bread and wine used in communion were transubstantiated only after the priest consecrated them over the *pedra d'ara*. The *pedra d'ara* also served as a "portable altar" for priests who might say mass in some location outside of their home church. The priest carried the *pedra d'ara* with him and placed it on the table over which he said mass, thereby consecrating the table as a holy altar.[34]

The magical power of the *pedra d'ara* was quickly recognized by Africans, who turned it into one of the most sought-after talismans in the African-Portuguese world. Rocks and other objects from the natural world, especially those with cavities for harnessing the power of spirits or special medicines, were widely recognized in Africa as having strong magical powers. For those who were enslaved in the Portuguese colonial world, the *pedra d'ara* fit into the same category of powerful talismans. The fact that they were regarded as sacred by the Catholic Church probably only enhanced their value. Rather than approaching these religious relics with awe and veneration, Africans tried time and again to steal them from the altars of various churches in Portugal and Brazil, attempting to harness their power for their own religious and temporal needs.

Pieces of *pedra d'ara* were most commonly carried inside *bolsas de mandinga*, the necklace-like pouches described in the previous chapter. The *pedra* was just one of the ingredients that protected the owner of the *bolsa* from injury in quarrels or fights. As early as 1690, when a Cape Verdean was accused of carrying pieces of *pedra d'ara* in Lisbon, the prosecutor noted that there was "in this land universal scandal from committing this crime much indulged in by people similar to Negroes . . . [for which] this Mesa already has some denunciations."[35] The "sacrilege" of stealing *pedras d'ara* and using them for evil intents was already being most clearly associated with peoples of African descent.

By the eighteenth century, the *pedra d'ara* was a common ingredient in the *bolsas* that were transported throughout the Portuguese colonial world. Francisco, one of the conspirators in the 1729 *bolsa* web that extended across Brazil and Portugal, was accused of carrying pieces of *pedra d'ara*, the bone of a dead person, and several orations inside of a *bolsa* that he sold to Luís de Lima in Pernambuco. Luís de Lima then carried the *bolsa* to Porto, where he eventually passed it on to José da Costa. The demand for *pedras* continued in Porto. There, another slave named José, also a friend of Luís de Lima's, stole pieces of *pedra d'ara* from an altar and sold them as "*Mandingas*."[36]

Some African slaves also believed that pieces of the consecrated host were endowed with magical powers. In 1773, in the Brazilian mining town of Vila Real do Sabará, a priest had just completed saying mass. When he returned to the altar to administer communion, he "heard a great whispering and saw a particle on the floor broken into two pieces." The priest picked up the two pieces and fastened them together, marking the spot on the floor where the host had fallen. He then completed the communion ceremony. Afterward, he cleaned up the remaining fragments of the host and ordered them thrown in a nearby river.

Just as the people were leaving the church, there was a great commotion, with a slave named Pedro Monjollo in the middle of a throng of angry people. After questioning several witnesses, the priest learned that while he had been gone from the altar, Pedro had stolen the host and put it in his mouth. When he tried to transfer the host from his mouth to his hat, he dropped it on the floor. Even after this mishap, Pedro still tried to recover some of the pieces by drawing them toward him with a truncheon. Only when the priest reemerged at the altar did Pedro cease in his attempts to reach the fragments of the host.[37]

Even though it was widely understood that Africans and their descendants were the most frequent manipulators of consecrated particles and *pedras d'ara* for "diabolical" purposes, some whites also embraced these meanings, especially in Brazil. In some areas, the use of *bolsas* had evidently become standard practice by the eighteenth century, and pieces of consecrated host were among their primary ingredients. Soldiers were the most likely to carry *bolsas* in order to protect themselves from knives and guns. In some instances, even the church was culpable in promoting what it labeled as "superstitious" beliefs. In 1714, a Pernambucan priest named Joseph Maurício, was accused of distributing little packets of consecrated particles for residents around Serinhaem to carry in their *bolsas*.[38] Despite official church policy that forbade the desecration of the sacred hosts and relics, some priests apparently chose to ignore mandates and followed the will of the majority of their parishioners.

Another way in which Africans gained a foothold in the Catholic faith was through the cult of Catholic saints. The pantheon of Catholic religious figures was, in many respects, analogous to the pantheon of African ancestral spirits. Jesus, the Virgin, and the saints were all living, breathing human beings who had once resided on earth. Their likenesses could be found everywhere in statues and relics. They had recognizable characteristics and personality traits. And they also possessed the magical power to transform the condition of those on earth.

Like African ancestral spirits, the saints could be called upon to help Africans address specific temporal concerns. The Virgin Mary as Our Lady of Childbirth helped women during difficult child labor. St. Sebastian assisted hunters. St. George protected men in street brawls. St. Lazarus cured skin diseases—leprosy, smallpox, and measles. St. Peter aided in finding thieves. St. Gonçalo answered prayers involving love, desire, and relationships. And the list went on.[39]

Africans did not allow the character of saints to be frozen by the Catholic Church. They often transformed the traits of the saints, making them more human and more amenable to the specific needs of their immediate community. In 1704, a twenty-year-old Kongolese woman named Dona Beatriz Kimpa Vita was possessed by the spirit of St. Anthony, who she claimed was "sent from God to [her] head to preach to the people." Dona Beatriz subsequently led a far-reaching movement across Kongo that touched thousands of people. As the living embodiment of St. Anthony, she healed the sick, cured infertility, and claimed that St. Anthony was second only to God in terms of spiritual power. She also claimed that Jesus was Kongolese, and she criticized Catholic priests for not promoting black saints. Ultimately, Dona Beatriz was burned at the stake for propagating heretical views, but the Antonian Movement survived her, perhaps even in Brazil.[40]

Africans in Brazil continued this trend of humanizing saints, sometimes utilizing them to challenge the sanctity of the orthodox church. For example, as early as the seventeenth century, St. Benedict the Moor emerged as one of the prime protectors of blacks in the Catholic world. Because of his brown skin and his power to heal, Africans immediately recognized him as a kindred spirit. But rather than placing him on an ethereal pedestal, Africans transformed St. Benedict into a being with secular faults and human frailties. In Bahia, in 1689, a processional float belonging to a black brotherhood depicted St. Benedict arguing with the Holy Virgin and acting in a "most indecent fashion."[41] Some years later, St. Benedict was memorialized by slaves in the following verse, which endowed him with some of the same stereotypical character flaws ascribed to slaves:

> Saint Benedict's a saint
> Whom every black adores.
> He drinks brandy,
> And when he sleeps, he snores.[42]

By humanizing Catholic saints and transforming them into protectors of slave causes, Africans turned these Catholic symbols into African-style ancestral spirits. Though the saints did not replace the African ancestral spirits, they took a place alongside them, providing a point of connection between African beliefs and Catholicism that would eventually contribute to the formation of a distinctly Afro-Brazilian Catholicism.

Among the most potent forces in the emergence of Afro-Brazilian Catholicism were the Catholic lay brotherhoods that were created by Africans and their descendants in the Portuguese world. These black lay brotherhoods were fraternal organizations dedicated to religious activities and social work in the black community. Members of the brotherhoods were given special privileges rarely accorded to blacks by their masters or by state authorities. When they died, members were promised a decent Christian burial, support for their dependent survivors, and masses said for their souls. The brotherhoods also aided members during times of illness. Some even provided financial and legal help in purchasing the freedom papers of slaves in their communities.[43]

The earliest black confraternities were established in the fifteenth century in Portugal. By the third decade of the sixteenth century, there were black brotherhoods spread across Portugal, as well as in São Tomé.[44] The first ones in Brazil were established as early as 1552.[45] These early black brotherhoods were dedicated to Our Lady of the Rosary, a trend that would persist over the entire colonial period. One survey of 165 confraternities in colonial Brazil found that eighty-six (52 percent) were dedicated to Our Lady of the Rosary. Other brotherhoods were dedicated to Senhor Bom Jesus, Nossa Senhora dos Remedios, and Nossa Senhora da Boa Porte.[46] The attraction of Our Lady of the Rosary is not altogether clear. Dominican missionaries encouraged devotion to Our Lady of the Rosary in Portuguese Africa during the fifteenth and sixteenth centuries, so prior knowledge may have contributed to the embrace of the rosary. But a more likely explanation is the object power of the rosary itself. The rosary functioned like so many other African talismans. Worn around the neck, the magical power of rosary beads served as a protective balm against the powers of evil, no doubt attracting Africans and their descendants.[47]

The formation of brotherhoods was encouraged by the church as a way of bringing newly arrived Africans into the Catholic fold. But the brotherhoods also provided Africans with the opportunity to forge their own social spaces within the repressive slave society. In Brazil, some brotherhoods functioned as little more than veiled ethnic societies. Membership was restricted to members of particular African nations, and the brotherhoods' activities included the perpetuation of African religious and social forms. For instance, during the seventeenth century, most of the black brotherhoods of Our Lady of the Rosary in Bahia admitted only Angolans.[48] Later, the Brotherhood of Our Lady of the Redemption was established for Dahomeans in Bahia.[49] The Brotherhood of Bom Jesus in the Carmelite Convent in Cachoeira, Bahia, was reserved for Dahomean Gejes.[50] And the Bahian brotherhood of Nossa Senhora da Boa Morte emerged as a Yoruba enclave, reserved for Africans from the Ketu nation.[51] Similar patterns of ethnic exclusivity in religious brotherhoods were repeated in Recife and Rio de Janeiro.

The impacts of these ethnic-based brotherhoods were profound for Africans. According to Mary Karasch, when a new African arrived in Brazil, he could find his own ethnic community (brotherhood) worshipping a powerful "idol" (the statue of a Catholic saint) in a shrine (as an altar in a church):

> The members of the brotherhood, he would learn, organized ceremonies in the saint's honor, dressed the statue in proper clothing and symbols of sainthood, carried it in procession, paid a priest to say Mass at its altar, prayed "fervently" before other statues of the saint in the street, carried the saint's image on their persons, and honored the image as long as it was forceful. . . . When the charm no longer fulfilled its purpose and dissension broke out because of witchcraft or sorcery and diseases plagued the brothers and their families, then one of the leaders led the brotherhood to a new saint, forming a new brotherhood.[52]

For some Africans, the ethnically exclusive brotherhoods might have seemed similar to the kinlike secret societies that they had known in Africa—for instance, the healing societies in Angola or the *kimpasi* religious societies in Kongo.[53] For others, the brotherhoods were simply a way to maintain ethnic ties and create a sense of oneness among their peers. Either way, Catholic symbols were transformed and integrated into African religious and social views of the world, not vice versa.

Over time, the brotherhoods provided space for the integration of even more Catholic symbols and probably, at least for some members, an eventual understanding of communion with the Christian God and other "mysteries of the faith." This process was facilitated by the integration of Brazilian-born blacks into some of the formerly ethnically exclusive brotherhoods. But even as some Africans gradually absorbed Catholic beliefs, they continued to hold closely to the African spiritual practices that sustained them in their homelands. This religious duality is clearly illustrated in a 1780 report describing the festival of Our Lady of the Rosary in Recife. Members of the black brotherhoods, most of whom were from the Mina coast, were accused of practicing "profane" African dances during the religious festival, but their "real" sins were of another order. The brotherhood members were alleged to be secretly worshipping African deities in religious houses, complete with clay idols, goats, and priestesses who anointed themselves with oils and animal blood. Thus, the Minas were both Christians and practitioners of African religious forms, a contradiction that was intolerable in the eyes of the Catholic Church, but which seemed perfectly reasonable to the majority of Africans.[54]

The black brotherhoods were not the sole preserve of religious duality. Parallel practices also occurred within all-African congregations that were far from white society's gaze. In 1754, Church officials were informed about one of these African "synagogues" (the term used in the Inquisition denunciation) in Itaubira, Minas Gerais, and they went to shut it down. As several priests approached the small house, they heard the Kongolese preacher, a slave named Pedro Congo, saying "mass." The Catholic priests pounded on the locked door, and when it was opened, they found a large group of slaves and freedmen. Of these, ten were identified as Mina women and one as a Mina man. In addition to these eleven, there were "many others" whom the priests did not recognize because they were from other parishes.

When the priests asked Pedro what he was preaching, Pedro responded that he was preaching the Christian doctrine. But a further examination revealed that Pedro was preaching an Africanized form of Christianity that was coupled with specific African religious beliefs and practices. The Christian aspects of Pedro's ministry included the general belief among the parishioners that the Holy Spirit spoke to Pedro any time he wanted Him to. This, of course, resonated with those Africans who were accustomed to the continuous revelation of African spirit possession. In exchange for four *vinteis* (eighty réis), Pedro also guaranteed that the souls of dead Africans on the Mina Coast and in Rio de Janeiro would enter Heaven. The orthodox church would have considered this a heresy, since many of those being offered passage into God's Kingdom were not even baptized Christians, but Pedro's prayers for African souls were just one more example of the way Africans transformed Christian practices. In addition to these beliefs, Pedro also preached that anyone who gave alms or performed charity for their *fazendas* was a "sinner," the implication being that any slave who performed uncoerced duties for his or her master was reinforcing the evil and sin that was slavery. Finally, before being denounced to the Inquisition, Pedro and his flock had purchased a Habit of Saint Francis to wear in an upcoming procession on the day of the kings, demonstrating that despite Pedro's unorthodox, Africanized teachings, he and his parishioners still considered themselves a part of the Catholic fold.

Even though Pedro and his Mina followers called themselves Christians, they also continued to practice what were clearly African rituals. The precise derivation of the rituals is difficult to discern, since Pedro was Kongolese and the majority, if not all, of his followers were Minas. Pedro no doubt tailored his ministry to resonate with his Mina flock, but there were also ritual elements that were clearly more broadly Central African. For example, one of Pedro's Mina adherents came to him complaining of an illness that was plaguing her. Pedro determined that she was suffering because her soul had flown off to Vila Rica. Pedro advised the woman that if she got on her knees and allowed him to make some orations, her soul would return to her body. In this case, Pedro's diagnosis appears to be of Central African origin. The independent will of the soul was a common belief among Central Africans, and it was understood that when the soul separated from the body, the body would begin to deteriorate.

Other rituals and beliefs are not as easily identifiable. Among other things, Pedro placed a pan of rotten eggs in the middle of the floor in his "synagogue" and ordered all of the women to pass over it for good luck. It was also rumored that on the night of a full moon, Pedro used his powers of witchcraft (*feitiçaria*) to make ritual sacrifices of human beings. The cryptic nature of the documentation does not allow us to probe these practices any more deeply, but it is clear that Pedro and his adherents relied upon a variety of religious streams.[55]

The complexity of the religion practiced by Pedro and his adherents was demonstrative of a trend that was probably becoming widespread in many African slave communities. As Africans of different ethnic stripes were thrown together in the various slave societies, they began to create a body of rituals and beliefs that would resonate with all Africans, regardless of ethnic background. The first generation, like Pedro's all-African congregation, certainly must have recognized the distinctions between the Christian, Kongolese, and Mina streams that were contributing to their ritual practices. Since religious worldviews were roughly similar across West and Central Africa, many rituals and practices could be easily exchanged and understood. Certain elements of Christianity were also adopted, especially those that were analogous to African beliefs. But in the final analysis, beliefs and practices like those of Pedro and his followers must be viewed as "African" forms of religion, since they were informed by a shared set of "African" core understandings.

This process of Africanization was a discrete step in the broader process of American-based creolization. Over time, as the Brazilian-born population grew, African ethnic and regional pasts became less pronounced in some places, and a more syncretic slave religion might have emerged. But in most of Brazil, this was an excruciatingly slow process that was always complicated by large importations of new Africans. These newly arrived Africans injected religious energy and vitality into slave communities throughout the colonial period, reinforcing specific African practices. When new rituals and beliefs were introduced into the community, some of these new ideas were embraced, while others were discarded. Still, every ritual had a specific, traceable origin that was probably recognizable to those who were practicing it. These religious streams remained discrete, with the various rituals (including Christian ones) operating as a spiritual "toolbox" for an increasingly heterogeneous group of African slaves who sometimes came together under the banner of a broadly shared cosmology to seek communion with their slave peers and address the trying conditions of the slave environment.

Blasphemy and Sacrilege among Slaves

One indicator of slaves' rejection of Christianity was the frequency of blasphemous statements and sacrilegious acts committed by them. Many of these libels against the church were committed under duress and were meant to be an affront to the master. Not surprisingly, mulatto and creole slaves were the most likely to transgress the boundaries set out by the church. These slaves were more aware of the sanctity of the church and were seeking to insult the master and his sacred institution. At the same time, their actions show that their commitment to the church was often only a superficial mask meant to appease their devout masters.

For example, in 1595, a mulatto slave named José was accused of blasphemy in Olinda, Pernambuco. José was a thirty-year-old kettleman on the sugar *engenho* of his master, Fernão Soares. Suffering from acute hunger, one day José entered his master's store and stole a small stack of sardines. He was caught by the master and sent to jail, where "with rage and fury" he stated that he was renouncing God and giving himself to all the devils.

On another occasion, José was doing some iron work, repairing the kettles that were used to hold the boiling cane liquid. Still experiencing bouts of extreme hunger, he asked his master's wife, Dona Caterina, if she would give him something to eat. Rejecting his pleas for food, Dona Caterina replied that he should eat the red-hot iron instead. Later that night, José again gave himself to the devils and told them that he would give up a body part if they would remove him from that house. José was reported to the Holy Office. As punishment for his blasphemy, José was sentenced to appear before the auto da fé and was publicly whipped in the streets of Lisbon.

Unfortunately, José's sad story does not end here. Several months after returning from Lisbon, he was again heard renouncing God and casting his lot with the devils. He confessed that he only gave himself to the devils because he "wanted them to carry him away, [and] that this was because of the bad treatment and bad life that he has in the house of Fernão Soares, who does not give food to his Negroes." For his hunger, malnutrition, and curses against the Catholic Church, José was again sentenced to a public whipping and was exiled for four years to the king's galleys.[56]

José's case was not unique. Whether suffering from hunger, disease, or brutality of a master, a slave had very little in life that could be considered worthy of blessing. Creolized slaves recognized the hypocrisy of their master's Christian message and reacted with scorn. In 1736, a thirty-year-old slave named Gracia Luzia confessed that she had renounced Jesus Christ, the Holy Trinity, and the purity of the Virgin Mary. Uprooted from the Bahian home that she had known for her entire lifetime, Gracia was a recent and unwilling arrival in Lisbon. Gracia claimed that before being sold away to Portugal, she requested to purchase her freedom and had made a "reasonable offer" to her Brazilian masters, who turned her down. Angry, frustrated, and alone in her new surroundings, Gracia lashed out at the Christian God. Eventually, Gracia saw the errors of her ways and confessed her sins before the Holy Office. The inquisitors were merciful with Gracia because she appeared voluntarily before them and because her blasphemous words were said in a "moment of desperation." She was ordered to renounce her sins and do penance.[57]

Abuses against God were not limited to words; slaves also committed a variety of deeds deemed sacrilegious. We have already mentioned how some Africans coveted the Sacred Host as a magical talisman, using pieces of it in their *bolsas de mandinga*. Other slaves desecrated the Host more directly, contemptuously rejecting its symbolic Christian meaning. In 1771, Francisco da Costa Xavier, a Bahian-born slave of a São Tomé father and a Geje mother,

Master beating his slave with a *palmatória*, a wooden paddle with holes in it, in Brazil, nineteenth century. Lithograph by Jean-Baptiste Debret, *Voyage pittoresque et historique au Brésil* (Paris, 1834).

was accused of desecrating the Host. As a boy, Francisco was ordered to the city of Salvador to be apprenticed as a shoemaker. Once he became proficient in his craft, Francisco worked as a *negro de ganho* (slave for hire), paying his master 1,280 réis at the end of every week. Because his master did not allow Francisco to rest and cared only about getting his weekly payment, Francisco decided to run away. But before he could flee, his master learned of his plot and had him locked up. Francisco was then sold away to Pará, in the far north of Brazil.

When he arrived in Pará, Francisco found that his new master was even more abusive than his previous one. Feeling "little compassion" for his slaves, the new master ordered each slave to produce six pairs of shoes per week, a workload that Francisco found intolerable. Francisco also had some disagreements with the mistress of the house, who ordered him to be punished with the *palmatória* (a wooden paddle with holes in it). When the mistress's husband returned home, he arranged for Francisco to be punished further.

In desperation, Francisco sought spiritual answers for the abuse he was receiving. He asked a priest if there were more than one God, and the priest replied that there was only one God. Francisco protested that this could not be true, since his master treated him contrary to what God ordered. Francisco believed that there had to be other gods. Francisco later asked another priest who made the world. The priest responded that God made the world. Again, Francisco begged to differ, asking how it was that God could have created a world where people (like Francisco's master) exercised more power than He did. Finally, still questioning his faith, Francisco received communion and removed the Host from his mouth "in order to see with his own eyes Jesus Christ in his hand." Ultimately, Francisco was caught with the Sacred Host and reported to the Inquisition. He was sentenced to appear before the auto de fé, publicly whipped, and exiled to ten years in the king's galleys.[58]

Like Francisco, other slaves also rejected the symbolic meaning of the Consecrated Host. In 1781, a thirty-year-old slave named Gracia Angola took communion in the small town of Marica near Rio de Janeiro. Since it was a common practice for slaves in Marica to keep the Sacred Host in their mouths and later remove it, steps were taken to curb these abuses. "Negroes and children" of the Igreja Paroquial of Marica were required to pass in front of a lay assistant and open their mouths to prove that they had consumed the Host. Gracia somehow evaded detection. As she exited the church, she spat the Sacred Form on the ground, without any regard for who might see her. At the urging of an elderly creole slave, Gracia picked up the soiled Host, put it in her mouth, and swallowed it. Gracia eventually was arrested and jailed by the Inquisition. Ultimately, she paid the supreme price for her "disrespect." She died four years after her arrest, still in jail for her sacrilegious act.[59]

Gracia's rejection of the symbolic body of Christ was a calculated act of defiance against the church, an unambiguous expression of resistance to the religion (or witchcraft?) of those who were keeping her in thrall. Other slaves chose mockery and humor as a way of challenging the sanctity of the Catholic Church. In 1593, Francisco, the slave son of a São Tomé father and a Kongolese mother, stole an image of the Virgin Mary from the altar of a church in Lisbon. Francisco took the statue with him to the house of two female acquaintances, a woman and her niece, who both commented that the image was better off in their house than on some dusty altar. The three friends began a long night of merry-making with the statue. They removed the image's clothes and kissed her on the face. The two women danced with the image of the Virgin on top of their heads, laughing hysterically at the new pleasures they were showing the Holy Mother. At one point, the older woman took the hand of the image and put it under her dress, sarcastically remarking to her niece, "Look sister, she doesn't have that!" Ultimately, the image was broken, but not before the three had exposed the Holy Virgin to some of the "mysteries" of the secular world.[60]

Slave masters also were not beyond playing sacrilegious tricks on the church, even at the expense of their slaves. In 1698, a Carmelite priest named Father Antônio da Conceição denounced an Angolan slave named Branca in Bahia. Father da Conceição accused Branca of proffering heretical propositions against the Catholic faith. Branca told the priest that Christ did not exist in the sacrament of the Eucharist, because she could not see Him with her own eyes. Branca also asserted that she could be saved in her faith just as the Catholics could be in theirs. She stated that the pope was not the successor of St. Paul, nor the Vicar of Christ, because St. Paul did not have a successor. Finally, she said that she "made a song" when she gave confession, because it was not the priest's place to act as Christ in absolving her. Asking Branca where she heard all of these "lies," Father da Conceição learned that her master, Capt. Fernando Pereira da Rocha, had taught her to be a nonbeliever. Father da Conceição went on to denounce Capt. Pereira da Rocha, but the captain and his allies had their own version of the story. Branca's heretical statements were all a cruel trick played against Father da Conceição.

Another priest, Father Antônio de Rosário, had accompanied Father da Conceição when the incident with Branca occurred, and he confessed that it was all a misunderstanding, a joke that went too far. Father de Rosário said that when they were out seeking alms, the two priests were given shelter at the house of Capt. Pereira da Rocha in Cachoeira. When Father da Conceição saw Branca, who was extremely fair-skinned and red-headed, he asked if she was from a foreign country. Realizing that Father da Conceição was a novice priest, the captain decided to play a trick on him. The captain told Father da Conceição that Branca was indeed from a foreign country and that she followed a religion other than Catholicism. After making his examination of Branca and becoming convinced that she was a nonbeliever, the trick was revealed to Father da Conceição. But "because of his simplicity," he remained unmoved in his opinion that both Branca and the captain were heretics. Father de Rosário, who was in on the joke, vouched for the captain, arguing that he knew him to be a faithful Catholic who often provided shelter to the priests when they were out collecting alms for their convent. Apparently, the Holy Office believed the captain and Father de Rosário. Neither Branca's nor the captain's case was ever brought to a full trial.[61]

If one reads between the lines of Branca's case, it seems that her lack of faith in the Catholic doctrine was profound and not something she conjured along with her master. But even if we accept that Branca's heretical statements were only a joke, we still must pause to consider the implications of such a joke. Both a slave master and a priest were willing to compromise the sanctity of the faith for a few moments of amusement. This hypocritical message could not have been lost on the slaves who were the objects of such frivolity. For many whites, priests included, slave souls were little more than a laughing matter.

Despite the many physical and philosophical obstacles that the church faced in its efforts to proselytize African slaves, a distinct Afro-Brazilian Catholicism emerged in the colonial period. The basic core of African beliefs remained unchanged, but elements of Catholicism were added to existing beliefs, enhancing and strengthening African ritual practices. This process of Africanizing Catholic symbols and beliefs permanently transformed the Catholic Church in Brazil, creolizing the church in such a way that even whites embraced some of the new meanings, including the increased temporal powers of the *pedra d'ara* and the cult of saints.

The creolization of religious forms was never a one-way street. As we have already suggested in earlier chapters, whites embraced elements of African religious beliefs. Seeking answers to questions that their God and saints could not provide, whites often sought out the remedies of African diviners and curers. Most of the time, whites only dabbled along the periphery of the "diabolical" African arts, continuing to assert the spiritual supremacy of the Catholic Church. But in some instances, whites supplemented their beliefs in the Church with "stronger" African remedies. In the next chapter, we analyze some of these cases, suggesting that the Portuguese embrace of African religious forms was in many respects no different than the African embrace of certain Catholic forms. Portuguese and Africans alike utilized one another's religious powers in accordance with their temporal and religious needs. We will also examine the ways in which certain Catholic priests responded to the challenges presented by African religious practices, modifying certain rituals while maintaining the essential Catholic core.

CHAPTER TEN

The Impacts of African Religious Beliefs on Brazilian Catholicism

Whereas Catholic missionaries and priests actively proselytized African slaves, vigorously attempting to bring them into the Christian fold, the majority of Africans never engaged in such a calculated conversion project among their masters. With the exception of some Islamic Africans, overt "conversion" simply was not a part of African religious understanding. Nonetheless, some whites still gravitated toward African forms of religion. One of the ironies of church difficulties in converting Africans to Catholicism in Brazil was the extent to which whites seemingly embraced so many elements of African religious beliefs and practices. The question is, why?

Africans did not need to "convert" the Portuguese to their system of beliefs because African religions proved themselves through temporal results. Where Catholic theology was abstract and ethereal to most Africans—requiring a heavy dose of faith—African divining, healing, and maladies caused by "witchcraft" were very real to many Portuguese. The efficacy of African rituals was proven on a daily basis through empirical means, as practitioners tested the strength and goodwill of various deities and ancestral spirits. Still, Portuguese and Africans shared certain religious symbols and ideas with one another. Some adopted only those symbolic elements that resonated with their worldviews, while others gradually came to embrace dual cosmologies. There were no inherent theological contradictions that precluded one from being both a Christian and a practitioner of African religions. But, in the wake of the Council of Trent, the Catholic Church had increasingly little tolerance for unorthodox beliefs and practices. Threatened on a number of fronts, both in Europe (with the rise of Protestantism) and in the colonial worlds, the church responded with a rigid codification of Catholic doctrine. Expanding upon existing notions of African "savagery" and "heathenism," Portuguese priests consistently declared African religious practices to be the work of the Devil. As we have seen, attempts to extirpate African practices and beliefs were a dismal failure. Nonetheless, priests succeeded in marginalizing, criminalizing, and exoticizing African religious practices, reifying the widely held belief in primitive African power.

Because many priests framed the struggle for African souls as a holy war between European agents of God and African agents of the Devil, those opting for African remedies were *ipso facto* casting their lot with the Devil. As we have already seen, many whites simply ignored the rigid dichotomy between God's work and the Devil's work. Masters used African slaves to divine the whereabouts of stolen objects and runaway slaves. They used African curers to heal them of various illnesses. Some even purchased African healers as prospective investments, expecting the slaves to return a handsome profit from their cures. Still other masters feared their slaves' religious powers and quickly sold away any slave suspected of practicing "witchcraft." All of these behaviors indicate a pervasive belief in African religious powers.

While these examples of the acknowledgement of African powers are impressive enough, even more remarkable are the ways in which specific African beliefs became woven into the everyday fabric of Brazilian society. Whites and mixed-race peoples embraced certain elements of African religions as if they were their own. For instance, Central African *calundú* rituals were not the sole preserve of Africans. In 1713, several mulattas emerged as important religious leaders in the slave community of Tapagipe de Riba in Bahia. Two women named Lourença, one a "negra" and the other a mulatta, performed *calundús*, "dancing to the sound of instruments from Angola that they call *canzás* and *tabaques*." When the spirits mounted them, both women spoke in the "language of Angola." Seated in a prominent place and observing the proceedings was another mulatta named Ignes, the aunt of Lourença Mulatta. João da Costa Barros, a pardo man who witnessed the ritual, asked why Ignes did not also dance the *calundús*. The other observers responded that Ignes was the Queen, and it was not necessary for her to dance. The spirit would enter her even as she sat still, without any dancing or other invocation. And thus it happened. After the two Lourenças had been possessed by their respective spirits, Ignes was possessed while seated. When Ignes was finished proffering her divinations and cures, everyone in the house was called to embrace her (or her spirit). The ceremony ended when the last man embraced her, lifting her from her seat and agitating her until the spirit left her body.[1]

The significance of this case lies not so much in the actual ritual, which, as we have seen, was fairly common. Rather, what makes it important are the cultural passageways that it reveals within a certain African-derived community. The two mixed-race women, Lourença and Ignes, did not try to distance themselves from the "savagery" and "sin" of their African ancestors. On the contrary, they were religious leaders in the best tradition of their African forefathers and mothers. The two mulattas not only practiced distinctly Central African rituals, but they performed them in the "language of Angola," insuring that very specific Central African ideas and structures would not die. Finally, we get a glimpse of how these ideas and practices were passed from generation to generation. As a Brazilian-born mulatta, Ignes was at least one generation removed from her nearest African ancestor. Ignes's initiation of her niece, Lourença, into the practices of the *calundeira* guaranteed that Central African language and religious beliefs would survive for at least a third generation, even in the mixed-race, Brazilian-born community.

Though one might expect some mixed-race offspring of African mothers to continue holding on to specific African rituals and beliefs, this same elasticity probably would not be expected to extend to the white community. Nonetheless, there was at least one case in which a white woman believed that she could be possessed by her own *calundús*. One night in 1694, the Bahian Captain Domingos Pinto Ferrás was in bed with his wife, Maria Pereira, when he was awakened by a loud clamor. He sat up and saw "his wife putting her finger on her head." The captain described the noise as "a rumbling in her head, like a fury of wind over dry leaves." Soon, Pinto Ferrás "felt in him a vehement ardor of sensuality" like those that he had experienced only before marrying Maria. When he informed her about his amorous feelings, she responded that "they must have been her *lundus*" that were making him feel that way.

Pinto Ferrás was convinced that his wife was a *feiticeira*. In fact, the captain believed that his wife had bewitched him. The captain had a strange odor coming from his body that he presumed to be "some balm of the devil." He was also suffering from an ailment that was making him "crazy." Pinto Ferrás called in an African curer from a neighboring property, but the African told him that he could not cure him because he was suffering from *caboclo* (Indian) *feitiços*. The captain later learned that his wife was trying to bewitch him by urinating on the corners of the doors of the house early in the morning before he awoke, a practice that was more in accordance with European than African witchcraft. The captain eventually resorted to beating his wife and his mother-in-law before finally denouncing them to the Inquisition.[2]

Maria Pereira drew from several religious traditions in formulating her responses to her husband. In addition to the *lundus* and the European *feitiços* that were a part of her spiritual arsenal, she also prayed various versions of the Hail Mary, including one that apparently was designed to assert the special place of women in God's kingdom. It went: "Hail Mary, full of grace. God is with you and the women. Amen." Maria embraced a set of beliefs that contained elements of Christianity, European witchcraft, and Central African spirit possession. These elements did not mix. Rather, they were drawn upon in specific contexts and circumstances as a way of addressing the misery suffered at the hands of her abusive husband.

Though Maria's adoption of three different spiritual traditions is interesting, what concerns us here is the specific nature of the African elements that she invoked. Maria did not appeal to an undifferentiated form of African spirit. She appealed to the spirits of her deceased ancestors, her *lundus*. By using the term "*lundu*," Maria was referring to a very specific Central African tradition, one that resonated even with her husband, who told the Inquisition that "in the language of the pretos from Guine," *lundus* were "demons or malignant spirits." As discussed in Chapter 7, the specialized rituals of the *calundeiros* apparently remained the provenance of Africans and their descendants. But the African belief in the power of deceased spirits (or "demons") became engrained in the broader Brazilian culture. The impact of African religious beliefs on white Catholics can be summed up in the disparate reactions of Maria Pereira and her husband. White Brazilians, even as early as the colonial period, were torn between an embrace of "exotic" African spiritual power and a rejection of this power as "diabolical" and "sinful."

Perhaps the most notable aspect of the white embrace of African religious traditions is the way African beliefs and practices impacted the Brazilian Catholic Church. We have already seen that priests provided pieces of consecrated hosts for *bolsas* in Pernambuco, that the Benedictine monastery in Olinda employed African healers, and that a priest in Bahia advised his ailing parishioners to send their slaves to *calundeiros* because Catholic exorcisms would not work against African forms of witchcraft. Usually, Catholic priests acknowledged African religious powers only as they might apply to other Africans, arguing that whites must avoid the taint of the Devil's remedies and cures. But sometimes, when the church's remedies were ineffective against so-called African "witchcraft," priests advised whites that their only hope for survival was consultation with an African diviner/healer.

In the 1780s, in the village of Iraruama, outside of Rio de Janeiro, a woman named Francisca de Sousa was suffering from an "evil spirit" that had taken over her body. The evil spirit was the result of witchcraft created by her mulatta slave, Clemência, and Clemência's spiritual adviser, a freed African named Boaventura.[3] Francisca's husband, Antônio da Assunção, called in a priest to exorcise her. The exorcism eased Francisca's pain but did not completely expel the evil spirit. After about a week, Antônio brought her some crystals that were supposed to counteract evil spirits. When Francisca took the crystals, the spirit loosened its grip on her body and through her wasted figure began screaming in a loud voice that Clemência and Boaventura were trying to kill her. Clemência denied that she was the one who bewitched Francisca, naming Boaventura as the culprit. Boaventura was immediately interrogated and jailed, but Francisca's illness persisted.

In the meantime, another exorcism was performed on Francisca. Father Francisco Gomes, coadjutor of the Igreja de Cabo Frio, presided over the ceremony. The priest worked diligently trying to remove the evil spirit from Francisca's body, but to no avail. During the course of the exorcism, Father Gomes learned that the spirit that possessed Francisca was under the complete control of Boaventura. Father Gomes ultimately advised Antônio that the evil spirit would not leave his wife's body without Boaventura's permission. Not believing Father Gomes, Antônio consulted a Franciscan priest who confirmed that "even though the Devil might be the father of all lies, sometimes he tells the truth." In other words, Boaventura was the master of the evil spirit that resided in Francisca, and neither the Devil nor the priest had the power to remove it on their own accord.

To free his wife from the malignant spirit, Antônio da Assunção was forced to throw himself on the mercy of the "criminal" who allegedly had created this evil. Antônio arrived at Boaventura's jail cell around midnight, carrying oranges and tobacco to ingratiate himself to the African. After giving Boaventura the gifts, Antônio told him that he would arrange to have him released from jail if he would free his wife from her suffering. Antônio begged Boaventura in the name of God and the Holy Virgin "to concede license to the devil to exit the body of my wife." But Boaventura was unmoved. He angrily responded that Antônio's prayers would not work against him, and he refused to release Francisca from her suffering. Eventually, Boaventura was sentenced to forced labor in the chain gangs.[4]

The case of Boaventura illustrates several important points about the nature of African religious strength in the colonial world. First, some Catholic priests conceded that exorcisms and other church remedies were no match for African spirits, even when they infected white Christians. When these priests advised their parishioners to utilize the services of African diviners and healers, they were providing a tacit recognition of African powers and weakening the position of the church as a temporal force in Brazil. Second, African religious power had the potential to invert the social order. Given the racial hierarchy of colonial Brazil, the image of the wealthy, white Antônio da Assunção entering Boaventura's jail cell, bearing gifts and soliciting his spiritual services, is a difficult picture to fathom. African religious power operated as one of the most powerful forms of resistance to slavery and racial oppression. Finally, the reactions of ecclesiastical and secular authorities to African "witches" only served to reinforce African religious strength. The prosecution and chain-gang sentence received by Boaventura was an admission that his powers were so formidable as to be criminal.

Catholic priests, like their parishioners, were not immune to the lure of African religious solutions. Sometimes priests strayed from the precepts of the church, becoming intimately involved in the personal and spiritual lives of their African charges. In 1702, Father Miguel da Assunção, Prior of the Carmelite convent in Goiana, Pernambuco, was involved in an intimate relationship with one of his slaves, a woman named Felícia. Felícia inexplicably fell ill, prompting Father Miguel to send for "a Negro *feiticeiro* to make certain divinations and *feitiçarias* in order for him to know who it was who made the evil for his negra." A freed black named Pedro arrived and began his ceremonies, using calabashes and a pan of water. Pedro determined that Felícia's illness was the result of witchcraft cast by another slave owned by the convent, a woman named Caterina. Father Miguel immediately began a campaign of retribution and torture against Caterina. In less than three months, Caterina was dead from the ill treatment and "rigorous punishments" meted out by Father Miguel.[5]

Presumably, Father Miguel did not abandon the core beliefs of the Catholic Church, but his actions demonstrate a belief in a competing set of African spiritual forces. As all of the foregoing cases show, instances of priests acknowledging the parallel power of the African spirit world were not isolated incidents of capitulation to African influences. Rather, they were expressions of deeper institutional struggles over the role of African religions in the shaping of the Brazilian Catholic Church. On the one hand were those priests who wanted to uphold the rigid orthodoxy of Trent, rejecting all African practices as the work of the Devil. Father Antonil, for instance, argued that the *feiticeiros* and curers were "deserving of abomination" and that those who sought their services were effectively "leaving God, from whom comes all remedies."[6] On the other hand were more pragmatic priests who recognized that conditions in Brazil demanded a more relaxed attitude toward African religious practices. As we have already noted, these priests urged their parishioners to consult African diviners and healers. The harsh physical conditions of the Brazilian environment took their toll on whites as well as blacks, and both groups sought out African diviners and curers who were experts at manipulating this forbidding environment.

While some Catholic priests saw no contradiction in Catholicism and African ritual practices, still others sought to "Africanize" church doctrine so that it would cohere with an emerging Brazilian worldview that emphasized the temporal as well as the spiritual realm in religious expressions. The core of church doctrine remained unchanged, but certain rituals were transformed to accommodate these new African-inspired imperatives. For example, in 1713, Father Alberto de Santo Tomás, a friar in the Convento de São Domingos in Lisbon, confessed that as a missionary in Brazil, he had made some adjustments to the church's prescribed method of healing those afflicted with evil spirits. Father Alberto said that he had embarked for Brazil around 1702. When he arrived in Bahia, he "observed that for all of those parts of the *sertão* (hinterlands) where he went preaching, those residents used many evils, vexing many people; and in order to free themselves from these, they called on some Negroes who were *feiticeiros*." Father Alberto noted that these *feiticeiros* divined many things for their clients, telling them who had caused the affliction and how to recognize its symptoms. Upon seeing these many "offenses," Father Alberto "tried in his sermons and conversations, as well as in confession, to exhort and admonish the people that they should not consult nor use the services of the said Negroes, nor of some other person who they might understand had dealings with the Devil; and that in order to free themselves from evil, they should use the exorcisms of the church, which were the most secure and efficacious remedy, and that they should appeal to [Father Alberto] who had a book to make the exorcisms." Father Alberto followed the book's direction in performing his exorcisms, which were not in any way extraordinary. After doing the exorcism, he always ordered that the clothes and the bed of the sick person be searched. These searches yielded dolls, little pieces of clothing of the ill person, and live beasts, all of which Father Alberto ordered burned. As a result of his good works, Father Alberto claimed that the people of Bahia stopped appealing to the "Negro *feiticeiros*."

In addition to providing directions on how to perform the exorcism ceremony, Father Alberto's book, *Práctica de exorcistas y ministros de la Iglesia*, also made a number of unorthodox prescriptions that went beyond the usual prayers and incantations.[7] The book, authored by Father Benito Remigio, recommended that the sick person provide the priest with myrrh, gold dust, wax, salt, olive leaves, and rue. Father Alberto blessed each one of these items. He then mixed them all together and separated them into four or more parts, putting each one into a little *bolsa*. Father Alberto then ordered that the *bolsas* be put in the corners of the mattress of the sick person and that one of the *bolsas* should be carried with the ill person at all times. The book also instructed that sick people should drink holy water and temper their food with consecrated salt. Holy water was also used in enemas, which Father Alberto claimed elicited such objects as pins, feathers, fishhooks, cords, cotton, wood, animal bones, skeletons, people's teeth, hairs, sand, animal skins, and other "filth" from the bodies of sick people. Finally, the book required that the priest bless all medicines taken by the ill person. Because Father Alberto was not always present when his patients were taking their medicines, he instructed them to sprinkle the mixtures with holy water in order to endow them with the power of God.

Father Alberto claimed that his remedies were successful across Brazil, so much so that when he was passing through Pernambuco, the municipal council (*câmara*) of Recife wanted to request a special commendation from the king, immortalizing him in that city. But Father Alberto rejected the accolades, noting that his success was due to the power of God and his book of exorcisms. Indeed, after revealing that his exorcisms came from a book, a number of people in Recife bought *Práctica de exorcistas* from a local store.

Despite Father Alberto's many successes, the Inquisition did not look kindly on the embellishments that he had made to the typical exorcism. After making his confession, Father Alberto was ordered to cease performing exorcisms and not to leave the city of Lisbon, pending an investigation. The details of Father Alberto's case were passed on to several ecclesiastical scholars for their judgments of his behavior. When the reports came back, the scholars were divided in their opinions.

Father Manuel Manso concluded that the mixtures put into the *bolsas* seemed "superstitious and a symbol of some tacit pact with the Devil in order to undo one *feitiço* with another." He suspected that these "counter-*feitiços*" were "instituted by the very Devil, disguised with the blessings of the church in order to trick those who are less erudite and circumspect." Father Manuel advised that no exorcist should be permitted "to exceed that which is ordered in any ritual approved by the Church." In keeping with the Inquisition's role as a public censor, he also insisted that the offending pages of *Práctica de exorcistas* should be removed from all surviving editions.

The two other priests who rendered opinions on Father Alberto's case were far more forgiving. Father Sebastião Ribeiro argued that "corporal" objects like salt, wax, myrrh, and so on, had no effect on "pure" spirits like the Devil. Natural remedies could not cure the illnesses that were caused by the Devil.

According to Father Sebastião, the efficacy of Father Alberto's cures probably lay in their natural healing properties. As such, Father Alberto was not substituting one *feitiço* for another. Rather, he was curing natural illnesses with natural remedies. Father Alberto's most sympathetic reader was Father Antônio de Santo Tomás. Father Antônio admitted that it was "indecent" to apply holy water to mixtures that were to be taken orally, but that this indecency was "only material and not formal, since the end that it carried was to achieve the remedy." Father Antônio concluded that Father Alberto's zeal in healing the sick was justified. Otherwise, the sick would have continued going to "the Negroes, who certainly cured by work of the Devil." Father Antônio reasoned that Father Alberto's unorthodox exorcisms curtailed these behaviors and kept whites under the umbrella of the Catholic Church. After some debate, Father Alberto's suspension finally was lifted, but he was ordered not to perform any exorcisms beyond those "ordered by the Roman Ritual, over penalty of being gravely punished."[8]

Clearly, Father Alberto put himself in a precarious position by Africanizing his exorcism rituals. The ambivalent decision rendered by the Inquisition demonstrates that there was a great deal of opposition to any deviation from the strict requirements of the Roman Church, yet ecclesiastical scholars in Lisbon ultimately determined that the religious ends justified Father Alberto's unorthodox means. The motives behind Father Alberto's expansion of the exorcism ritual were clear enough. To remain an important and vital part of the everyday lives of many Brazilians, the church had to find ways of addressing the harsh physical realities of the colony. The uncertainties faced by most Brazilians compelled them to embrace African remedies that often provided more visible and immediate results than prayer and faith. Father Alberto's elaborate rituals were a logical way of meeting the African religious challenge. The use of medicinal materials from the natural world, the various blessings, and the *bolsas* must have resonated with people who were accustomed to consulting African diviners and curers. By naturalizing certain African religious principles, Catholic priests were able to meet the changing needs of their parishioners. And though specific Catholic rituals were Africanized, core beliefs remained unchanged.

Ultimately, the adoption of African spiritual elements by Catholic priests was no different from the African embrace of Catholic elements discussed in the last chapter. Africans and Europeans exchanged religious ideas in Brazil, naturalizing elements of each other's belief systems for their own distinct purposes. At the same time, both groups were forced to recast certain elements of their own belief systems to explain the conditions they each faced in Brazil. As the nexus of various African and European worlds, colonial Brazil was neither Portuguese nor African in its religious and cultural essence. But neither was it an undifferentiated, creolized mixture. Rather, Brazil was the sum of its separate, often incongruent parts.

Conclusion

The preceding chapters have provided a broad outline of the cultural and religious practices of Africans in the Portuguese colonial world from the sixteenth to the eighteenth century—from Islamic Wolof slaves in sixteenth-century Portugal, to Ndembu slaves in seventeenth-century Bahia, to Arda slaves in eighteenth-century Pernambuco, to Benguela slaves in eighteenth-century Rio de Janeiro. Despite my best attempts to provide some sense of the ethnic heterogeneity of the African-Portuguese world and the changes that occurred over time and space, the dominant cultural stream considered in this work is the one from Central Africa to Brazil. That Central African beliefs and practices would have survived in Brazil should come as no surprise. Between 1600 and 1770, more than two-thirds of the approximately 1.5 million slaves that arrived in Brazil hailed from Congo and Angola. But what may surprise many is that the beliefs and practices of Central African slaves were more than culturally detached and diluted "survivals." The argument posited here is that an essential character or worldview, based on the cultural values of a specific African region, was transferred to the Americas and survived in large measure.

The most commonly practiced rituals of Brazilian slaves in the seventeenth and eighteenth centuries were probably Mbundu in origin. In addition to the expressions of concern over various *calundús*, Catholic priests and other observers throughout Brazil commented on an array of very specific Mbundu ritual practices and beliefs. These included the ordeal of Golungo and the ordeal of *jaji* (to divine who committed some crime), *tambes* (ritual burial ceremonies), *quitecles* (ancestor worship through small statues or dolls), *quigillas* (dietary taboos), *quimbandas* (same-sex, kinlike secret religious societies), as well as other specific beliefs, practices, and lineage structures that went un-named.

Taken together, these findings challenge widely held notions that African slaves were unable to replicate specific African institutions in the Americas. Scholars have argued that the removal from one's specific cultural milieu in Africa and the devastating experience of the Middle Passage effectively diluted distinct African cultural systems. As noted earlier, Sidney Mintz and Richard Price's seminal work, *The Birth of African-American Culture*, suggests that, at best, particular African "retentions" and "survivals" merged with the beliefs of other African ethnic groups, as well as the beliefs of the larger colonial society to form new syncretic or creolized cultures. Even as recently as 1998, the authors of a work on slave religion in the United States and the British Caribbean articulated this same sentiment when they wrote: "Nowhere in the Americas would Africans be able to duplicate their traditional religious systems. What they were able to do, and often very successfully, was to piece together new systems from the remnants of the old."[1]

For early colonial Brazil, this clearly was not the case. Not only did the broad contours of Mbundu rituals remain intact, but uniquely Angolan implements of spiritual invocation made their way across the Atlantic. One of the central arguments made by the creolization school is that Africans were unable to replicate the necessary conditions to recreate African cultural forms. But the use of Kimbundu-language signifiers in the Portuguese records indicates that Central Africans were utilizing numerous ideas and material objects that had no analogous terms in Portuguese. Conceptually, the *quilundo*, the *nganga nzambi*, and the *nganga wisa* had no Portuguese equivalents. Even material terms like *canzá*, *atabaque*, *engoma*, *mpemba*, and *ualuá* defied Portuguese descriptors. Finally, the ceremonies themselves usually were conducted in the Kimbundu language, limiting the complete understanding of the rituals to those who were Kimbundu speakers. Where creolization occurred in Brazilian slave communities during the seventeenth century, it most often occurred among various Central African ethnic groups that shared remarkably similar cultural and linguistic cores. Philosophically and structurally, seventeenth-century Brazilian slave culture must be characterized as essentially Central African, with a variety of specific ethnic practices and beliefs—Ndongo, Ndembu, Kongo, Mbata and so on—resonating in the slave community, much as they did in Central Africa. Slave culture in Brazil during the seventeenth century was never creolized or diluted, any more so than culture in Central Africa was creolized. And the passage of these religious, cultural, and linguistic practices through generations of Brazilian slaves and free blacks, even to mixed-race African descendants in the mid-eighteenth century, demonstrates the tenacity of Central African culture. The so-called "Angolan" stream of Brazilian slave culture remained strong throughout the colonial period.

While I concede that some elements of Central African culture were gradually transformed or lost in Brazil, particularly after 1700, when large numbers of Mina slaves arrived in the slave communities, it is no longer evident that we should start from a premise of creolization when analyzing slave culture in the diaspora. Rather, we should assume that specific African cultural forms and systems of thought survived intact. We should then assess these disparate cultural and ethnic streams and attempt to chart the *process* of creolization. Historians do not dispute the specific Portuguese cultural roots of Brazil, or the specific English cultural roots of British North America. Yet the same is not true of the Africans who arrived in the diaspora. The deductive and additive processes of creolization took place extraordinarily slowly, and African beliefs and practices were often quite resistant to changes imposed from the "outside."

One of the first discernible changes to Central African rituals in Brazil was the involvement of Portuguese whites. None of the documents that I have consulted suggest that whites actually became diviners or played integral roles in the ceremonies, but very early on, whites consulted African diviners and healers to seek redress from a variety of maladies. According to Mintz and Price, slaves were able to create institutions only "*within* the parameters of the master's monopoly of power, but *separate from* the master's institutions."[2] As we have shown, slave masters did co-opt the strength of their spiritually powerful slaves, consulting them on a variety of matters—from ferreting out runaway slaves to exposing pilferers and thieves on the plantation. But there were instances in Brazil where the master class not only ceded elements of power to their slaves, but actually adopted the slaves' institutions, especially in the realms of divination and healing.

This widespread belief in African religious practices among whites raises serious questions about power dynamics and the nature of slave resistance in the diaspora. In light of the evidence presented here, it seems clear that much of the African struggle against slavery occurred in the religious realm. Fighting their inhumane conditions with religious rituals may help explain why Africans did not resort to overt violence as often as might have been expected. In their worldview, violence was neither as powerful nor as effective a tool. We must recognize that African ritual behaviors were as much secular and political as religious exercises. By monopolizing direct access to the power of the spirit world, Central Africans were able to undermine their servitude on a regular basis. As conduits to the spirit world, Africans not only held the power to divine and to cure, but they could also manipulate the spirits to help them maim and kill livestock, other slaves, or even the master himself. Unlike direct physical resistance, these rituals and practices were stealthy killers, provoking constant paranoia and fear on the parts of whites. Some might argue that this was psychological resistance, but the physical effects were very real, especially for those who believed that their own physical deterioration was due to the malefic curses of their slaves. In the final analysis, Africans used the most potent weapons at their disposal to shield themselves from and retaliate against the brutalities of slavery. Religious remedies were efficacious because the Portuguese had no antidote to the African spiritual arsenal.

Central African religious power was firmly entrenched in seventeenth- and eighteenth-century Brazilian society. The Portuguese constantly affirmed the power of specific divination and healing practices. By acknowledging the "diabolical" qualities of Central African religious practices, the Portuguese reinforced the spiritual power of slaves and free blacks. Ironically, the main impetus for the reification of African religious power was the Catholic Church. In their attempts to eradicate "heathen" practices like "idolatry," "fetishism," and "witchcraft," the church actually energized these alternative, counter-hegemonic spiritual forces, especially in the white community. African behaviors that might have been dismissed simply as superstition were transformed into a reality that challenged elements of Catholicism and the broader social order.

While there were certainly Africans in Brazil who gradually adopted elements of Christianity, I would argue that the impact of Christianity on Africans was no greater than the impact of African beliefs on Christians. Those who emphasize the Christian core of African slave communities obscure our understanding of African religious meanings. As the Inquisition and other records show, there were at least some Africans in Brazil who practiced African religious forms in an almost unadulterated form, recasting their belief systems only as a way of addressing the new sources of misfortune caused by slavery. These African beliefs were independent systems of thought that ran parallel and counter to Catholicism, challenging the temporal power of the dominant society and leaving the indelible imprint of Central Africa on the emerging Brazilian nation.

NOTES

Introduction

1. See, for example, Lovejoy, "The African Diaspora"; Palmer, "Defining and Studying the Modern African Diaspora"; Gomez, "African Identity and Slavery in the Americas"; and Sweet, "Teaching the Modern African Diaspora."

2. Though Fernando Ortiz, Nina Rodrigues, Manuel Querino, and Artur Ramos all did pioneering work on the African backgrounds of African American cultures at the beginning of the twentieth century, it was not until the publication of Melville J. Herskovits, *The Myth of the Negro Past* (1941) that American scholars began to debate the merits of "survivals" or "Africanisms." American readers were quickly exposed to a Brazilian interpretation of African "survivals" with the English-language edition of Gilberto Freyre, *The Masters and the Slaves* (1946). The study of "survivals" continues to flourish. For instance, see Roger Bastide, *African Civilizations in the New World*, and more recently, the series of essays edited by Joseph E. Holloway, *Africanisms in American Culture*.

3. Eltis, "Volume and Structure of the Transatlantic Slave Trade"; Curtin, *Atlantic Slave Trade*, 207, 268.

4. The term "flux and reflux" is borrowed from Verger, *Flux et reflux*.

5. Thornton, *Africa and Africans*, 184–92.

6. For the importance of the Angola/Brazil nexus in the emergence of modern South Atlantic economy and society, see Alencastro, *O Trato dos Viventes*.

7. S. B. Schwartz, *Sugar Plantations*. For Schwartz's finest work on African culture, see "Rethinking Palmares."

8. See, for instance, Mott, *Escravidão, homossexualidade, e demonologia* and *O sexo proibido*; Vainfas, *Trópico dos pecados*; and Souza, *O diabo e a terra de Santa Cruz*.

9. Mott, "Acontundá," *Rosa Egipcíaca*, and "Cotidiano e vivência religiosa."

10. Even for the nineteenth century, research on slavery can sometimes be quite difficult. Many of the documents were destroyed after emancipation. In 1890, the abo-

litionist, Rui Barbosa, ordered that all documents pertaining to slavery housed in the Ministry of the Treasury in Rio de Janeiro be burned. On what survived the conflagrations, see Slenes, "O que Rui Barbosa não queimou."

Chapter One

1. I am grateful to John Thornton and Wyatt MacGaffey, who used their knowledge of Kikongo and Kimbundu to help me decipher this passage. None of these words can be traced directly to contemporary Kimbundu or Kongolese; however, all of the Central African scholars that I consulted acknowledged that the words constitute a curse deriving from some Central African language. With Thornton and MacGaffey's help, I have arrived at a tentative translation based on the following: (1) *carinsca = carimisca = kadimisca* (from the root *dima*) = "may you be charmed"; (2) *casundeque = kasundike* (from the root *sunda*) = "may you be overcome"; (3) *carisca = cadisca = kadisca* (from the root *disa*) = "may you be eaten." It should be noted that in Kimbundu and Kongolese orthography, after the eighteenth century, the letter "r" was often rendered as a "d." Hence, the shifts in the above translations.

2. From the Kongolese root *zama*, meaning "to rise to one's feet," the word *cazamficar* was clearly used to break the spells that were harming Caterina Maria's victims. Again, thanks to John Thornton for translation help.

3. During the seventeenth and eighteenth centuries, the Portuguese Holy Office frequently banished convicted criminals to one of Portugal's less desirable overseas colonies. Because of poor health conditions in places like Angola, these exiles rarely returned home alive. See Coates, "Exiles and Orphans," 97–103.

4. For more on dreams as tools of Central African divination, see Chapters 5 and 6.

5. ANTT, Inquisição de Lisboa, Processos, No. 6286.

6. It should be noted that the Portuguese were also facilitators of an Atlantic trade within Africa during this period. Between 1500 and 1535, the Portuguese transported 10,000 to 12,000 slaves across the Bight of Benin, selling slaves from the Slave Coast to the Akan peoples of the Gold Coast. In return for these Igbo and Benin slaves, the Akan offered gold, ivory, and pepper, which Portuguese traders carried on to Portugal. Iliffe, *Africans*, 129.

7. Elbl, "Volume of the Early Atlantic Slave Trade." The volume of the slave trade up to the early part of the sixteenth century has been the subject of a great deal of guesswork on the part of scholars. Curtin's classic study, *The Atlantic Slave Trade*, suggests that only 78,000 slaves arrived in foreign ports before 1525, half the number suggested by Elbl. Elbl's is the first study to utilize quantitative archival sources in an attempt to estimate the volume of the trade. Using customs records and tax records, she provides the most convincing argument yet posited on the volume of the early trade. For other estimates, see Godinho, *Os Descobrimentos*, 4:161; Boxer,*Portuguese Seaborne Empire*, 31; Tinhorão, *Os Negros em Portugal*, 80.

8. Donnan, *Documents*, 1:42.

9. Eltis, "Volume and Structure of the Transatlantic Slave Trade." Also see Palmer, *Slaves of the White God*, 13–30; and Vilar, "Large-scale Introduction."

10. Curtin, *Atlantic Slave Trade*, 116. Curtin estimates that 76,100 slaves entered São Tomé prior to 1600.

11. Birmingham, *Trade and Conflict in Angola*; Thornton, *Africa and Africans*, 100–101, 114–15, 120–22; Miller, *Way of Death*, 140–69. For the Kongo civil wars, see Thornton, *Kingdom of Kongo*. For an overview of Central Africa's role in the slave trade, see Miller, "Central Africa during the Era of the Slave Trade."

12. While scholars generally agree on the proportion of Central Africans that arrived in Brazil in the seventeenth century, there remains debate over the exact numbers. Eltis and the other authors of *The Transatlantic Slave Trade: A Database* conclude that 327,000 Africans arrived in Brazil. These figures have been persuasively contested by Luiz Felipe de Alencastro, who arrives at a "conservative" estimate of 560,000. See Alencastro, *O Trato dos Viventes*, esp. 375–80.

13. S. B. Schwartz, *Sugar Plantations*, 339.

14. Miller, *Way of Death*, 452.

15. Richardson, "Slave Exports from West and West-Central Africa." From 1720 to 1770, Central African imports recovered, outnumbering Mina imports 702,000 to 221,000, a ratio of better than 3:1.

16. S. B. Schwartz, *Sugar Plantations*, 341.

17. Pigafetta, *Reporte of the Kingdome of Congo*, 57.

18. Sandoval, *De Instauranda*, 89, 96. Also see Thornton, *Africa and Africans*, 191.

19. Robert Slenes has coined the term "Bantu proto-nation" to describe the Central African presence in early nineteenth-century Brazil. See Slenes, "'Malungu, Ngoma Vem!'"

20. In looking at parish records from Rio de Janeiro, one notes that "Guinea" slaves predominated in the seventeenth century, even though we know that the majority of Rio's slaves were Central African. In these parishes, the term "Guinea" fades from common usage by the second and third decades of the eighteenth century and is replaced by "Angola" and "Mina." My interpretation of this shift is that some Brazilian whites did not feel the need to make distinctions during the seventeenth century, since it was understood during that time that the majority of "Guinea" (read "African") slaves were from Central Africa. Only when significant numbers of slaves from Lower Guinea began appearing was it necessary to make distinctions between "Angolas" and "Minas."

21. Miller has noted that the runaway status of the "Ndembu" was not unlike that of maroon communities in the Americas. Miller, "Central Africa during the Era of the Slave Trade," 46–47.

22. Ibid., 47–48.

23. For discussions of the shifting nature of ethnicity in Africa and the diaspora, see Miller, "Central Africa during the Era of the Slave Trade," and "History and Africa/Africa and History."

24. These included "Loango," "Benguela," "Cabinda," "Ajudá," and the fort at Sõ Jorge de "Mina."

25. See Byrd, "Constructing Identities"; Matory, "Jeje" and "English Professors of Brazil"; and Reis, "Identidade e Diversidade Étnicas."

26. For the meaning and importance of "nation" among Africans in Brazil at the end of the colonial period, see Karasch, "'Minha Nação.'"

27. Instituto do Açúcar e do Alcool, *Documentos para a história do açúcar*, 3:89-96. Throughout the period of the Atlantic slave trade, masters often referred to their slaves simply as "escravos de Guine." The term "Guine" was extremely imprecise. Sometimes it referred quite literally to the Upper Guinea coast. At other times it referred to the entire west coast of Africa from Senegambia to the Angolan coast.

28. Ibid., 3:40-49, 54-55, 63-64.

29. The transition from Indian to African slaves is outlined in S. B. Schwartz, "Indian Labor and New World Plantations."

30. ANTT, CSJ, Maço 13, No. 3. Of twenty-nine African adults, thirteen are listed with Central African ethonyms. One is called "Guine." The remaining fifteen are listed by their first names only.

31. Ibid., Maço 30, No. 3, f. 1040.

32. Ibid., Maço 17, No. 49.

33. Ibid., Maço 15, No. 12.

34. Mauro, *Portugal, o Brasil e o Atlântico*, 239. A number of contemporary observers came up with similar numbers for Bahia, including Father Joseph de Anchieta, Father Fernão Cardim, and Gabriel Soares de Sousa. The same figures were also cited by Father Cristóvão Gouveia in ARSI, Brasilia 26; VFL Roll 159, ff. 333-39.

35. Anchieta, *Cartas*, 410; Padre Cristóvão Gouveia, Enformacion de la Provincia del Brasil para Nuestro Padre (1583), ARSI, Brasilia 26; VFL Roll 159, ff. 333-39.

36. Cardim estimated only 2,000 Africans for Pernambuco, while Soares counted between 4,000 and 5,000.

37. ARSI, Brasilia 26; VFL Roll 159, ff. 333-39.

38. The ethnicities listed in this inventory include Mabanga, Mandongo, Amboella, Zenza, Monjolla, Quibinda, Quibaqua, Casumba, Robollo, Gangella, Bondo, and Congo.

39. ANTT, CSJ, Maço 30, No. 3, f. 1040.

40. Ibid., Maço 30, No. 3, f. 1214v.

41. Ibid., Maço 17, No. 24. The solitary slave who was not from Central Africa was Mozambican.

42. Bergad, *Slavery and the History of Minas Gerais*, 151-52.

43. ANTT, CSJ, Maço 17, Nos. 28 and 29.

44. S. B. Schwartz, *Sugar Plantations*, 348. The sample includes 469 African slaves.

45. ANTT, CSJ, Maço 15, No. 23.

46. Miller, *Way of Death*, 463.

47. ANRJ, Primeiro Ofício de Notas do Rio de Janeiro, Livro de Notas, No. 123, ff. 98v.-99v.

48. Ibid., Livro de Notas, No. 121, ff. 168–168v.

49. ANRJ, Segundo Ofício de Notas do Rio de Janeiro, Livro de Notas, No. 65, ff. 110v.–111v.

50. Alden has suggested that Engenho Santana was made up entirely of Brazilian-born slaves by 1674, but this simply cannot have been the case with ethnic signifiers like Mabanga, Quibinda, Ambuella, Gangella, Congo, and so on, scattered throughout the inventory. Alden, *Making of an Enterprise*, 520.

51. ANTT, CSJ, Maço 30, No. 3, f. 1057.

52. Ibid., Maço 54, No. 7.

53. Ibid., Maço 15, No. 23.

54. The majority of slaves listed in the Santana inventories have no ethnic or national signifier. Thus, there is no way of knowing whether they were African born or Brazilian born. As already noted, Alden missed a number of Africans in his reading of the 1674 inventory for Santana. For the 1730 Santana inventory, he claims that there were only two Africans on the property. By my count there were at least six — three Gejes, one Angola, one Congo, and one Ganguella. Alden, *Making of an Enterprise*, 521.

55. Ibid., 523.

56. ANTT, CSJ, Maço 17, Nos. 28 and 29.

57. The average price of the fourteen *"ladino"* and "creole" slaves in my sample was 125 mil-réis. The lowest price paid for any of them was 100 mil-réis, for a *ladina* suffering from smallpox. Meanwhile, the average price of healthy, unacculturated Africans was 87 mil-réis. Among the remaining fifty-two slaves whose identity remains uncertain, thirty-four were purchased for less than 100 mil-réis, suggesting their status as newly arrived from Africa.

58. During 1750–1751 Petinga purchased five Geje men, one Geje woman, and one Angolan man. ANTT, CSJ, Maço 54, No. 36. And during 1753–1754 Sergipe purchased only three Mina men. Ibid., Maço 54, No. 57.

59. ARSI, Brasilia 4; VFL Roll 157, ff. 75–75v.

60. ADB/UM, CSB 138.

61. Ibid., f. 261. This 2:1 ratio in slaves received to slaves sold is probably also an indicator of the degree to which Benedictine properties were creolized, since creolized slaves possessing some skills were more valuable than their newly arrived, "unskilled," African counterparts.

62. ADB/UM, CSB 134, f. 187.

63. Most *engenhos* spent upwards of 20 to 25 percent of their annual outlay on salaries, while the Benedictines spent only around 14 percent of their annual budget on salaries for skilled employees. On the comparatively small amounts that the Benedictines paid for salaries, see S. B. Schwartz, *Sugar Plantations*, 222–23. Schwartz argues that the Benedictines were successful largely because of their progressive attitudes in the treatment of their slaves. While there is some element of truth to these arguments, I would suggest that much of the Benedictine success can be attributed to the charity that flowed in their direction, especially in the form of skilled slaves. See Schwartz, "Plantations of St. Benedict," 18–22.

Chapter Two

1. ANRJ, Primeiro Ofício de Notas do Rio de Janeiro, Livro de Notas, No. 121, ff. 136v-137. Also see Sweet, "Manumission in Rio de Janeiro."

2. Palmer, "From Africa to the Americas," 230-31.

3. ANTT, CSJ, Maço 17, No. 24.

4. Thornton, *Africa and Africans*, 197-205.

5. ANRJ, Segundo Ofício de Notas do Rio de Janeiro, Livro de Notas, No. 66, f. 140, and No. 67, f. 16v.

6. ANRJ, Primeiro Ofício de Notas do Rio de Janeiro, Livro de Notas, No. 125, ff. 29v.-30. Evidence from the nineteenth century (1790-1890) suggests that as many as 11 percent of Africans in Salvador, Bahia, had contact with members of their African natal kin group. See Oliveira, "Viver e Morrer."

7. The idea of slavery as a form of social death is described in Patterson, *Slavery and Social Death*.

8. Slenes, "'Malungu, Ngoma Vem!'"; S. B. Schwartz, *Slaves, Peasants, and Rebels*, 124.

9. Miller, *Kings and Kinsmen*, 55-56.

10. ANTT, Inquisição de Lisboa, Cadernos do Promotor, No. 72, Livro 266, ff. 302-303v. This rite of passage was called *Guicumbe*.

11. Merolla, *Breve e succinta relatione*, 147.

12. ANTT, Inquisição de Lisboa, Cadernos do Promotor, No. 20, Livro 221, ff. 392-94. April 7, 1631.

13. Cadornega, *História geral*, 260-61.

14. Also see Pigafetta, *Reporte of the Kingdome of Congo*, 31; Cortona, "Breve Relatione," 153; and Balandier, *Daily Life in the Kingdom of the Kongo*, 215.

15. ANTT, Conselho Geral, "Santo Ofício Tomo XXXI (1720)," Livro 272, ff. 123-123v.

16. Cavazzi, *Descrição Histórica*, 1:85. Also see the chronicle of Father Merolla, who noted that many women in Central Africa were loathe to marry their partners. Merolla, *Breve e succinta relatione*, 140.

17. ACMRJ, Nossa Senhora do Loreto de Jacarepaguá, Batismos de Escravos (1691-1725). From a sample of 439 total births, 270 were to unmarried mothers.

18. S. B. Schwartz, *Sugar Plantations*, 389.

19. ACMRJ, Paroquia de São José, Batismos de Escravos (1751-1790). From a sample of 811 total births, 694 were to unmarried mothers. Angolans accounted for 226 of births to unmarried mothers.

20. Venâncio, "Nos limites da sagrada família," 115.

21. ACMRJ, Nossa Senhora do Loreto de Jacarepaguá, Batismos de Escravos (1691-1725), f. 2.

22. ANTT, Inquisição de Lisboa, Processos, No. 502. João and Guiomar lived on a rural *fazenda* outside of Jacobina, Bahia, and were the slaves of Manuel Correia do Lago.

23. On the legal status of "natural"-born children in Brazil, see Lewin, "Natural and Spurious Children."

24. ACMRJ, Santíssimo Sacramento, Batismos de Escravos. Total births to African women equaled 363: 218 to unmarried women with no father named, 121 to women with the father's name provided, and 24 to married women.

25. Cavazzi, *Descrição Histórica*, 1:85.

26. ARSI, Brasilia 26; VFL Roll 159, ff. 333–39.

27. ARSI, Brasilia 8 (I); VFL Roll 159, ff. 250–51. The language problem was a persistent one in the early years. Another letter from 1620 notes that the fathers in Bahia were awaiting the arrival of two young priests who were relocating from Angola who could minister to the Angolan slaves in their own language. ARSI, Brasilia 8 (II); VFL Roll 159, ff. 311v.–312.

28. ARSI, Brasilia 10 (I); VFL Roll 160, ff. 19–21v.

29. S. B. Schwartz, *Sugar Plantations*, 347.

30. ADB/UM, CSB 134, ff. 75–76; ADB/UM, CSB 138, ff. 66–67. On Benedictine efforts to maintain gender balance and encourage "family" formation, see S. B. Schwartz, "Plantations of St. Benedict."

31. For sex ratios on eighteenth-century Bahian *engenhos*, see S. B. Schwartz, *Sugar Plantations*, 348.

32. ACMRJ, Nossa Senhora de Candelaria, Óbitos, November 2, 1738, last will and testament of João Ignacio Alvares.

33. ACMRJ, Nossa Senhora de Candelaria, Óbitos, April 2, 1748, last will and testament of Salvador Ferreira; ANRJ, Primeiro Ofício de Notas do Rio de Janeiro, Livro de Notas, No. 121, ff. 147v.–149.

34. ANRJ, Primeiro Ofício de Notas do Rio de Janeiro, Livros de Notas. The sample included thirty males and ten females.

35. ARSI, Brasilia 28; VFL Roll 157, f. 29v. Similarly, in Piauí in 1697 there were 203 male slaves and only 7 females on 129 cattle ranches. Mott, *Piauí colonial*, 75.

36. In Vila Rica the sex ratio was almost 11:1; in Mariana, 13:1; in São João del Rei, 27:1. Bergad, *Slavery and the History of Minas Gerais*, 104.

37. On the impact of the slave trade on sex ratios in Angola, see Thornton, "Sexual Demography," 39–48.

38. ARSI, Brasilia 8 (I); VFL Roll 159, ff. 270–270v. During this mission, 308 slave couples were married.

39. ADB/UM, CSB 134, f. 274.

40. ARSI, Brasilia 8 (I); VFL Roll 159, ff. 270–270v.

41. S. B. Schwartz, *Sugar Plantations*, 385.

42. Antonil, *Cultura e opulência do Brasil*, 124–25.

43. Anchieta, *Cartas*, 399.

44. S. B. Schwartz, *Sugar Plantations*, 354–55.

45. Willeke, "Atas capitulares," 128–29.

46. ANTT, CSJ, Maço 54, No. 7.

47. ADB/UM, CSB 37.

48. Quoted from Archbishop of Bahia, Don Sebastião Monteiro da Vide in Conrad, *Children of God's Fire*, 160.

49. Antonil, *Cultura e opulência do Brasil*, 124–25.

50. ACMRJ, Nossa Senhora da Candelária, Casamentos de pessoas livres e escravos (1751–1761).

51. ANTT, Inquisição de Lisboa, Processos, No. 11283. The auto da fé was a public spectacle, usually held in the main square of Lisbon, where those found guilty by the Inquisition were paraded in front of thousands of people. The accused wore penitential clothing, went barefoot, and carried candles. The alleged crimes of each person were read aloud by officials of the Inquisition for all to hear. *Citra sanguinis effusionem* was a Latin term meaning "until the blood flows," usually around fifty lashes. Castro-Marim is a Portuguese town in the extreme east of the Algarve, near the border with Spanish Andalusia. See Mott, *"Justitia et Misericordia,"* 719–21.

52. ANTT, Registos Paroquiais, Concelho de Lisboa, Sé, Casamentos, Livro 1, Part 2, f. 28v. (May 18, 1616).

53. Some scholars point to high incidences of polygyny in other parts of the Americas. I did not find similarly large numbers of polygyny cases for the Portuguese world. See, for instance, Palmer, "From Africa to the Americas," 236.

54. ANTT, Inquisição de Lisboa, Cadernos do Promotor, No. 39, Livro 238, ff. 1–13v.

55. ANTT, Inquisição de Lisboa, Processos, No. 9110.

56. In recent years, there has been a vigorous debate in Brazilian historiography relating to the place of "family" in nineteenth-century slave society. For the argument that marriage and Western-style families functioned to subdue slaves and bring peace to the slave quarters, see Florentino and Goés, *A Paz das Senzalas*. For a contrary view that emphasizes the transmission of culture and resistance through "family," see Slenes, *Na Senzala, Uma Flor*.

57. For similar statistical outcomes to those outlined below, see M. Soares, *Devotos da Cor*, 125.

58. ANTT, CSJ, Maço 15, No. 23 (June 30, 1730 to June 30, 1731); ANTT, CSJ, Maço 54, No. 52 (November 13, 1752).

59. The ecclesiastical estates were exceptional in this regard. As we have already noted, the majority of slaveholdings were overwhelmingly African and male, with very few "marriages." At least four of the seventeen marriages on Santana in 1674 were between Africans and creoles. There were also twenty-five children under the age of sixteen on the property. ANTT, CSJ, Maço 54, No. 7.

60. When Father Pedro Teixeira took over Santana in 1731, he was exasperated to learn that his predecessor, Father Manuel de Figueiredo, opposed slave marriages. This had produced a slave population that was living in "sin." S. B. Schwartz, *Sugar Plantations*, 355.

61. For statistical details on the household structure of Santana from 1731 to 1752, see S. B. Schwartz, *Sugar Plantations*, 394–406.

62. For the development of the *ki-lombo* in Central Africa, see Miller, *Kings and Kinsmen*, 112–75.

63. For a provocative comparison of the institutions created by the Central African Imbangala and those created by the residents of Palmares, see S. B. Schwartz, "Rethinking Palmares."

64. This is not to suggest that these kinlike corporate structures were limited to African men. On the contrary, women were also integral parts of these corporate hierarchies. However, the *quilombos* were mostly male domains, and their replication in Brazil was certainly one way of addressing the absence of natal kinship networks.

65. The modern, Western term "homosexual" is entirely problematic in this context. In fact, what I mean is "homosexual behavior." The idea of the "homosexual" as a discrete "species" does not emerge until the twentieth century. This Western view assumes that everyone who engages in homosexual behavior is a homosexual, but behavior does not necessarily imply exclusivity. Moreover, examination of same-sex practices across cultures demonstrates that these behaviors take place in a wide range of social and cultural contexts that often transcend the sexual acts themselves. See Katz, *Invention of Heterosexuality*; and Murray, "Homosexual Categorization in Cross-Cultural Perspective."

66. While many have neglected the topic, Brazilian scholar Luiz Mott has written pioneering works on homosexuality in the Brazilian slave community. See for instance, Mott, *Escravidão, homossexualidade, e demonologia* and *O sexo proibido*, as well as numerous articles.

67. Like "homosexuality," the term "heterosexual" is also problematic because of its modern connotations. See Katz, *Invention of Heterosexuality*.

68. See, for instance, the case of the slave named João, who lived in the Portuguese countryside outside of Évora. In 1574, he was accused of having sex with three goats, three sheep, two donkeys, a mare, and a mule. Mott, *O sexo proibido*, 38–39.

69. These visitations include Bahia, Pernambuco, and Pará. Mott, *O sexo proibido*, 40.

70. ARSI, Brasilia 26; VFL Roll 159, ff. 333–39.

71. ANTT, Inquisição de Lisboa, Denuncias, Livro 779, ff. 128–129v.

72. Ibid., ff. 129v.–130v.

73. ANTT, Inquisição de Lisboa, Cadernos do Promotor, No. 24, Livro 224, ff. 313–16. The term "negro de Brasil" was a term usually used to describe Indians during this period, so the couple described in this case were probably an Indian and an African.

74. Mott, *O sexo proibido*, 41.

75. ANTT, Inquisição de Lisboa, Processos, No. 4815.

76. Ibid., No. 10868.

77. While I can find no evidence of gender inversion for sixteenth-century Benin, later chronicles suggest that the young sons of prominent families were recruited by the King of Dahomey and raised as "women." These trans-gendereds guarded the king's wives and carried out other important political roles. Fleuriot de Langle, "Croisières à la côte d'Afrique (1868)," 243.

78. Mott, "*Justitia et Misericordia*," 705–9; Trexler, *Sex and Conquest*, 167–72.

79. ANTT, Inquisição de Lisboa, Denúncias, Livro 779, ff. 128–129v. Also see Sweet, "Male Homosexuality and Spiritism."

80. The Kikongo rendering of this word is *kimbanda*, while the Kimbundu is *quimbanda*. In some areas, for instance Lwena/Luvale, this word would sound strikingly similar to *jinbandaa* (i.e., "tshinbanda"). In all cases, the word means "medicine man," "healer," and/or "spirit medium." Guthrie, *Comparative Bantu*, 28.

81. Viegas, *Relação Anual*, 1:414.

82. Cadornega, *História Geral*, 3:259.

83. Cavazzi, *Descrição Histórica*, 1:202.

84. Historian Joseph Miller argues that these groups of diviners, healers, hunters, and so on were a "supra-descent group network of contacts and served to transmit skills and knowledge widely throughout society." Miller, *Kings and Kinsmen*, 50.

85. I would suggest that the liminality represented in the blurring of the male/female gender roles is symbolic of other polarities in Central African cosmology, especially the divide between water spirits and earth spirits, the world of the dead and the living, and so on. By representing both the male and the female in a single human vessel, the transvested "homosexual" becomes a living conduit between two vastly different worlds—male/female, living/dead, and so on, and is thus spiritually very powerful. Some scholars have suggested a universal psychological link between homosexual transvestism and shamanism. See, for instance, La Barre, *Ghost Dance*, 106–9. In Native American societies, the transvested, homosexual *berdache* possessed spiritual powers similar to those of the Central African *quimbanda*. See Williams, *Spirit and the Flesh*; and Gutiérrez, *When Jesus Came, the Corn Mothers Went Away*.

Chapter Three

1. ANTT, CSJ, Maço 54, No. 42. The capture and incarceration of Gaspar cost the Jesuits a total of 10$860—10 mil-réis for his actual capture, 320 réis for his jailing, and 540 réis for his food during the nine days of incarceration. Jacinta was purchased at auction for 100 mil-réis. Thus, the Jesuits spent 110$860 to appease the runaway slave, Gaspar.

2. ANTT, CSJ, Maço 54, No. 52. In this 1752 inventory of Santana, Gaspar and Jacinta are listed as a married couple occupying a single household.

3. There was, however, precedence for uniting separated slave couples on Jesuit properties. In the 1630s, the Jesuits on Engenho Sergipe purchased the "wives" of two male slaves. Each of the men was accused of fleeing the estate dozens of times per year in order to be with their loved ones. According to the Jesuits, the women were bought "in order to appease and serve" their respective mates. ANTT, CSJ, Maço 14, No. 1.

4. ANTT, CSJ, Maço 54, No. 43. The Jesuits paid 440 réis to have Jacinta cured.

5. Ibid., No. 56.

6. Miller, *Way of Death*, 440–41.

7. For a description of African enslavement and the Middle Passage in the South Atlantic, see Miller, *Way of Death*, 379–442.

8. Thus, from capture in the interior of Africa until fully seasoned in Brazil, only about 30 percent of Africans survived. Miller, *Way of Death*, 440–41.

9. For detail on smallpox, see Alden and Miller, "Out of Africa."

10. Quoted from Joachim John Monteiro, *Angola and the River Congo*, 2 vols. (1875; reprint, London, 1968), 2:252–53 in Karasch, *Slave Life in Rio de Janeiro*, 151. Karasch suggests that *mal de bicho* might have been schistosomal dysentery.

11. S. B. Schwartz, *Sugar Plantations*, 137–39.

12. ADB/UM, CSB 134, ff. 55–56.

13. Ibid.

14. Koster, *Travels in Brazil*, 213.

15. Kiple and King, "Slave Child Mortality," 287, 298.

16. ANTT, CSJ, Maço 15, No. 9.

17. ARSI, Brasilia 26; VFL Roll 159, f. 433.

18. ARSI, Brasilia 8 (I); VFL Roll 159, ff. 250–51.

19. ANTT, CSJ, Maço 14, No. 1. Compounding the problem of slave mortality on Sergipe were illness and disease. A 1628 report noted that among the *engenho*'s eighty adult slaves, only forty-six were fit for service. The other thirty-four were "old and infirm." Thus, only 60 percent of Sergipe's adult labor force was strong enough to work. ANTT, CSJ, Maço 14, No. 52.

20. ARSI, Brasilia 3 (I); VFL Roll 161, ff. 273–74. In 1640, the Jesuit College of Rio owned more than 600 slaves. Boxer, *Salvador de Sá*, 134.

21. ADB/UM, CSB 134, f. 95. There is no indication as to how these deaths were distributed among the inherited and the newly purchased, but it seems safe to assume that the majority occurred among recently purchased Africans.

22. ADB/UM, CSB 138.

23. These findings correspond closely to Katia Mattoso's estimate that the annual replacement rate for slaves on Brazilian plantations prior to 1640 was 6.3 percent. Mattoso, *To Be a Slave in Brazil*, 42–43. On Central African mortality rates, see Miller, *Way of Death*, 381–82.

24. ANTT, CSJ, Maço 68, No. 306.

25. Ibid., No. 307. Of the forty slaves, there were twenty-eight males and twelve females. Salvador de Sá, who was also a member of Portugal's Overseas Council, made vows to the Society of Jesus but never received sacral orders. Father Franco's close relationship to the politically powerful Sá is outlined in Alencastro, *O Trato dos Viventes*, 270, 282.

26. ANTT, CSJ, Maço 68, No. 308.

27. Ibid., Maço 70, No. 390.

28. Ibid., Maço 15, No. 25.

29. Ibid., Maço 70, No. 428 (September 20, 1733).

30. ADB/UM, CSB 134, f. 244.

31. Ibid., CSB 135, f. 148.

32. S. B. Schwartz, *Sugar Plantations*, 367.

33. Klein and Engerman, "Fertility Differentials." Extended lactation has a contraceptive effect that lasts for the duration of the time the child breastfeeds. Caldwell and Caldwell, "Role of Marital Abstinence."

34. Stillbirths were apparently quite common among the slave population. In Maranhão in 1798, the ratio of stillbirths to total births in the slave population was 10:3. Comparable ratios among whites and free pardos were, respectively, 5:7 and 6:3. S. B. Schwartz, *Sugar Plantations*, 370.

35. ARSI, Brasilia 2; VFL Roll 161, ff. 142–142v.

36. ANTT, CSJ, Maço 54, No. 7. The four who died were Maria, eleven and a half years old; Anna, six years old; Andre, one and a half years old; and Bastião, *moleque*. The term *moleque/moleca* applied to those slaves up to the age of adulthood. Though flexible, it usually meant a child between the ages of eight and sixteen.

37. These were Anna, seven years old; Agustinho, three years old; and Joaquim, a three-year-old mulatto.

38. Francisco, small *moleque*; João small *moleque*; and Maria, small *moleca*.

39. Death, disease, and orphanage also took a steep toll on the rice plantations of nineteenth-century America. Between 1833 and 1855, an astonishing 90 percent of slave children who were born or imported into Gowrie plantation in South Carolina did not live to see their sixteenth birthday. Of children who survived, only one in four reached adulthood with both parents still living. See Dusinberre, *Them Dark Days*, 50–56, 118–21, 235–47, 410–16, 445–51.

40. Though scholarship aimed specifically at slave children has increased in recent years, few scholars have considered the work of developmental psychologists in their definitions of "childhood," and even fewer have considered how African cultural meanings might have been transformed by American slavery. For the experiences of slave children in Brazil, see Neves, "Infância de faces negras." For those in the United States, see King, *Stolen Childhood*; M. J. Schwartz, *Born in Bondage*; and Dusinberre, *Them Dark Days*. Also see the following articles of Steckel: "A Peculiar Population"; "A Dreadful Childhood"; "Birth Weights and Infant Mortality."

41. Freyre, *Masters and the Slaves*, 349–50.

42. Ibid., 350.

43. Ibid.

44. For the custom of giving chickens, wine, and other sought-after foods to the parents of newborn slaves, see the numerous entries in the account books of the *engenhos* in ANTT, CSJ, Maço 54. On slave fathers threatening Jesuit administrators with flight, see ANTT, CSJ, Maço 54, No. 55.

45. ANTT, Inquisição de Lisboa, Cadernos do Promotor, No. 96, Livro 289, ff. 412–end (unnumbered page)

46. ANTT, CSJ, Maço 70, No. 89. Also see S. B. Schwartz, *Sugar Plantations*, 353–54.

47. Scheper-Hughes, *Death Without Weeping*. The benign resignation to the loss of newborn children was also evident among the slave populations of America's rice

swamps. In 1839, Frances Kemble described the reaction of slave parents whose new-born had just died on Butler Plantation in Georgia: "The father and mother, and old Rose, the nurse, who was their little baby's grandmother, all seemed apathetic, and apparently indifferent to the event. The mother merely repeated over and over again: 'I've lost many; they all goes so'; and the father, without word or comment, went out to his enforced labor." As quoted in Dusinberre, *Them Dark Days*, 245.

48. ACMRJ, Nossa Senhora do Loreto de Jacarepaguá, Batismos de Escravos (1691–1725), f. 6.

49. ACMRJ, Santíssimo Sacramento, Óbitos, July 9, 1739.

50. Miller, *Way of Death*, 387.

51. Eltis, Behrendt, Richardson, and Klein, *Trans-Atlantic Slave Trade: A Database*. Statistics come from Eltis, *Rise of Slavery in the Americas*, 105.

52. See, for instance, ANTT, Inquisição de Lisboa, Processos, Nos. 254, 348, 502, 8464, 9110, 11767, 11970; Inquisição de Coimbra, Processos, No. 54, 7840.

53. See, for instance, the 1743 inventory from Engenho Sergipe, which states: "The old people serve to watch over the children while their mothers go to work." ANTT, CSJ, Maço 70, No. 109.

54. ANTT, Inquisição de Lisboa, Processos, No. 16687. Also see Luiz Mott, "Terror na Casa da Torre." Some children succumbed to their beatings, even on supposedly well-run plantations like those of the Benedictines. For instance, see the case of Pedro, who Father Bento de Santa Barbara of the Benedictine monastery in Bahia "visibly killed with the great punishment that he gave him, inappropriate not only for a man, but even more so for a child." ADB/UM, CSB 322, ff. 324–33 (December 9, 1800).

55. S. B. Schwartz, *Sugar Plantations*, 377.

56. ADB/UM, CSB 322, f. 191; S. B. Schwartz, *Sugar Plantations*, 143.

57. Freyre, *Masters and the Slaves*, 454.

58. For an account of the remarkable life of Rosa Egipcíaca, see Mott, *Rosa Egipcíaca*.

59. ANTT, Inquisição de Lisboa, Processos, No. 16687. Also see Mott, "Terror na Casa da Torre."

60. Because of the Portuguese aversion to male sodomy, the documentary evidence of male rape is actually richer than that for female rape. Females were almost certainly sexually assaulted more frequently than males, but the cultural legitimacy of female rape insured that the perpetrators would not be prosecuted in the same way that male rapists were. The regularity of female rape has been noted by Gilberto Freyre, who wrote that "girls of twelve or thirteen years . . . were given to white lads already rotting with . . . syphilis." According to Freyre, it was widely believed that sexual intercourse with a young virgin slave girl could cure venereal disease. Freyre, *Masters and the Slaves*, 324–25.

61. Mott, *Rosa Egipcíaca*, 20.

62. França and Siqueira, *Segunda visitação do Santo Ofício*, 444–46.

63. ANTT, Inquisição de Lisboa, Cadernos do Promotor, No. 98, Livro 291, un-numbered pages (October 9, 1727).

64. ANTT, Inquisição de Lisboa, Cadernos do Promotor, No. 12, Livro 213, ff. 429–34.

65. ANTT, Inquisição de Lisboa, Cadernos do Promotor, No. 29, Livro 228, ff. 83–83v.

66. Mott suggests that newly arrived (*boçal*) slaves were preferred because they were unfamiliar with white customs and were more likely to accept "sexual seduction" as part of their duties as slaves. Since *boçal* Africans did not know that sodomy was a crime and were unable to speak Portuguese, the masters ran little risk in seeking to have their way with newly arrived slaves. Mott, *O sexo proibido*, 44.

67. ANTT, Inquisição de Lisboa, Cadernos do Promotor, No. 29, Livro 228, ff. 93–93v.

68. See, for example, Shengold, *Soul Murder*; Sanford, *Strong at the Broken Places*; Wyatt, "Aftermath of Child Sexual Abuse." For a historical analysis of the psychological impacts of abuse in U.S. slave communities, see Painter, "Soul Murder and Slavery."

69. ANTT, Cadernos do Nefando, No. 20, f. 149; Mott, *O sexo proibido*, 55–56. This was a sentiment held by many slave masters throughout the Americas. For an example from the United States, see McLaurin, *Celia*.

70. ANTT, CSJ, Maço 70, No. 89; S. B. Schwartz, *Sugar Plantations*, 353–54. Father Matias reported that the white men were removed from the plantation.

71. ANTT, Inquisição de Lisboa, Cadernos do Promotor, No. 24, Livro 224, ff. 96–125v.

72. Ibid., Cadernos do Promotor, No. 75, Livro 269, ff. 201–3.

73. ADB/UM, CSB 321, ff. 116–20.

74. ANTT, Inquisição de Lisboa, Processos, No. 15097.

75. Ibid., Processos, No. 6478. Also see the source cited in note 74 (Processo No. 15097) and Cadernos do Promotor, No. 77, Livro 271, ff. 240–242v.

76. ANTT, Inquisição de Lisboa, Cadernos do Nefando, No. 20, f. 364, as quoted in Mott, *O sexo proibido*, 47–48.

77. ANTT, Inquisição de Lisboa, Processos, No. 45.

78. Lapa, *Livro da visitação do Santo Ofício*, 261–65. Five of the Africans died from their wounds.

79. ANTT, Inquisição de Lisboa, Processos, No. 17759.

80. Joannes de Laet, "História ou anais dos feitos de companhia privilegiada das Indias Ocidentais," *Anais da Biblioteca Nacional de Rio de Janeiro* 41 (1925), 86, cited in J. A. Goulart, *Da palmatória ao patíbulo*, 82.

81. J. A. Goulart, *Da palmatória ao patíbulo*, 99.

82. Many of these punishments and tortures are chronicled in Goulart, *Da palmatória ao patíbulo*. For contemporary commentaries on the severity of slave punishments, see Benci, *Economia cristã dos senhores*, 136.

83. Pereira, *Compendio Narrativo*, 1:158.

84. *Documentos históricos*, 32:393–95.

85. S. B. Schwartz, *Sugar Plantations*, 134–35.

86. Ibid., 134.

87. ANTT, CSJ, Maço 69, Nos. 75 and 83 (same document).

88. ADB/UM, CSB 321 (unnumbered pages), Treslado da sindicação que se tirou do Muito Reverendo Padre Mestre ex-Abbe Frei Salvador dos Santos (October 20, 1750). Complaints against the Benedictines continued through the end of the eighteenth century. During the last three years of the century, the friars in the monastery of Bahia were accused of a series of atrocities. A creole child named Pedro was beaten to death by Father Bento de Santa Barbara. Another slave, named Cristóvão, was beaten to death, even as he was suffering from a fever. And the slave João Ramos was confined to the *tronco* without clothes for four years, during which time he came down with smallpox. He eventually "lost his mind." ADB/UM, CSB 322, ff. 324-33, Sindicação do Muito Reverendo Padre Mestre ex-Abbe Frei João da Trinidade Soares do tempo em que governou este Mosteiro (December 9, 1800).

89. ANTT, Inquisição de Lisboa, Cadernos do Promotor, No. 54, Livro 251, ff. 293-302v.

90. ANTT, Inquisição de Lisboa, Processos, No. 2780.

91. Ibid., Processos, No. 13264.

92. ANRJ, Primeiro Ofício de Notas do Rio de Janeiro, Livro de Notas, No. 121, ff. 162-162v.

93. Ibid., Livro de Notas, No. 117, ff. 112-13.

94. Ibid., Livro de Notas, No. 123, ff. 130-31. The granting of manumission in exchange for other slaves was not unusual and was one way of actually increasing the master's wealth. In a case similar to the one cited here, Mariana Mina was freed by her master, Antônio dos Reis Franco, in exchange for two Mina women. ANRJ, Quarto Ofício de Notas do Rio de Janeiro, Livro de Notas, No. 49, ff. 132-132v. (1753). For the exchange of slaves for freedom papers in Bahia, see S. B. Schwartz, "Manumission of Slaves in Colonial Brazil," 625-26.

95. Pereira, *Compendio Narrativo*, 1:157.

96. ANRJ, Primeiro Ofício de Notas do Rio de Janeiro, Livro de Notas, Nos. 117-21; Segundo Ofício de Notas do Rio de Janeiro, Livro de Notas, Nos. 62, 65-68, 70; Quarto Ofício de Notas, Nos. 44, 46-49.

97. Such practices were widespread across the Americas. Father Alonso de Sandoval, a Jesuit priest residing in Cartagena from 1605 to 1617, wrote that masters would free their sick slaves for the period of their illness, just so they would not have to incur the cost of curing the slave. Once the slave regained his health, he was required to return to service. Sandoval, *De Instauranda*, 197.

98. Many of the works on American slavery written in the past twenty-five years provide a sanitized view of the institution. Slaves have been depicted as overwhelmingly resilient in withstanding the pain and cruelty of slavery. These works have stressed the vibrancy of slave culture, economy, and society, largely neglecting the physical and psychological tolls that the institution took on the majority of the enslaved. See, for instance, Genovese, *Roll, Jordan, Roll*; Owens, *This Species of Property*; Joyner, *Down by the Riverside*; and, more recently, Berlin, *Many Thousands Gone*. Several recent works have begun to assault the idea of "teflon-coated" slaves who used culture to

defend themselves from the brutalities of slavery. See, for instance, Palmer, "Rethinking American Slavery." Dusinberre, *Them Dark Days*, demonstrates the bitter physical effects suffered by slaves on America's Low Country rice plantations. Dusinberre's work implicitly refutes many of the assertions made by Joyner.

99. ADB/UM, CSB 134, f. 112.

100. ANTT, CSJ, Maço 70, No. 425; S. B. Schwartz, *Sugar Plantations*, 405–6.

101. ANTT, CSJ, Maço 82, No. 14.

102. Ibid., Maço 54, No. 34.

103. ANTT, Chanceleria D. Filipe III, Perdões e Legits (Proprios), Livro 12, f. 5v.

104. There is a rich literature on runaway communities in Brazil. See, for instance, Carneiro, *O quilombo dos Palmares*; S. B. Schwartz, "Rethinking Palmares;" and Reis and Gomes, *Liberdade por um fio*.

Chapter Four

1. Cadamosto, *Voyages of Cadamosto*, 31.

2. Even today, these two belief systems coexist among the Wolof of the Senegambia. Gratton, "Wolof."

3. These wars and their outcomes are chronicled in Barry, *Senegambia and the Atlantic Slave Trade*; and Boulègue, *Le Grand Jolof*.

4. Saunders, *Social History of Black Slaves and Freedmen*, 161–62; ANTT, Inquisição de Lisboa, Denúncias, Livro 2, ff. 124v.–125v.; Livro 3, ff. 94v.–95v.; Livro 4, ff. 18–18v.

5. Zambo, who arrived in Portugal around 1561, was probably enslaved in the wars that led to the collapse of the Jolof Confederation. His reference to the "Moors" who enslaved him might be a specific reference to the Kajoor Moors, or it could be a more general reference to peoples from any of the Muslim provinces under the former rule of the Jolof. See Barry, *Senegambia and the Atlantic Slave Trade*, 35, 82.

6. The *shahada* is the First Pillar of Islam, and any person reciting it with sincerity is considered a Muslim. Zambo recited it in the Arabic: "*La-ilaha ill'l-Lah Muhammadan rasul-ul-lah*" ("There is no God but God and Mohammed is the Prophet of God").

7. ANTT, Inquisição de Lisboa, Processos, No. 10870.

8. Deive, *La esclavitud del negro en Santo Domingo*, 2:445–54.

9. Saunders, *Social History of Black Slaves and Freedmen*, 137; ANTT, Chanceleria D. Manuel I, 46, f. 146.

10. During the *festas dos negros*, blacks sang, danced, played instruments, ate, and drank wine. In 1559, these parties were effectively outlawed when blacks were prohibited from gathering within a 4.5 kilometer radius of the center of Lisbon. Saunders, *Social History of Black Slaves and Freedmen*, 106.

11. ANTT, Inquisição de Lisboa, Processos, No. 7565.

12. Ibid., Processos, No. 10845.

13. Ibid., Processos, No. 10870.

14. The religious solidarity of Senegambian Muslims extended to the Americas as

well. Father Alonso de Sandoval, the Jesuit priest in Cartagena, noted that among the Jolofs, Mandingas, and Fulanis, there were diverse languages and customs. Despite these differences, Sandoval claimed that "all of these nations" were united by their membership in "the cursed sect of Muhammed." Sandoval, *De Instauranda*, 91.

15. ANTT, Inquisição de Lisboa, Processos, No. 13006.

16. Ibid., Processos, No. 5964.

17. ANTT, Inquisição de Coimbra, Processos, No. 54.

18. ANTT, Inquisição de Lisboa, Processos, No. 11970. Only the denunciations and a summary of Thomas's case appear in the packet, thereby implying that the case was never turned into a full trial.

19. According to legend, St. Veronica wiped the bleeding face of Jesus on the way to Calvary. Catholics used white cloths with the image of Jesus and red "blood" streaks as religious relics that they carried with them. Other religious relics and medals that could be worn around the neck also were called "veronicas." On Jesuits using veronicas to reward slaves on Engenho Santana in Brazil, see ANTT, CSJ, Maço 70, No. 104.

20. ANTT, Inquisição de Lisboa, Processos, No. 6600.

21. Ibid., Processos, No. 5393.

Chapter Five

1. The association of bodies of water with the world of the dead was prevalent throughout Central Africa. Cavazzi describes the "ridiculous and superstitious" ceremonies that engaged Central Africans before they crossed lakes or rivers. Arriving at the edge of a body of water, Central Africans would drink a little of the water. They would then take clay (*mpemba*) from the bottom and "trace some mysterious signals on their chests" before diving in. Cavazzi, *Descrição Histórica*, 1:118.

2. It should be noted that despite a strong emphasis on the continuity of the soul in the other world, there was a diversity of beliefs about the nature of the afterlife in Central Africa. Some believed that, at death, souls passed from husbands to wives, unless the widow completed a ritual at a lake or a river, "drowning" her husband's spirit. Cavazzi, *Descrição Histórica*, 1:130. Others believed that the soul died along with the body. And still others believed in reincarnation. See Thornton, "Religious and Ceremonial Life," 74–75.

3. On the ritual preparation of bodies to aid the souls in their passage to the other world, see Cavazzi, *Descrição Histórica*, 1:125, 128–31; and "Ritos gentilicos," 373. For descriptions of spirits of the dead causing illness in Angola and Benguela in the eighteenth century, including remedies of feasts in their honor, see ANTT, Inquisição de Lisboa, Cadernos do Promotor, No. 94, Livro 287, ff. 371–74; and ANTT, Inquisição de Lisboa, Cadernos do Promotor, No. 92, Livro 285, ff. 250–83. Also see Cavazzi, 1:203–5; and "Ritos gentilicos," 372–73.

4. On the importance of dreams, see Cavazzi, *Descrição Histórica*, 1:116; Cadornega, *História Geral*, 3:259–60.

5. On offerings to the dead and idol houses located at cemeteries in Dongo in the

seventeenth century, see the chronicle of Padre Pero Tavares, "Carta e verdadeira relação." For similar beliefs among the Jaga, see Cavazzi, *Descrição Histórica*, 1:203–5.
Also see Hilton, *Kingdom of Kongo*, 11.

6. On souls being "eaten" by malevolent spirits in eighteenth-century Angola, see
ANTT, Inquisição de Lisboa, Cadernos do Promotor, No. 94, Livro 287, ff. 371–74.
Cavazzi noted that "the worst trick" that Kongolese healers (*ngombos*) played on people
was having them believe that illness and death could only be caused by the "malevolence" of witches. Cavazzi, *Descrição Histórica*, 1:93.

7. For descriptions of Central African poison ordeals, see Cavazzi, *Descrição Histórica*, 1:103–6; and Battell, *Strange Adventures of Andrew Battell*, 62.

8. Cavazzi, *Descrição Histórica*, 1:121; Hilton, *Kingdom of Kongo*, 15–18.

9. I have borrowed the term "devout" scholars from Horton, *Patterns of Thought in
Africa and the West*, 162. Horton argues that scholars like Victor Turner, E. E. Evans-
Pritchard, John Mbiti, E. Bolaji Idowu, and others have failed to capture the true
essence of African religions because of the deep influence of Christianity in their approach to the scholarship. Horton also uses the term "theologians" to describe these
scholars. Horton has been widely criticized for his iconoclastic approach to the study
of African religions, but his is one of the only approaches that attempts to place Africans at the center of their own spiritual world. The following theoretical descriptions
draw heavily from Horton's work, in particular Chapter 6, "Judaeo-Christian Spec-
tacles," 161–93.

10. Thornton, *Kongolese Saint Anthony*, 114–15.

11. Greene, "Religion, History and the Supreme Gods of Africa," 122–38.

12. In at least one society, there was no supreme being at all. According to Okot
p'Bitek, the Luo of Tanzania and Uganda maintain no supreme deity in their traditional
religious thought. p'Bitek, *Religion of the Central Luo*.

13. p'Bitek, *African Religions in Western Scholarship*, 109.

14. Horton views religious thought and scientific theory as operating on the same
explanatory plane. Despite the value-laden nature of religion and science in Western
society, the two operate in remarkably similar ways in most parts of the world. For
more on Horton's "Similarity Thesis," see Horton, *Patterns of Thought in Africa and
the West*, 347–54.

15. Thornton, *Africa and Africans*, 257.

16. Ibid., 255–62.

17. For a clear articulation of Kongolese Christianity in the seventeenth and eighteenth centuries, see Thornton, *Kongolese Saint Anthony*. Also see Thornton, "Development of an African Catholic Church"; Thornton, *Kingdom of Kongo*, 56–68; and,
most recently, Thornton, "Religious and Ceremonial Life in the Kongo and Mbundu
Areas."

18. Prior to the Council of Trent, the Catholic Church was more tolerant of everyday forms of revelation similar to those found in Africa, but this changed quickly in
the second half of the sixteenth century, as the church embraced an elaborate theory
of witchcraft, prosecuting diviners and healers who were believed to be in league with

the Devil. On the emergence of witchcraft in the Portuguese world, see Bethencourt, *O Imaginário da magia*; and Paiva, *Bruxaria e superstição*. As we will see in the chapters that follow, African religious forms were particularly suspect as the work of the Devil.

19. Thornton, *Africa and Africans*, 260.

20. ANTT, Corpo Chronológico, Parte 1, Maço 115, No. 136. Carta de Frei Manuel Baptista, Bispo do Congo e Angola dando conta a Rey estara genteo daquella terra incapaz de se esperar servissem a Deus e ao mesmo Sr. El Rey do Congo . . . 10 July 1612.

21. Cavazzi, *Descrição Histórica*, 1:87.

22. On the burning of African sacred objects and houses of worship from the year 1606, see Viegas, *Relação Anual*, 1:413; from the year 1674, Propaganda Fide, Scritture referite nei Congressi, Serie Africa, 1; VFL Roll 11481, ff. 302–303v.; from the year 1699, Thornton, *Kongolese Saint Anthony*, 72–73; from the year 1752, ANTT, Inquisição de Lisboa, Processos, No. 16414. The public burning of African sacred objects continued in Brazil. See, for instance, Pereira, *Compendio Narrativo*, 1:128.

23. Inquisição de Lisboa, Cadernos do Promotor, No. 86, Livro 279, ff. 39–40.

24. Thornton argues that Catholic priests took an "inclusive" approach to Kongolese conversion, tolerating numerous aspects of indigenous religion. See Thornton, *African and Africans*, 256–57.

25. Kimpa Vita, who claimed that she was permanently possessed by Saint Anthony, gained a widespread following in Kongo between 1704 and 1706 with her messages of Kongolese unity and redemption of the war-torn kingdom of Mbanza Kongo. Among other things, she argued that Jesus was Kongolese; she charged that European priests intentionally ignored black saints; and she rejected Catholic sacraments as mere symbols. In 1706, she was burned at the stake. See Thornton, *Kongolese Saint Anthony*.

26. The phrase "explanation, prediction, and control" is Robin Horton's way of succintly explaining the primary aim of African religion. I have borrowed this from him. See Horton, *Patterns of Thought in Africa and the West*.

27. Thornton, *Kongolese Saint Anthony*, 17, 28–29.

28. Thornton persists in referring to "African Christians" in nearly all of his most recent work. Yet, throughout *Kongolese Saint Anthony* he demonstrates the distinct nature of African Christianity and the attempts by the Kongolese to recast Christianity according to Kongolese tradition. The conflict between the two traditions permeates the work. In short, I believe Thornton is correct in arguing for a distinct form of African Christianity, but his findings demand alternative terminologies or theoretical paradigms.

29. Thornton, *Africa and Africans*, 255–56.

30. Parallel beliefs were not uncommon in the Portuguese world during the sixteenth and seventeenth centuries. See the examples of China and some parts of India in Boxer, *Portuguese Seaborne Empire*, 238–45.

31. Thornton, "Development of an African Catholic Church," 148.

32. Thornton, *Kingdom of Kongo*, 120.

33. MacGaffey, "Dialogues of the Deaf." Similar misunderstandings occurred between Europeans and the indigenous peoples of the Americas. James Lockhart has called the phenomenon "Double Mistaken Identity." Lockhart, "Some Nahua Concepts in Postconquest Guise."

34. This process is well chronicled in Thornton, *Kongolese Saint Anthony* and "Religious and Ceremonial Life."

35. Barnes, "Introduction," 11.

36. As quoted in Thornton, "Perspectives on African Christianity," 180.

37. This "creolization" argument is most clearly articulated in Mintz and Price, *Birth of African-American Culture*. More recently, see Frey and Wood, *Come Shouting to Zion*; and Berlin, *Many Thousands Gone*. For Brazil, see Souza, *O diabo e a terra de Santa Cruz*.

38. The pioneering work on African "survivals" was Herskovits, *Myth of the Negro Past*. The notion of broadly conceived "survivals" or "Africanisms" can also be found in Bastide, *African Civilizations in the New World*; Blassingame, *Slave Community*; and Holloway, *Africanisms in American Culture*. Other investigations, like Klein, *African Slavery in Latin America and the Caribbean*, 163–87, also describe a culturally disconnected, homogenized "African" culture. Some Brazilianists have been more attentive to the specifics of the African past. See, for instance, Slenes, "'Malungu Ngoma Vem!'" and *Na Senzala, Uma Flor*. Also see Reis, "Magia jeje na Bahia," and *Rebelião escrava no Brasil*.

39. Thornton, *Africa and Africans*, 320.

40. Gomez, *Exchanging Our Country Marks*, has argued that Africans in North America exchanged their ethnic identities for a collective one centered on race, admitting that it is a "complex matter . . . how such unity was achieved." While I would not quibble with Gomez's conclusions, I would reformulate his proposal somewhat. Before African slaves could come to identify themselves according to race, they first had to overcome those social and cultural obstacles that distinguished them from slaves of other backgrounds. Thus, I would argue that distinct ethnic/national identities were first transformed into a collective "African" identity. Through negotiation and exchange between Africans of various backgrounds, broadly shared core "African" beliefs emerged in slave communities. Still, African ethnic distinctions persisted where demographic conditions allowed. Even as a collective "African" identity was forged, distinct ethnic identities retained their primacy in many slave communities, resulting in a hierarchy of identity that was more narrow at the top (African ethnicity) and broader at the bottom (race). For Brazilian expressions of collective "African" identities, see Reis, *Rebelião escrava*; and Prandi, "De Africano a Afro-Brasileiro."

Chapter Six

1. Devisch, "Divination and Oracles."

2. In nearly all the Inquisition cases in which Central Africans are key figures, there are references to the use of African languages in rituals and ceremonies. Usually these

references appear as "in his/her language," or "in the language of Angola." Given the large numbers of Africans who attended these divining and healing ceremonies and who apparently understood the orations, it appears that a creolized Kimbundu/Kikongo lingua franca developed in the slave communities of Brazil. It is likely that this process of linguistic creolization began on the African coast. As we have already noted, there were only slight differences between Kimbundu and Kikongo. Joseph Miller suggests that Kimbundu supplanted Kikongo at the main slaving port of Luanda only during the seventeenth century and after, as Europeans brought large numbers of Kimbundu-speaking slaves from the interior to the coast. Miller, *Kings and Kinsmen*, 39; *Way of Death*, 403; and "Worlds Apart." Enslavement and the Middle Passage no doubt hastened the search for linguistic common ground.

3. ANTT, Inquisição de Lisboa, Processos, No. 8464. Also see Cadernos do Promotor, No. 59, Livro 256, ff. 130-130v.

4. Wealth and prosperity were considered indicators of religious strength, but over-abundance — or, in the case of a slave community, relative "overabundance" — was very likely believed to be the result of malevolence or "witchcraft." See Geschiere, *Modernity of Witchcraft*.

5. Russell-Wood, *Black Man in Slavery and Freedom*, 45-46, 51-52, 134-35.

6. Henri Junod, *The Life of a South African Tribe*, Vol. 2: *Mental Life*, 2d ed. (London, 1927), 571, as quoted in Peek, *African Divination Systems*, 69.

7. Peek, "African Divination Systems: Non-Normal Modes of Cognition," in Peek, *African Divination Systems*, 195.

8. Cavazzi, *Descrição Histórica*, 1:109.

9. Merolla, *Breve e succinta relatione*, 98. Cadornega also describes this ritual in his *História Geral*, 3:319-20, as does the anonymous author of "Ritos gentilicos," 372.

10. MacGaffey, "Dialogues of the Deaf," 255.

11. The name Gunza comes from the Kimbundu and Kikongo *ngunza*, which means "prophet." Bentley, *Dictionary and Grammar of the Kongo Language*, 375.

12. ANTT, Inquisição de Lisboa, Cadernos do Promotor, No. 29, Livro 228, ff. 10-11.

13. Ibid., Cadernos do Promotor, No. 18, Livro 219, ff. 305-13. This same ceremony with the cord and ball was still practiced by the Ndembu and Lunda in the middle of the twentieth century. See Turner, *Revelation and Divination in Ndembu Ritual*, 337.

14. ANTT, Inquisição de Lisboa, Cadernos do Promotor, No. 92, Livro 285, ff. 396-401.

15. MacGaffey as quoted in Thompson, *Flash of the Spirit*, 108. The cross is to be read as a symbol — with God at the top, the dead at the bottom, and water in between.

16. Divination by "casting lots" with various symbolic objects was, and continues to be, common throughout Central and Southern Africa. For the most detailed description of these divinations and the symbolic meanings of the objects, see Turner, *Revelation and Divination in Ndembu Ritual*.

17. Thompson, *Flash of the Spirit*, 142-45. For a discussion of Kongo-derived bottles in contemporary Haiti, see McAlister, "Sorcerer's Bottle."

18. Several of these divination rituals, along with burial practices, healing rituals, dietary restrictions, and other practices of Angolan slaves, are described in a document written in Rio de Janeiro in 1720. The list of ten "pagan rites of Angola" and an unsigned letter, requesting more priests to help instruct the Angolan slaves in Rio, can be found in ANTT, Conselho Geral, "Santo Ofício Tomo XXXI (1720)," Livro 272, ff. 123–123v., 231, 235–235v.

19. Ibid., Livro 272, ff. 123–123v., 235–235v. I have found no detailed description of the ritual as it was practiced in Brazil. Likewise, there is no specific reference to the ordeal of Golungo in Central African sources. Golungo is probably a reference to the Angolan town by the same name, located near Ambaca, between the Lucala and Zenza Rivers.

20. Nieuhof, *Memorável Viagem*, 309.

21. Lopes, *Dicionário Banto do Brasil*, 212.

22. Thomas, *Religion and the Decline of Magic*, 212–14.

23. Paiva, *Bruxaria e superstição*, 118.

24. The other confession was that of Bernardo Teixeira, a twenty-three-year-old white man, who stated that as a boy in Bahia, he took part in the *quibando* ritual, "which was popular in the said city." ANTT, Inquisição de Lisboa, Cadernos do Promotor, No. 59, Livro 256, ff. 237–39.

25. Ibid., Cadernos do Promotor, No. 59, Livro 256, ff. 235–36.

26. Ibid., Cadernos do Promotor, No. 91, Livro 284, ff. 535–536v.

27. For a description of the *quibando* ritual in Goa, see ibid., Cadernos do Promotor, No. 74, Livro 268, ff. 37–48 (November 22, 1701).

28. Again, the uncertainty of ethnic background in the term "Guinea" further complicates any attempt to draw out specific cultural meanings in the divination ceremony.

29. ANTT, Inquisição de Lisboa, Denúncias, Livro 779, ff. 47v.–48v.

30. Ibid., Cadernos do Promotor, No. 263, Livro 263, f. 278v.

31. Ibid., Processos, No. 14089.

32. Herskovits, *Dahomey*, 2:240. It should be noted that these symbolic understandings of bodies of water were remarkably similar to those of many Central Africans, probably facilitating cultural exchange between the two groups in the diaspora.

33. ANTT, Inquisição de Lisboa, Processos, No. 16753. The small stick used by Joseph was also common in Dahomean vodun. See Herskovits, *Dahomey*, 2:263–88.

34. Ibid., Processos, No. 16995.

35. In the early eighteenth century, English trader William Snelgrave noted that the snake was the "principal god" of Dahomey. Snelgrave, *A New Account of Some Parts of Guinea*, 10–14. Similarly, in 1788, Paul Erdmann Isert stated that the snake was the "superior godhead" of Dahomey. See Isert, *Journey to Guinea*. For a more recent description of snake worshipers on the "Mina" coast, see Herskovits, *Dahomey*, 2:245–55.

36. On divination with snakes to bring "goods and riches" on the Guinea coast near Cacheu, see ANTT, Inquisição de Lisboa, Processos, No. 2079.

37. Ibid., Processos, No. 14577. For a description of the use of snakes in divining

and healing in nineteenth-century Brazilian slave communities, see Bastide, *African Religions of Brazil*, 132–34.

38. See Chapter 7 for a fuller explication of this argument.

39. Herskovits, *Dahomey*, 2:18. It must be noted that there is no way of determining exactly when the *amízoka* ceremony began being practiced in Dahomey. Herskovits's descriptions are based on oral histories taken in the early 1930s.

40. Cavazzi, *Descrição Histórica*, 1:116.

41. Ellis, *Ewe-Speaking Peoples of the Slave Coast*, 95–96.

42. ANTT, Inquisição de Lisboa, Cadernos do Promotor, No. 29, Livro 228, ff. 13–14.

43. Ibid., Cadernos do Promotor, No. 18, Livro 219, ff. 305–13.

44. Ibid., Processos, No. 15484.

45. The term *boçal* (plural *boçais*) was used to refer to slaves who were newly arrived from Africa. Its literal meaning is "rude, stupid, or loutish."

46. ANTT, Inquisição de Lisboa, Cadernos do Promotor, No. 59, Livro 256, ff. 237–39.

47. Ibid., Livro 784, ff. 113–14.

48. Ibid., Processos, No. 252.

49. For a similar argument, see D. Ramos, "A influência africana," 149.

50. Schwartz has noted that justice in colonial Brazil was constantly threatened by "an unruly . . . society, great power in the hands of individuals and families, and broad sectors of the population unable or unwilling to comply with the social norms." In addition, he has written that the law applied to slaves "more as an object lesson than as the application of justice." S. B. Schwartz, *Sovereignty and Society in Colonial Brazil*, 246–47.

51. For the argument that slaves were able to create institutions only "within the parameters of the master's monopoly of power . . . separate from the master's institutions," see Mintz and Price, *Birth of African-American Culture*, 39.

Chapter Seven

1. Cavazzi, *Descrição Histórica*, 1:204–5.

2. Caltanissetta also recounts the tremors and great pains in the head allegedly suffered by a *nganga ngombo* who was given baptismal water on his head. Caltanissetta concluded that the devil in the *nganga*'s head was causing his pain. Caltanissetta, "Relatione della missione fatta nel regno di Congo," 254–55, 259–60.

3. Cavazzi, *Descrição Histórica*, 1:93.

4. ANTT, Inquisição de Lisboa, Cadernos do Promotor, No. 85, Livro 278, ff. 132–49.

5. Ibid., Processos, No. 3641.

6. Desch-Obi, "Combat and the Crossing of Kalunga," 358.

7. By the nineteenth century, the *jogo da capoeira* had emerged as a combination of dance and martial arts performed by male slaves, almost always in tandem. The martial

aspects of the "dance" made it appear to be a faux fight between the two contestants. For the most recent treatment of *capoeira* and its links to Central Africa, see Desch-Obi, "Engolo"; and C. Soares, *A capoeira escrava*. Also see Karasch, *Slave Life in Rio de Janeiro*, 245.

8. ANTT, Inquisição de Lisboa, Livro 784, ff. 81–82v. Also see ff. 65–66v. Although the ethnic description of these slaves is "Guiné," their ceremonies appear to be Central African in origin.

9. Cavazzi, *Descrição Histórica*, 1:209. These Central African possession rituals also occurred in other parts of the African diaspora. In St. Domingue, they were known as *calenda* and were widely practiced among the colony's slaves in the seventeenth and eighteenth centuries. See Métraux, *Voodoo in Haiti*, 32–35; Fick, *Making of Haiti*, 40–41.

10. "Ritos gentilicos," 371–73. This is part of a larger article entitled, "Exploração á Africa nos ineditos da Biblioteca de Evora," which provides edited transcriptions of African sources to be found in the Library of Évora. The editor of the larger article suggests that the likely author of this document was D. Luiz Simões Brandão, Bishop of Angola, who wrote similar tracts around the turn of the eighteenth century.

11. See Souza, *O diabo e a terra de Santa Cruz*, 263–69. Instead of recognizing *calundú* as a Kimbundu word describing a very particular type of spirit possession, Souza sees *calundú* as a broad category of possession ritual, into which she places some ceremonies that "seem to be *calundú*." There is no attempt on her part to unravel the specific African backgrounds of particular ceremonies. Souza also claims that *calundús* "thrived in Minas [Gerais] more than in any other point in the colony in the 18th century,." However, of the dozen *calundú* cases that I examined for the eighteenth century, only two were from Minas Gerais. Nine came from Bahia. By the late eighteenth century, *calundú* apparently was transformed into a more universal "African" belief system, at least in the minds of those born outside of Africa. Reis notes that in 1785, a large group of Jeje (Ewe-Fon) slaves were accused of *calundú* in Cachoeira. Reis, "Magia Jeje na Bahia."

12. ANTT, Inquisição de Lisboa, Livro 784, ff. 81–81v.

13. Ibid., Cadernos do Promotor, No. 18, Livro 219, ff. 305–13.

14. ADB/UM, CSB 138, ff. 49, 87. Between 1660 and 1666, the monastery paid 144$120 for "medicines and Negro curers."

15. ANTT, Inquisição de Lisboa, Processos, No. 3723. Also see the discussion of Souza, *O diabo e a terra de Santa Cruz*, 263–64.

16. Ibid., Cadernos do Promotor, No. 59, Livro 256, ff. 130–130v.

17. Ibid., Cadernos do Promotor, No. 82, Livro 275, ff. 421–22.

18. Ibid., Cadernos do Promotor, No. 83, f. 202. Calmon made a similar complaint the following year in 1716.

19. ANTT, Conselho Geral, "Santo Ofício Tomo XXXI (1720)," Livro 272, ff. 123–123v. and 235–235v(two copies of document in same livro).

20. From Mattos's *Satirica*, as quoted in Bastide, *African Religions of Brazil*, 134–35.

21. Pereira, *Compendio Narrativo*, 1:123–26.

22. ANTT, Inquisição de Lisboa, Cadernos do Promotor, No. 81, Livro 274, ff. 239–48.

23. In other instances, Central African drums known as *ngomas* were used. See, for instance, ANTT, Conselho Geral, "Santo Ofício Tomo" XXXI (1720), Livro 272, ff. 123–124v.

24. Jacobson-Widding, *Red-White-Black as Mode of Thought*, 50.

25. See *aluá* in Lopes, *Dicionário Banto do Brasil*, 30. *Ualuá* is sometimes translated as "beer"; however, it is not the barley- and hops-based beer that most Westerners are familiar with. Rather, *ualuá* is similar to other African "beers" made from sorghum, millet, corn, and so on.

26. The headdress of feathers and ribbons was common among Central African diviner/healers until very recently. The feathered crest was probably symbolic of those worn by the great chiefs. See Turner, *Revelation and Divination in Ndembu Ritual*, 146, 291.

27. ANTT, Inquisição de Lisboa, Cadernos do Promotor, No. 59, Livro 256, ff. 130–130v. For descriptions of remarkably similar practices in Central Africa, see Cavazzi, *Descrição Histórica*, 1:213.

28. ANTT, Inquisição de Lisboa, Cadernos do Promotor, No. 80, Livro 273, ff. 29–29v.

29. Ibid., Cadernos do Promotor, No. 67, Livro 261, ff. 311–320v.

30. Ibid., Cadernos do Promotor, No. 91, Livro 284, ff. 41–41v.

31. For the view that masters wielded unmitigated control over their slaves, see Gorender, "Questionamentos." The idea of the "peasant breach" is articulated most clearly in Cardoso, *Escravo ou campônes*.

32. ANTT, Inquisição de Lisboa, Cadernos do Promotor, No. 18, Livro 219, ff. 305–13.

33. Ibid., Processos, No. 12658.

34. The *negro de ganho* was "free" to seek out his own labor arrangements as long as he paid his master a set percentage of his earnings.

35. ANTT, Inquisição de Lisboa, Cadernos do Promotor, No. 76, Livro 270, ff. 86–87.

36. Ibid., Cadernos do Promotor, No. 67, Livro 261, ff. 311–320v.

37. Ibid., Cadernos do Promotor, No. 59, Livro 256, ff. 135–45.

38. Cavazzi, *Descrição Histórica*, 1:203.

39. ANTT, Inquisição de Lisboa, Cadernos do Promotor, No. 94, Livro 287, ff. 371–74.

40. For cures using *Zumbi* in Benguela in 1722, see ANTT, Inquisição de Lisboa, Cadernos do Promotor, No. 92, Livro 285, ff. 250–83. Also see Merolla, *Breve e succinta relatione*, 391–92.

41. ANTT, Conselho Geral, "Santo Ofício Tomo XXXI (1720)," Livro 272, ff. 123–123v., 235–235v.

42. ANTT, Inquisição de Lisboa, Cadernos do Promotor, No. 67, Livro 261, ff. 311–320v.

43. Ibid., Processos, No. 14723. The average price of a prime male slave in Minas Gerais in 1789 was 108 mil-réis. Bergad, *Slavery and the History of Minas Gerais*, 188, 199.

44. ANTT, Conselho Geral, "Santo Ofício Tomo XXXI (1720)," Livro 272, ff. 123–123v. and 235–235v.

45. ANTT, Inquisição de Lisboa, Cadernos do Promotor, No. 66, Livro 260; folios are unnumbered, but between ff. 256 and 257.

46. Ibid.

47. ANTT, Inquisição de Évora, Processos, No. 7759.

48. The Mina, Domingos Álvares, also "passed chickens over the heads" of his ailing clients in Rio de Janeiro. See ANTT, Inquisição de Évora, Processos, No. 7759.

49. According to Voeks, the seeds of *pimenta da costa* have "magical" powers which continue to be utilized by adherents of Candomblé. Voeks notes that this West African plant has been used by Africans in Brazil "at least since the mid-1800s." My findings push the date back to at least 1770. Voeks, *Sacred Leaves of Candomblé*, 112–13.

50. ANTT, Inquisição de Lisboa, Processos, No. 14158.

51. Métraux, *Voodoo in Haiti*, 172.

52. For the significance of herbal baths in curing physical and social illness in the Dahomean tradition, see Herskovits, *Dahomey*, 2:263; and Métraux, *Voodoo in Haiti*, 309–12. On herbal baths in Angola, see Cadornega, *História Geral*, 3:258.

53. Among some Angolans, particularly the Imbangala, the palm tree (along with its fruit and wine) were considered sacred. On the importance of palm trees, see Battell, *Strange Adventures*, 28–35. On the worship of palms and Catholic priests cutting them down in Angola, see ANTT, Inquisição de Lisboa, Cadernos do Promotor, No. 96, Livro 289, ff. 412–end (unnumbered). Stuart Schwartz has suggested that Brazil's most famous *quilombo* (slave runaway community) was called Palmares because of Imbangala influence in Brazil. See S. B. Schwartz, "Rethinking Palmares," 127.

54. ANTT, Inquisição de Lisboa, Processos, No. 7759.

Chapter Eight

1. The idea of witchcraft was usually captured in words and concepts that meant "religious powers." See, for instance, the description of Kongolese *kindoki* (religious powers/"witchcraft") in Bockie, *Death and the Invisible Powers*, 43–57.

2. Much of this theoretical framework is drawn from the works of Peter Geschiere on witchcraft discourses in modern Cameroon. Though the changing variables of "modernity" certainly transform meanings over time, the basic theoretical foundation of Geschiere's work applies equally to parts of precolonial Africa and, as we shall see, even to the diaspora. See Geschiere, *Modernity of Witchcraft* and "Witchcraft and Sorcery." Also see Bockie, *Death and the Invisible Powers*.

3. See, for example, a letter written by four Jesuits describing slave baptisms in Luanda in 1622. Some slaves believed the baptismal ceremony was "a thing of witchcraft in order for the Spaniards to eat them"; Sandoval, *De Instauranda*, 348. For an-

other description of the Angolan belief in white cannibals, see Leitão, "Uma viagem a Cassange," 20–21. For the connection between cannibalism and slave trading in Central Africa, see Thornton, "Cannibals and Slave Traders"; for a broader discussion of "white cannibals," see Piersen, *Black Legacy*, 5–12.

4. Debien, "La traite nantaise," 210; Debien, "Le journal de traite de la *Licorne*," 105–6.

5. Cosme, "Tractado das queixas endemicas," 264.

6. Taunay, *Subsídios para a história do tráfico africano no Brasil*, 139–40; Sandoval, *De Instauranda*, 348. Also see the letter of Jesuit Father Pedro Tavares, "Carta e verdadeira relação," 353.

7. See the provocative works of Comaroff and Comaroff, *Modernity and Its Malcontents*; Shaw, "Production of Witchcraft/Witchcraft as Production." For Central Africa, see MacGaffey, *Religion and Society in Central Africa*, 62.

8. For one of the first arguments describing American slavery as a form of witchcraft, see Schuler, "Afro-American Slave Culture." Also see Palmer, *Passageways*, 1:243, 251; and more recently, Palmié, *Wizards & Scientists*, 176–81.

9. Houdard, *Les sciences du diable*.

10. For Portuguese understandings of witchcraft, see Paiva, *Bruxaria e superstição*.

11. In particular, see Moura, *De incantationibus seu ensalmis*; and Lacerda, *Memorial e antídoto*. Moura and Lacerda were deputies of the Inquisition in Évora and Lisbon during the early seventeenth century. Both of these treatises are discussed at length in Paiva, *Bruxaria e superstição*, 25–36.

12. Paiva, *Bruxaria e superstição*, 26–30, 162–63. Women were the overwhelming targets of malefic witchcraft accusations in Portugal. Between 1600 and 1774, Paiva found that women were the accused in 83 percent of malevolent witchcraft cases heard by the Inquisition. Single women were especially suspect. Because they were not attached to a man, they were suspected of being morally lax and therefore vulnerable to the Devil's vices.

13. Ibid., 66–70.

14. Ibid., 37–38.

15. ANTT, Inquisição de Lisboa, Cadernos do Promotor, No. 29, Livro 228, ff. 4–4v.

16. ARSI, Brasilia 10 (I); VFL Roll 160, ff. 19–21v.

17. Souza, *O diabo e a terra de Santa Cruz*, 206–7; ANTT, Inquisição de Lisboa, Processos, No. 11163. The power of rubbings from the soles of shoes was a common popular belief in Europe, even as early as the sixteenth century. Africans and their descendants probably learned these rituals from Europeans and Moorish slaves.

18. ANTT, Inquisição de Coimbra, Processos, No. 1630.

19. ANTT, Inquisição de Lisboa, Cadernos do Promotor, No. 59, Livro 256, ff. 258–262v.

20. Ibid., Cadernos do Promotor, No. 76, Livro 270, ff. 41–42v.

21. Ibid., Cadernos do Promotor, No. 59, Livro 256, ff. 135–45.

22. Antonil, *Cultura e opulência do Brasil*, 130–33.

23. ANTT, Inquisição de Lisboa, Processos, No. 254.

24. Ibid., Cadernos do Promotor, No. 29, Livro 228, ff. 9–10.

25. Ibid., Cadernos do Promotor, No. 29, Livro 228, ff. 3v.–4.

26. Ibid., Processos, No. 3825.

27. The number of witchcraft cases in Portugal began to decline after 1750. The end of official persecution came in 1774 with the publication of the Regimento da Inquisição. Paiva, *Bruxaria e superstição*, 12, 363.

28. ANTT, Inquisição de Lisboa, Cadernos do Promotor, No. 18, Livro 219, ff. 299–300.

29. *Documentos históricos* 67:132–33.

30. ANTT, Inquisição de Lisboa, Processos, No 8464. See also ibid., Cadernos do Promotor, No. 59, Livro 256, ff. 130–130v.

31. Ibid., Cadernos do Promotor, No. 59, Livro 256, ff. 135–45.

32. Ibid., Cadernos do Promotor, No. 69, Livro 263, f. 282.

33. Ibid., Processos, No. 12658.

34. Ibid., Cadernos do Promotor, No. 71, Livro 265, ff. 430–430v.

35. Ibid., Cadernos do Promotor, No. 87, Livro 280, ff. 45–46.

36. Ibid., Processos, No. 3641.

37. See, for instance, ibid., Cadernos do Promotor,, No. 44, Livro 241, ff. 118–138v.; No. 76, Livro 270, ff. 86–87. But these social distinctions were often perpetuated by the master. Thus, one way to get back at both slave and master was to bewitch the deviant slave.

38. Ibid., Cadernos do Promotor, No. 18, Livro 219, ff. 301–3.

39. Ibid., Cadernos do Promotor, No. 71, Livro 265, ff. 430–430v.

40. Ibid., Processos, No. 3641.

41. Ibid., Cadernos do Promotor, No. 99, Livro 292, ff. 283–300v.

42. Ibid., Cadernos do Promotor, No. 64, Livro 259, ff. 33–33v.

43. Ibid., Cadernos do Promotor, No. 96, Livro 289, ff. 397–407v.

44. On such practices in Africa, see Cavazzi, *Descrição Histórica*, 1:121; and Hilton, *Kingdom of Kongo*, 15–18. On similar European practices, see Souza, *O diabo e a terra de Santa Cruz*, 171–72; and Paiva, *Bruxaria e superstição*, 97–98.

45. ANTT, Inquisição de Coimbra, Processos, No. 6821.

46. ANTT, Inquisição de Lisboa, Processos, No. 631. Also see Souza, *O diabo e a terra de Santa Cruz*, 239.

47. Licking a small stick and making a wish was a potent ritual in Dahomean vodun. See Herskovits, *Dahomey*, 2:283–84.

48. ANTT, Inquisição de Lisboa, Processos, No. 15628.

49. Cavazzi, *Descrição Histórica*, 1:179. See also the anonymous report, "Ritos gentilicos," 373.

50. Merolla, *Breve e succinta relatione*, 146.

51. Pereira, *Compendio Narrativo*, 1:133.

52. ANTT, Conselho Geral, "Santo Ofício Tomo XXXI (1720)," Livro 272, ff. 123–123v. and 235–235v. For slaves who adhered to these dietary restrictions, nutritional

deficiencies certainly were exacerbated. Since almost all meats were prohibited, protein deficiencies must have been particularly acute. Whether these Angolans were able to substitute beans, eggs, or other protein-rich foods for meat remains uncertain.

53. Pereira, *Compendio Narrativo*, 1:133.

54. ANTT, Inquisição de Lisboa, Cadernos do Promotor, No. 72, Livro 266, ff. 39–41v. (August 5, 1698—Luanda).

55. Cavazzi, *Descrição Histórica*, 1:128–29.

56. In seventeenth-century Cartagena, Colombia (New Granada), the Jesuit Father Pedro Claver noted that funerals were "social occasions" where "certain assemblies of Moors of the same nation [*stripe*] meet when someone of their nation dies." Similarly, in seventeenth-century Virginia, slaves gathered "in great numbers in makeing and holding of Funneralls for Dead Negroes." Thornton, *Africa and Africans*, 202, 228.

57. Russell-Wood, *Black Man in Slavery and Freedom*, 132. For Central African reactions to bones found in Brazilian waters, see Slenes, "Great Porpoise-Skull Strike."

58. See, for example, ANTT, Inquisição de Lisboa, Cadernos do Promotor, No. 55, Livro 252, ff. 367–397v. (May 30, 1678—Sergipe do Conde). Also see a 1731 case from Minas Gerais, cited in D. Ramos, "A influência africana," 155.

59. From Zacharias Wagener's *Thierbuch*, as quoted in Teixeira, *Dutch Brazil*, 2:20.

60. ANTT, Conselho Geral, "Santo Ofício Tomo XXXI (1720)," Livro 272, ff. 123–123v. and 235–235v.

61. Ibid. (Ritos gentilicos de Angolla). The passage that describes this ritual reads: "Quando foge algum escravo se sabem aporta por donde fugio vião de certas medidas de cordeis, e dentro dos dias sinalados, se recolhe o do escravo a casa do Senhor."

62. For descriptions of *kanga* in Kongo, see Thornton, *Kongolese Saint Anthony*, 133–34, 213. For the explicit use of *kanga* in eighteenth-century St. Domingue, see Fick, *Making of Haiti*, 57–58. For contemporary interpretations of *kanga* in Haiti, see Rey, "Kongolese Catholic Influences on Haitian Popular Catholicism," 280–84.

63. ANTT, Inquisição de Lisboa, Cadernos do Promotor, No. 68, Livro 262, ff. 176–183v.

64. On the use of *bolsas* in Mazagão, North Africa, see ibid., Cadernos do Promotor, No. 70, Livro 264, f. 205 (March 18, 1698); on *bolsas* in India, see ibid., Cadernos do Promotor, No. 66, Livro 260, ff. 42–57 (1689).

65. The use of "witchcraft" to escape from slavery apparently was not uncommon. In 1705, in a letter to King Dom Pedro II, Governor-General Dom Luis Cesar de Meneses noted that slaves in Brazil who could not convince their masters or the courts to free them through legal means would resort to *feitiçaria* in order to coerce friends in Lisbon to intervene on their behalf and secure their freedom by "extraordinary means." Presumably, these intermediaries would "bewitch" the king so that he would pardon them from their servitude. Russell-Wood, "'Acts of Grace,'" 322.

66. On early uses of *bolsas* in Europe, see Souza, *O diabo e a terra de Santa Cruz*, 211–12; Paiva, *Bruxaria e superstição*, 113–14.

67. ANTT, CSJ, Maço 68, No. 119. One can find a similar description of Mandingo pouches in Jobson, *Golden Trade*, 67.

68. ANTT, Inquisição de Lisboa, Processos, No. 2079.

69. One *tostão* was equal to 100 *réis*.

70. ANTT, Inquisição de Lisboa, Cadernos do Promotor, No. 51, Livro 248, ff. 283–285v.

71. For a description of the public demonstrations, see Paiva, *Bruxaria e superstição*, 113–14.

72. ANTT, Inquisição de Lisboa, Cadernos do Promotor, No. 72, Livro 266, ff. 77–91.

73. Ibid.

74. ANTT, Inquisição de Lisboa, Processos, No. 5477 (November 4, 1716).

75. ANTT, Inquisição de Coimbra, Processos, No. 1630. For another case that is linked with Luís de Lima's, see ANTT, Inquisição de Coimbra, Processos, No. 7840 (Pedro José, single slave, born on the Mina Coast, resident in Porto). Still another case from Lisbon in 1731 is ANTT, Inquisição de Lisboa, Processos, No. 16479.

76. ANTT, Inquisição de Lisboa, Processos, No. 9972. Also see Souza, *O diabo e a terra de Santa Cruz*, 217.

77. ANTT, Inquisição de Lisboa, Processos, No. 11774 (Processo de José Francisco Pedroso); Processos, No. 11767 (Processo de José Francisco Pereira). Also see Souza, *O diabo e a terra de Santa Cruz*, 217–18.

78. ANTT, Inquisição de Lisboa, Cadernos do Promotor, No. 79, Livro 272, ff. 397–397v. *Cartas de tocar*—literally, "touch letters"—were of European origin. They were pieces of paper with various orations and drawings that were reputed to draw the sexual interest of any person who was touched by them. Souza, *O diabo e a terra de Santa Cruz*, 228–30. African slaves used *cartas de tocar* in their *bolsas de mandinga* as another form of talisman.

79. For the Portuguese view of Brazil as a place alternating between heaven, purgatory, and hell, see Souza, *O diabo e a terra de Santa Cruz*, esp. 371–78. The "ambiguity" of Brazilian "popular" religion rendered the colony a veritable purgatory in the minds of most Portuguese religious thinkers.

80. The *bolsa* was the most common form of *mandinga*, but any object or talisman that was reputed to protect or bring luck could be referred to as a "*mandinga*."

81. ANTT, Inquisição de Coimbra, Processos, No. 1630.

82. ANTT, Inquisição de Lisboa, Novos Maços, Maço 27, No. 41.

83. Ibid., Processos, No. 15628. It is not clear whether the *mandinga* offered by Domingos was a *bolsa* or some other talisman.

84. Ibid., Processos, No. 502. Two years earlier, in 1750, three other slaves were accused of carrying *bolsas de mandinga* in the Bahian village of Jacobina. See Souza, *O diabo e a terra de Santa Cruz*, 220–21, from the following cases: ANTT, Inquisição de Lisboa, Processos, Nos. 508, 1131, and 1134.

85. Gronniosaw (1770) as quoted in Gates and Andrews, *Pioneers of the Black Atlantic*, 114–15.

86. For a discussion of African encounters with "the word," see Gates and Andrews,

in *Pioneers of the Black Atlantic*, 1–29. For a very different reaction to an encounter with "the word" among the Inca in Peru, see Seed, "'Failing to Marvel.'"

87. Taussig, *Shamanism, Colonialism, and the Wild Man*, 465.

Chapter Nine

1. Thornton, *Kongolese Saint Anthony*, 27–35.

2. ANTT, Inquisição de Lisboa, Cadernos do Promotor, No. 98, Livro 291, (unnumbered folios).

3. Ibid., Cadernos do Promotor, No. 72, Livro 266, ff. 36–41v.

4. Cadornega, *História Geral*, 3:267–68.

5. ANTT, Inquisição de Lisboa, Processos, No. 16414. Correa's case was related by Father Gaspar Borges Cardozo, who argued that Correa was falsely accused. Father Gaspar noted that large numbers of people were the victims of similar trumped up charges. According to the priest, these accused either died in prison or were sold into the Brazilian slave trade.

6. Thornton, *Kongolese Saint Anthony*, 149–50. Thornton describes this phenomenon near the town of Mbanza Soyo in eastern Kongo in 1705.

7. Cavazzi, *Descrição Histórica*, 1:352–53.

8. Thornton, *Kongolese Saint Anthony*, 17.

9. The belief in salt as a witchcraft repellent continues to be widespread across Central and Southern Africa. Those who believe that they are being attacked by malevolent witchcraft will spread rock salt around their yards and on top of their houses to ward off evil spirits. Personal observation by author.

10. Cavazzi, *Descrição Histórica*, 1:353.

11. ANTT, Inquisição de Lisboa, Cadernos do Promotor, No. 98, Livro 291 (unnumbered).

12. Sandoval, *De Instauranda*, 348, 352. Similar mass baptisms continued at least through the middle of the eighteenth century. See Miller, *Way of Death*, 402–4.

13. Sandoval, *De Instauranda*, 349, 363–64.

14. For discussions of the African-Catholic influence in the diaspora, see the numerous works of Thornton. Also see Vanhee, "Central African Popular Christianity"; and Rey, "The Virgin Mary and Revolution in Saint-Domingue." On the nature of Christian beliefs among Central Africans in the Danish West Indies, see the chronicle of the missionary C. G. A. Oldendorp. Oldendorp wrote: "The Negroes from the Congo nation who came to the West Indies as slaves usually have for the most part some knowledge of the true God and of Jesus Christ, and they are more intelligent and better mannered than other Blacks. For this they have to thank the Portuguese who, since their settlement along this coast, have made a great effort to enlighten and improve these ignorant people with Christian teachings. In this endeavor, they have been partially successful with those who dwell nearby. However, those who live further inland and are far removed from the Portuguese have a religion that combines heathen superstition

and Christian ritual." Oldendorp, *History of the Mission of the Evangelical Brethren*, 168.

15. Carli, "A Curious and Exact Account of a Voyage to Congo," 152.

16. Cavazzi, *Descrição Histórica*, 2:146; Merolla, *Breve e succinta relatione*, 101–2.

17. ARSI, Brasilia 26; VFL Roll 159, ff. 333–39.

18. ARSI, Brasilia 8 (I); VFL Roll 159, ff. 250–51.

19. ARSI, Brasilia 8 (I); VFL Roll 159, ff. 270–270v. Slaves were catechized before being baptized so they would understand the substance of their baptism. For instructions on the catechism, see "Constituições Primeiras do Arcebispado da Bahia," as quoted in Conrad, *Children of God's Fire*, 154–58.

20. ARSI, Brasilia 8 (II); VFL Roll 159, ff. 311v.–312.

21. ARSI, Brasilia 26; VFL Roll 160, f. 386v.

22. ARSI, Brasilia 3 (II); VFL Roll 156, ff. 115–115v.

23. ANTT, Conselho Geral, "Santo Ofício Tomo XXXI (1720)," Livro 272, f. 231.

24. Antonil, *Cultura e opulência do Brasil*, 124–27.

25. The questions posed to Father Antonil were strikingly similar to those asked of Capuchin priests in Central Africa. For instance, in the 1650s, Capuchin priest Sarafino da Cortona noted that "it is universal error among these people to believe that there is no other life than this one; and so they say that it is a lie what we preach about death, the Judgement, Hell, and Heaven. And [they ask] how does a person get to Heaven or Hell after dying?" Cortona, "Breve Relatione," 168.

26. Benci, *Economia christã dos senhores*, 71–78.

27. ANTT, Inquisição de Lisboa, Cadernos do Promotor, No. 24, Livro 224, ff. 96–125v.

28. ARSI, Brasilia 8 (I); VFL Roll 159, ff. 270–270v. (1619).

29. ARSI, Brasilia 10 (I); VFL Roll 160, ff. 19–21v. (1702).

30. Pereira, *Compendio Narrativo*, 1:155.

31. As quoted in Bastide, *African Religions of Brazil*, 134.

32. ARSI, Brasilia 9; VFL Roll 158, f. 342.

33. See, for instance, the remarkable story of the African-born Courana slave, Rosa Egipcíaca, who was brought to Brazil as a child. Rosa was thoroughly creolized and eventually was brought before the Inquisition for her continuous visions and heretical claims. Among other things, she claimed that she was Jesus's wet-nurse, that she would be the bride of the Holy Trinity, and that she would birth the baby Jesus on his second coming. Mott, *Rosa Egipcíaca*.

34. Souza, *O diabo e a terra de Santa Cruz*, 214. The description of the *pedra d'ara* as a "portable altar" comes from the *Constituições Primeiras do Arcebispado da Bahia* (1707).

35. ANTT, Inquisição de Lisboa, Processos, No. 3670.

36. Ibid., Processos, No. 1630.

37. Ibid., Processos, No. 14826.

38. Ibid., Cadernos do Promotor, No. 79, Livro 272, ff. 397–397v.

39. Karasch, *Slave Life in Rio de Janeiro*, 268–75; Bastide, *African Religions of Brazil*, 260–72.

40. Thornton, *Kongolese Saint Anthony*. On the importance of St. Anthony in Brazil, see Mott, "Santo Antônio," 110–38. Though Mott demonstrates that Central Africans appealed to St. Anthony in several healing and curing ceremonies after 1739, he also shows that whites called upon St. Anthony to help them recover runaway slaves from as early as the seventeenth century. It is unclear whether the slaves' appeals to St. Anthony were born of the Antonian Movement in Central Africa or of understandings of St. Anthony learned in Brazil. The documents from Brazil remain silent on this issue.

41. Bastide, *African Religions of Brazil*, 116.

42. Romero, *Contos Populares do Brasil*, as quoted by Bastide, *African Religions of Brazil*, 116.

43. For instance, in 1754, Antônio, a Courana slave in Rio de Janeiro, was purchased by the Irmandade de Santo Elesbão e Efigênia for 89$600. ANRJ, Segundo Ofício de Notas do Rio de Janeiro, Livro de Notas, No. 70, ff. 27–27v.

44. Saunders, *Social History of Black Slaves and Freedmen*, 151–52.

45. Mulvey, "Black Brothers and Sisters," 254.

46. Mulvey, "Slave Confraternities in Brazil," 61.

47. On the rosary as an African talisman, see Saunders, *Social History of Black Slaves and Freedmen*, 152; Mulvey, "Black Brothers and Sisters," 256.

48. Mulvey, "Black Brothers and Sisters," 262–63.

49. Bastide, *African Religions of Brazil*, 119.

50. Mulvey, "Black Brothers and Sisters," 263.

51. Verger, *Flux et Reflux*, 528.

52. Karasch, *Slave Life in Rio de Janeiro*, 272.

53. For Angola, see Miller, *Kings and Kinsmen*, 50. For Kongo, see Thornton, *Kongolese Saint Anthony*, 56–58.

54. Mulvey, "Black Brothers and Sisters," 261.

55. ANTT, Inquisição de Lisboa, Processos, No. 16001. It should be noted that Pedro and his Mina adherents did not respond kindly to the intrusion made by the Catholic priests. After the priests had seen Pedro's "synagogue" and made their departure, Pedro and a number of Mina women marched "scandalously" through the streets until they arrived at the house of Father Manuel Ribeiro Soares. The group proceeded to enter the priest's house, threatening him with a gun and a club.

56. ANTT, Inquisição de Lisboa, Processos, No. 2556.

57. Ibid., Processos, No. 433.

58. Ibid., Processos, No. 719.

59. Ibid., Processos, No. 3641.

60. Ibid., Processos, No 9676.

61. Ibid., Cadernos do Promotor, No. 73, Livro 267, ff. 86–93v.

Chapter Ten

1. ANTT, Inquisição de Lisboa, Cadernos do Promotor, No. 80, Livro 273, ff. 32–32v.

2. Ibid., Cadernos do Promotor, No. 68, Livro 262, ff. 176–183v.

3. Based on the descriptions of his rituals and practices, Boaventura was probably a Kongolese *nganga ngombo*. See Chapter 7, passim.

4. ANTT, Inquisição de Lisboa, Processos, No. 3641.

5. Ibid., Cadernos do Promotor, No. 75, Livro 269, ff. 201–3.

6. Antonil, *Cultura e opulência do Brasil*, 102–3.

7. The complete citation for the book is Benito Remigio Noydens, *Práctica de exorcistas y ministros de la Iglesia, en que con mucha erudición y singular claridad se trata de la instrucción de los exorcismos para lanzar y ahuyentar los demonios y curar espiritualmente todo género de maleficios y hechizos* (Madrid: Andrés Garcia de la Iglesia, 1678).

8. ANTT, Inquisição de Lisboa, Processos, No. 597.

Conclusion

1. Frey and Wood, *Come Shouting to Zion*, 39–40.

2. Mintz and Price, *Birth of African-American Culture*, 39.

BIBLIOGRAPHY

This study relies upon a range of ecclesiastical and state records, the majority of them housed in Portuguese and Brazilian archives. In Portugal, I examined marriage records, criminal pardons, Jesuit- and Benedictine-related materials, and records of Inquisition cases. In Brazil, I looked at marriage records, baptismal records, and notarial papers. I also consulted the Jesuit missionary reports at the Vatican Film Library at St. Louis University.

In some instances, I have retraced the steps of other scholars, examining many of the same documents but through a distinctly African prism. Stuart Schwartz and Dauril Alden have both done magisterial works using the Jesuit materials in the Arquivo Nacional da Torre do Tombo. Indeed, Professor Alden's notations in that collection served as a helpful road map for negotiating the lack of order that characterizes the collection. Professor Schwartz's work also served as a guide for my research in the Benedictine collection at the Arquivo Distrital de Braga. Their studies made my research far easier.

Though I have built upon the works of other scholars, by far the most important collection that I consulted for this project was one that has been used only sparingly by colonial Brazilianists—the collection of documents of the Portuguese Holy Office of the Inquisition. The Inquisition records provide some of the richest ethnographic accounts available describing the Portuguese and their colonial subjects. Included in the collection are detailed descriptions of those African religious practices that the Portuguese defined as "witchcraft." The collection also includes descriptions of the practices of Muslim slaves. In addition to detailed accounts of African religious practices, there are data on sacrileges, blasphemies, separation from families and kinship units, same-sex relationships, abuses by masters, work patterns, economic opportunities, and many other aspects of slave life.

The collection has remained inaccessible to many scholars because it is so immense and, until recently, almost completely uncatalogued. The *processos* (cases that were actually brought to trial) are slowly being entered into a computer data base. The data base allows the researcher to perform searches according to a wide range of criteria, including names, ages, birthplaces, types of crimes, social status, marital status, verdicts/punishments, and so on. But the slow pace at which this information is being entered means that research still can be excruciatingly difficult.

During the time that this research was being undertaken, the data base was far from complete. In most cases, the *processo* number and the name of the suspect were the only information available. Thus, in my searches for peoples of African descent, I engaged in a strategy of informed guesswork. Since most slaves lacked surnames, I scanned all of the data bases for the Coimbra, Évora, and Lisboa tribunals, searching for those suspects who were listed by only a first name. Once I had compiled a list of all of the suspects with first names only, I systematically examined each of these cases to determine whether Africans were among the accused. This strategy elicited a number of cases involving African slaves, but it was certainly not a foolproof way of finding Africans and their descendants. Despite my best efforts, there are very likely a number of cases involving Africans that remain to be discovered.

Though the *processos* provide the most complete and detailed ethnographic descriptions in the Inquisition collection, perhaps the best starting point for any student of the Portuguese colonial world are the *Visitações* (Visitations) and the *Cadernos do Promotor* (Prosecutor's Notebooks). Included among the papers of the Lisbon tribunal of the Inquisition are the various confessions, denunciations, and reports from Portugal's colonial possessions. The Inquisition made official visitations to the Azores and Madeira (1591–1593), Bahia (1591–1595 and 1618–1620), Pernambuco (1593–1595), and Grão Pará (1763–1769), during which they heard confessions and denunciations. In addition to these visitations, officials of the Holy Office heard confessions and denunciations on a regular basis in the colonies and sent them to Lisbon for review. The surviving confessions, denunciations, and reports are kept in the more than one hundred books of the *Cadernos do Promotor*.

The *Cadernos* have been largely ignored by historians and anthropologists, but their potential as a source of social and cultural history for the Portuguese colonial world is enormous. The *Cadernos* are organized chronologically. Within each book (*livro*) might be confessions, denunciations, and reports from a variety of locations in Portugal, Africa, Brazil, Asia, and India—in other words, the entire Portuguese colonial world. Thus, a single *livro* might cover a five-year period and be comprised of twenty pages of denunciations from Goa, followed by fifteen pages of denunciations from São Tomé, followed by fifty pages of denunciations from Bahia, followed by sixty pages of denunciations from Luanda. The typical *livro* is around 500 pages in length. For those interested in the cultural beliefs and practices of the peoples who comprised the Portuguese colonial world, the *Cadernos* are a rich and underutilized source.

Archival Primary Sources

Brazil

Arquivo da Curia Metropolitana do Rio de Janeiro (ACMRJ)

This is the archive for the archbishopric of Rio, where the old parish records are collected. The collections include marriage, baptismal, and burial records for slaves and free blacks. The documents provide vital information on the marriage choices of Africans and their descendants. I consulted records from the following parishes:

Nossa Senhora do Loreto do Jacarepaguá
  Batismos de escravos, 1691–1725
Paroquia de São José
  Batismos de escravos, 1751–1790
Nossa Senhora da Candelária
  Casamentos de pessoas livres e escravos, 1751–1761
  Óbitos, 1737–1740
Freguesia de S. Salvador do Mundo de Guaratiba
  Casamentos de escravos, 1763–1794
Santíssimo Sacramento
  Batismos de escravos, 1709–1714
  Óbitos, 1737–1740

Arquivo Nacional do Rio de Janeiro (ANRJ)

Here, in the national archives of Brazil, I consulted notarial records, which included letters of emancipation and slave inventories. The letters of emancipation reveal important information like the sex, age, and ethnicity of the emancipated slave, who purchased the slave's freedom, for how much, under what terms, and so on. Slave inventories give the researcher data on the ethnic and gender compositions of particular slave properties. The documents I consulted may be found in the following collections:

Primeiro Ofício de Notas do Rio de Janeiro (1749–1754)
  Livro de Notas, Nos. 117–121, 123–125
Segundo Ofício de Notas do Rio de Janeiro (1749–1754)
  Livro de Notas, Nos. 62, 65–68, 70
Quarto Ofício de Notas do Rio de Janeiro (1749–1754)
  Livro de Notas, Nos. 44, 46–49

Portugal

Arquivo Distrital de Braga/Universidade de Minho (ADB/UM)

The Benedictines of Brazil submitted triennial reports to their mother house in Tibães, near the city of Braga. These reports are now housed in the district archives and reveal important information on slave mortality rates, slave treatment, and slave purchase and inheritance patterns of the congregation. I consulted all of the *livros* of the following collection:

Congregação de São Bento (CSB)

Arquivo Nacional da Torre do Tombo, Lisbon (ANTT)

The National Archive of Portugal houses the majority of the surviving records of the Portuguese Inquisition, discussed above. It is also the depository for some of the papers of the Portuguese Society of Jesus (Jesuits), including those who operated sugar plantations in Bahia. The Jesuit records are among the only surviving plantation records for early colonial Brazil and reveal indispensable information on the African origins of slaves, slave purchasing patterns, work patterns, living conditions, birth and mortality rates, and kinship patterns. I also consulted the marriage records of several Lisbon parishes; however, unlike in the parish records that I consulted in Rio de Janeiro, there was no ethnic or genealogical information listed in the records of slaves and free blacks. Finally, I looked at the criminal pardons issued by Dom Filipe III. These pardons show the "criminal" behaviors of slaves and free blacks, including assaults, murders, gambling, and "illicit relationships" (*amancebados*) between males and females. The collections I consulted were the following:

Cartório dos Jesuítas (CSJ)
 Maços 5–19, 26–27, 30, 33, 35–38, 51–54, 68–70, 82–83
Chancelaria D. Filipe III
 Perdões e Legits (Proprios)
Corpo Cronológico
 Parte 1
Registos Paroquiais
 Concelho de Lisboa
  Sé—Casamentos, Livros 1–3
  Nossa Senhora da Conceição—Casamentos, Livros 1–4
Santo Ofício
 Conselho Geral
  Inquisição, Livro 272
 Inquisição de Coimbra
  Processos
 Inquisição de Évora
  Processos
 Inquisição de Lisboa
  Processos
  Cadernos do Promotor
  Novos Maços
  Visitações

United States

Saint Louis University/Vatican Film Library (VFL)

Saint Louis University houses a microfilm collection of numerous Vatican and other church-related documents. Among their collection are the papers of the Society of Jesus, taken from the Archivum Romanum Societatis Iesu (ARSI) in Rome. These papers include missionary reports from across Brazil during the early colonial period. The missionary reports provide valuable commentaries on the religious practices of African slaves as well as reports on the attempts of Catholic priests to proselytize Africans. The mission priests commented on a number of important issues, including language difficulties, the shortage of priests, slave mortality, gender imbalance in the slave population, and the difficulties of administering the sacraments to Africans. The citations in my text refer to the ARSI collection of reports from Brazil by book number, as well as the Vatican Film Library (VFL) microfilm roll number. I consulted all of the microfilms in the Brasilia collection.

Archivum Romanum Societatis Iesu (ARSI)
   Brasilia

Published Primary Sources

Abreu, João Capistrano de, ed. *Primeira visitação do Santo Officio às partes do Brasil pelo Licenciado Heitor Furtado de Mendonça. Confissões da Bahia, 1591-1592.* Rio de Janeiro: F. Briguiet, 1935.

———. *Primeira visitação do Santo Ofício às partes do Brasil pelo Licenciado Heitor Furtado de Mendonça. Denunciações da Bahia, 1591-1593.* São Paulo, 1925.

Anchieta, Padre Joseph de, S.J. *Cartas, Informações, Fragmentos Históricos e Sermões do Padre Joseph de Anchieta, S.J. (1554-1594).* Edited by Afranio Peixoto. Rio de Janeiro: Civilização Brasileira, 1933.

Antonil, André João. *Cultura e opulência do Brasil por suas drogas e minas.* Edited by Andrée Mansuy. Paris: Institut des hautes études de l'Amérique latine, 1968.

Arquivo Nacional. *Guia brasileiro de fontes para a história da Africa, da escravidão, e do negro na sociedade actual.* 2 vols. Brasília: Departamento da Imprensa Nacional, 1988.

Battell, Andrew. *The Strange Adventures of Andrew Battell of Leigh.* Edited by E. G. Ravenstein. London: Hakluyt Society, 1901.

Benci, Jorge. *Economia cristã dos senhores no governo dos escravos (1700).* Edited by Serafim Leite. 2d ed. Porto: Livraria Apostolado da Imprensa, 1954.

Bosman, Willem. *A New and Accurate Description of the Coast of Guinea.* London: Frank Cass, 1967.

Brasío, António, ed. *Monumenta Missionaria Africana.* Lisbon: Agência Geral do Ultramar, 1952- .

Brito, Domingos Abreu e. *Um inquérito a vida administrativa e económica de Angola e do Brasil em fins do século XVI. 1591.* Edited by Alfredo de Albuquerque Felner. Coimbra: Imprensa da Universidade, 1931.

Cadamosto, Alvise da. *The Voyages of Cadamosto and Other Documents.* Translated and edited by G. R. Crone. London: Hakluyt Society, 1937.

Cadornega, Antônio de Oliveira. *História geral das guerras angolanas, 1680.* 3 vols. Lisbon: Agência Geral das Colónias, 1940–1942.

Caltanisetta, Luca da. "Relatione della missione fatta nel regno di Congo per il padre Fra Luca da Caltanissetta per lo spatio di anni undici in circa sino all fine del 1701." In *Il Congo agli inizi del settecento nella relazione di P. Luca da Caltanissetta,* edited by Romain Rainero. Florence: La Nuova Italia, 1972.

Cardim, Fernão. *Tratados da terra e gente do Brasil.* 1583. 3d ed. São Paulo: Companhia Editora Nacional, 1978.

Carli, Dionigio de. "A Curious and Exact Account of a Voyage to Congo in the Years 1666 and 1667." In *A general collection of the best and most interesting voyages and travels in all parts of the world, many of which are now first translated into English, digested on a new plan.* Vol. 16, edited by John Pinkerton. London, 1808–1814.

Cavazzi, Padre Giovanni António. *Descrião Histórica dos Três Reinos do Congo, Matamba e Angola.* 2 vols. Edited and translated by Padre Graciano Maria de Leguzzano. Lisbon: Junta de Investigações do Ultramar, 1965.

Collecção de Noticias para a Historia e Geografia das Nações Ultramarinas, que Viven nos Dominios Portuguezes, ou lhes São Visinhas. Lisbon: Academia Real das Sciencias, 1812.

Cortona, Serafino da. "Breve Relatione dei riti gentilichi e ceremonie diaboliche e superstitioni del infelice Regno di Congo." In *Sogno: Bamba, Pemba, Ovando e altre contrade dei Regni di Congo, Angola e adiacenti,* edited by Paolo Collo and Silvia Benso, 151–72. Milan: Fernando Ricci, 1986.

Cosme, Dr. Francisco Damião. "Tractado das queixas endemicas, e mais fataes nesta Conquista," edited by Luis de Pina. *Studia* 20–22 (1967): 119–268.

Dapper, Olfert. *Objets Interdits.* Paris: Fondation Dapper, 1989.

Documentos históricos, Biblioteca Nacional de Rio de Janeiro. Rio de Janeiro, 1928– .

Debret, Jean Baptiste. *Voyage Pittoresque et Historique au Brésil, ou Séjour d'un Artists Français au Brésil, depuis 1816 jusqu'en 1831.* 3 vols. Paris, 1834–1839.

Donnan, Elizabeth, ed. *Documents Illustrative of the Slave Trade to America.* 4 vols. Washington, D.C.: Carnegie Institution, 1930–35.

Dussen, Andrien van der. *Relatório sôbre as capitanias conquistadas no Brasil pelos holandeses.* Edited by José Antônio Gonçalves de Mello. Rio de Janeiro: Instituto do Açúcar e do Alcool, 1947.

Ellis, A. B. *The Ewe-Speaking Peoples of the Slave Coast of West Africa: Their Religion, Manners, Customs, Laws, Languages, &c.* London, 1890; reprint, New York: Anthropological Publications, 1970.

Evreux, Yves d'. *Voyage au Nord du Brésil fait en 1613 et 1614.* Edited by Hélène Clastres. Paris: Payot, 1985.

Fleuriot de Langle, A. J. R. "Croisières à la côte d'Afrique (1868)." *Le tour du monde* 31 (1876): 241–304.

França, Eduardo d'Oliveira, and Sonia Siqueira, eds. *Segunda visitação do Santo Ofício* ás partes do Brasil pelo inquisidor e visitador o Licenciado Marcos Teixeira. *Livro das Confissões e Ratificações da Bahia—1618-1620.* Anais do Museu Paulista, vol. 17.

Garcia, Rodolfo, ed. *Primeira visitação do Santo Ofício às partes do Brasil pelo Licenciado Heitor Furtado de Mendonça. Denunciações de Pernambuco, 1593-1595.* São Paulo, 1929.

————. *Segunda visitação do Santo Ofício às partes do Brasil. Denunciações da Bahia, 1618—Marcos Teixeira.* Anais da Biblioteca Nacional do Rio de Janeiro 49 (1927).

Guinness, H. Gratten. *Grammar of the Congo Language as Spoken in the Cataract Region Below Stanley Pool.* London: Stodder and Stoughton, 1882.

Instituto do Açúcar e do Alcool. *Documentos para a história do açúcar.* 3 vols. Rio de Janeiro, 1954-1963.

Isert, Paul Erdmann. *Journey to Guinea and the Caribbean Islands in Columbia (1788).* Edited by Selena Axelrod Wisnes. Oxford: Oxford University Press, 1992.

Jobson, Richard. *The Golden Trade; or, A discovery of the River Gambra, and the golden trade of the Aethiopians.* London, 1623; reprint, New York: Da Capo, 1968.

Julião, Carlos. *Riscos Iluminados de Figurinhos Brancos e Negros dos Uzos do Rio de Janeiro e Serro do Frio.* Rio de Janeiro: Biblioteca Nacional, 1960.

Koster, Henry. *Travels in Brazil.* London: Longman, Hurst, Rees, Orme, and Brown, 1816.

Lacerda, Manuel de. *Memorial e antídoto contra os pós venenosos que o Demónio inventou e per seus confederados espalhou, em odio da christandade.* Lisbon, 1631.

Lapa, José Roberto Amaral, ed. *Livro da visitação do Santo Ofício da Inquisição ao Estado do Grão Pará—1763-1769.* Petrópolis: Vozes, 1978.

Leitão, Manuel Correia. "Uma viagem a Cassange nos meados do século XVIII," edited by Gastão Sousa Dias. *Boletim da Sociedade de geografia de Lisboa* 56 (1938): 3-30.

Leite, Serafim, ed. *Cartas do Brasil e mais escritos do P. Manuel da Nóbrega (ópera omnia).* Coimbra: Universidade de Coimbra, 1955.

————. *Diálogo sobre a conversão do gentio* (por Manuel de Nóbrega). Lisbon, 1954.

————. *Monumenta Brasiliae.* 5 vols. Rome: Monumenta Historica Societatis Iesu, 1956-1960.

Léry, Jean de. *Histoire d'un voyage faict dans la terre du Brésil.* 2 vols. Edited by Paul Gaffarel. Paris: Alphonse Lemerre, 1880.

Mello, J. A. Gonsalves de, ed. *Primeira visitação do Santo Ofício às partes do Brasil pelo Licenciado Heitor Furtado de Mendonça. Confissões de Pernambuco.* Recife: Universidade Federal de Pernambuco, 1970.

Merolla, Girolamo. *Breve e succinta relatione del viaggio nel regno di Congo nell'Africa Meridionale.* Naples, 1692.

Moura, Manuel do Vale. *De incantitionibus seu ensalmis.* Évora, 1620.

Nieuhof, Joan. *Memorável Viagem Marítima e Terrestre ao Brasil (1682).* Introduction by José Honório Rodrigues. São Paulo: Livraria Martins, 1951.

Oldendorp, C. G. A. *History of the Mission of the Evangelical Brethren on the Caribbean Islands of St. Thomas, St. Croix, and St. John.* Edited by Johann Jakob Bossard, translated by Arnold R. Highfield and Vladimir Barac. Barby, 1770; English ed., Ann Arbor: Karoma, 1987.

Peixoto, Afranio, ed. *Cartas Jesuitas*. Vol. 2: *Cartas avulsas, 1550–1568*. Rio de Janeiro: Officina Industrial Graphica, 1931.

Pereira, Nuno Marques. *Compendio Narrativo do Peregrino da America (1728)*. 6th ed. 2 vols. Rio de Janeiro: Academia Brasileira de Letras, 1939.

Pigafetta, Philippo. *A Reporte of the Kingdome of Congo, a region of Africa. And of the countries that border rounde about the same*. Translated by Abraham Hartwell. London, 1597; reprint, New York: Da Capo, 1970.

Purchas, Samuel. *Purchas his Pilgrimes*. 5 vols. London, 1625.

"Ritos gentilicos, e superstições, que observão os negros do gentio do Reyno de Angola desde o seu nascimento athe a morte." *Boletim da Sociedade de Geografia de Lisboa* 5–6 (1885): 371–74.

Sandoval, Alonso de. *De Instauranda Aethiopum Salute: El Mundo de la Esclavitud Negra en America*. Bogotá: Empresa Nacional de Publicaciones, 1956.

Snelgrave, William. *A New Account of Some Parts of Guinea and the Slave Trade*. London, 1734; reprint, London: Frank Cass, 1971.

Soares de Sousa, Gabriel. *Tratado descritivo do Brasil em 1587*. São Paulo: Companhia Editora Nacional, 1971.

Staden, Hans. *Duas viagens ao Brasil*. São Paulo: Editora de Universidade de São Paulo, 1974.

Taunay, Affonso Escragnolle de. *Subsídios para a história do tráfico africano no Brasil*. São Paulo: Imprensa Oficial do Estado, 1941.

Tavares, Pedro. "Carta e verdadeira relação dos successos do Padre Pedro Tavares da Companhia de Jesus em suas missões dos Reinos de Angola e de Congo, tudo tambem composto pollo mesmo padre em quanto a saude lhe deu lugar porquanto depois por rezão de gravissimas doenças ocasionadas do grande trabalho das missoins foi mandado pela santa obediencia e ordem dos medicos a se curar a Portugal." *Boletim da Sociedade de Geografia de Lisboa* 5–6 (1885): 352–54.

Viegas, Artur, ed. *Relação Anual das Coisas que Fizeram os Padres da Companhia de Jesus nas suas Missões do Japão, China . . . Angola, Guiné, Serra Leoa, Cabo Verde e Brasil nos anos de 1600 a 1609 e do processo da conversão e cristandade daquelas partes: tirada das cartas que os missionários de lá escreveram. Pelo Padre Fernão Guerreiro da Companhia de Jesus, Natural de Almodovar de Portugal*. 3 vols. Coimbra: Imprensa da Universidade, 1930.

Secondary Sources

Alden, Dauril. *The Making of an Enterprise: The Society of Jesus in Portugal, Its Empire, and Beyond, 1540–1750*. Stanford, Calif.: Stanford University Press, 1996.

Alden, Dauril, and Joseph C. Miller. "Out of Africa: The Slave Trade and the Transmission of Smallpox to Brazil, ca. 1560–ca. 1830." *Journal of Interdisciplinary History* 18 (1987): 195–224.

Alencastro, Luiz Felipe de. *O Trato dos Viventes: a formação do Brasil no Atlântico Sul, séculos XVI e XVII*. Rio de Janeiro: Companhia das Letras, 2000.

Amiel, Charles. "The Archives of the Portuguese Inquisition: A Brief Survey." In *The Inquisition in Early Modern Europe: Studies on Sources and Methods*, edited by Gustav Henningsen and John Tedeschi, 79–99. Dekalb: Northern Illinois University Press, 1986.

Aufderheide, Patricia. "True Confessions: The Inquisition and Social Attitudes in Brazil at the Turn of the Seventeenth Century." *Luso-Brazilian Review* 10 (1973): 208–40.

Austen, Ralph A. "The Trans-Saharan Slave Trade: A Tentative Census." In *The Uncommon Market: Essays in the Economic History of the Atlantic Slave Trade*, edited by Henry A. Gemery and Jan S. Hogendorn, 23–76. New York: Academic, 1979.

Balandier, Georges. *Daily Life in the Kingdom of the Kongo from the Sixteenth to the Eighteenth Century*, translated by Helen Weaver. New York: Allen and Unwin, 1968.

Barnes, Sandra T. "Introduction: The Many Faces of Ogun." *Africa's Ogun: Old World and New*, edited by Sandra T. Barnes. Bloomington: University of Indiana Press, 1989.

Barry, Boubacar. *Senegambia and the Atlantic Slave Trade*. Translated by Ayi Kwei Armah. Cambridge, U.K.: Cambridge University Press, 1998.

Bastide, Roger. *African Civilizations in the New World*. New York: Harper and Row, 1971.

———. *The African Religions of Brazil*. Translated by Helen Sebba. Baltimore, Md.: Johns Hopkins University Press, 1978.

Bentley, Rev. W. Holman. *Dictionary and Grammar of the Kongo Language*. London, 1887; reprint, London: Farnborough, Gregg, 1967.

Bergad, Laird W. *Slavery and the Demographic and Economic History of Minas Gerais, Brazil, 1720–1888*. Cambridge, U.K.: Cambridge University Press, 1999.

Berlin, Ira. *Many Thousands Gone: The First Two Centuries of Slavery in North America*. Cambridge, Mass.: Belknap Press of Harvard University Press, 1998.

Bethencourt, Francisco. *História das Inquisições Portugal, Espanha e Itália*. Lisbon: Círculo de Leitores, 1994.

———. *O Imaginário da magia. Feiticeiras, saludadores e nigromantes no século XVI*. Lisbon: Projecto Universidade Aberta, 1987.

Birmingham, David. *Trade and Conflict in Angola: The Mbundu and their Neighbors Under the Influence of the Portuguese, 1483–1790*. Oxford, U.K.: Clarendon, 1966.

Blassingame, John W. *The Slave Community: Plantation Life in the Antebellum South*. Oxford: Oxford University Press, 1979.

Bockie, Simon. *Death and the Invisible Powers*. Bloomington: Indiana University Press, 1993.

Boeck, Filip de, and René Devisch, "Ndembu, Luundu, and Yaka Divination Compared: From Representation and Social Engineering to Embodiment and World Making." *Journal of Religion in Africa* 24 (1994): 98–133.

Boulègue, Jean. *Le Grand Jolof, XIIIe-XVIe siècle: Les Anciens royaumes Wolof*. Paris: Karthala, 1987.

Boxer, Charles R. *The Dutch in Brazil, 1624-1654*. Oxford, U.K.: Clarendon, 1957.

———. *The Portuguese Seaborne Empire, 1415-1825*. London: Hutchinson, 1969.

———. *Race Relations in the Portuguese Colonial Empire, 1415-1825*. Oxford, U.K.: Clarendon, 1963.

———. *Salvador de Sá and the Struggle for Brazil and Angola, 1602-1686*. London: University of London, 1952.

Brásio, António. *Os prêtos em Portugal*. Lisbon: Agência Geral das Colónias, 1944.

Brooks, George E. *Landlords and Strangers: Ecology, Society, and Trade in Western Africa, 1000-1630*. Boulder, Colo.: Westview, 1993.

Byrd, Alexander X. "Constructing Identities in the African Diaspora." Unpublished paper, delivered at "The African Diaspora: A Symposium," Schomburg Center for Research in Black Culture, New York, N.Y., May 4, 2001.

Calainho, Daniela Buono. "Jambacousses e gangazambes: feiticeiros negros em Portugal." *Afro-Ásia* 25-26 (2001): 141-76.

Caldwell, J. C., and Pat Caldwell. "The Role of Marital Abstinence in Determining Fertility: A Study of the Yoruba of Nigeria." *Population Studies* 31 (1977): 193-217.

Cardoso, Ciro Flamarion S. *Escravo ou campônes. O protocampesinato negro nas Américas*. São Paulo: Editora Brasiliense, 1987.

Carneiro, Edison. *O quilombo dos Palmares*. 3d ed. Rio de Janeiro: Civilização Brasileira, 1966.

Castro, Yeda Pessoa de. *Os falares africanos na interação social do Brasil colônial*. Salvador: Universidade Federal da Bahia, 1980.

Coates, Timothy J. "Exiles and Orphans: Forced and State-Sponsored Colonizers in the Portuguese Empire, 1550-1720." Ph.D. thesis, University of Minnesota, 1993.

Coelho, António Borges. *Inquisição de Évora dos Promórdios a 1668*. 2 vols. Lisbon: Caminho, 1987.

Comaroff, Jean, and John Comaroff, eds. *Modernity and its Malcontents*. Chicago: University of Chicago Press, 1993.

Conrad, Robert Edgar. *Children of God's Fire: A Documentary History of Black Slavery in Brazil*. Princeton, N.J.: Princeton University Press, 1987.

Curtin, Philip D. *The Atlantic Slave Trade: A Census*. Madison: University of Wisconsin Press, 1969.

Cuvelier, J. *L'ancien royaume de Congo*. Bruges and Paris: Desclée de Brouwer, 1946.

Debien, Gabriel. "Le journal de traite de la *Licorne* au Mozambique, 1787-1788." In *Etudes africaines offertes à Henri Brunschwig*, 91-116. Paris: Edition de l'Ecole des hautes études en sciences sociales, 1982.

———. "La traite nantaise vue par un Nantaise." In "Documents sur la traite (XVII-XIX siècles)." *Enquêtes et documents* (Centre de Recherches sur l'Histoire de la France Atlantique) 2 (1972): 203-12.

Deive, Carlos Esteban. *La esclavitud del negro en Santo Domingo*. 2 vols. Santo Domingo: Museo del Hombre Dominicano, 1980.

Desch-Obi, Thomas J. "Combat and the Crossing of Kalunga." In *Central Africans and Cultural Transformations in the American Diaspora*, edited by Linda M. Heywood, 353–70. Cambridge, U.K.: Cambridge University Press, 2002.

———. "Engolo: Combat Traditions in African and African Diaspora History." Ph.D. thesis, University of California–Los Angeles, 2000.

Devisch, René. "Divination and Oracles." In *Encyclopedia of Africa South of the Sahara*, edited by John Middleton, 1:493–97. New York: C. Scribner's Sons, 1997.

Dusinberre, William. *Them Dark Days: Slavery in the American Rice Swamps*. Oxford: Oxford University Press, 1996.

Elbl, Ivana. "Cross-Cultural Trade and Diplomacy: Portuguese Relations with West Africa, 1441–1521." *Journal of World History* 3 (1992): 165–204.

———. "The Volume of the Early Atlantic Slave Trade, 1450–1521." *Journal of African History* 38 (1997): 31–75.

Elkins, Stanley M. *Slavery: A Problem in American Institutional and Intellectual Life*. Chicago: University of Chicago Press, 1959.

Eltis, David. *The Rise of African Slavery in the Americas*. Cambridge, U.K.: Cambridge University Press, 2000.

———. "The Volume and Structure of the Transatlantic Slave Trade: A Reassessment." *William and Mary Quarterly* 58 (2001): 17–46.

Eltis, David, Stephen D. Behrendt, David Richardson, and Herbert Klein, eds. *The Trans-Atlantic Slave Trade: A Database on CD ROM*. Cambridge, U.K.: Cambridge University Press, 2000.

Farinha, Maria do Carmo Jasmins Dias. *Os Arquivos da Inquisição*. Lisbon: Arquivo Nacional da Torre do Tombo, 1990.

Fick, Carolyn E. *The Making of Haiti: The Saint Domingue Revolution from Below*. Knoxville: University of Tennessee Press, 1990.

Florentino, Manolo, and José Roberto Goés. *A Paz das Senzalas: Famílias escravas e tráfico atlântico, Rio de Janeiro, c. 1790–1850*. Rio de Janeiro: Civilização Brasileira, 1997.

Frazier, E. Franklin. *The Negro Family in the United States*. Chicago: University of Chicago Press, 1939.

Frey, Sylvia, and Betty Wood. *Come Shouting to Zion: African-American Protestantism in the American South and British Caribbean to 1830*. Chapel Hill: University of North Carolina Press, 1998.

Freyre, Gilberto. *The Masters and the Slaves*. Translated by Samuel Putnam. New York: Knopf, 1946.

Garfield, Robert. "A History of São Tomé Island, 1470–1655." Ph.D. thesis, Northwestern University, 1971.

Gates, Henry Louis, Jr., and William L. Andrews, eds. *Pioneers of the Black Atlantic: Five Slave Narratives from the Enlightenment, 1772–1815*. Washington, D.C.: Civitas, 1998.

Genovese, Eugene. *Roll, Jordan, Roll: The World the Slaves Made*. New York: Pantheon, 1974.

Geschiere, Peter. *The Modernity of Witchcraft: Politics and the Occult in Postcolonial Africa*. Charlottesville: University Press of Virginia, 1997.

———. "Witchcraft and Sorcery." In *Encyclopedia of Africa South of the Sahara*, edited by John Middleton, 4:376–81. New York: C. Scribner's Sons, 1997.

Godinho, Vitorino Magalhães. *Os descobrimentos e a economia mundial*. 4 vols. Lisbon: Editora Arcádia, 1963–1981.

Gomez, Michael A. "African Identity and Slavery in the Americas." *Radical History Review* 75 (1999): 111–20.

———. *Exchanging Our Country Marks: The Transformation of African Identities in the Colonial and Antebellum South*. Chapel Hill: University of North Carolina Press, 1998.

Gorender, Jacob. *O escravismo colonial*. 2nd ed. São Paulo: Editora Atica, 1985.

———. "Questionamentos sobre a teoria econômica do escravismo colonial." *Revista de Estudos Econômicos* 13 (1983): 7–40.

Goody, Jack, ed. *The Character of Kinship*. Cambridge, U.K.: Cambridge University Press, 1973.

Goulart, José Alípio. *Da palmatória ao patíbulo*. Rio de Janeiro: Conquista, 1971.

Goulart, Maurício. *A escravidão africana no Brasil: das origens à extinção do tráfico*. 3d ed. São Paulo: Editora Alfa-Ômega, 1975.

Gratton, Nancy E. "Wolof." In *Encyclopedia of Africa South of the Sahara*, edited by John Middleton, 4:381–82. New York: C. Scribner's Sons, 1997.

Greene, Sandra E. "Religion, History and the Supreme Gods of Africa: A Contribution to the Debate." *Journal of Religion in Africa* 26 (1996): 122–38.

Gudeman, Stephen, and Stuart B. Schwartz. "Cleansing Original Sin: Godparentage and the Baptism of Slaves in Eighteenth Century Bahia." In *Kinship Ideology and Practice in Latin America*, edited by Raymond T. Smith, 35–58. Chapel Hill: University of North Carolina Press, 1984.

Guthrie, Malcolm. *Comparative Bantu: An Introduction to the Comparative Linguistics and Prehistory of the Bantu Languages*. London: Farnborough, Gregg, 1971.

Gutiérrez, Ramón. *When Jesus Came, the Corn Mothers Went Away: Marriage, Sexuality, and Power in New Mexico, 1500–1846*. Stanford: Stanford University Press, 1991.

Gutman, Herbert G. *The Black Family in Slavery and Freedom, 1750–1925*. New York: Pantheon, 1976.

Guyer, Jane I. "Household and Community in African Studies." *African Studies Review* 24 (1981): 87–138.

Heleno, Manuel. *Os escravos em Portugal*. Lisbon, 1933.

Henningsen, Gustav, and John Tedeschi, eds. *The Inquisition in Early Modern Europe: Studies on Sources and Methods*. Dekalb: Northern Illinois University Press, 1986.

Herculano, Alexandre. *História da Origem e Estabelecimento da Inquisição em Portugal*. Lisbon: Ailland e Bertrand, 1858.

Herskovits, Melville J. *Dahomey: An Ancient West African Kingdom*. 2 vols. New York: J. J. Augustin, 1938.

————. *The Myth of the Negro Past*. New York: Harper and Brothers, 1941.

Higgins, Kathleen J. *"Licentious Liberty" in a Brazilian Gold-Mining Region: Slavery, Gender, and Social Control in Eighteenth-Century Sabará, Minas Gerais*. University Park: Pennsylvania State University Press, 1999.

Higman, Barry W. "African and Creole Slave Family Patterns in Trinidad." In *Africa and the Caribbean: The Legacies of a Link*, edited by Margaret E. Crahan and Franklin W. Knight, 41–64. Baltimore, Md.: Johns Hopkins University Press, 1979.

Hilton, Anne. *The Kingdom of Kongo*. Oxford: Clarendon, 1985.

Holloway, Joseph E., ed. *Africanisms in American Culture*. Bloomington: Indiana University Press, 1990.

Horton, Robin. *Patterns of Thought in Africa and the West: Essays on Magic, Religion, and Science*. Cambridge, U.K.: Cambridge University Press, 1993.

Houdard, Sophie. *Les sciences du diable: Quatre discours sur la sorcellerie*. Paris: Editions du Cerf, 1992.

Iliffe, John. *Africans: The History of a Continent*. Cambridge, U.K.: Cambridge University Press, 1995.

Jacobson-Widding, Anita. *Red-White-Black as Mode of Thought: A Study of Triadic Classification of Colours in the Ritual Symbolism and Cognitive Thought of the Peoples of the Lower Congo*. Uppsala, 1979.

Joyner, Charles. *Down by the Riverside: A South Carolina Slave Community*. Urbana: University of Illinois Press, 1984.

Karasch, Mary C. "'Minha Nação': Identidades Escravas no Fim do Brasil Colonial." In *Brasil: Colonização e Escravidão*, edited by Maria Beatriz Nizza da Silva, 127–35. Rio de Janeiro: Nova Fronteira, 1999.

————. *Slave Life in Rio de Janeiro, 1808–1850*. Princeton: Princeton University Press, 1987.

Katz, Jonathan Ned. *The Invention of Heterosexuality*. New York: Penguin, 1995.

King, Wilma. *Stolen Childhood: Slave Youth in Nineteenth-Century America*. Bloomington: Indiana University Press, 1995.

Kiple, Kenneth F. "The Nutritional Link with Slave Infant and Child Mortality in Brazil." *Hispanic American Historical Review* 69 (1989): 677–90.

Kiple, Kenneth F., and Virginia H. King. "Slave Child Mortality: Some Nutritional Answers to a Perennial Puzzle." *Journal of Social History* 10 (1977): 284–309.

Klein, Herbert. *African Slavery in Latin America and the Caribbean*. Oxford: Oxford University Press, 1986.

————. "African Women in the Atlantic Slave Trade." In *Women and Slavery in Africa*, edited by Claire C. Robertson and Martin A. Klein, 29–38. Madison: University of Wisconsin Press, 1983.

————. "A demografia do tráfico atlântico de escravos para o Brasil." *Estudos Econômicos* 17 (1987): 129–50.

Klein, Herbert, and Stanley L. Engerman. "Fertility Differentials between Slaves in the United States and the British West Indies: A Note on Lactation Practices." *William and Mary Quarterly*, 3d ser., 35 (1978): 357–74.

La Barre, Weston. *The Ghost Dance: Origins of Religion.* Garden City, N.Y.: Doubleday, 1970.

Lara, Silvia Hunold. *Campos de violência. Escravos e senhores na capitania do Rio de Janeiro, 1750-1808.* Rio de Janeiro: Paz e Terra, 1988.

Leite, Serafim. *História da Companhia de Jesus no Brasil.* 10 vols. Rio de Janeiro: Livraria Portugália, 1938-1950.

Lewin, Linda. "Natural and Spurious Children in Brazilian Inheritance Law from Colony to Nation: A Methodological Essay." *The Americas* 48 (1992): 351-96.

Lockhart, James. "Some Nahua Concepts in Postconquest Guise." *History of European Ideas* 6 (1985): 465-82.

Lopes, Nei. *Dicionário Banto do Brasil: repertório etimológico de vocábulos Brasileiros originários dos centro, sul, leste e sudoeste africanos.* Rio de Janeiro: Imprensa da Cidade, 1996.

Lovejoy, Paul E. "The African Diaspora: Revisionist Interpretations of Ethnicity, Culture and Religion under Slavery." *Studies in the World History of Slavery, Abolition and Emancipation* 2 (1997): 1-23.

———. *Transformations in Slavery: A History of Slavery in Africa.* 2d ed. Cambridge, U.K.: Cambridge University Press, 2000.

MacGaffey, Wyatt. "Dialogues of the Deaf: Europeans on the Atlantic Coast of Africa." In *Implicit Understandings: Observing, Reporting, and Reflecting on the Encounters Between Europeans and Other Peoples in the Early Modern Era,* edited by Stuart B. Schwartz, 249-67. Cambridge, U.K.: Cambridge University Press, 1994.

———. "Lineage, Structure, Marriage, and Family Amongst the Central Bantu." *Journal of African History* 24 (1983): 173-87.

———. *Religion and Society in Central Africa.* Chicago: University of Chicago Press, 1986.

Marques, A. H. de Oliveira. *A History of Portugal: From Lusitania to Empire.* New York: Columbia University Press, 1972.

Matory, J. Lorand. "The English Professors of Brazil: On the Diasporic Roots of the Yoruba Nation." *Comparative Studies in Society and History* 41 (1999): 72-103.

———. "Jeje: Repensando Nações e Transnacionalismo." *Mana* 5 (1999): 57-80.

Mattoso, Katia M. de Queiros. *To Be a Slave in Brazil, 1550-1888.* Translated by Arthur Goldhammer. New Brunswick, N.J.: Rutgers University Press, 1986.

Mauro, Frédéric. *Portugal, o Brasil e o Atlântico, 1570-1670.* Lisbon: Editorial Estampa, 1988.

Mbiti, John. *African Religions and Philosophy.* Garden City, N.Y.: Anchor, 1970.

McAlister, Elizabeth. "A Sorcerer's Bottle: The Visual Art of Magic in Haiti." In *Sacred Arts of Haitian Vodou,* edited by Donald J. Consentino, 304-21. Los Angeles: University of California Press, 1995.

McLaurin, Melton Alonza. *Celia: A Slave.* Athens: University of Georgia Press, 1991.

Metcalf, Alida. "Vida familiar dos escravos em São Paulo no século dezoito: o caso de Santana de Paranaíba." *Estudos Econômicos* 17 (1987): 229-43.

Métraux, Alfred. *Voodoo in Haiti*. Translated by Hugo Charteris. New York: Schocken, 1972.

Miers, Suzanne, and Igor Kopytoff, eds. *Slavery in Africa: Historical and Anthropological Perspectives*. Madison: University of Wisconsin Press, 1977.

Miller, Joseph. "Central Africa during the Era of the Slave Trade." In *Central Africans and Cultural Transformations in the African Diaspora*, edited by Linda M. Heywood, 21–69. Cambridge, U.K.: Cambridge University Press, 2002.

———. *Kings and Kinsmen: Early Mbundu States in Angola*. Oxford: Clarendon, 1976.

———. "History and Africa/Africa and History." *American Historical Review* 104 (1999): 1–32.

———. "The Paradoxes of Impoverishment in the Atlantic Zone." In *History of Central Africa*, 2 vols., edited by David Birmingham and Phyllis M. Martin, 1:139–43. London: Longman, 1983.

———. *Way of Death: Merchant Capitalism and the Angolan Slave Trade, 1730–1830*. Madison: University of Wisconsin Press, 1988.

———. "Worlds Apart: Africans' Encounters and Africa's Encounters with the Atlantic in Angola, Before 1800." In *Actas do Seminário "Encontro de povos e culturas em Angola*, 227–80. Lisbon: Comissão Nacional para as Comemorações dos Descobrimentos Portugueses, 1997.

Mintz, Sidney W., and Richard Price. *The Birth of African-American Culture: An Anthropological Perspective*. Boston: Beacon, 1992.

Mott, Luiz R. B. "Acontundá: raizes setecentistas do sincretismo religioso afro-brasileiro." *Revista do Museu Paulista* (new ser.) 31 (1986): 124–47.

———. "Cotidiano e vivência religiosa: entre a capela e o calundu." In *História da vida privada no Brasil: cotidiano e vida privada na América portuguesa*, vol. 1, edited by Laura de Mello e Souza, 155–220. Rio de Janeiro: Companhia das Letras, 1997.

———. *Escravidão, homossexualidade, e demonologia*. São Paulo: Icone, 1988.

———. "*Justitia et Misericordia*: A Inquisição Portuguesa e a Repressão ao Nefando Pecado de Sodomia." In *Inquisição: Ensaios sobre mentalidade, heresias e arte*, edited by Anita Novinsky and Maria Luiza Tucci Carneiro, 703–38. São Paulo: Universidade de São Paulo, 1992.

———. *Piauí colonial: População, economia e sociedade*. Teresina: Projeto Petrônio Portella, 1985.

———. *Rosa Egipcíaca: Uma Santa Africana no Brasil*. Rio de Janeiro: Bertrand Brasit, 1993.

———. "Santo Antônio, o Divino Capitão do Mato." In *Liberdade por um fio: História dos quilombos no Brasil*, edited by João José Reis and Flávio dos Santos Gomes, 110–38. São Paulo: Companhia das Letras, 1996.

———. *O sexo proibido: escravos, gays e virgens nas garras da Inquisição*. Campinas: Papirus Editora, 1988.

———. "Terror na Casa da Torre." In *Escravidão e Invenção da Liberdade*, edited by João José Reis, 17–32. São Paulo: Editora Brasiliense, 1988.

Mulvey, Patricia. "Black Brothers and Sisters: Membership in the Black Lay Brother-hoods of Colonial Brazil." *Luso-Brazilian Review* 17 (1982): 253–79.

———. "Slave Confraternities in Brazil: Their Role in Colonial Society." *The Americas* 39 (1982): 39–68.

Murray, Stephen O. "Homosexual Categorization in Cross-Cultural Perspective." In *Latin American Male Homosexualities*, edited by Stephen O. Murray, 3–32. Albuquerque: University of New Mexico Press, 1995.

Neves, Maria de Fátima Rodrigues. "Infância de faces negras: a criança escrava brasileira no século XIX." Ph.D. thesis, Universidade de São Paulo, 1993.

Oliveira, Maria Inês Cortês de. "Viver e Morrer no Meio dos Seus." *Revista USP* 28 (1996): 174–93.

Ortiz, Fernando. *Los negros esclavos*. Havana: Revista bimestre cubana, 1916.

Owens, Leslie Howard. *This Species of Property: Slave Life and Culture in the Old South.* Oxford: Oxford University Press, 1976.

Painter, Nell I. "Soul Murder and Slavery: Toward a Fully Loaded Cost Accounting." In *U.S. History as Women's History: New Feminist Essays*, edited by Linda K. Kerber, Alice Kessler-Harris, and Kathryn Kish Sklar, 125–46. Chapel Hill: University of North Carolina Press, 1995.

Paiva, José Pedro. *Bruxaria e superstição num país sem "caça às bruxas," 1600–1774.* Lisbon: Editorial Notícias, 1997.

Palmer, Colin A. "Defining and Studying the Modern African Diaspora," *Perspectives* 36 (1998): 1, 22–25.

———. "From Africa to the Americas: Ethnicity in the Early Black Communities of the Americas." *Journal of World History* 6 (1995): 223–36.

———. *Passageways: An Interpretive History of Black America.* 2 vols. Fort Worth, Tex.: Harcourt Brace, 1998.

———. "Rethinking American Slavery." In *The African Diaspora*, edited by Alusine Jalloh and Stephen E. Maizlish, 73–99. College Station: Texas A&M University Press, 1996.

———. *Slaves of the White God: Blacks in Mexico, 1570–1650.* Cambridge, Mass.: Harvard University Press, 1976.

Palmié, Stephan. *Wizards and Scientists: Explorations in Afro-Cuban Modernity and Tradition.* Durham, N.C.: Duke University Press, 2002.

Patterson, Orlando. *Slavery and Social Death.* Cambridge, Mass.: Harvard University Press, 1982.

p'Bitek, Okot. *African Religions in Western Scholarship.* Nairobi: East African Literature Bureau, 1971.

———. *Religion of the Central Luo.* Nairobi: East African Literature Bureau, 1971.

Peek, Philip M., ed. *African Divination Systems: Ways of Knowing.* Bloomington: Indiana University Press, 1991.

Piersen, William D. *Black Legacy: America's Hidden Heritage.* Amherst: University of Massachusetts Press, 1993.

Prandi, Reginaldo. "De Africano a Afro-Brasileiro: Etnia, identidade, religião." *Revista USP* 46 (2000): 52–65.

Querino, Manuel. *Costumes africanos no Brasil*. Rio de Janeiro: Civilização Brasileira, 1938.

Ramos, Artur. *As culturas negras no novo mundo*. Rio de Janeiro: Civilização Brasileira, 1937.

———. *O negro brasileiro. Ethnographia, religiosa, e psychanalyse*. 2d ed. São Paulo: Companhia Editora Nacional, 1940.

Ramos, Donald. "A influência africana e a cultura popular em Minas Gerais: um comentário sobre a interpretação da escravidão." In *Brasil: Colonização e Escravidão*, edited by Maria Beatriz Nizza da Silva, 142–62. Rio de Janeiro: Nova Fronteira, 1999.

Rau, Virginia, and Jorge de Macedo, eds. *O açúcar de Madeira no fins do século XV*. Funchal: Junta Geral do Distrito Autónomo de Funchal, 1962.

Reis, João José. "Identidade e Diversidade Étnicas nas Irmandades Negras no Tempo da Escravidão." *Tempo* 3 (1997): 6–32.

———. "Magia jeje na Bahia: A Invasão do Calundu do Pasto de Cachoeira, 1785." *Revista Brasileira de História* 8 (1988): 57–81.

———. *Rebelião escrava no Brasil. A história do levante dos Malês (1835)*. São Paulo: Brasiliense, 1986.

Reis, João José, and Flávio dos Santos Gomes. *Liberdade por um fio: História dos quilombos no Brasil*. São Paulo: Companhia das Letras, 1996.

Rey, Terry. "Kongolese Catholic Influences on Haitian Popular Catholicism: A Sociohistorical Exploration," In *Central Africans and Cultural Transformations in the American Diaspora*, edited by Linda M. Heywood, 265–85. Cambridge, U.K.: Cambridge University Press, 2002.

———. "The Virgin Mary and Revolution in Saint-Domingue: The Charisma of Romaine-la-Prophétesse." *Journal of Historical Sociology* 11 (1998): 341–69.

Ribeiro, Victor. *A Santa Casa da Misericordia de Lisboa subsídios para a sua história, 1498-1898*. Lisbon: Academia Real das Sciencias, 1902.

Richardson, David. "Slave Exports from West and West-Central Africa, 1700–1810." *Journal of African History* 30 (1989): 7–22.

Rodrigues, Nina. *Os africanos no Brasil*. Edited by Homero Pires. São Paulo: Companhia Editora Nacional, 1932.

Rout, Leslie B., Jr. *The African Experience in Spanish America, 1502 to the Present Day*. Cambridge, U.K.: Cambridge University Press, 1976.

Russell-Wood, A. J. R. "'Acts of Grace': Portuguese Monarchs and Their Subjects of African Descent in Eighteenth-Century Brazil." *Journal of Latin American Studies* 32 (2000): 307–32.

———. "Before Columbus: Portugal's African Prelude to the Middle Passage and Contribution to Discourse on Race and Slavery." In *Race, Discourse, and the Origin of the Americas: A New World View*, edited by Vera Lawrence Hyatt and Rex Nettleford, 134–68. Washington, D.C.: Smithsonian Institution Press, 1996.

————. "Black and Mulatto Brotherhoods in Colonial Brazil: A Study in Collective Behavior." *Hispanic American Historical Review* 54 (1974): 567–602.

————. *The Black Man in Slavery and Freedom in Colonial Brazil*. New York: St. Martin's, 1982.

————. "Iberian Expansion and the Issue of Black Slavery: Changing Portuguese Attitudes, 1440–1770." *American Historical Review* 83 (1978): 16–44.

Sanford, Linda Tschirhart. *Strong at the Broken Places: Overcoming the Trauma of Childhood Abuse*. New York: Random House, 1990.

Saunders, A. C. de C. M. *A Social History of Black Slaves and Freedmen in Portugal, 1441–1551*. Cambridge, U.K.: Cambridge University Press, 1982.

Scarano, Julita. "Black Brotherhoods: Integration or Contradiction?" *Luso-Brazilian Review* 16 (1979): 1–17.

————. *Devoção e escravidão: a Irmandade de Nossa Senhora do Rosário dos Pretos no distrito Diamantino no século XVIII*. São Paulo: Companhia Editora Nacional, 1976.

Scheper-Hughes, Alice. *Death Without Weeping: The Violence of Everyday Life in Brazil*. Berkeley: University of California Press, 1992.

Schuler, Monica. "Afro-American Slave Culture." In *Roots and Branches*, edited by Michael Craton, 121–37. New York: Pergamon, 1979.

————. *'Alas, Alas Kongo': A Social History of Indentured African Immigration into Jamaica, 1841–1865*. Baltimore, Md.: Johns Hopkins University Press, 1980.

————. "Liberated Central Africans in Nineteenth-Century Guyana." In *Central Africans and Cultural Transformations in the American Diaspora*, edited by Linda M. Heywood, 319–52. Cambridge, U.K.: Cambridge University Press, 2002.

Schwartz, Marie Jenkins. *Born in Bondage: Growing Up Enslaved in the Antebellum South*. Cambridge, Mass.: Harvard University Press, 2000.

Schwartz, Stuart B. "Indian Labor and New World Plantations: European Demands and Indian Responses in Northeastern Brazil." *American Historical Review* 83 (1978): 43–79.

————. "The Manumission of Slaves in Colonial Brazil: Bahia, 1684–1745." *Hispanic American Historical Review* 54 (1974): 603–35.

————. "The Plantations of St. Benedict: The Benedictine Sugar Mills of Colonial Brazil." *The Americas* 39 (1982): 1–22.

————. "Rethinking Palmares: Slave Resistance in Colonial Brazil." In *Slaves, Peasants, and Rebels: Reconsidering Brazilian Slavery*, edited by Stuart B. Schwartz, 103–36. Urbana: University of Illinois Press, 1992.

————. *Slaves, Peasants, and Rebels: Reconsidering Brazilian Slavery*. Urbana: University of Illinois Press, 1992.

————. *Sovereignty and Society in Colonial Brazil: The High Court of Bahia and Its Judges, 1609–1751*. Berkeley: University of California Press, 1973.

————. *Sugar Plantations in the Formation of Brazilian Society. Bahia 1550–1835*. Cambridge, U.K.: Cambridge University Press, 1985.

Scott, James C. *Weapons of the Weak*. New Haven, Conn.: Yale University Press, 1985.

Seed, Patricia. "'Failing to Marvel': Atahualpa's Encounter with the Word." *Latin American Research Review* 26 (1991): 7–32.

Shaw, Rosalind. "The Production of Witchcraft/Witchcraft as Production: Memory, Modernity, and the Slave Trade in Sierra Leone." *American Ethnologist* 24 (1997): 856–76.

Shengold, Leonard. *Soul Murder: The Effects of Childhood Abuse and Deprivation.* New Haven, Conn.: Yale University Press, 1989.

Silva, A. da. *Trent's Impact on the Portuguese Patronage Missions.* Translated by Joaquim da Silva Godinho. Lisbon: Centro de Estudos Históricos Ultramarinos, 1969.

Siqueira, Sonia A. *A Inquisição Portuguesa e a sociedade colonial.* São Paulo: Ática, 1978.

Slenes, Robert W. "The Great Porpoise-Skull Strike: Central African Water Spirits and Slave Identity in Early-Nineteenth-Century Rio de Janeiro." In *Central Africans and Cultural Transformations in the American Diaspora,* edited by Linda M. Heywood, 183–208. Cambridge, U.K.: Cambridge University Press, 2002.

———. "'Malungu Ngoma Vem!': African Encoberta e Descoberta no Brasil," *Revista USP* 12 (1991–1992): 48–67.

———. *Na Senzala, Uma Flor: Esperanças e recordações na formação da família escrava.* Rio de Janeiro: Nova Fronteira, 1999.

———. "O que Rui Barbosa não queimou: novas fontes para o estudo da escravidão no século XIX." *Estudos Econômicos* 13 (1983): 117–49.

Soares, Carlos Eugênio Líbano. *A capoeira escrava e outras tradições rebeldes no Rio de Janeiro.* Campinas: Editora da UNICAMP, 2001.

Soares, Mariza de Carvalho. *Devotos da Cor: Identidade étnica, religiosidade e escravidão no Rio de Janeiro, século XVIII.* Rio de Janeiro: Editora Civilização Brasileira, 2000.

Souza, Laura de Mello e. *Declassificados do ouro—a pobreza mineira do século XVIII.* Rio de Janeiro: Graal, 1982.

———. *O diabo e a terra de Santa Cruz: feitiçaria e religiosidade popular no Brasil colonial.* 4th ed. São Paulo: Companhia das Letras, 1994.

———. *Inferno Atlântico: Demonologia e colonização, séculos XVI–XVIII.* São Paulo: Companhia das Letras, 1993.

Steckel, Richard H. "Birth Weights and Infant Mortality among American Slaves." *Explorations in Economic History* 23 (1986): 173–98.

———. "A Dreadful Childhood: The Excess Mortality of American Slaves." *Social Science History* 10 (1986): 427–65.

———. "A Peculiar Population: The Nutrition, Health, and Mortality of American Slaves from Childhood to Maturity." *Journal of Economic History* 46 (1986): 721–41.

Sweet, James H. "Male Homosexuality and Spiritism in the African Diaspora: The Legacies of a Link." *Journal of the History of Sexuality* 7 (1996): 184–202.

———. "Manumission in Rio de Janeiro, 1749–1754: An African Perspective." *Slavery and Abolition* 24 (2003): 79–95.

———. "Teaching the Modern African Diaspora: A Case Study of the Atlantic Slave Trade." *Radical History Review* 77 (2000): 106–22.

Tannenbaum, Frank. *Slave and Citizen: The Negro in the Americas*. New York: Knopf, 1947.

Taussig, Michael T. *Shamanism, Colonialism, and the Wild Man: A Study in Terror and Healing*. Chicago: University of Chicago Press, 1987.

Teixeira, Dante Martins. *Dutch Brazil*. 2 vols. Rio de Janeiro: Editora Index, 1998.

Thomas, Keith. *Religion and the Decline of Magic: Studies in Popular Beliefs in Sixteenth Century England*. New York: Scribner, 1971.

Thompson, Robert Farris. *Flash of the Spirit: African and Afro-American Art and Philosophy*. New York: Vintage, 1984.

Thornton, John. *Africa and Africans in the Making of the Atlantic World, 1400-1800*. 2nd ed. Cambridge, U.K.: Cambridge University Press, 1998.

———. "African Roots of the Stono Rebellion." *American Historical Review* 96 (1991): 1101-13.

———. "Cannibals and Slave Traders in the Atlantic World." Unpublished manuscript.

———. "The Chronology and Causes of the Lunda Expansion to the West, c. 1700 to 1852." *Zambia Journal of History* 1 (1981): 1-14.

———. "The Development of an African Catholic Church in the Kingdom of Kongo, 1491-1750." *Journal of African History* 25 (1984): 147-67.

———. "'I Am the Subject of the King of Congo': African Political Ideology and the Haitian Revolution." *Journal of World History* 3 (1993): 181-214.

———. *The Kingdom of Kongo: Civil War and Transition, 1641-1718*. Madison: University of Wisconsin Press, 1983.

———. *The Kongolese Saint Anthony: Dona Beatriz Kimpa Vita and the Antonian Movement, 1684-1706*. Cambridge, U.K.: Cambridge University Press, 1998.

———. "On the Trail of Voodoo: African Christianity in Africa and the Americas." *The Americas* 55 (1988): 261-78.

———. "Perspectives on African Christianity." In *Race, Discourse, and the Origins of the Americas: A New World View*, edited by Vera Lawrence Hyatt and Rex Nettleford, 169-98. Washington, D.C.: Smithsonian Institution Press, 1995.

———. "Religious and Ceremonial Life in the Kongo and Mbundu Areas, 1500-1700." In *Central Africans and Cultural Transformations in the American Diaspora*, edited by Linda M. Heywood, 71-90. Cambridge, U.K.: Cambridge University Press, 2002.

———. "Sexual Demography: The Impact of the Slave Trade on Family Structure." In *Women and Slavery in Africa*, edited by Claire C. Robertson and Martin A. Klein, 39-48. Madison: University of Wisconsin Press, 1983.

Tinhorão, José Ramos. *Os Negros em Portugal. Uma presença silenciosa*. Lisbon: Caminho, 1988.

Trexler, Richard C. *Sex and Conquest: Gendered Violence, Political Order, and the European Conquest of the Americas*. Ithaca, N.Y.: Cornell University Press, 1995.

Turner, Victor. *The Drums of Affliction: A Study of Religious Processes among the Ndembu of Zambia*. Oxford: Clarendon, 1968.

————. *The Forest of Symbols: Aspects of Ndembu Ritual.* Ithaca, N.Y.: Cornell University Press, 1967.

————. *Revelation and Divination in Ndembu Ritual.* Ithaca, N.Y.: Cornell University Press, 1975.

Vainfas, Ronaldo. *Trópico dos pecados: moral, sexualidade e Inquisição no Brasil.* Rio de Janeiro: Editora Campus, 1989.

————, ed. *História e sexualidade no Brasil.* Rio de Janeiro: Graal, 1986.

Vanhee, Hein. "Central African Popular Christianity and the Making of Haitian Vodou Religion." In *Central Africans and Cultural Transformations in the American Diaspora,* edited by Linda M. Heywood, 243–64. Cambridge, U.K.: Cambridge University Press, 2002.

Vansina, Jan. *Kingdoms of the Savanna.* Madison: University of Wisconsin Press, 1966.

————. *Paths in the Rainforests.* Madison: University of Wisconsin Press, 1990.

Venâncio, Renato P. *Ilegitimidade e concubinato no Brasil colonial.* Rio de Janeiro: Universidade de São Paulo, 1986.

————. "Nos limites da sagrada família: ilegitimidade e casamento no Brasil colonial." In *História e sexualidade no Brasil,* edited by Ronaldo Vainfas, 107–24. Rio de Janeiro: Graal, 1986.

Verger, Pierre. *Flux et reflux de la traite des nègres entre le golfe de Bénin et Bahia de Todos os Santos du XVII au XIX siécle.* Paris: La Haye, Mouton, 1968.

Vilar, Enriqueta Vila. "The Large-scale Introduction of Africans into Veracruz and Cartagena." In *Comparative Perspectives on Slavery in New World Plantation Societies,* edited by Vera Rubin and Arthur Tuden, 267–80. New York: New York Academy of Sciences, 1977.

Voeks, Robert A. *The Sacred Leaves of Candomblé: African Magic, Medicine, and Religion in Brazil.* Austin: University of Texas Press, 1997.

Walker, Timothy. "Doctors, Folk Medicine and the Inquisition: The Persecution of Popular Healers in Portugal during the Enlightenment Era." Ph.D. thesis, Boston University, 2000.

Willeke, Venâncio. "Atas capitulares da Província Franciscana de Santo Antônio do Brasil (1649–1893)." *Revista do Instituto Histórico e Geográfico Brasileiro* 286 (1970): 92–222.

Williams, Walter L. *The Spirit and the Flesh: Sexual Diversity in American Indian Culture.* Boston: Beacon, 1986.

Wyatt, Gail Elizabeth. "The Aftermath of Child Sexual Abuse of African-American and White American Women: The Victim's Experience." *Journal of Family Violence* 5 (1990): 61–81.

Yai, Olabiyi B. "Survivals and Dynamism of African Cultures in the Americas." In *From Chains to Bonds: The Slave Trade Revisited,* edited by Doudou Diène, 344–56. New York: Berghahn, 2001.

INDEX

element in, 185–86; containing *pedra d'ara*, 203–4; containing consecrated host, 204–5
Borges, Caterina, 193–94
Bournou, 186
Bragança, Portugal, 159
Brandão, Luiz Simoes, 144
Brotas, Brazil, 28
Brotherhoods, Catholic, 206–8
Buçal, André, 129
Burials, 56, 176–79, 206

Cabo Frio, Brazil, 173, 221
Cabral, Manuel Álvares, 73–74
Cachoeira, Brazil, 207, 214
Cacheu, Guinea-Bissau, 97, 181
Cadamosto, Alvise da, 88
Cadornega, Antônio de Oliveira, 35, 56
Calmon, João, 146
Caltanissetta, Luca da, 140–42
Calundú. See Spirit possession
Canary Islands, 94
Canzás. See Musical Instruments
Cape Verde, 24, 97
Capoeira, 142–43
Capuchins, 34, 56, 140, 167, 192, 196, 197, 198
Carahí, Brazil, 79
Cardim, Fernão, 23
Cardosa, Maria, 44
Caribbean, 89, 228
Carli, Dionigio de, 197
Carmelites, 72, 78, 145, 158, 207, 214, 222
Cartas de tocar, 184, 260 (n. 78)
Carvalhal, Sebastiana de, 174
Carvalho, Julia de, 134–35
Carvalho, Manuel, 184
Castro, Franciso Serrão de, 74
Castro Marim, Portugal, 42, 159
Cavazzi, Giovanni Antônio, 35, 37, 56, 110, 122–23, 131–32, 140, 142, 175–78, 196, 198

Cazado, Domingos Álvares, 36–37
Ceuta, Morocco, 2, 92, 93
Chagas, Domingos das, 146
Children: out-of-wedlock, 35–37, 49; baptized, 46–47; malnutrition and, 61–62; birth rates of, 65; mortality of, 65–66; physical and psychological abuse of, 66–67, 69–72, 243 (n. 54); and meanings of childbirth, 67; abandonment of, 68; rape of, 70–71; and long-term impact of abuse, 81–82; souls of, called in divination ceremonies, 145, 148. *See also* Orphans
Christianity: as lens for understanding African beliefs, 106–9; Central African, 109–15, 191–97, 249 (n. 28), 261 (n. 14); and obstacles to missions in Brazil, 198–202; African-Brazilians naturalize, 202–10; and blasphemy, 210–11; and sacrilege, 211–15; responses of, to African challenges in Brazil, 219–26. *See also* Baptism; Brotherhoods, Catholic; Marriage
Circumcision: in Angola, 34–35; in Brazil, 35; of Islamic slaves, 93, 94
Coelho, Domingos, 153
Coimbra, Portugal, 183
Conceição, Antônio da, 214
Congo, Antônio (of Engenho Santana), 49
Congo, Antônio (of Itatiayo), 155
Congo, Gracia, 121–23
Congo, Pedro, 208–10
Congo, Simão, 120–22, 170
Cordeiro, Amaro de França, 42–43
Correa, Sebastião Fernandes, 194–95
Correia, Maria, 44
Costa, Antônio da, 77–78
Costa, Domingos Alves da, 134
Costa, Gaspar da, 170
Costa, José da, 204
Council of Trent, 96, 218, 222, 248 (n. 18)

Creole slaves, 24, 25–29, 47, 49, 61, 64, 78, 172, 210

Creolization: critique of, 115–17, 227–30

Criolla, Antônia (of Santana), 40, 65

Criolla, Antônia (of Rio de Janeiro), 68

Criollo, Antônio, 65

Cuna, Gonçalo de, 170

Cunha, João da, 148

Dahomey, 131

Dance, 144, 148, 151, 154, 202, 208

Dembo, Francisco, 125, 133, 145, 152

Desch-Obi, T. J., 142

Diaspora, African, 1–2, 229–30

Diet: Catholic restrictions, 97; Mbundu restrictions (quijila), 175–76. See also Malnutrition

Disease, 60–61, 64, 65, 241 (n. 19); Central African interpretations of, 105

Divination: role in Africa, 119–20; Central African forms of, in the diaspora, 120–28; ordeals, 120–25, 126; hand in boiling water (jaji/amízoka), 121–23, 131; needle in arm, 123–24; ball and cord, 125; casting lots, 125–26; with bottles, 126; of future, 126–27; European forms Africanized (quibando), 127–28, 184; Mina forms in the diaspora, 128–30, 156–57; in water, 129–30, 135; with snakes, 130; omens, 131–32; and resistance, 134–36; using string of shells, 184; Catholic priest calling on African to perform, 222

Divino, Domingas do Amor, 79

Dominicans, 206

Dongo, Pedro, 170

Dreams, 14, 98, 104, 109

Dutch, 24, 62, 95, 186, 202

Egipcíaca, Rosa, 70, 262 (n. 33)

Elches, 93

Encarnação, Maria de, 79

Engenhos, 38, 44, 62, 74, 77, 198, 199, 202, 210; Sergipe, 22–27, 32, 40, 62, 64, 67, 72, 75, 82, 240 (n. 3); Santana, 22–27, 40, 47, 59, 62, 64, 65, 66, 81; Petinga, 27, 64; Musurepe, 38, 70; Guaguasú, 38, 81; Ilha, 39; São Bernardo, 72; Capanema, 75

England, 94, 96–99, 127

Equiano, Olaudah, 186

Espírito Santo, Brazil, 170

Ewe, 107

Exorcism, 145–46, 166, 167, 221, 223–24

Family, 57–58; African constructions of, 36–37, 46–47; impact of sex imbalance on, 38–39; impact of abusive masters on, 72–77; impact of slave sales on, 77–78; impact of manumission on, 78–80. See also Ancestors; Kinship; Marriage

Faria, Manuel de, 70

Faya, Manuel, 71

Feathers, 149, 185

Feira, Manuel Leite, 170

Fernandes, Luís, 165

Fernandes, Manuel, 27

Fernandes, Mariana, 67

Fernandes, Miguel, 123

Ferrás, Domingos Pinto, 179, 219–20

Fez, Morocco, 93

Figueiredo, João de, 41

Filipe (king of Ndongo), 151

Flamengo Island, 82

Fon, 107

Fonseca, Francisco da, 43–44

Franciscans, 40

Franco, Filipe, 64

Freed Blacks, 122, 167

French Guyana, 32

Freyre, Gilberto, 66–67

Funerals. See Burials

Kisama, 16, 194

Kitekes. See Spirit possession: ancestral figurines

Kongo, 54, 107, 155, 205, 207; Christianity in, 109–15, 191–93; cosmogram, 126; spirit possession, 140–42; kingship, 151; baptism in, 195–96, 197

Koster, Henry, 61

Labor: brickmaking, 24, 38; carpentry, 29; cattle ranching, 38; manioc farming, 38, 121; net making, 24; sugar mill, 24, 70, 210–11; barber, 79; boatmen, 90; mariners, 94; divining and curing, 152–54; shoemaking, 212–13

Ladinos, 27, 28, 199

Lago, Francisco Pereira do, 166

Language, 53, 133, 134, 135, 147, 151, 220, 232 (nn. 2, 3); Kikongo, 19, 20; Kimbundu, 19, 20, 33, 127–28, 144, 149, 228; and difficulties for missionaries in Brazil, 37, 198–99; "language of Angola," 125, 148, 155, 199, 218–19, 250 (n. 2)

Lapa, Lourença Correia, 42–43

Lima, Luís de, 183, 184, 204

Lima, Pedro de Oliveira, 78–79

Lisbon, Portugal, 13, 14, 42, 44, 52, 53, 71, 77, 78, 79, 82, 89–91, 94, 97, 146, 154, 165, 172, 173, 175, 181, 182, 183, 184, 185, 204, 211, 213

Lomas, Juan de, 32

London, England, 94, 98

Lovejoy, Paul, 1

Luanda, Angola, 16

Lucca, Lorenzo da, 110–11

Luís, João, 132–33

Lunda, 16

Luzia, Gracia, 211

MacGaffey, Wyatt, 113, 123, 126, 232 (n. 1)

Machado, Pedro Pais, 75

Madeira, 166, 179, 182

Malnutrition, 61–62, 65, 210–11. *See also* Diet

Malumba a Cambolo, 194

Malungo, 33, 50

Mandingo, Sebastião, 129

Manicongo, Francisco, 54, 57

Manso, Manuel, 224

Manumission, 31–32; impact on marriage and family, 78–80; of old and infirm, 80, 245 (n. 97); by lay brotherhoods, 206; and attempt at self-purchase, 211

Manriques, Paulo, 53

Maranhão, 38, 129

Maria, Antônio de Jesus, 40–41

Maria, Juliana, 78–79

Marica, Brazil, 213

Marriage: African attitudes toward, 35–37; performed by missionaries in Brazil, 37–38; impediments to, 38–40; coerced by masters, 41–42; African regional endogamy in, 44–50; forced by runaway slaves, 59; and impacts of sale of spouse, 77–78; and impacts of manumission, 78–80; performed by Kongolese priest, 193. *See also* Family; Kinship

Marimba, João, 74

Martel, Gaspar Afonso, 95

Masangano, Antônio, 36

Mascarenhas, Antônio, 166

Masters: attitudes of, toward slave marriage, 39–41; cutting slave rations, 61; abuse of slave children by, 69–70; use of African diviners by, 120–30, 134–36; attitudes of, toward spirit possession, 145–48, 151–52, 219–20; opposition of, to missionary efforts, 200–202. *See also* Punishment; Rape

Matamba, 16

Matos, Mateus de, 133

Mattos, Alvaro de, 165
Mattos, Gregório de, 146–47
Maurício, Joseph, 205
Mauritania, 15
Mazagão, Morocco, 2, 93, 179
Mbata, 195
Mbundu, 7, 33, 146, 175–76, 227–28
Medical care: conditions of, 64
Medicine, herbal, 105, 126, 129, 149, 151, 157, 165, 169
Medina, André Gomes de, 120–22, 170
Mendes, Fernão, 77–78
Mendes, João, 185
Mendonça, Mariana de, 134–35
Merolla, Girolamo, 34, 123, 176, 198, 236 (n. 16)
Mexico City, Mexico, 32
Middle Passage, 32, 33, 60, 115, 116, 197
Miller, Joseph, 33
Mina, Antônio (slave of King João V), 37
Mina, Antônio (of Rio de Janeiro), 79–80
Mina, Gonçalo, 167
Mina, José, 130
Mina, Joseph, 129–130
Mina, Maria, 37
Mina, Romana, 168
Mina, Teresa, 36
Minas Gerais, Brazil, 18, 24, 38, 70, 73, 134, 135, 147, 151, 165, 208
Mintz, Sidney, 228, 229
Mobanga, Pedro, 65
Modena, Joseph de, 154
Monasteries, 28–29, 41, 75
Monjollo, Pedro, 204
Morais, Barbara, 125
Morais, Vicente de, 183
Moreira, Matias, 52, 54
Morena, Joana, 43
Moribeca, Brazil, 156
Morocco, 91–93

Mortality: in Brazil, 59–60, 62–64; in Central Africa, 60, 63; child, 65–66
Mott, Luiz, 6
Mozambique, Antônio, 173, 175
Mpemba, 148–49, 151
Mulattoes, 27, 72, 126, 133, 166, 210, 218–19, 220–21
Musical instruments, 143, 148–49, 151, 155, 178, 202, 218

Nangô, 157
Nazaret, Luís da, 145–46
Ndembu, 16, 20, 233 (n. 21)
Ndongo, 16
Negros de ganho, 153–54, 212
Nganga: ngombo, 140–42; *quilundo*, 144, 148–49; *nzambi*, 154–55; *wisa*, 155. See also Spirit possession
Ngangela, 20
Ngunza, 123
Nieuhof, Johan, 127
Nogueira, Antônia, 44
Nogueira, Félix José, 31
Nunes, Mateus, 148
Nzambi mpungu, 107, 113, 126

Olinda, Brazil, 28, 29, 63, 70, 75, 125, 130, 145, 158, 198, 202, 210
Oliveira, Manuel Francisco de, 174
Orphans, 66, 68, 78
Ouidah (Dahomey), Benin, 183–84

Pais, Estevão, 79
Paiva, Francisco de, 94
Paiva, Gonçalo de, 82
Palmares, 50
Palmer, Colin, 1
Pará, Brazil, 74, 212
Paraíba, Brazil, 74, 130
Parishes: Santíssimo Sacramento, 36; Saubara, 36; São José, 36, 47; Jacarepaguá, 36, 68; Nossa Senhora de Candelária, 44; Guaratiba,

46; Santo Amaro de Pitanga, 120;
Cotegipe, 121; São Gonçalo, 142;
Matoim, 170; Marica, 213
Partana, Fidélis de, 167–68
Pascoal, Gregório, 193–94
Passube, Joseph, 49
Pavia, Andrea da, 115
P'Bitek, Okot, 108
Pedra d'ara. See Talismans
Pedroso, José Francisco, 183
Pelouro, Manuel Nunes, 72
Pereira, Domingos João, 125
Pereira, Gaspar, 129
Pereira, João, 165
Pereira, José Francisco, 183
Pereira, Maria, 179, 219–20
Pereira, Nuno Marques, 80
Pereira, Sebastião de Prado, 127
Perico, Manuel da Costa, 31–32
Pernambuco, Brazil, 16, 18, 23, 38, 44,
72, 74, 130, 156, 157, 170, 178, 183,
197, 199, 202, 204, 205, 210, 222,
224
Piedade, Manuel de, 183
Pimentel, Pedro Coelho, 153
Pina, João Rodrigues, 31
Pinheiro, Antônio Coelho, 167
Pinheiro, Mariana, 127
Pinheiro, Simão, 199
Pinta, Luzia, 135
Piracy, 94, 95
Pires, Antônio, 146
Pires, Diogo, 91
Pires, Felícia, 148–49
Poincepe, Brazil, 129
Poisoning, 39, 105, 142, 145, 166, 167–
69. See also Witchcraft
Polyandry, 43
Polygyny, 38, 42, 43
Porto, Portugal, 95, 98, 99, 183, 184,
204
Price, Richard, 228, 229

Prostitution, 53, 61, 70, 201
Punishments, 99, 222, 245 (n. 88);
torture, 69–70, 75, 157; whipping,
74–75, 97, 98, 185, 212

Quibando. See Divination: European
forms Africanized
Quijila. See Diet: Mbundu restrictions
Quilombos. See Runaways
Quimbandas, 54–57

Rama, Miguel Gomes da, 181–82
Ramos, Jacinta, 59–60
Ramos, Maria de, 79
Rape: of females, 67, 70, 72–73; of chil-
dren, 70–71; of males, 70–71, 73–74,
243 (n. 60), 244 (n. 66); by Catholic
priests, 71; of newly arrived Africans,
71, 73–74
Religion: Central African, 104–6; and
Western science, 108–9. See also
Anglicanism; Christianity; Divination;
Islam; Spirit possession; Witchcraft
Recife, Brazil, 127, 167, 207, 208, 224
Resistance, 6–7, 82–83, 159–60, 213–14,
229–30. See also Witchcraft
Ribeiro, Antônio, 79
Ribeiro, Francisco, 133
Ribeiro, Sebastião, 224–25
Rio da Prata, Brazil, 70
Rio das Contas, Brazil, 59
Rio das Mortes, Brazil, 72
Rio de Janeiro, Brazil, 13–14, 18, 24, 27,
29, 36, 38, 39, 41, 42, 44, 52, 62, 64,
68, 71, 77, 78, 79, 80, 81, 82, 129,
130, 146, 155, 157, 170–71, 172, 173,
176, 178, 183, 200, 207, 209, 213, 220
Rio Real, Brazil, 148, 151, 155
Rocha, Fernando Pereira da, 214
Rodeio, Brazil, 151
Rodrigues, Antônio, 62
Rodrigues, Estevão, 42